THE BRITISH ISLES AND
THE WAR OF AMERICAN INDEPENDENCE

The British Isles
and the War of
American Independence

STEPHEN CONWAY

OXFORD
UNIVERSITY PRESS

*This book has been printed digitally and produced in a standard specification
in order to ensure its continuing availability*

OXFORD
UNIVERSITY PRESS

Great Clarendon Street, Oxford OX2 6DP

Oxford University Press is a department of the University of Oxford.
It furthers the University's objective of excellence in research, scholarship,
and education by publishing world-wide in

Oxford New York

Auckland Bangkok Buenos Aires Cape Town Chennai
Dar es Salaam Delhi Hong Kong Istanbul Karachi Kolkata
Kuala Lumpur Madrid Melbourne Mexico City Mumbai Nairobi
São Paulo Shanghai Taipei Tokyo Toronto

Oxford is a registered trade mark of Oxford University Press
in the UK and in certain other countries

Published in the United States
by Oxford University Press Inc., New York

ISBN 0-19-925455-9

Printed in Great Britain by

Antony Rowe Ltd., Eastbourne

Acknowledgements

WRITING a book is in many ways a solitary, introspective activity; yet it would be impossible to bring the process to fruition without the help of others. Historical monographs, based on intensive research in archives, would never see the light of day were it not for the willingness of a great many people to lend their assistance. I gratefully acknowledge my debt to the owners and custodians of the manuscript collections that I have consulted in preparing this book, particularly Viscount Barrington; Mr A. C. Bell-Macdonald; Dr J. L. Campbell of Canna; Lt.-Col. R. M. P. Campbell-Preston; Captain C. T. F. Fagan; Olive, Countess Fitzwilliam's Wentworth Settlement Trustees; Mr S. W. Fraser; the Duke of Grafton; Mr F. E. Hart; the Rt. Hon. Baron Home of the Hirsel; the Rt. Hon. Lady Lucas; Mr A. R. Maitland; the Mellish trustees; the Duke of Northumberland; Mr Oliver Russell; the Earl of Verulam; and the Marquis of Zetland.

I offer my thanks also to the many archivists and librarians whose knowledge and patience made my task much easier than it might otherwise have been, particularly those at Aberdeen University Library, the American Philosophical Society, Bedfordshire Record Office, Berkshire Record Office, Birmingham City Archives, the Bodleian Library, Boston Public Library, the British Library, the Brotherton Library, Buckinghamshire Record Office, Calderdale Archives, Cambridgeshire Record Office, the Centre of South Asian Studies, Cornwall Record Office, the Corporation of London Record Office, Cumbria Record Office, Devon Record Office, Dr Williams's Library, East Suffolk Record Office, East Sussex Record Office, Essex Record Office, Glasgow University Library, Gloucestershire Record Office, Hampshire Record Office, Hertfordshire Record Office, Historical Society of Pennsylvania, Horsham Museum, Hull Record Office, Hull University Library, the India Office Library and Records, Kent Archives Office, Lancashire Record Office, Leeds Archives, Leicestershire Record Office, Library of Congress, Lichfield Record Office, Lincolnshire Archives Office, Liverpool Record Office, Massachusetts Historical Society, National Army

Museum, National Library of Ireland, National Library of Scotland, National Library of Wales, New-York Historical Society, New York Public Library, Norfolk Record Office, Northumberland Record Office, North Yorkshire Record Office, Nottingham University Library, Nottinghamshire Archives, Pembrokeshire Record Office, the Public Record Office, the Public Record Office of Northern Ireland, Queen's Lancashire Regiment Museum, Reading University Library, the Royal Fusiliers Museum, the Royal Society, the Scottish Record Office, Sheffield Archives, Society of Friends Library, Somerset Record Office, Staffordshire Record Office, Trinity College Dublin Library, University College London Library, Warwickshire Record Office, West Suffolk Record Office, West Sussex Record Office, West Yorkshire Archives Service, Whitehaven Library, William L. Clements Library, William Salt Library, Wiltshire Record Office, Worcestershire Record Office, and York City Archives.

It will be apparent from my bibliography and from my footnotes that I owe a good deal to the work of fellow historians. Scholarship advances incrementally, building on the foundations laid by others; even when our findings appear to contradict earlier wisdom, we benefit from the insights of those who have prepared the ground. We profit, likewise, from the endeavours of colleagues working in very different fields, and I have been fortunate to work and learn alongside historians of the highest calibre both in my own department and across the University of London.

An anonymous referee made helpful comments on my original book proposal, and these steered me towards many new areas of enquiry, for which I offer my thanks. Three historians very kindly took on the burden of reading my first draft—Professor Martin Daunton of Churchill College, Cambridge; Professor David French of University College London; and Professor P. J. Marshall of King's College London. They all made suggestions for changes and corrected errors. I thank them for an attention to detail and an engagement with my text that greatly exceeded what could reasonably be expected of very busy people. Needless to say, the mistakes remaining are my responsibility, not theirs.

Parts of this book draw on material I published earlier in scholarly periodicals, though in every case I have revised and extended the originals. I thank the editors for permission to reproduce (albeit in amended form) articles, or parts of articles, that appeared first in their journals; namely, 'Locality, Metropolis and Nation: The Impact of the Military Camps in England during the American War', *History*, 82 (1997), 547–62; 'The Politics of British Military and Naval Mobilization, 1775–1783', *English Historical Review*, 112 (1997), 1179–1201; and 'British Mobilization in the War of American Independence', *Historical Research*, 72 (1999), 58–76. Some of the material in Chapter 9 appeared earlier in my chapter of *The Oxford History of the British Empire*, ii. *The Eighteenth Century*, ed. P. J. Marshall (Oxford, 1998), 325–46, and I thank Peter Marshall for permission to employ it in this new context. Likewise, parts of the 'Conclusions' are based on parts of my essay on 'British Governments and the Conduct of the American War' for H. T. Dickinson (ed.), *Britain and the American Revolution* (London, 1998), 155–79; I am grateful to Harry Dickinson for allowing me to recast it for this book.

Once a work of this kind has been submitted to the publisher, there remains much to be done. In this regard I wish to thank Ruth Parr, the History Editor at Oxford University Press and her colleagues, particularly Rowena Anketell, Anne Gelling, and Sarah Ridgard. I am also grateful to Ruth's predecessor, Tony Morris, who worked with me at the beginning of this project. Finally, I must express my gratitude to my family for their understanding, support, and encouragement over the years it has taken to translate my first thoughts into this final product. As a small token of my thanks and my love I dedicate it to them.

S.R.C.

Contents

List of Maps

List of Figures

Abbreviations

The following abbreviations are used in the footnotes:

ADM	Admiralty Papers, Public Record Office
BL	British Library
BM	British Museum, Department of Prints and Drawings
HMC	Historical Manuscripts Commission
HO	Home Office Papers, Public Record Office
NLI	National Library of Ireland
NLS	National Library of Scotland
NLW	National Library of Wales
PH	*The Parliamentary History of England*, ed. William Cobbett and J. Wright (36 vols., London, 1806–20)
PRO	Public Record Office
PRONI	Public Record Office of Northern Ireland
RO	Record Office
SP	State Papers, Public Record Office
SRO	Scottish Record Office
T	Treasury Papers, Public Record Office
VCH	Victoria County History
WO	War Office Papers, Public Record Office

Map I.1. The British Isles in 1775

Introduction

ON 19 APRIL 1775 the constitutional dispute between Britain and its North American colonies finally erupted into open war. For the next thirty months or so, Lord North's government was able to devote much of the military resources at its disposal to crushing the rebellion. But although Washington's Continental army suffered defeats in the field, notably on Long Island, New York, in August 1776 and at Brandywine Creek, Pennsylvania, in September 1777, the Americans could not be subdued. At length, following the capitulation of a British force under General Burgoyne at Saratoga, New York, in October 1777, the French brought forward their plans to enter the conflict on the side of the new United States, and became belligerents in the early summer of 1778. The next year the Spanish joined the French, and at the end of 1780 the Dutch also became enemies of the British. A colonial rebellion had turned into a world war. The fighting continued in North America, but spread to the Caribbean, Central America, Europe, West Africa, and even India. After the defeat and surrender in October 1781 of another of their armies at Yorktown, Virginia, the British suspended offensive operations in North America and concentrated on salvaging what they could of the rest of their empire. The outcome of the war was not as disastrous as it might have been for the British, thanks largely to the staunch defence of Gibraltar and Admiral Rodney's victory at the battle of the Saintes in April 1782, which saved Jamaica. Nonetheless, in the peace treaties of 1782–3 Britain was obliged to give up most of the mainland North American colonies and to cede territory to France and Spain.

The American war has not lacked historians. Scholars from the United States, not surprisingly, have studied the struggle from the perspective of the birth and early development of their nation.[1]

[1] See e.g. Willard M. Wallace, *Appeal to Arms* (New York, 1951); Christopher Ward, *The War of the American Revolution*, ed. John R. Alden (2 vols., New York, 1952); Howard H. Peckham, *The War for Independence* (Chicago, 1958); John R. Alden, *A History of the American Revolution* (London, 1969); Don Higginbotham, *The War of American Independence* (New York, 1971); Marshall Smelser, *The Winning of Independence* (New York, 1973); Robert Middlekauf, *The Glorious Cause* (New York, 1982).

British historians, equally unsurprisingly, have tended to emphasize its international and imperial dimensions, if only to explain the magnitude of the task confronting the British government and armed forces.[2] But the role of the American war in domestic British and Irish history has attracted less attention than the military campaigns and the strategic dimensions. Granted, the politics of the period have been examined in some detail, both within and beyond the British and Irish parliaments, at 'high' and popular levels.[3] Some suggestive work has also been done on the economic consequences for various areas;[4] and work has commenced on the influence of the conflict on contemporary culture and on attitudes to empire.[5] But no truly wide-ranging effort has been made to explore the impact of this war on the British Isles.[6]

---

[2] See esp. Piers Mackesy's unsurpassed classic *The War for America 1775–1783* (London, 1964). Stephen Conway, *The War of American Independence* (London, 1995) also attempts to adopt a broad approach. By contrast, Christopher Hibbert, *Rebels and Redcoats: The War for America, 1770–1781* (London, 1990) and Jeremy Black, *War for America* (Stroud, 1991), confine their attention almost exclusively to the American theatre of the struggle.

[3] e.g. Herbert Butterfield, *George III, Lord North and the People* (London, 1949); Ian Christie, *The End of North's Ministry* (London, 1958) and *Wilkes, Wyvill and Reform* (London, 1962); Maurice O'Connell, *Irish Politics and Social Conflict in the Age of the American Revolution* (Philadelphia, 1965); Frank O'Gorman, *The Rise of Party in England: The Rockingham Whigs 1760–1782* (London, 1975) and 'The Parliamentary Opposition to the Government's American Policy 1760–1782', in H. T. Dickinson (ed.), *Britain and the American Revolution* (London, 1998), 97–123; Colin Bonwick, *English Radicals and the American Revolution* (Chapel Hill, NC, 1977); R. B. McDowell, *Ireland in the Age of Imperialism and Revolution 1760–1801* (Oxford, 1979); James E. Bradley, *Popular Politics and the American Revolution in England* (Macon, Ga., 1986), *Religion, Revolution and English Radicalism* (Cambridge, 1990), and 'The British Public and the American Revolution: Ideology, Interest and Opinion', in Dickinson (ed.), *Britain and the American Revolution*, 124–54.

[4] Such as M. L. Robertson, 'Scottish Commerce and the American War of Independence', *Economic History Review*, 2nd ser., 9 (1956–7), 123–31; Peter L. Wickens, 'The Economics of Privateering: Capital Dispersal in the American War of Independence', *Journal of European Economic History*, 13 (1984), 375–95; T. M. Devine, *Exploring the Scottish Past* (East Linton, 1995), ch. 6.

[5] See Dror Wahrman, '*Percy*'s Prologue: From Gender Play to Gender Panic in Eighteenth-Century England', *Past & Present*, 159 (1998), 113–60; and Eliga H. Gould, 'A Virtual Nation: Greater Britain and the Imperial Legacy of the American Revolution', *American Historical Review*, 104 (1999), 476–89.

[6] *Britain and the American Revolution*, a collection of essays edited by Harry Dickinson, to which reference has already been made, contains a number of contributions which relate to the domestic face of the war, but its scope is not confined to the war and it does not attempt to be comprehensive in its coverage. As the editor writes in his introduction (p. 13), 'British historians have so far largely neglected the impact of the war on British society'.

Contexts

This omission owes much to the long shadow cast by the wars of 1793–1815. Until recently, it was generally assumed that the French Revolutionary and Napoleonic Wars were very different in scale and impact from all the eighteenth-century conflicts that preceded them. Mass mobilization in France in 1793 certainly had dramatic effects on that country's society, politics, and economy; and, despite the enormity of the ramifications, sooner or later all of the new republic's enemies were obliged to some extent to follow in its footsteps. By comparison with this great and cataclysmic struggle, the conflicts of the pre-French Revolution period seemed insipid and unobtrusive. They tended to be portrayed as much tamer 'limited' wars, struggles that were restricted in terms of their means, ends, and impact. Such wars, historians argued, were contested by relatively small professional armies and navies. They lacked the ideological fervour of the religious conflicts of the seventeenth century and the wars of nationalism inaugurated by the French Revolution. They were fought not for the benefit of peoples but for the carefully defined purposes of expanding princely or oligarchical power. And because the people were for the most part excluded from participation, it was assumed that they should be immunized as much as possible from the harsh reality of war; it has often been claimed that the wars of this period impinged only to a limited extent on the lives of civilians. At its most extreme, this view of *ancien régime* warfare presented a picture of decorous, restrained, and often indecisive military operations that touched the lives of remarkably few contemporaries beyond the competing armed forces.[7]

In the last few years the work of many scholars has qualified, modified, or even overturned received wisdom on the nature of eighteenth-century wars in Europe. The crucial role of the regiments of the old royal army in the battlefield successes of the new French revolutionary regime is now properly recognized.[8] We now

---

[7] See Carl von Clausewitz, *On War*, ed. and trans. Michael Howard and Peter Paret (Princeton, 1976), 589–91 for one of the classic expressions of this view. For echoes in more recent work see Eric Robson, 'Armed Forces and the Art of War', in *The New Cambridge Modern History*, vii. *The Old Regime, 1713–1763* (Cambridge, 1957), 163–76; J. F. C. Fuller, *The Conduct of War 1789–1961* (London, 1961), ch. 1; Clive Emsley, *British Society and the French Wars 1793–1815* (London, 1979), 2, 11.

[8] S. F. Scott, *The Response of the Royal Army to the French Revolution* (Oxford, 1978); Alan J. Forrest, *Conscripts and Deserters: The Army and French Society during the Revolution and Empire* (New York, 1989).

know that nationalism, so long thought to be a product of the French Revolution and its war, was developing in France and other European states long before 1789.[9] Work on continental Europe has revealed the intrusive and incredibly destructive face of the wars of the *ancien régime*. Civilians were far from left alone. In many places they were exposed to forced 'contributions' of money, supplies, or transport; and there were areas that were systematically laid waste, such as the Rhineland in 1689 and Bavaria in 1704.[10] Drawing on recent research, several historians have been able to deliver some telling blows to the 'limited war' model.[11]

Studies of eighteenth-century Britain have similarly cast doubt on the view that conflicts before the French Revolution were small-scale and had minimal effect. John Brewer has argued that successive wars led to the emergence of a 'fiscal-military state' in Britain, revolutionizing taxation and public credit.[12] His work has stimulated enquiry in a wide range of areas; a collection of essays edited by Lawrence Stone sets out to explore the implications of Brewer's ideas.[13] Linda Colley, in her influential book on the formation of British national identity, devotes a good deal of attention to the part played by war, particularly war against France;[14] while Kathleen Wilson, in her work on national and political consciousness in eighteenth-century Britain, also highlights the importance of armed conflict.[15] A reflection of the progress of this process of revision is Huw Bowen's summary of the findings of a burgeoning literature in an accessible overview of the impact of war on Britain between 1688 and 1815.[16]

[9] e.g. M. S. Anderson, *War and Society in Europe of the Old Regime, 1618–1789* (London, 1989), 200–2. Adrian Hastings, *The Construction of Nationhood: Ethnicity, Religion and Nationalism* (Cambridge, 1997), argues that nationalism long predates the 18th cent.

[10] e.g. Martin van Creveld, *Supplying War: Logistics from Wallenstein to Patton* (Cambridge, 1977), 26–39; C. R. Friedrichs, *Urban Society in an Age of War: Nordlingen, 1580–1720* (Princeton, 1979); Myron P. Gutmann, *War and Rural Life in the Early Modern Low Countries* (Princeton, 1980).

[11] See esp. John Childs, *Armies and Warfare in Europe 1648–1789* (Manchester, 1982) and Jeremy Black, *European Warfare, 1660–1815* (London, 1994).

[12] John Brewer, *The Sinews of Power: War, Money and the English State 1688–1783* (London, 1989).

[13] Lawrence Stone (ed.), *An Imperial State at War: Britain from 1689 to 1815* (London, 1994).

[14] Linda Colley, *Britons: Forging the Nation 1707–1837* (New Haven 1992).

[15] Kathleen Wilson, *The Sense of the People: Politics, Culture and Imperialism in England, 1715–1785* (Cambridge, 1995).

[16] H. V. Bowen, *War and British Society, 1688–1815* (Cambridge, 1998).

The current book, by concentrating on the impact on the British Isles of the last significant conflict before the French Revolution, should add something to the increasingly well-established case against the traditional, 'limited war' view of eighteenth-century armed struggles. It should also, I hope, make a contribution to the historiographical debates caused by the work of Brewer and Colley. Brewer's concept of the 'fiscal-military state', the efficient war-making machine responsible for Britain's rise to Great Power status, while generally well received, does not appear to sit easily alongside Paul Langford's very different picture of an England characterized by vigorous localism and the diffusion of power amongst property-owners of varying social background, who were often remote from or unconnected to the central state.[17] J. E. Cookson's stimulating study of the mobilization of British and Irish manpower in the long wars against revolutionary and Napoleonic France highlights the difficulties of reconciling these interpretations, and comes down on the side of Langford. Cookson concludes that in his period local initiatives and local power were important counters to central authority, and that wartime activity by the state ultimately depended on the cooperation of a whole host of interests not directly under its control. In his account, the British state is presented as weak rather than strong, even in the key area of national defence. Cookson also seeks to correct what he sees as Colley's overemphasis on the emergence of an overarching and unifying sense of Britishness. He argues that she understates the very different motives that led many varying groups to proclaim their patriotism. His picture is again much more fragmented and variegated than the one offered by the author he criticizes.[18] Other historians, working to different agendas, have suggested that Colley's focus on national consciousness obscures the much more important divisions generated by eighteenth-century wars.[19] Material in various chapters in this book should shed further light on these debates, and in the conclusion an attempt will be made to see what the British and

---

[17] Paul Langford, *Public Life and the Propertied Englishman 1689–1798* (Oxford, 1991).

[18] J. E. Cookson, *The British Armed Nation 1793–1815* (Oxford, 1997). See his introduction for the establishment of his argument and its relationship to existing interpretations.

[19] See e.g. Douglas Hay and Nicholas Rogers, *Eighteenth-Century English Society* (Oxford, 1997), ch. 10.

Irish experience in the American war tells us about the different interpretations.

Starting Points and Ending Points

Before the layout of this book is explained, a few words on its approach and scope might be in order. I came to this project as a historian interested both in the American war and in eighteenth-century British history. But I came to it above all as a historian fascinated by the effects of armed conflict and armed forces on the societies that produce and sustain them. Brought up in a century which has witnessed two world wars and a host of smaller but nonetheless intrusive conflicts, I have perhaps been conditioned to see war not just as a series of battles and campaigns but as a dynamic process impinging on many aspects of life. Over the last twenty years I have, needless to say, been influenced enormously by the work of a veritable army of other scholars, and I have consciously or unconsciously sought to apply their insights to my own period and subject. I have also immersed myself in a mass of primary material, which in some respects has overturned, often has modified or reshaped, and nearly always has broadened my understanding of the impact of the American war. Even so, my opening assumption was that the conflict's effects were multifarious and profound, and that assumption has inevitably influenced my approach to the sources used in this book.

It is, of course, both impossible and undesirable to isolate the impact of the war from the effects of other contemporary developments. It needs to be seen alongside those developments, and as a contributor to change rather than as its sole or exclusive agent. To understand the importance of the American conflict, we have to place it in its appropriate settings. If this means making lateral connections, it also requires the war to be viewed in the context of medium- or even long-term trends, as accelerating or retarding processes already underway, and which sometimes came to fruition much later. The chronological focus of the work is therefore not confined to the war years 1775–83. It ranges, where appropriate, from the close of the Seven Years War in 1763 to the outbreak of the war against revolutionary France in 1793, or on some occasions into the nineteenth century.

If the time-span requires explanation, so does the geographical area under consideration. This study considers the impact of the War of American Independence not just on Britain but on the British Isles. This might be regarded as a response to fashion; and there is no gainsaying that the 'Four Nations' version of British history is in vogue.[20] Yet the decision to opt for this broad approach was not reached easily. British historians, like British politicians, have to grapple with the issue of Ireland, and it must be said that the case for excluding Ireland from the focus of the current work is in some senses a strong one.[21] Ireland on the eve of the American Revolution had its own parliament and though George III was the monarch, he ruled as king of Ireland not of Great Britain. In practice Ireland was less a 'sister kingdom' than a colonial dependency, for the Irish Parliament was subject to considerable restrictions on its freedom of action and ultimately subordinate to the Westminster Parliament. Irish trade, moreover, was controlled by British legislation, which severely restricted Irish commercial access to the British colonies. But whether we regard Ireland as 'sister kingdom' or colony, it was clearly separate from Britain; not until the creation of the United Kingdom of Great Britain and Ireland in 1800 can we think in terms of a constitutionally common story, and even then increasing Irish resistance to incorporation reminds us of the continuing importance of a distinctive Irish history.

Yet this approach ignores the parallel nature of developments in Britain and Ireland during the American war, which were themselves products of the very strong ties that make it difficult neatly to divide the two. Ireland's Protestants, who dominated the country's politics and landownership, were very proud of their 'Irishness' in so far as they resented British attempts to limit their autonomous power; but they still valued and celebrated their links with Britain. The internal dynamics and party alignments of the Irish Parliament were remarkably similar to those of its British counterpart.[22] There was even some overlap in terms of personnel. The Church of Ireland, the

---

[20] A recent example is David L. Smith, *A History of the Modern British Isles 1603–1707: The Double Crown* (Oxford, 1998). For more chronologically ambitious works of the genre see Hugh Kearney, *The British Isles: A History of Four Nations* (Cambridge, 1989) and Jeremy Black, *A History of the British Isles* (London, 1996).

[21] See e.g. the arguments in Keith Robbins, *Great Britain: Identities, Institutions and the Idea of Britishness* (London, 1998), 5–6, 277–84.

[22] See David Lammey, 'The Growth of the "Patriot Opposition" in Ireland during the 1770s', *Parliamentary History*, 7 (1988), 257–81.

established church, was the Irish version of the Church of England; indeed, many of its senior clergy were British rather than Irish in origin. In 1775 the bishop of Clogher, John Garnett, was from Lambeth; the bishop of Killaloe, Robert Fowler, was from Lincolnshire; and John Cradock, the archbishop of Dublin, was a native of Wolverhampton. Even some of the Irish-born bishops had strong English links: Charles Agar, bishop of Cloyne, and Robert Downes, bishop of Raphoe, were Dubliners, but they had both been educated at Christ Church, Oxford.[23] Nor was the British connection confined to the Anglican elite. The Presbyterians of Ulster, who tended to be particularly resentful of British restrictions, were themselves closely associated with the Church of Scotland; a good number of prominent Irish Presbyterians were educated at Scottish universities.[24] Even the Catholic majority was not necessarily and inevitably alienated.[25] Catholic loyalty, as we shall see, was much debated during the American war. But on one important level Irish Catholics showed themselves to be British as well as Irish — very considerable numbers of them served in the army or navy during the conflict. Indeed, it makes little sense to focus on the mobilization of manpower without bringing Ireland into the picture; the regular armed forces depended heavily upon the Irish contribution. The case for Irish inclusion, then, is arguably more compelling than the case for exclusion. Inclusion, it must be confessed, leads to occasional awkwardness. But the alternative would surely have created still greater difficulties.

Structure

The structure of the book is, I hope, straightforward. The first chapter addresses mobilization of manpower for the war, considering the scale and breadth of participation in the armed forces, official

[23] See the list of bishops and archbishops of the Church of Ireland in *A New History of Ireland*, ix. *Maps, Genealogies, Lists*, ed. T. W. Moody, F. X. Martin, and F. J. Byrne (Oxford, 1984), 391–438. Details of birth and education were taken from the *Dictionary of National Biography* and *Alumni Oxonienses . . . 1715–1886*, ed. Joseph Foster (4 vols., Oxford and London, 1887–8).

[24] See Graham Walker, *Intimate Strangers: Political and Cultural Interaction between Scotland and Ulster in Modern Times* (Edinburgh, 1995), ch. 1.

[25] See S. J. Connolly, 'Varieties of Britishness: Ireland, Scotland and Wales in the Hanoverian State', in Alexander Grant and Keith J. Stringer (eds.), *Uniting the Kingdom? The Making of British History* (London, 1995), 193–207.

and unofficial. This is an important starting point, because the magnitude of mobilization, which has usually been greatly underestimated, had important and multifarious ramifications. The next chapter explores the war's economic impact, mainly concentrating on the situation during the struggle itself, but considering also the post-war picture. The key areas examined are the destruction and loss of capital assets, taxation and public borrowing, overseas trade, pay and prices, and war-related public expenditure. Chapter 3 looks at the impact of the war on society and culture. The themes with which it seeks to deal are the ways in which the conflict affected women and gender relations, the social mobility and social conflict generated by the war, patterns of crime and changes in penal policy, social reform, military enthusiasm, and finally the influence of the armed struggle on literature and the arts. The fourth chapter is devoted to the political battles within the British Isles associated with the conflict, and explores the depth and bitterness of the division, the backgrounds of the antagonists, and the issues of contention. From division we turn to unity. The purpose of the fifth chapter is to consider whether the war promoted an overarching sense of Britishness. The connection between war and national identity and the timing or even the reality of the emergence of a popular identification with Britain have been hotly contested by historians in recent years, and an exploration of these issues in the context of the American conflict should add something to the debates. Chapters 6 and 7 deal with constitutional issues. Chapter 6 focuses on the parliaments of the British Isles. The Westminster Parliament saw its authority curbed, most obviously in relation to America but also over the rest of the empire. The Dublin Parliament, by contrast, benefited to the extent that Ireland was given limited legislative independence. Both parliaments, however, faced internal challenges, in that movements for parliamentary reform, stimulated by wartime developments, emerged in Britain and Ireland. In Britain there was also a concerted and successful campaign for 'economical reform'—the reduction of the number of offices at the disposal of the executive—which in time was to transform the very nature of politics. Chapter 7 concentrates on the religious side of the constitution. In this area there were a number of significant wartime reforms. Catholics in England, Wales, and Ireland received limited relief; only in Scotland did they continue to be subject to the full panoply of restrictions imposed by the penal laws. Protestant

Dissenters in England and Wales were likewise given some concessions, and those in Ireland were even admitted to public office from 1780. The motives behind these reforms have been a matter of much debate. This chapter summarizes the arguments and adds some further suggestions. It also explores resistance to change, which, like the reforms themselves, owed much to the impact of the war. The eighth chapter comprises a set of local studies, designed to bring together some of the points made earlier in the book. The areas chosen vary considerably in terms of type and geography — from small towns like Brentwood in Essex, Lichfield in Staffordshire, and Strabane in County Tyrone, to Hull, a medium-sized English east coast port, Glasgow, the great Scottish entrepôt, and a largely rural county, Berkshire. Chapter 9 considers the ways in which the American conflict affected attitudes to war in general, and how it contributed to changing views on empire. The conclusion returns to the historiographical debates about the nature of eighteenth-century warfare before the French Revolution, the power and efficiency of the British state, and the importance we should attach to Britishness as an overarching and unifying force.

I

Mobilization

BRITAIN'S MILITARY FORCES in the American war depended heavily on peoples from beyond the British Isles. In India, particularly, the British armies were only nominally 'British': a handful of regular regiments fought alongside a much larger number of locally raised sepoys in the service of the East India Company. In North America, native warriors acted as British auxiliaries on the frontier of the rebel colonies; while within the colonies themselves, white loyalists were organized into provincial regiments and local militias, and even small numbers of black slaves were armed to fight alongside British troops. German regiments, hired from their rulers, were also used—as in earlier wars—to extend British military resources. In the American conflict, German units were added to the British forces in North America, the Mediterranean, and India. Recent scholarship has drawn attention to this reliance on external sources of manpower, either to highlight the desperate situation which confronted the British from 1778, when the war became a global struggle, affecting almost every area of European involvement, or as part of a wider account of changing perceptions of empire and British attitudes to hitherto marginal or excluded peoples.[1]

Historians have focused rather less on an associated and equally important development—the considerable mobilization of British and Irish manpower in the American conflict. This mobilization was central to the British experience in the war, and an appreciation of its scale is therefore an essential starting point for any study of the impact of the struggle. This chapter will try to establish just two

---

[1] See e.g. Jeremy Black, *War for America* (Stroud, 1991), ch. 2, and *Britain as a Military Power, 1688–1815* (London, 1999), 275–6; P. J. Marshall, 'A Nation Defined by Empire, 1755–1776', in Alexander Grant and Keith J. Stringer (eds.), *Uniting the Kingdom? The Making of British History* (London, 1995), 208–22. Linda Colley pursued the same theme as Professor Marshall, and sought to relate it directly to the American war, in her lectures on 'The Frontier in British History' delivered at Cambridge and Belfast in 1997.

fundamentals: the number of Britons and Irishmen who served in a military capacity, and the sections of society from which they came. Other related matters, such as the political debates over mobilization, its geographical basis within the British Isles, its social and economic consequences, and the problems associated with demobilization, will be examined in later chapters.

The generally accepted view is that, before the French Revolution, eighteenth-century wars in western and central Europe were fought by small professional armed forces, drawn very largely from two social classes: those at the top and those at the very bottom. The officers are taken to have been members of landed families—aristocrats, gentry, or their sons—and the rank and file are assumed to have been recruited from those groups that society could manage without: particularly criminals, vagrants, and paupers. To make up the numbers without disrupting economic life, foreigners were employed, either in specially hired regiments or as individual entrants into the armies and navies.[2] Modern scholarship, while questioning many aspects of the received view of the impact of war on eighteenth-century Britain, offers little to challenge this picture of the composition of the armed forces. Stress still tends to be laid on aristocratic officers, a rank and file comprised largely of the scapings of society, and the considerable dependence on European, and particularly German, mercenaries.[3]

The pattern of mobilization in Britain and Ireland during the American conflict corresponds in some respects to this model. For the first three years of the struggle, when the rebellious colonies were the only enemy, the armed forces grew only slowly, and there was a heavy reliance on German auxiliaries. But from early 1778, when the war took on the character of a worldwide contest, with

---

[2] e.g. Geoffrey Best, *War and Society in Revolutionary Europe, 1770–1870* (London, 1982), chs. 2 and 3; M. S. Anderson, *War and Society in Europe of the Old Regime, 1618–1789* (London, 1988), esp. 121, 164–5.

[3] See John Brewer, *The Sinews of Power: War, Money and the English State, 1688–1783* (London, 1989), esp. 41–2; 'Introduction', in Lawrence Stone (ed.), *An Imperial State at War: Britain from 1689 to 1815* (London, 1994), esp. 6, 10, 20. Linda Colley, *Britons: Forging the Nation, 1707–1837* (New Haven, 1992) discusses mobilization of British manpower in 18th-cent. wars, but devotes most of her coverage to the struggle against revolutionary and Napoleonic France. See also her 'The Reach of the State, the Appeal of the Nation', in Stone (ed.), *Imperial State at War*, 165–84. J. E. Cookson, *The British Armed Nation 1793–1815* (Oxford, 1997), ch. 1, explores antecedents to the mass mobilization of the French Revolutionary and Napoleonic Wars, and gives some attention to the American war; but he still understates, in my judgement, the 'evolutionary' argument.

France, Spain, and finally the United Provinces becoming Britain's opponents, the whole tempo of the war effort changed. By 1781 only 9% of the money voted by Parliament for the army was earmarked for German auxiliaries, compared with 24% in 1760, at the height of the Seven Years War, and 25% in the War of Spanish Succession (1702–13).[4] The Germans had become proportionately less important because more Britons and Irishmen than ever before went into uniform, and significant numbers of these British and Irish soldiers, sailors, marines, militiamen, and volunteers came from social and occupational backgrounds not normally associated with eighteenth-century military or naval service.

The Expansion of the Armed Forces

When the first shots were fired at Lexington and Concord, there were less than 16,000 seamen in the Royal Navy. The army, with an establishment strength of 48,647 officers and men, could probably muster only about 36,000 troops. Some 8,000 of these were under the command of General Thomas Gage, the commander-in-chief in North America. As early as November 1774 Gage, aware that a violent clash was becoming very likely, had warned that the force at his disposal was inadequate. The rebellion that he believed was already starting in Massachusetts could only be suppressed by a much larger military force: an army of 20,000 was imperative in Gage's estimation.[5] This was not the response expected by Lord North, the prime minister. He thought Gage's request for reinforcement was unreasonable. The dispatch of so many troops, North complained, 'will require us to put our army almost upon a war establishment'.[6] Not until hostilities had begun—not, indeed, until the summer of 1775—did the government recognize that it had to conduct a war rather than a more limited police operation. Even then, North was unwilling fully to mobilize the Royal Navy in case such a move provoked the French, and because he was keen to limit the rise in public expenditure that such a mobilization would

---

[4] *Journals of the House of Commons*, xxviii. 636–9; xxxviii. 33–9; Brewer, *Sinews of Power*, 32. See also David French, *The British Way in Warfare* (London, 1990), 59, 87.
[5] K. G. Davies (ed.), *Documents of the American Revolution* (21 vols., Shannon, 1972–81), viii. 221.   [6] Staffordshire RO, Dartmouth MSS, D(W) 1778/II/1073.

inevitably involve.[7] In November 1775 the naval estimates presented to the British House of Commons increased the number of seamen and marines for the following year, but only to 28,000 men.[8] It took persistent reports of a French naval build-up to persuade the cabinet in October 1776 to heed the advice of the admiralty and authorize the impressment of seamen; and it was not until the eve of hostilities with France that mobilization of the Royal Navy began in earnest.[9]

After a lively debate within government circles, it was decided that the chief instrument for the crushing of the American rebellion should be the army. A land war was chosen partly because it was thought that it would be more likely than a naval blockade to bring speedy success, and was therefore less likely to provide an opening for the French, who were assumed to be waiting for an appropriate opportunity to avenge their defeat in the Seven Years War. The American loyalists also influenced official thinking. British ministers, convinced that the rebellion was the work of a conspiratorial minority that had duped many colonists, believed that a substantial number of Americans were 'friends to government'. These 'good Americans' could be used to help put down the insurrection and restore British control—but only in the aftermath of the defeat of the American forces and so long as the loyalists were sustained by a British military presence.[10] A significant army was needed, then, for operations in America. Yet the army's expansion was hardly more rapid than the navy's. In belated response to Gage's plea, the government resolved to have 20,000 regular troops in the rebel colonies in the spring of 1776. Lord Barrington, the secretary at war, warned that this timetable was overly ambitious: 'I not only fear, but am confident,' he told the king, 'the proposed augmentation cannot possibly be raised, and ought not to be depended on'.[11] The king dismissed such advice as tainted: Barrington was one of the

---

[7] Nicholas Tracy, *Navies, Deterrence and American Independence* (Vancouver, 1988), ch. 6; Daniel A. Baugh, 'The Politics of British Naval Failure, 1775–1777', *American Neptune*, 52 (1992), 221–46.   [8] *PH* xviii. 842.

[9] N. A. M. Rodger, *The Insatiable Earl: A Life of John Montagu, 4th Earl of Sandwich* (London, 1993), 225–37.

[10] See Baugh, 'Politics of British Naval Failure'; BL, Hardwicke Papers, Add. MS 35427, fo. 19.

[11] Shute Barrington, *The Political Life of William Wildman, Viscount Barrington* (London, 1814), 158–9. See also WO 4/96, p. 258.

ministers who favoured a purely naval subjugation of the Americans.[12] But Barrington's pessimism was justified, not least because the king insisted on adding troops to existing regiments rather than allowing new ones to be formed. It seems likely that if George had been a little more flexible on this point his army would have grown much more quickly. The one exception he made was certainly a success story. The king consented in 1775 to the formation of the Seventy-first, or Fraser's Highlanders, which became a two-battalion regiment. The corps was raised by offering commissions to those who recruited a stipulated number of men: Thomas Campbell, for instance, was told that he had to provide eighteen men in three months to qualify for an ensigncy.[13] He would have had to cover some incidental recruiting expenses, but the sums involved were modest in comparison with the cost of an ensign's commission, which would have been £400. So raising regiments for rank, as this system was called, had the obvious advantage of giving potential officers a strong incentive to seek out men as quickly as possible. Charles Campbell of Ardchattan, who became a lieutenant in the Seventy-first, used his father's services to enlist men in Edinburgh;[14] while Patrick Campbell of Barcaldine, hoping to raise enough soldiers for a captain's commission, even paid a recruiting agent in Newcastle.[15] Yet, despite the encouraging example of the Seventy-first Highlanders, George refused to countenance any further applications to raise new corps until the end of 1777. His motives were commendable—he wanted to protect the interests of officers in the old regiments and prevent the rapid promotion of militarily inexperienced new appointments. But George's scruples meant that, in the first years of the war, the army's expansion was fractional rather than exponential. Only about 11,000 troops were raised for the British establishment between September 1775 and September 1776. The next twelve months produced a mere 6,882 more.[16]

Rather than striving to the uttermost to recruit men in Britain and

[12] *The Correspondence of King George III*, ed. Sir John Fortescue (6 vols., London, 1927–8), iii. 250.

[13] HMC, *Laing MSS* (2 vols., London, 1914–25), ii. 487.

[14] Ardchattan Priory, Campbell Preston Papers, box 34, bundle 514, Campbell to his father, 7 Mar. 1776.

[15] New York Public Library, Bayard-Campbell-Pearsall Papers, box 13, 'Capt. Campbell's Recruiting Instructions', 15 Dec. 1775.

[16] BL, Liverpool Papers, Add. MS 38344, fo. 162.

Ireland, the government turned, in the first years of the war, to external sources of manpower. An agreement was concluded with Georg Scheiter, a Hanoverian officer, to raise 2,000 troops in Germany; those that he eventually enlisted were distributed amongst understrength British regiments.[17] More importantly, whole units of foreign troops were added to the British payroll. Initially, approaches were made to Catherine the Great to secure Russian auxiliaries, then to the Dutch to enlist the services of their Scots brigade. In the end, however, it was Germany that provided the manpower. George III, in his capacity as elector of Hanover, lent five battalions to release for American service some of the British troops in garrison at Gibraltar and Minorca. Further regiments were hired from the princes of Brunswick, Hesse-Cassel, Hesse-Hanau, Waldeck, Anspach-Bayreuth, and Anhalt-Zerbst, who signed treaties with the British government between January 1776 and October 1777. A large number of these German auxiliaries—about 18,000 of them—were available for the 1776 campaign, which meant that the British army received an immediate and invaluable reinforcement of ready-trained and well-equipped men. When, at the close of that campaign, General Sir William Howe, Gage's successor, requested reinforcements, the cabinet promptly agreed that another 4,000 Germans should be sought.[18]

The full mobilization of British resources was seen as imperative only from 1778, when French intervention radically changed the nature of the war. The entry of the French, then in 1779 the Spanish, and at the end of 1780 the Dutch, transformed a rebellion in Britain's mainland North American colonies into a world war. The Caribbean, the Mediterranean, India, and even Africa became arenas of conflict, as the British tried to defend their own far-flung outposts and take advantage of the perceived weaknesses of their opponents. A greatly extended imperial contest made additional manpower imperative. But what gave particular urgency to British efforts was the threat posed to the British Isles themselves. In March 1778, with a French war imminent, plans were drawn up to counter a descent on Ireland. The southern and western coasts were seen as particularly vulnerable, with Cork, Waterford, Limerick, and Galway

---

[17] T 1/514, fos. 127, 130–1. For the distribution of Scheiter's Germans see WO 4/96, pp. 257, 389, 462; WO 4/99, p. 198.

[18] PRO, Granville Papers, 30/29/3/7, fo. 617.

identified as likely landing places, though even the arrival of enemy troops in Ulster was regarded as possible.[19] The following April and May the defences of Cornwall were strengthened; the batteries at Pendennis and St Mawes were put in good order and at Mevagissey a battery was constructed to defend the harbour.[20] Arrangements were also made to meet a landing in Sussex or Kent, with emphasis placed on removing livestock and food from the coastal districts to deprive an invading French army of resources and to create magazines to supply the British defenders.[21] Plans of this kind continued to be penned at times of crisis until the end of the war. In the summer of 1779, for instance, the lord-lieutenant of the East Riding of Yorkshire divided his part of the coast into districts, requested small arms from the government, and named 'particular Gentlemen . . . for the Country People to flock to in case of alarm';[22] and in 1781 further preparations were made along the Sussex coast.[23]

The response to this new situation was impressive. The Royal Navy's sixty-six ships of the line in 1778 increased to ninety in 1779 and ninety-five in 1780. The number of seamen and marines paid for by the British Parliament rose from 60,000 in 1778 to 100,000 in 1782. The naval estimates for 1783, approved by the British House of Commons on 12 December 1782, envisaged 110,000 seaborne personnel serving in the Royal Navy (see Fig. 1.1).[24] These figures, it must be stressed, do not necessarily correspond to the numbers recruited. Securing the requisite men was never easy; compulsory enlistment of trained mariners by naval press-gangs was unpopular and led to considerable friction between the navy and local authorities. Magistrates who were opposed to the war against the Americans, as we shall see, sometimes refused to cooperate on the grounds that impressment was illegal.[25] And resistance could go beyond official obstruction; members of press-gangs were often attacked and occasionally killed in the course of their duty. In April 1778, for instance, Lucy Goddard saw a press-gang set upon by a crowd in Dublin;[26] and the next year an officer on the impress

---

[19] NLI, MS 14306, 'Considerations with regard to the Invasion, and Defence of Ireland', 27 Mar. 1778, a paper drawn up by David Dundas, the Irish quartermaster-general.

[20] Cornwall RO, DDX 517/24, Ordnance Office Letter-book, 1774–9, pp. 112, 150.

[21] BL, Pelham Papers, Add. MS 33118, fos. 33–56.

[22] BL, Leeds Papers, Add. MS 27918, fo. 11.

[23] East Sussex RO, Add. MS 2535.   [24] *PH* xxiii. 292.   [25] See below, Ch. 4.

[26] *Hamwood Papers*, ed. Eva Mary Bell (London, 1930), 36.

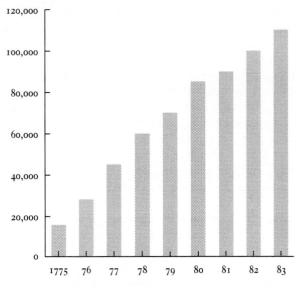

Fig. 1.1. The growth of the navy. The figures represent the number of seamen and marines for whom the British Parliament made financial provision, the estimates being presented in the November or December of the preceding year

Source: *PH*, xviii–xxiii; supplemented by William Laird Clowes, *The Royal Navy: A History* (7 vols., London, 1897–1901), iii. 327

service was shot dead on board a collier on the Medway at Rochester.[27] But there was a ready reserve of trained merchant seamen, many of whom were conscripted by naval press-gangs, and apparently no shortage of volunteers, both mariners and landmen. Indeed, despite the difficulties in securing men, and complaints that 'seafaring men grow very scarce',[28] in 1782 it seems that 106,000 actually served in the navy or marines, rather than the 100,000 envisaged by the British Parliament.[29] At the end of 1781, when the navy was supposed to be 90,000 strong, it mustered 99,831 seamen and marines, or nearly 11% over establishment.[30]

The army was never able to meet its establishment strength, let

[27] *Gentleman's Magazine*, 49 (1779), 213.
[28] ADM 1/2391, Capt. John Rushworth to Philip Stephens, 28 May 1778.
[29] *PH* xxiii. 292.
[30] *The Private Papers of John, Earl of Sandwich*, ed. G. R. Barnes and J. H. Owen (4 vols., London, 1932–8), iv. 290, 313.

alone exceed it;[31] nonetheless, expansion was similarly spectacular. The changed circumstances obliged the king to put aside his hostility to the creation of new corps. He accepted, though with some reluctance,[32] offers from the governing bodies of the towns and cities of Liverpool, Manchester, Glasgow, and Edinburgh, and from several influential landowners, especially in the Scottish Highlands. In all, twelve infantry battalions were added to the establishment in the spring of 1778; another fourteen in 1779, together with four regiments of light dragoons. Between September 1777 and September 1778 some 24,000 men were recruited for the British establishment alone.[33]

By 1783 there were 118 battalions of infantry (excluding the Guards), compared with only seventy-two in 1774. Three regiments of fencibles—corps confined to home defence—were raised, and another was formed on the Isle of Man. The army estimates for 1782 envisaged the British Parliament paying for nearly 112,000 men in the British regiments or corps (see Fig. 1.2). In England and Wales the militia, which had been reformed during the previous conflict by the 1757 Militia Act, was embodied, or called out for active service, in 1778. An attempt to double the militia in 1779 was abandoned, but additional companies raised by voluntary enlistment increased the size of many units. By the end of the war there were sixty-six militia corps in existence. In several counties this was the first time that the new militia had been embodied; this was the case with five of the thirteen Welsh shires, and a swathe of Midland counties in England (see Map 1.1). The militia mobilization of 1778–83 was accordingly a much more impressive affair than the turnout in the Seven Years War. In Scotland, where there was no militia, four substantial fencible regiments were created. They played an important part in coastal defence—fenciblemen, for example, constructed and manned the defences at Lerwick in Shetland.[34] In Ireland, where the militia was not revived for lack of money, volunteer corps

---

[31] John Houlding, *Fit for Service: The Training of the British Army, 1715–1795* (Oxford, 1981), 126, states that in wartime British infantry regiments were, on average, at 83% of establishment strength, and cavalry regiments at 94%.

[32] In Apr. 1778 e.g. the king refused an offer to raise a corps of light cavalry, on the grounds that the old regiments were still under strength: see North Yorkshire RO, Zetland (Dundas) MSS, ZNK X2/1/32.

[33] BL, Liverpool Papers, Add. MS 38344, fo. 162.

[34] *The Diary of the Reverend John Mill*, ed. Gilbert Goudie (Scottish History Society, vol. v, Edinburgh, 1889), 63.

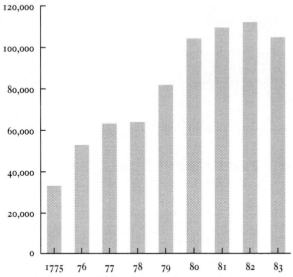

Fig. 1.2. The growth of the army. These figures, which are taken from the estimates presented to the British Parliament at the end of the preceding year, should be seen as indicative rather then precise (see below, n. 64, for further refinement). They exclude all foreign regiments, and the regiments in Ireland and India

Source: *Journals of the House of Commons*, xxxv–xxxix

were established among the Protestant population. Belfast formed companies in the spring of 1778,[35] and soon many other areas in Ulster and beyond followed suit. By the summer of 1779 it was said that 'The country is arming from one end to the other'.[36] The Irish volunteers, as we shall see later, were not simply a military force; their political demands became increasingly obvious and alarming to the British government. But the authorities at Dublin Castle recognized that, with Ireland's garrison of regulars depleted to help the war in North America, the volunteers could play a useful role in the event of an invasion. In 1779 the Irish quartermaster-general envisaged the volunteers acting as auxiliaries to the regulars, harassing

[35] *Belfast News-letter*, 17–21 Apr. 1778.
[36] *The Correspondence of the Right Hon. John Beresford*, ed. William Beresford (2 vols., London, 1854), i. 44.

Map 1.1. English and Welsh counties embodying their militia for the first time in 1778

Source: J. R. Western, *The English Militia in the Eighteenth Century* (London, 1965), 158

an enemy army as it tried to advance from its coastal landing points.[37]

Volunteering was less important beyond Ireland, but still of some significance. Senior army officers were generally sceptical about the value of arming untrained civilians; it was assumed that they would

---

[37] NLI, MS 14306, 'Memorandum', 1 July 1779—another paper by David Dundas. See also his report in the same volume on 'Irish Military Associations', 2 Feb. 1780.

never be able to resist French regulars.[38] There were also, as we shall see, political considerations that inhibited the government. North's ministry was nervous about arming the people in Britain, especially at a time when the Irish volunteers were using their position to press for commercial and constitutional reforms. But, despite official ambivalence, or even discouragement, it was difficult to stop local initiatives. Volunteer units came into being, with or without official approval. One was formed in Bath in 1779,[39] a number in Cornwall,[40] others in Devon—where arms were distributed to local gentry by the governor of Plymouth in the crisis days of August,[41] and a militia officer reported in October that almost every village had raised a company.[42] Sussex produced twenty-four companies at the same time,[43] while at Dover more than 300 men agreed to associate in a volunteer corps.[44] The Duke of Queensbury reported that in Dumfries a county meeting had offered to raise volunteer companies, and similar offers came from Cardigan, Anglesey, and Pembrokeshire.[45] That summer and autumn, military associations were formed at Stockton, County Durham, and at Bradford, Scarborough, and Kirkby Moorside in Yorkshire.[46] The metropolis also responded to the emergency, with volunteer units emerging in Westminster and Middlesex, and the officers and artificers of the Board of Works agreeing to incorporate from amongst their body 300 volunteers in four companies.[47] By the end of 1779 there were said to be about 150 companies in England, of at least fifty men each;[48] but this is almost certainly an underestimate that takes no account of those units formed without official sanction. Some of

---

[38] WO 34/116, fo. 196. A plan drawn up in July 1779, and presented to the commander-in-chief, was more positive about the role of civilians, envisaging that men in all the parishes from Essex to Cornwall be prepared to 'make a Stand against the Enemy', those with arms harassing them, and those without, and the women and boys, blocking the roads and driving off the cattle. See WO 34/153, fo. 514.

[39] *Bath Chronicle*, 19 Aug. 1779.

[40] SP 41/33, fos. 20, 47, 53, 78, 89–90, 92, 101, 153, 157, 266, 277; Cornwall RO, Tremayne of Heligan Papers, DDT 1892/1, and Rogers of Penrose Papers, DDRP 43.

[41] *Papers of Earl of Sandwich*, ed. Barnes and Owen, iii. 74.

[42] Wiltshire RO, Savernake MS 9, Lt. Matthew Bentham to Lord Ailesbury, 10 Oct. 1779.

[43] HO 42/205, fos. 156–8; BL, Pelham Papers, Add. MS 33127, fo. 33.

[44] WO 34/116, fos. 1–2.

[45] WO 34/155, fo. 15; *Journals of the House of Commons*, xxxvii. 514–15.

[46] *York Courant*, 24 and 31 Aug., 5 Oct. 1779.

[47] WO 34/116, fos. 20–1; WO 34/154, fos. 540, 548–9.

[48] Herbert Butterfield, *George III, Lord North and the People* (London, 1949), 55.

these volunteer bodies were ephemeral—most of those in Middlesex and Westminster had disbanded by September 1780—but even after the immediate danger of an enemy landing receded, volunteer units continued to emerge. By July 1780 there was a corps of volunteer artillery in King's Lynn;[49] Great Yarmouth formed a volunteer force in response to the Dutch entry into the war,[50] as did Aberdeen, which had been refused permission to raise volunteers in 1778, when enemy privateers menaced the coast.[51] In the same year, 1781, the Edinburgh Defensive Band was created; the Caledonian Band followed in 1782.[52] Indeed, the encouragement given to volunteering by the new Rockingham government meant that 1782 saw another wave of enthusiasm. Lewes in Sussex, which already had raised two companies in 1779, agreed to form three more;[53] a company was established at Leeds;[54] another in Sheffield;[55] Liverpool pledged to raise ten companies of at least sixty men each;[56] York, five companies;[57] while in Birmingham the rules for the town's 'Independent Volunteers' were published in the local press.[58] That September, when a Dutch descent on the east coast seemed a real possibility, 'The Old Norfolk Squires . . . all turned military',[59] and a cavalry unit, the Norfolk Rangers, was formed.[60] A different source suggests that there were other volunteer corps raised in the county at this time.[61]

This vogue for volunteering was not entirely new—volunteer units had emerged during previous invasion scares in 1745 and 1759—but it anticipated, on a more modest scale, what was to happen during the French Revolutionary and Napoleonic Wars.

---

[49] *Ipswich Journal*, 22 July 1780.

[50] SP 41/33, fo. 301; HO 42/205, fo. 132. See also Norfolk RO, Great Yarmouth Corporation Records, Y/TC/36/20/10.

[51] SP 54/47, fos. 135, 137, 151; SP 54/48, fos. 103, 105, 107, 125, 127.

[52] John Robertson, *The Scottish Enlightenment and the Militia Issue* (Edinburgh, 1985), 137–8.

[53] HO 42/205, fos. 152–4; BL, Pelham Papers, Add. MS 33128, fo. 79; V. Smith (ed.), *The Town Book of Lewes 1702–1837* (Sussex Record Society, vol. lxix, Lewes, 1973), 68–9.

[54] *Leeds Intelligencer*, 21 and 31 Dec. 1782.   [55] HO 42/205, fo. 111.

[56] Ibid., fo. 113.

[57] York City Archives, Acc. 163, Diary of Dr William White, 14, 16 and 21 May 1782.

[58] *Aris's Birmingham Gazette*, 12 Aug. 1782.

[59] Leeds Archives, Ramsden Papers, Rockingham Letters, vol. 3b, Rev. William Palgrave to William Weddell, 2 Sept. [1782].

[60] Ian J. F. Beckett, *The Amateur Military Tradition 1558–1945* (Manchester, 1991), 70.

[61] *Mary Hardy's Diary*, ed. Basil Cozens-Hardy (Norfolk Record Society, vol. xxxvii, Norwich, 1968), 43.

Indeed, while conflict with the Bourbons and the Dutch was in many senses a 'traditional' imperial contest, its impact on British mobilization pointed the way to the 1790s rather than merely repeated the experience of earlier eighteenth-century struggles. There were, of course, considerable obstacles to the full-scale mobilization of manpower. Military considerations, as we have already seen, played a part in determining the speed with which expansion of the armed forces took place, and the nature of that expansion. Political issues, as we shall see later, also influenced both the scale and the form of military and naval participation. Economic interests were important, too. Employers were often reluctant to lose valuable workers or servants to the militia, which was raised by a ballot of eligible men, and some masters even paid a fine rather than see a trusted man taken away.[62] On a more general level, sensitivity to the labour requirements of landowners and their tenant farmers helped to scupper plans to double the size of the militia.[63] But, despite these countervailing pressures, the growth of the armed forces, official and unofficial, was spectacular. By the close of the American war more than a quarter of a million of George III's British and Irish subjects were serving in the official armed forces (about 100,000 in the army,[64] 107,000 in the navy, and around 46,000 in the English and Welsh militia and the English and Scottish fencibles). Another 60,000 or so Irishmen were active in volunteer units,[65] and perhaps

---

[62] e.g. *Correspondence of the Reverend Joseph Greene*, ed. Levi Fox (Dugdale Society Publications, vol. xxiii, London, 1965), 125; Hampshire RO, Diaries of John Thorp of Preston Candover, 65 M82/2, p. 145.

[63] BL, Hardwicke Papers, Add. MS 35660, fo. 181; *The Correspondence of Edmund Burke*, ed. Thomas W. Copeland et al. (10 vols., Cambridge, 1958–78), iv. 109. See also NLW, Bute MS L93/13, where Lord Mountstuart expresses the view, even before the militia is embodied, that its assembling 'will be very detrimental to the hay harvest'.

[64] Precision is impossible. This figure is based on the estimates presented to the House of Commons in Feb. 1783 (*Journals of the House of Commons*, xxxix. 203, 242–4), which exclude foreign and American loyalist auxiliaries. From these estimates I have deducted those British regular regiments known to have been made up largely of Germans or American loyalists (such as the 60th, 84th, and 105th Regiments of Foot). I have made some additions, as well, for the regiments on the Irish establishment (paid for by the Irish Parliament, and therefore not included in the British estimates) and those serving in India, the costs of which were met by the East India Company. Finally, I have adjusted the total to take account of John Houlding's calculations of the actual — as opposed to establishment — strength of the different corps at this time (see above, n. 31).

[65] Peter Smyth, '"Our Cloud-Cap't Grenadiers": The Volunteers as a Military Force', *Irish Sword*, 13 (1977–9), 195.

half as many Britons (this is no more than a guess, and quite probably too cautious).

But aggregating these figures merely provides a snapshot of the armed forces at their peak; an indication of how many men were serving at a given moment. There are, of course, considerable difficulties involved in trying to calculate the total number of men who served at one time or another. The practice of drafting soldiers from one regiment to another muddies the water somewhat. In January 1775 the government proposed to bring the army at Boston up to strength with a mixture of new recruits and men drafted from corps based in Britain and Ireland.[66] Once the war had begun, the regiments in America, though they received a steady stream of recruits raised in the British Isles, took in large numbers of drafts from regiments ordered home. Early in 1776, for example, the Eighteenth and Fifty-ninth regiments of Foot distributed their rank and file among the corps remaining behind, and the officers and sergeants came back to the British Isles to raise their regiments afresh. But drafting was only a temporary expedient, not a substitute for raising more soldiers. By leaving their rank and file in America, the Eighteenth and Fifty-ninth had saved government the expense of shipping out the equivalent number of recruits. New entrants were still required, though, to rebuild the Eighteenth and Fifty-ninth. By November 1777 the Fifty-ninth, according to a newspaper report, was again nearly 500-strong.[67] Drafting, then, while it meant that at any given time there might be one or two regiments that were no more than skeletons, did not ultimately reduce the demand for new enlistments.

But there are other problems involved in trying to calculate the numbers who served in the various services, official and unofficial, throughout the war. Some men spent time in more than one branch of the armed forces. Privates William Tilbery and Thomas Jones of the Northern battalion of the Hampshire militia turned out to be deserters from the navy.[68] The lieutenant-colonel of the Cambridgeshire militia reported that his regiment had 'Recd some men as Substitutes, that have been Discharged from the Regulars'.[69] There was trade in the opposite direction, too; a Staffordshire militia officer believed it

---

[66] SP 41/26, Earl of Rochford to Barrington, 23 Jan. 1775.
[67] *Leeds Intelligencer*, 4 Nov. 1777.
[68] ADM 1/2392, Rushworth to Stephens, 25 Mar. 1779.
[69] BL, Hardwicke Papers, Add. MS 35660, fo. 210.

'more than probable' that some of the men discharged as unfit from his regiment 'have Enlisted among the new Corps'.[70] Officers also moved. Vere Hunt, first a major in an Irish volunteer corps, then an ensign in the Fifth Foot, and finally a major in an Irish provincial or fencible unit, might have been exceptional;[71] even so, there were several officers who transferred from the militia to the regulars, such as Lieutenant James Ogden of the West Middlesex militia, who became an ensign in the newly formed Ninety-sixth Foot.[72] But, while we need to be aware of the problem of double-counting, the numbers in these categories were probably not very great—in the Cambridgeshire militia only one officer out of twenty-eight serving in the war left to join a regular regiment—and it should be remembered that at this time the regulars and the navy were forbidden to recruit militiamen.[73]

If some men served twice, many more passed in and out just once. A large number of enlistees taken into the service after the start of the war were no longer present at its end. For the Royal Navy to increase its manpower from 16,000 men in 1775 to 107,000 in 1783 required far more than 91,000 recruits, because in the course of the conflict staggeringly large numbers of sailors were lost through death, desertion, or discharge, most of whom would have been replaced with new entrants. According to one source, just in the years 1774–80 the navy was deprived of the services of more than 60,000 men.[74] Losses were probably not so high for the army, but they were still significant. Between 1775 and 1779 alone, at least 19,000 British troops in North America died, or deserted, or were discharged or captured.[75] In proportionate terms, the regiments employed in the disease-ridden Caribbean theatre suffered even more. St Lucia, occupied by the British from December 1778, was a veritable graveyard: 'this horrid Island', one officer wrote, 'they say

---

[70]   Staffordshire RO, Paget Papers, D 603/0/2/8.

[71]   Limerick City Archives, Vere Hunt Papers, Diaries, 1780–2 (microfilm in NLI).

[72]   BL, Rainsford Papers, Add. MS 23654, fo. 135.

[73]   J. R. Western, *The English Militia in the Eighteenth Century* (London, 1965), 265. See also Tower of London, Royal Fusiliers Museum, MS R-29(b), 'Recruiting Instructions for the Royal Fuziliers', 27 Nov. 1775. Henry Penrud Wyndham, a Salisbury magistrate, suggested in July 1779 a plan by which the regulars could be recruited by volunteers from the militia; but nothing came of the proposal (BL, Liverpool Papers, Add. MS 38211, fo. 186).

[74]   Michael Duffy, 'The Foundations of British Naval Power', in id. (ed.), *The Military Revolution and the State* (Exeter, 1980), 72.

[75]   BL, Liverpool Papers, Add. MS 38375, fos. 74–5.

is the most unhealthy in the whole West Indies';[76] another commented that St Lucia 'has almost destroyed the few troops that came from America, and the recruits of new Corps are fast following them'.[77] If disease was responsible for the large loss of men in the Caribbean, in Ireland desertion was the primary problem. The regiments based there found it particularly difficult to keep recruits, not least, it was said, because the local population was only too happy to protect deserters.[78] Charles Jenkinson, Barrington's successor as secretary at war, told the king that in Ireland 'not above half of those who are Enlisted are brought to the Publick Service'; and in October 1780 the lord-lieutenant reported that 'In the last two months the desertions, &c., has exceeded the recruits by 27.'[79]

To calculate the number of men who served at one time or another, we need, then, to combine the number raised during the war with the number already in the army and navy when the fighting started. A very cautious estimate suggests that something over 100,000 men were recruited by the army;[80] perhaps about 171,000 by the navy.[81] Adding these to the existing strengths in 1775 (about 36,000 and 16,000 respectively) gives a total of 323,000 soldiers and sailors. Then there is the militia to consider. No militiaman was killed in action, but some died of disease in the camps established to concentrate troops to counter an invasion, others were discharged, and still others deserted.[82] More significantly, in statistical terms, militiamen were required to serve only for three years once their unit had been embodied, which meant that in theory a whole new cohort would have been raised in 1781 and 1782. In practice, it

[76] SRO, Dalguise Muniments, GD 38/2/19, Lt. William Robertson to his father, 17 Jan.–1 Feb. 1779.
[77] SRO, Broughton and Cally Muniments, GD 10/1421/7/338.
[78] HMC, *Stopford Sackville MSS* (2 vols., London, 1904–10), i. 245; BL, Buckingham Papers, Add. MS 40178, fos. 29–30.
[79] *Correspondence of George III*, ed. Fortescue, iii. 194; HMC, *Stopford Sackville MSS* i. 277.
[80] Extrapolated from figures in BL, Liverpool Papers, Add. MS 38344, fo. 162.
[81] This may well be an underestimate. Duffy, 'Foundations of British Naval Power', 72, states that there were 175,990 enlistments from 1774 to 1780 alone. On the other hand, this figure must include men who joined one ship, were discharged, and then joined another. For the problems of estimating numbers of men recruited—as opposed to the number of enlistments—see N. A. M. Rodger, *The Wooden World: An Anatomy of the Georgian Navy* (London, 1986), ch. 5.
[82] For deaths at Warley Camp see below, Ch. 8. For Coxheath Camp see Western, *English Militia*, 396. For militia deserters see e.g. *Reading Mercury and Oxford Gazette*, 20 July 1778 and NLW, Bute MS L93/88i.

appears that some militiamen agreed to serve a second term on payment of a bounty.[83] There were certainly many fresh entrants, though: of the eighty-one men entering the Bedfordshire militia between 25 December 1781 and 24 June 1782, only twenty-four (just under 30%) had re-enrolled.[84] Without further information, we can only speculate on the number of militiamen who served in the war; but 60,000 is probably a cautious estimate. If we say that 80,000 is an appropriate figure for the Irish volunteers, and maybe 30,000 for their British counterparts, we have around half a million men under arms in the course of the conflict.

The population of the British Isles in 1775 was perhaps twelve million. There were an estimated 6.7 million English, around 0.4 million Welsh, maybe 1.4 million Scots, and about 3.6 million Irish.[85] If we say that a quarter of this number was made up of adult males of military age—say between 16 and 50[86]—we have three millions. The quantity potentially available between the beginning and the end of the war would, of course, have been much greater, for every year a fresh cohort of males joined the group as 16-year-olds. If 3% of the male population became this age every year,[87] we need to add 3% per year to our original three millions. This produces a total of 3.8 million men who were theoretically available at some stage between 1775 and 1783. If half a million actually served in this period, the military participation ratio

---

[83] For an example of a private arrangement see the agreement between James Smith and Thomas Adams, a serving substitute 'soon to be discharged', 4 Mar. 1780: Hampshire RO, Jervoise Collection, 44 M60 030.   [84] WO 13/99.

[85] E. A. Wrigley and R. S. Schofield, *The Population History of England 1541–1871* (Cambridge, 1989), 208 (table 7.8) and 566 n. 20; B. R. Mitchell, *British Historical Statistics* (Cambridge, 1988), 8; K. H. Connell, *The Population of Ireland 1750–1845* (Oxford, 1950), 25. For the problems in calculating the Scottish population in the 18th cent. see Michael Flinn et al., *Scottish Population History from the Seventeenth Century to the 1930s* (Cambridge, 1977), 4.

[86] The militia laws specified that only men between 18 and 45 were eligible to be balloted (Western, *English Militia*, 247), but there were some 16- and 17-year-olds in the army and navy, and some men over 45. There were, it must be admitted, a few entrants below 16, such as drummer boys in the army and officers' servants in the navy; but they were not numerically significant (see David Baker, 'The Inhabitants of Cardington in 1782', *Bedfordshire Historical Record Society Publications*, 52 (1973), 57; Sylvia Frey, *The British Soldier in America: A Social History of Military Life in the Revolutionary Period* (Austin, Tex. 1981), 23–6; Rodger, *Wooden World*, app. vii, pp. 360–4).

[87] This may be an overestimate, but better to exaggerate than to understate in this instance. See the population pyramids in R. D. Lee and R. S. Schofield, 'British Population in the Eighteenth Century', in Roderick Floud and Donald McCloskey (eds.), *The Economic History of Britain since 1700* (2 vols., Cambridge, 1981), i. 23 (fig. 2.2).

was between one in seven and one in eight. This is less than the one in four (or five or six) calculated for the Napoleonic Wars,[88] let alone the one in two for the First World War.[89] But it exceeds the ratios for earlier eighteenth-century conflicts—perhaps one in nine or ten for the Seven Years War and maybe as low as one in sixteen for the War of Austrian Succession[90]—and suggests that the 'British Armed Nation' of the 1790s and early 1800s should be seen less as a revolutionary departure from past practice and more as a development and intensification of existing trends.

Who Served?

The level of mobilization in the American war posited here sits somewhat uneasily with the received image of the composition of the British armed forces in the eighteenth century. But when each branch of the services is examined in turn, it becomes clear that the established view of their make-up is in need of considerable revision. Foreigners played only a limited role in easing the pressure for recruits, and many different types of Britons and Irishmen took up arms between 1775 and 1783.

It should be reiterated that the calculations made earlier of the number of men in the army—about 100,000 in 1783 and somewhere in the region of 136,000 at one time or another during the war—were confined to those serving in regular British army units; they exclude both the German auxiliary regiments and all other allies of the British, whether native or colonial, organized in their own formations. The estimates even exclude a small number of British

---

[88] Linda Colley, 'Whose Nation? Class and National Consciousness in Britain 1750–1830', *Past & Present*, 113 (1986), 101 and n. 12; Cookson, *British Armed Nation*, 95.

[89] John Bourne, 'Goodbye to all that? Recent Writing on the Great War', *Twentieth Century History*, 1 (1990), 97.

[90] These are my calculations, based on the methods used to produce a military participation ratio for the American war. Douglas Hay and Nicholas Rogers, *Eighteenth-Century English Society* (Oxford, 1997), 228, drawing on material in Roderick Floud, Kenneth Wachter, and Annabel Gregory, *Height, Health and History: Nutritional Status in the United Kingdom, 1750–1980* (Cambridge, 1990) and other sources, suggest that the American war saw a lower ratio of military and naval involvement than the Seven Years War. I suspect, however, that they, like many other historians, have mistaken figures for men in British pay with the number of Britons and Irishmen in the armed forces. Earlier 18th-cent. wars, as we have seen, involved the employment of considerable numbers of foreign troops in nominally British armies—a much higher proportion than in the American war.

units known to have contained large numbers of men from beyond the British Isles, such as the Royal American Regiment, which was made up largely of German soldiers and German and Swiss officers, and the Eighty-fourth and One-hundred-and-fifth regiments, which were manned predominantly by American loyalists.[91]

This, admittedly, does not draw a line under the foreign contribution. Account must be taken of German enlistees, such as those raised by Colonel Scheiter, who were used to top up understrength British regiments in the first years of the conflict. Other foreigners were also incorporated into British units as the war progressed, such as the Frenchman Alexandre Naire, who came to England in 1779 and promptly joined a new corps, deserted to join another, and was finally packed off to serve abroad with the Royal Americans.[92] Nor should we forget that American loyalists, as well as serving in their own specially raised provincial corps, were to be found in several regular regiments. Thomas Taylor Byrd, a junior officer in the Sixteenth Foot, was a member of the famous Virginia family, while Leverett Saltonstall, from an equally famous New England dynasty, became a lieutenant in the Royal Welch Fusiliers. But the numbers involved were not sufficiently large to change the character of the British regiments, or noticeably to lessen the demand for recruits in the British Isles.[93] In four infantry battalions based in Canada at the end of the war, all of which had received German troops to bring them up to strength, foreigners comprised a mere 6% of the total; in four cavalry regiments inspected in 1775, they made up no more than 2%.[94] When the Twenty-second Light Dragoons were inspected in 1779, there were only two foreigners out of 240 troopers, or less than 1%,[95] while in all the regular infantry and cavalry regiments in Britain in 1781 there were a mere sixty-four foreigners out of 8,849 rank and file, or 0.72%.[96]

The standard social portrait of the army also requires much modification. There were certainly many officers from aristocratic

---

[91] Though the 105th was given permission to recruit in Ireland in the closing stages of the war: see NLI, Kilmainham Papers, MS 1001, Hillsborough to the lord-lieutenant, 21 Mar. 1782.　　　　　　　　[92] SP 41/28, Weymouth to Amherst, 25 Oct. 1779.

[93] It should be added that there were also Britons and Irishmen who served in units raised in the colonies. See e.g. *The Diary of the Revd. William Jones*, ed. O. F. Christie (London, 1929), 58; Cumbria RO, Rauthmell Letters, WD/AG/Box 3, Robert Rauthmell to his aunt, 6 July 1778.　　　　　　　　[94] Frey, *British Soldier*, 23–6.

[95] East Sussex RO, Sheffield Papers, A2714/265, 'General Return'.

[96] WO 27/47.

or gentry families. In the senior ranks, for instance, there were Hugh, Earl Percy, colonel of the Fifth Foot, heir to the Duke of Northumberland and estates worth about £50,000 a year;[97] General Henry Seymour Conway, the second son of Lord Conway and the brother of the Earl of Hertford; Sir Henry Clinton, commander-in-chief in North America 1778–82, the grandson of the Earl of Lincoln and cousin of the Duke of Newcastle; the Hon. William Howe, Clinton's predecessor, the second son of the first Viscount Howe. At the other end of the officer scale we find amongst the subalterns the likes of Lord Dunglass, heir of the Earl of Home, an ensign in the Guards; and the Hon. Edward Finch, fifth son of the Earl of Aylesford, a cornet in the Twentieth Dragoons. Even in less fashionable regiments there were plenty of sons of the aristocracy and gentry. The Hon. George Damer, second son of Lord Milton, was the major of the Eighty-seventh Foot, while Hew Dalrymple, son of a Scottish baronet of the same name, became a captain in the Ninety-second Foot after having served in the Royal Scots.

Even so, the British army did not have any equivalent of the four-quartering system that operated in the French army from 1781, by which officers above the rank of lieutenant had to prove the nobility of all four of their grandparents. Nor did the British army's proportion of aristocratic officers begin to compare with that in other European armies. In 1780 30% of British army officers had titles, while in Piedmont-Sardinia in 1767 nearly 75% of infantry officers were nobles, and 93% of cavalry officers; in the Prussian army in 1786 a mere 3% of officers of the rank of major or above were commoners.[98] It might be imagined that the purchase of commissions in the British army—with the cheapest ensigncy selling at £400—would have limited access to those with substantial property,[99] but there was no landed requirement, and money from commerce, or even manufacturing, could buy a commission. The purchase system, furthermore, did not necessarily keep out those with limited means. Officers could borrow to progress in the service: Mervyn Murray of the Seventeenth Foot purchased his lieutenancy with money loaned by fellow officers;[100] while Nisbet Balfour was

[97] John Cannon, *Aristocratic Century* (Cambridge, 1984), 146.

[98] Christopher Storrs and H. M. Scott, 'The Military Revolution and the European Nobility, c.1600–1800', *War in History*, 3 (1996), 15–17.

[99] See Anthony Bruce, *The Purchase System in the British Army, 1660–1871* (London, 1980), 13.   [100] WO 1/1008, p. 1053.

able to gain promotion only by going 'monstrously in debt'.[101] And entry and advancement in wartime could be obtained without purchase. The new regiments were raised, as we have seen, by rank, which meant that officers could acquire a commission much more cheaply. There were even almost cost-free means of entry and advancement: volunteers served with the rank and file in the hope of stepping into a subaltern vacancy;[102] and a battle could boost the career prospects of many an existing officer by allowing him to move up the promotion ladder without spending any money.[103]

Whatever the theory, then, in practice officers came from a bewildering variety of backgrounds. Aristocratic and gentry officers rubbed shoulders with the likes of Frederick Mackenzie of the Royal Welch Fusiliers, the son of a Dublin merchant; George Dunlop of the Seventy-fourth Foot, a junior member of a Glasgow mercantile family; and Gilbert Waugh of the Thirty-fifth Foot, by repute the son of an Edinburgh baker. Some officers were even promoted from the ranks. This seems to have been particularly so in the Royal Artillery, where purchase was not permitted and technical expertise was required. In the artillery contingent with the army at Boston in 1775–6 at least two sergeants were made second-lieutenants.[104] But the practice was certainly not confined to the artillery. Lieutenant George Hutchinson of the King's Own Regiment had been a drill sergeant in the Guards;[105] William Ralston, the son of a Glasgow hosier, after serving as a sergeant in the Seventy-first Foot, in 1780 became a lieutenant in the newly raised One-hundredth;[106] and in 1781 Sergeant Matthew O'Hea of the Twenty-fourth Foot became an ensign in the Ninety-sixth.[107]

---

[101] Bedfordshire RO, Lucas Collection, Polwarth Papers, L 30/12/3/4.

[102] Barrington complained that the volunteers commissioned after Bunker Hill were 'all without a farthing' (East Suffolk RO, Barrington Papers, HA 174/1026/107, p. 315). Gage sought to reassure him that 'They were all Gentlemen's Sons Strongly recommended' (ibid., HA 174/1026/6a (2)); but other sources suggest that Barrington's fears were justified: Brig.-Gen. James Grant was persuaded to take 'a reduced Custom-House Officer' as a volunteer in his regiment (Ballindalloch Castle, Macpherson Grant Papers, bundle 772, Grant to A. Mackenzie, 4 June 1776).

[103] NLS, Robertson-MacDonald Papers, MS 3945, fo. 52. See also, below, Ch. 3.

[104] Library of Congress, Peter Force MSS, Order-book, 43rd Foot, 10 Feb. 1776; WO 55/1537, fo. 62.

[105] Bedfordshire RO, Lucas Collection, Polwarth Papers, L 30/12/17/2.

[106] Francis J. Grant (ed.), *The Commissariot of Edinburgh: Consistorial Processes and Decreets, 1658–1800* (Scottish Record Society, vol. xxxiv, Edinburgh, 1909), 64.

[107] BL, Liverpool Papers, Add. MS 38217, fo. 173.

Nor was the rank and file itself recruited predominantly from the very bottom strata of society. Officers might complain of the 'dregs of mankind' with which they had to contend,[108] or observe that 'At this glorious time, Jails are purged, and ye. Gallows defrauded, to defend G:B',[109] but closer inspection suggests a rather different composition. Convicted or putative offenders were certainly enlisted: legal records show that conditional royal pardons were employed to offer criminals the choice of service in the army, and that others were given the option by judges and magistrates; the army's muster rolls confirm that some of these offenders arrived in the ranks.[110] But the numbers do not appear to have been great. In England and Wales some 500 convicts were offered pardons conditional on serving in the army between the beginning of the war and the end of 1781, and another 200 were given pardons that included army service among other choices. The impression conveyed by the records is that the number of offenders entering the army by other means was also limited: in the period 1775–81 Essex justices offered twelve criminals the chance to join the army, and another twenty the opportunity to enlist in the army or navy; but in Warwickshire the total was only five,[111] in Hertfordshire and Cambridgeshire three,[112] in Shropshire two, and in the City of London one. Assize court judges and magistrates in smaller boroughs seem to have been similarly disinclined to dispatch criminals to the army: no such cases appear in the records for the Norfolk Circuit, while Lichfield's wartime quarter sessions sent only two.[113] The number of paupers compelled to join the army by the Recruiting Acts of 1778 and 1779 seems likewise to have been small,[114] and they were clearly regarded

---

[108] Stephen Payne Ayde, *Treatise on Courts Martial* (London, 1778), 15.

[109] BL, Napier Papers, Add. MS 49092, fo. 8.

[110] Stephen Conway, 'The Recruitment of Criminals into the British Army, 1775–1781', *Bulletin of the Institute of Historical Research*, 58 (1985), 46–58. The material on offenders produced below is from this source unless otherwise stated; but note that in the article the marines were treated as associated with the army, while here they are seen as a branch of the navy.

[111] Warwickshire RO, Sessions Order-books, QS 32/1–2; Minute-book, QS 39/8.

[112] Cambridgeshire RO, Sessions Order-books, QS 07, pp. 453–5; QS 08, p. 101.

[113] Lichfield RO, Sessions Order-book, D 25/1/1, fo. 104; WO 4/96, p. 354.

[114] WO 34/119, fos. 217–19; WO 1/1004, Capt. John Money to Jenkinson, 13 Mar. 1779; WO 1/1005, Lord Percy to Jenkinson, 8 Mar. 1779. Most of the men raised seem to have been collected in the metropolis: see T 1/549, fo. 71. The Acts, it should be added, were seen as a means of stimulating voluntary recruitment, and they seem to have succeeded in this respect: BL, Liverpool Papers, Add. MS 38306, fo. 108.

as very different from normal recruits: the secretary at war confessed that impressed men were not 'precisely what a Commanding Officer would approve in the ordinary course of Recruiting'.[115]

Even unskilled labourers were not present in such numbers as one might suppose. Before the war, a surprisingly large proportion of recruits had been artisans or craftsmen,[116] and changes in conditions of recruitment during the conflict itself probably encouraged still more such men to enter the army. Particularly important in this regard were the reduction of the period of service to three years or the duration of the war and the substantial augmentation of bounty money. With the passing of the 1779 Recruiting Act there was another inducement for skilled men. The act sought to encourage recruitment by promising that voluntary entrants would be eligible to exercise their trade in any town in the country after the war. Captain John Moore of the newly formed One-hundred-and-fourth Foot focused on this pledge when he advertised for recruits in Reading in June 1782: 'Tradesmen serving in this battalion during the war', he announced, 'will be qualified in time of peace to exercise their trade without molestation, in any town corporate throughout Great Britain and even in the city of London'.[117]

Only a few recruiting returns seem to have survived, but these give the clear impression that the army's rank and file was made up of men from widely varying backgrounds. A sample of 285 men taken into the newly raised Ninety-sixth Foot between 1779 and 1782 reveals that while 52% were classified as labourers, the rest had all pursued trades of one type or another, from glassblowing and flax-dressing to tailoring and stay-making; there were even millers and clerks in the regiment's ranks.[118] Again, of sixty-seven men recruited for the Forty-sixth Foot in Ireland in the winter of 1775–6, more than half were labourers, but amongst the remainder were several weavers, cordwainers, and butchers, together with a former schoolmaster.[119]

---

[115] WO 4/966, p. 144.
[116] Corporation of London RO, Miscellaneous MSS, box 206, applicants to Sir John Langham's Charity; Library of Congress, Peter Force MSS, George Chalmers Collection, Journal of Walter Home, Nov. 1772, 'Description of Lord Robt. Berties Company Royal Fuziliers'.
[117] *Reading Mercury and Oxford Gazette*, 10 June 1782. The 1779 Act made it clear that volunteers entering under its provisions would not be removable from the parish in which they set up trade unless they became a charge on the local poor rates (19 Geo. III, c.10, s. xli).
[118] WO 25/537.
[119] WO 1/992, 'List of recruits Rais'd for the 46th Regiment', 9 Feb. 1776.

A return of twenty-two men raised for the Third Foot Guards at about the same time contains only six labourers, but two shoemakers, three weavers, a gardener, a tailor, and a failed merchant.[120] Among twenty-five troops recruited by Lieutenant Allan Macdonald of the Seventy-sixth Foot there was a similar occupational distribution: six labourers, twelve weavers, two smiths, a shoemaker, a nailer, an ostler, and a gardener.[121] In two companies of an English fencible regiment raised in Yorkshire, sixty-nine of the men (or 43%) were described as former labourers; but the majority were skilled or semi-skilled, and included carpenters, blacksmiths, cordwainers, wheelwrights, tailors, masons, bricklayers, and weavers, together with a gunsmith, a brewer, and a grocer.[122] The Northern Regiment of Scottish fencibles likewise contained a significant number of farmers and merchants in its ranks, as well as labourers.[123] Other sources add to this picture of diversity. We can perhaps discount as politically motivated the claim that there were privates in the Edinburgh and Glasgow regiments 'worth some hundred pounds';[124] but we can be confident that Edward Kirkham, who joined the Third Foot Guards as a private in 1778, was the son of a Staffordshire freeholder, who himself had enlisted in the last war. Edward's brother was a plumber and glazier in Lichfield and his sister was married to a butcher in Rugeley.[125] Letters to the secretary at war and his staff mention enlisted men who were freemen eligible to vote in borough elections, or who were 'by no means of the lowest Class of the Country, but some of condition & property, Sons of freeholders &c', the 'genteel' sons of a linen draper 'of no despicable Means', and even the son of 'a reputable Clergyman'.[126]

Similar observations can be made about the Royal Navy. Foreigners of every description were to be found on ships' musters— volunteers, pressed men, and even enemy prisoners (Captain James

---

[120] BL, Loudoun Papers, Add. MS 44084, fo. 231.

[121] Rammerscales House, Bell-Macdonald Papers, Macdonald's Day-book, 1781–2.

[122] WO 68/203.

[123] John Malcolm Bulloch, *Territorial Soldiering in the North-East of Scotland during 1759–1814* (Aberdeen, 1914), 119–23.   [124] *Gentleman's Magazine*, 48 (1778), 362.

[125] The property of Edward's father was acquired in 1778 by the Littleton family after a dispute over ownership—hence the survival of a good deal of interesting biographical material on the Kirkhams. See Staffordshire RO, Littleton Papers, D 260/MT/5/52.

[126] WO 4/111, p. 164; WO 1/1010, Major James Barker to Matthew Lewis, 6 Apr. 1781; BL, Liverpool Papers, Add. MS 38212, fo. 81; WO 1/1005, Major George Reynolds to ——, 24 May 1779.

Cumming informed the admiralty in August 1781 that his vessel had taken on board several volunteers from the prison ships at New York).[127] The Danish consul in London complained in 1778 of the 'great Number of our Seamen pressed';[128] and among the sailors who left the *Dolphin* in 1775–6—dead, discharged, or deserted—there were Dutchmen, Swedes, and Portuguese.[129] But the numbers again need to be put into proper perspective. Foreigners—in this case Portuguese and Americans—accounted for less than 5% of all those who left the *Bristol* in November 1776.[130] Only 5% of the crew of the newly commissioned *Cumberland* was foreign in June 1778; and foreigners comprised no more than 6% of the men mustered on the *America* the previous March.[131] In these cases, it must be conceded, we are dealing with small numbers; three out of sixty-five, four out of eighty-four, and four out of sixty-nine, respectively. But statistically more meaningful examples produce no more significant proportions. Of the 377 men entering the *Prince George* between the beginning of February and the end of March 1778, only twenty-four (6%) were foreign; and of the 451 men taken on to the *Elizabeth* between 1 April and 31 May 1778, only ten (just over 2%) came from beyond the British Isles.[132]

The navy's officers were nearly as much of a mixed bag as the army's. True, aristocrats and members of gentry families dominated the higher ranks, perhaps to an even greater extent than in the army. Among the senior officers at the time of the American war Admiral Keppel was the second son of the Earl of Albemarle, Admiral Howe was himself an Irish viscount, Captain the Hon. William Cornwallis was the fourth son of the first Earl Cornwallis, and Captain the Hon. Charles Phipps was the second son of Baron Mulgrave. But there were many officers of lesser birth, some of whom were the sons of tradesmen in the dockyards and others who had been officers on merchant ships. Lieutenant Samuel Codd was the son of the town clerk of Hull, who himself was the son of a bricklayer.[133] We should also note that marine officers tended to be of distinctly lower status than many of their naval colleagues, not least because promotion was slow and well-connected young men regarded the marines as an inferior service. A good many marine officers appear to have come

---

[127] ADM 1/1613, Cumming to Philip Stephens, 21 Aug. 1781.
[128] ADM 1/5118/21, fo. 520.   [129] ADM 36/7583.   [130] ADM 34/116.
[131] ADM 36/9026 and 9087.   [132] ADM 36/8205 and 8017.
[133] BL, Journal of Marmaduke Strother, 1784–5, Egerton MS 2479, fo. 51.

from struggling untitled gentry families, or, like Henry Norton Gamble, the son of a Leicester alderman, were middle class in background.[134] To talk of promotions from the ranks in the navy makes little sense, as all commissioned officers had to spend time mustered as common seamen before they qualified. But we can differentiate between those sons of gentlemen who usually started their maritime career as an officer's servant, gained the minimum six years' experience, and then passed the lieutenant's examination in their early twenties,[135] and men from more humble backgrounds who stayed for much longer on the lower decks and became officers later in life. We can be fairly confident, for example, that William Cox was not well connected. He served almost the whole of the Seven Years War as an able seaman on the *Dunkirk*, and then left the navy. He rejoined in 1778 as an able seaman on the *Jupiter*, and rose steadily to midshipman and master's mate, before passing his lieutenant's examination, aged 45, in April 1781.[136] Similarly, Robert Gill, appointed lieutenant in December 1780, had served throughout the Seven Years War as a gunner's mate. He rejoined the navy as an able seaman in July 1778, and was 52 when he was commissioned.[137]

The ratings, and the rank and file of the marines, also defy easy social categorization. Criminals were present on board ship, just as they were in the army's regiments; men like John Bolton, found guilty of counterfeiting a halfpenny at York in 1779;[138] Joseph Reynolds, who joined the marines after being charged with stealing from a shop in Essex;[139] and Samuel Parry and Richard Jones, 'sent to sea in his Majestys service' by Hampshire magistrates.[140] Smugglers, it should be added, were sometimes rounded up by naval officers on the impress service. Captain Francis Richards seized one while recruiting in Norfolk,[141] while Lieutenant Joseph Bradby,

---

[134] Gamble's father, John, was a grocer by trade, but also owned land and was reputed to be a man of considerable wealth. See Henry Hartopp, *Roll of the Mayors of the Borough and Lord Mayors of the City of Leicester* (Leicester, [1936?]), 162–3; Marion Balderston and David Syrett (eds.), *The Lost War: Letters from British Officers during the American Revolution* (New York, 1975), 112, 113, 115, 117, 118.

[135] Such as Sir John Reid, who passed his examination in Feb. 1781, aged 20. ADM 107/8, p. 114. [136] ADM 6/89.

[137] ADM 6/88.

[138] PRO, Clerk of Assize Papers, ASSI 42/9, Gaol Book, City and County of York, 6 Mar. 1779. [139] Essex RO, Sessions Book, Q/SMg 23, 13 Jan. 1778.

[140] Hampshire RO, Sessions Order-book, Q1/19, p. 123.

[141] ADM 1/2390, Richards to Stephens, 15 Mar. 1777.

on his way to Brighton at night to search for mariners to press, 'fell in with a Gang of Smugglers, and brought five out of seven with him'.[142] Again, however, we have to be careful not to exaggerate the importance of criminal entrants. No more convicted or suspected offenders seem to have gone into the navy or marines than into the army.[143] Unskilled labourers were to be found in large numbers in the marines; but, judging by an examination of the Description Books of the Portsmouth Division, more than half the ordinary marines had formerly been employed in skilled or semi-skilled occupations.[144] Joseph Evans, a private in the Plymouth Division, was perhaps typical of such men: prior to joining the marines he had been a journeyman broad-weaver in several different places.[145] Many of the navy's ratings were forcibly recruited by press-gangs ashore or afloat. In the vast majority of cases, impressed men were seafarers or employed in riverine activities. By definition they were nearly all skilled. Volunteers might come from the same backgrounds, or from a bewildering variety of places and occupations unconnected with the sea. Nearly a third of the 570 men recruited by Captain James Alms in Sussex by the end of 1779 were volunteer landmen;[146] and a staggering 78% of the men noted by Captain Martin Cole in a Dublin return of 20–7 February 1782 came in this category.[147] The crew of the *Elizabeth*, commanded by Captain the Hon. Frederick Maitland, included a great many men who must have been his local dependants or personal connections; no less than a quarter of the ship's company came from Fife, the county in which Maitland's estates were situated.[148] Other landmen were recruited in much the same way as many soldiers and marines—by parties on the impress service operating in village inns, county towns, and at country fairs—and came from similarly diverse backgrounds.

The militia, it could be argued, approximated more closely to the idea of an armed force led by the cream of society but for the most part made up of its sediment. Although militiamen were selected by ballot, balloted men rarely served in person: they made up 15% of

---

[142] ADM 1/1446, Capt. James Alms to Stephens, 24 July 1779.

[143] Conway, 'Recruitment of Criminals', 55.

[144] J. A. Lowe (ed.), *Records of the Portsmouth Division of Marines, 1764–1800* (Portsmouth Record Series, Portsmouth, 1990), p. lxiii.

[145] Phyllis Hembry (ed.), *Calendar of the Bradford-on-Avon Settlement Examinations and Removal Orders 1725–1798* (Wiltshire Record Society, vol. xlvi, Trowbridge, 1990), 54.

[146] ADM 1/1446.   [147] ADM 1/1614.   [148] Rodger, *Wooden World*, 156–7.

those who enrolled in the Ilford Division for the Essex militia in 1779–80,[149] and a mere 5% of those who joined the Bedfordshire regiment in the first six months of 1782.[150] Men of means could avoid service by hiring a substitute, and, as we have seen, employers often took it upon themselves to pay for substitutes for favoured workers or servants. Indeed, militia subscription clubs were formed to provide the insured parties with the money to hire a substitute.[151] It should also be noted that parishes sometimes helped less affluent but valued members of the community to hire substitutes; militia law allowed up to half the cost of hiring a replacement to be met by the local rates.[152] The net result was that the militia ballot produced less of a cross-section of contemporary society than might be imagined. And if the rank and file of the militia was not as socially mixed as it could have been, the officers were, in theory at least, confined to the landed elite of the county. The 1757 Militia Act set property qualifications for the different officer ranks which appear to have been designed to exclude all but those with substantial acres.

Yet, as with other branches of the armed services, closer investigation reveals a rather different picture. Principals—the men who served in person—were not always poor labourers who had little choice. Samuel Pearce, a shoemaker, and Samuel Sampson, a pewterer, both of Helston, were principals in the Cornwall militia, as was William Mallet, a tailor of Falmouth.[153] Likewise, substitutes might have agreed to become militiamen only under financial duress, but this does not necessarily mean that they were members of an eighteenth-century underclass. In the Hertfordshire militia there were substitutes like John Apthorp, a watchmaker of Ware; John Halding, a blacksmith, and William Williamson, a baker, both of Aspenden; and William Flood, a shoemaker of Bushy.[154] In one of the companies of the Sussex militia, made up almost entirely of substitutes, 60% of the men were probably agricultural labourers, but among the rest were seven shoemakers, two tailors, two carpenters, two butchers, and a

[149] Essex RO, D/DHt T145/4, List of men sworn and enrolled, Ilford subdivsion, 17 Apr. 1779–16 Feb. 1780.　　　　　　　　　　　　　　　　　　　　[150] WO 13/99.
[151] See e.g. Staffordshire RO, D 1727/4, 7, Diary of Samuel Pipe Wolferstan, 9 June, 14 Aug. 1779, 12 and 30 May 1782.
[152] e.g. Cornwall RO, St Erme Parish Records, DP P5/15.
[153] Ibid., DDX 534, Militia Roll, Kerrier Hundred, 1781–2.
[154] Hertfordshire Family and Population History Society: *Hertfordshire Militia Lists: Ware, A-C* (Militia series, no. 25, 1992), 5; *Aspenden* (Militia series, no. 35, 1992), 11, 25; *Bushey* (Militia Series, no. 41, 1994), 14.

miller.[155] The presence of skilled men in the militia ranks becomes more understandable when one realizes that militiamen, including substitutes, enjoyed certain privileges denied to regular soldiers, and this made militia service—maybe for no more than three years—an attractive option for men in acute but perhaps unaccustomed difficulty, or who sought a temporary escape from the tedium of their humdrum lives. Crucially, militiamen's wives and families were supported during their absence by the local authorities. In Berkshire, for example, the wife and child of John Wells of Kingston Bagpuize, who was serving as a substitute for William Bosher of St Nicholas, Abingdon, received two shillings a week.[156]

Militia officers, for their part, were by no means always drawn from the most prestigious county families. Admittedly, militia colonelcies tended to be held by leading aristocrats like the Duke of Richmond in Sussex; Lord Paget and then Lord Lewisham, the heir of the Earl of Dartmouth, in Staffordshire; and Lord Algernon Percy, second son of the Duke of Northumberland, in Northumberland. But it was impossible to fill the more junior officer ranks with men who met the property qualifications imposed in 1757, and it remained very difficult even after the qualifications were eased in 1762 and again in 1769. When the militia regiments were embodied from 1778, a noticeable number of aristocrats resigned their commissions, leaving the way open to even more men of middling station. The degree of non-elite penetration varied, of course, from county to county. In Sussex, Lucius Concannon, an adventurer of obscure background but probably the son of an Irish grocer, served alongside members of well-established local families such as Godfrey Webster, the son of a baronet, and Thomas Pelham, the heir to a barony.[157] But the situation in Buckinghamshire was probably typical. Here most of the junior officers had very small estates, many of which had been recently acquired, or they qualified only by virtue of non-landed property.[158] In Cambridgeshire, the lieutenant-colonel complained that 'Gentlemen are not to be found in this part

---

[155] East Sussex RO, Sheffield Papers, A 2714/265, Muster of Major Holroyd's company, [1778].

[156] Berkshire RO, Abingdon St Nicholas Parish Records, D/P2/17/1/3.

[157] See *The Early Journals and Letters of Fanny Burney*, ed. Lars E. Troide and Stewart J. Cooke (3 vols. to date, Kingston, 1988–), iii. 272–3 and nn., 275 and nn.

[158] Paul Langford, *Public Life and the Propertied Englishman 1689–1798* (Oxford, 1991), 298–9.

that will Enter for the good of their Country—many having been Used
to a sedentary life, or Else too fond of the Sports of the Field to leave
them'.[159] While the postmaster of Walden, 'who turns out to be a
Common Barber', was refused a commission, the regiment's officers
included Captain Thomas Baxter Aveling, qualified by virtue of a
landed estate but a former upholsterer from Wisbech, and Lieutenant
Thomas Miles Cotton, the son and heir of a Cambridge grocer and
tallow chandler.[160] Some militia officers appear to have been still more
lowly in status. When Lieutenant and Adjutant John Hall of the
Westmorland regiment died in 1779, his widow was left 'without
any means of Subsistence Whatsoever' to bring up four children.[161]

The volunteers depart most markedly from the stereotypical
image of the social make-up of an eighteenth-century military force.
Consider first the Irish volunteers. Traditional leaders of landed
society were certainly willing to play their part: in Ulster Lord
Charlemont was colonel of the Armagh Volunteer regiment, and
the two MPs for the county were lieutenant-colonels of the northern
and southern battalions. But there were many officers from non-elite
backgrounds, especially in the urban areas. In a company raised in
the city of Cork, one of the leading lights was a clothier.[162] Waddell
Cunningham, a merchant, was an officer in the Belfast First
Volunteer Company; in Belfast Third Company Lieutenant Robert
Hyndman was almost certainly a local tobacconist. Men of this type
became increasingly important in the volunteer movement, and even
started to eclipse landed officers.[163] Many of the rank and file seem
also to have been middle class. While aristocratic patrons like the
Marquis of Rockingham might offer to underwrite the costs of
particular companies,[164] or subscriptions might be raised to allow
poorer men to join,[165] there is some evidence that ordinary volunteers were often men of means. The lord-lieutenant believed 'most
of the Private men' to be 'either tradesmen or Farmers'.[166] The 100

[159] BL, Hardwicke Papers, Add. MS 35660, fo. 263.

[160] Ibid., Add. MSS 35659, fo. 280; 35660, fos. 126, 138. See also fo. 243.

[161] BL, Liverpool Papers, Add. MS 38342, fo. 290.

[162] Richard Caulfield (ed.), *The Council Book of the Corporation of the City of Cork*
(Guildford, 1876), 932.

[163] See Eileen Black, 'Volunteer Portraits in the Ulster Museum, Belfast', *Irish Sword*,
13 (1977–9), 181–4.   [164] Sheffield Archives, Rockingham MSS, R1/1854a.

[165] PRONI, Abercorn Papers, D/623/A/44/10.

[166] NLI, Heron Papers, MS 13038, Buckinghamshire to Sir Richard Heron, 9 July
1779.

volunteers from in and around Limavady, County Londonderry, were described as all freeholders, who were willing 'at their own Expence [to] furnish themselves with Arms and Uniform'.[167] The company formed at Rathfriland, County Down, was said to comprise 'men in business'.[168] In 1782 Lord Pembroke, writing from Belfast, announced that 'Each Volunteer equips himself, the horsemen at the expence of nearly £80; the foot soldiers about £20, for all they have is of the best kind.'[169]

The British volunteers were also socially distinct from the army and militia. Again, the landed elite provided some of the leadership. In Essex Sir Robert Smyth of Berechurch, MP for Colchester, offered to raise a corps for local defence;[170] while in Scotland 'the Earl of Buchan and several other Gentlemen appeared in the uniform of the Caledonian Band'.[171] But, as in Ireland, such corps could not have existed without the active participation of members of the middle and artisan classes of society. The Leeds volunteers were led by local merchants;[172] Lieutenant William Tremayne of the volunteer company raised in the Cornish parish of Phillack was probably the William Tremayne who managed the smelting works at Angarrack;[173] while the officers of the Great Yarmouth companies were mainly members of the town's mercantile and trading community.[174] The 'middling sort' seem likewise to have predominated in the rank and file. In the Scarborough companies there were some labourers, but most of the ordinary volunteers were local farmers or tradesmen.[175] The Penryn volunteers appear to have been much the same. While some of them were described as 'poor Inhabitants & Labourers', clothed by a subscription raised in the town, the others provided their own apparel and were said to be men with 'avocations', who could spare only a limited amount of time from their business commitments to drill.[176] The Great Yarmouth volunteers

---

[167] Trinity College Dublin, Conolly Papers, MS 3976/523.

[168] PRONI, Downshire Papers, D/607/B/91.

[169] *Pembroke Papers*, ed. Lord Herbert (2 vols., London, 1939–50), ii. 206.

[170] Essex RO, Smyth Family Papers, D/DFg Zi, Shelburne to Smyth, 11 June 1782.

[171] SRO, Logan Home of Edrom Muniments, GD 1/384/7/19.

[172] Emily Hargrave, 'The Early Leeds Volunteers', Thoresby Society, *Publications*, 28 (1923–7), 262.

[173] SP 41/33, fo. 277; Davies Gilbert, *The Parochial History of Cornwall* (4 vols., London, 1838), iii. 343.   [174] SP 41/33, fo. 301.

[175] North Yorkshire RO, Scarborough Corporation Records, DC/SCB, Return of volunteer companies, 1781.

[176] Ibid., Chaytor Papers, Z2H 11/2/58; WO 34/138, fo. 256.

seem to have come from the same background as their officers; they were described as 'Merchants and tradesmen'.[177] In Leeds, the volunteer corps projected in June 1782 was to be unpaid, the members to provide uniforms at their own expense, and training was to take place in the evening to allow the volunteers to pursue their occupations during the day.[178] A surviving roll of the Dover volunteers provides some interesting insights. Of the 316 volunteers listed, only eighteen were unable to sign their names. The kinship connections between the officers and men were striking: the Allen family provided two officers and three rank and file volunteers; the Ladds three of each. Amongst the ordinary volunteers were Thomas Gilbee, a draper and tailor; John Childers and William Sturgis, saddlers; George Jennings, a plumber and glazier; William Webb, a tallow-chandler; Jeffrey Marphew, John Johnson and John Brett, grocers; and Richard Rouse, a wine merchant.[179] The Norfolk Rangers was reported to be 'a very respectable body of gentlemen, farmers and tradesmen'.[180] The corps in Perth was so well heeled that many young men 'in decent stations did not enrol . . . from a dread of its turning out an expensive business'.[181] In London, bankers and merchants seem to have been prominent in the Light Horse Volunteers and the London Foot Association, and a corps was formed by the barristers and students of the Middle and Inner Temples.[182] It would be difficult to envisage military units more remote from the accepted picture of an eighteenth-century fighting force.

The British war effort, in terms of the number of men mobilized, officially or unofficially, was clearly considerable. Such a large-scale mobilization almost inevitably meant that many men from middling or artisan backgrounds performed some form of armed service, not just aristocrats and gentry at one end of the social spectrum and labourers and paupers at the other. If we locate the mobilization of the American war in a broader context, it can be seen to fit into a pattern of steadily increasing participation. The Seven Years War

---

[177] HO 42/205, fo. 132.   [178] *Leeds Mercury*, 25 June 1782.
[179] WO 34/116, fos. 1–2. Occupations are taken from *Bailey's British Directory . . . for the Year 1784* (4 vols., London, 1784), iii. 343, which, while providing information on the situation five years later, is probably a tolerably good guide.
[180] *Norfolk Mercury*, 14 Sept. 1782, cited in Beckett, *Amateur Military Tradition*, 70.
[181] HMC, *Laing MSS*, ii. 512.   [182] *London Chronicle*, 13–15, 17–20 June 1780.

had seen an advance on the War of Austrian Succession, and the American war carried on the upward trajectory. Viewed in this way, the importance of British and Irish mobilization in the American war lies in its being part of a process that culminated in the still greater mobilization in the wars of 1793–1815. But the scale and breadth of the mobilization in the American war also had an immediate importance. It played a major part, alongside other war-related developments, in ensuring that the impact of the conflict on the British Isles would be great. With something like one in seven or eight males of the appropriate age serving at one time or another in the army, navy, militia, or volunteers, it could hardly be otherwise.

2

The Economic Impact

HISTORIANS ARE DIVIDED over the impact on the economy of eighteenth-century wars. A. H. John, in a pioneering article published many years ago, concluded that the armed struggles of the first half of the century should, on the whole, be viewed as exerting a beneficial influence.[1] D. W. Jones's book on the response of the English economy to the wars of 1689–1713, while downplaying the stimulus provided by the manufacture of munitions and other war *matériel*, emphasizes the access to new markets facilitated by these struggles.[2] Some studies of the French Revolutionary and Napoleonic Wars have been similarly positive in their assessments. J. L. Anderson, for instance, sees these long conflicts as not merely conducive to British economic growth, but as 'fundamental' to an understanding of the process;[3] and Larry Neal boldly proclaims that the Industrial Revolution was directly linked to the Napoleonic War.[4] Phyllis Deane, adopting a more cautious tone, suggests that the conflicts of 1793–1815 did not impede the upward trajectory of the British economy.[5] Patrick O'Brien, while giving ample regard to the deleterious effects of war in the eighteenth century, has pointed out that British military success, by protecting the homeland from invasion and expanding its horizons, was one of the preconditions for economic growth.[6] Paul Langford, in another general assessment,

[1] A. H. John, 'War and the English Economy, 1700–1763', *Economic History Review*, 2nd ser. 7 (1954–5), 329–44.

[2] D. W. Jones, *War and Economy in the Age of William III and Marlborough* (Oxford, 1988).

[3] J. L. Anderson, 'Aspects of the Effect on the British Economy of the Wars against France, 1793–1815', *Australian Economic History Review*, 12 (1972), 18.

[4] Larry Neal, *The Rise of Financial Capitalism: International Capital Markets in the Age of Reason* (Cambridge, 1990), 218.

[5] Phyllis Deane, 'War and Industrialisation', in J. M. Winter (ed.), *War and Economic Development: Essays in Memory of David Joslin* (London, 1975), 100–1.

[6] Patrick O'Brien, 'Political Preconditions for the Industrial Revolution', in id. and Roland Quinault (eds.), *The Industrial Revolution and British Society* (Cambridge, 1993), 135–49.

suggests that the British economy advanced as a result of the stimulus provided by frequent wars to certain sectors of the economy *and* the stimulus provided to other sectors by the intervening periods of peace; the overall effect being progress across a broad front.[7] By contrast, T. S. Ashton, writing at about the same time as A. H. John, had no hesitation in categorizing war as distorting and damaging in its impact. He even claimed that without the armed struggles of the eighteenth century 'the Industrial Revolution might have come earlier'.[8] More recently Jeffrey Williamson has portrayed the French wars of 1793–1815 as slowing down the growth of the British economy;[9] and he and Joel Mokyr and N. E. Savin have seen these conflicts as depressing living standards for most of the people.[10] Other historians, recognizing the immense difficulties involved in weighing up the positive and negative aspects, have limited themselves simply to describing the pros and cons and eschewed any general conclusion.[11]

To attempt an assessment of the impact of the American war on the British and Irish economies would seem, then, a hazardous, perhaps even a foolhardy, undertaking. But if the macroeconomic picture is very hazy, there are some general points that can be made. There were some obvious negatives, such as destruction and loss of capital assets and the sharp contraction of overseas trade, and some possible positives, notably the stimulus provided by a substantial increase in government spending.[12] The negatives and the positives may well have almost counterbalanced each other, leading to a broadly neutral or only slightly damaging impact. The swift and sustained growth of the British economy after the American war certainly suggests that any deleterious effects were short-lived. If we look, however, at the microeconomic level—at the level of indivi-

---

[7] Paul Langford, *A Polite and Commercial People: A History of England 1727–1783* (Oxford, 1989), 636.

[8] T. S. Ashton, *Economic Fluctuations in England, 1700–1800* (London, 1959), 83.

[9] Jeffrey Williamson, 'Why was British Growth So Slow during the Industrial Revolution?', *Journal of Economic History*, 44 (1984), 687–712.

[10] J. Mokyr and N. E. Savin, 'Stagflation in Historical Perspective: The Napoleonic Wars Revisited', *Research in Economic History*, 1 (1976), 198–259.

[11] See e.g. Peter Mathias, *The First Industrial Nation: An Economic History of Britain 1700–1914* (London, 1969), 43–8. H. V. Bowen, *War and British Society, 1688–1815* (Cambridge, 1998), ch. 5, on which much of the foregoing paragraph is based, provides a judicious overview of the debates.

[12] The figures in this chapter, unless otherwise stated, are taken from B. R. Mitchell, *British Historical Statistics* (Cambridge, 1988).

duals and companies and even sectors of the economy—we can see more clearly the dramatic changes caused by the war. There is abundant evidence that contemporaries were acutely aware of its intrusive nature. This chapter will attempt to give due consideration to both the micro- and macro-pictures, by looking at destruction and loss, taxation and public borrowing, overseas trade, pay and prices, and government spending.

Destruction and Loss

The British Isles were not the scene of significant fighting between the belligerents, and so avoided the fate of territories that are the seat of military campaigns. Jersey was attacked by the French, the pro-American arsonist 'Peter the Painter' caused a ripple of alarm after he burnt the rope-works at Plymouth and destroyed some warehouses at Bristol, and a number of coastal settlements were attacked by John Paul Jones, the American privateer; but there was no laying waste large tracts of land, or widespread burning of villages and towns, such as was experienced in continental Europe in other eighteenth-century wars and in North America between 1775 and 1781.[13]

This is not to say that British and Irish property-owners escaped unscathed. Even before French intervention, merchant shipping was exposed to the attacks of American privateers, especially in the Caribbean and North American waters. In November 1776 the coast of Florida near St Augustine was said to be 'Infested' with American privateers trying to intercept valuable cargoes of indigo destined for Britain.[14] The following June, Lord Macartney, governor of Grenada, noted that 'our Seas swarm with American Privateers'.[15] The House of Lords was told in February 1778 that since the commencement of hostilities 733 vessels had been lost by capture, 559 of which remained in rebel hands. The value of these prizes,

[13] For an estimate of the damage caused by the British in South Carolina see Gloucestershire RO, Lloyd Letters, D 1628, bundle 2, John Lloyd to ——, 20 Apr. 1783; for an account of the impact of war on a much-contested European region see Myron P. Gutmann, *War and Rural Life in the Early Modern Low Countries* (Princeton, 1980).

[14] Ballindalloch Castle, Macpherson Grant Papers, bundle 772, Maj.-Gen. James Grant to [Robert Grant], 24 Nov. 1776.

[15] NLI, Fitzpatrick Papers, MS 8012, Macartney to Lady Ossory, 15 June 1777. See also Alan G. Jameson, 'American Privateers in the Leeward Islands, 1776–1778', *American Neptune*, 43 (1983), 20–30.

including cargoes, amounted 'upon a very moderate calculation' to in excess of £1.8 million.[16] Once the French joined the conflict, the danger to shipping increased markedly. Barmouth, on the coast of West Wales, was said by February 1780 to have lost four of its twenty vessels to the French, 'to the ruin of many inhabitants'.[17] By the end of the war the Americans alone had taken British prizes to the value of around £18 million.[18] Even in December 1782, months after offensive operations had ceased in North America, it was still thought unsafe for merchant ships to cross to New York without the protection of a convoy.[19]

There were also Britons and Irishmen who held property in North America or the West Indies and were therefore detrimentally affected by the disturbances across the Atlantic. When the French took Dominica in 1778, British planters were allowed to keep their estates, and even to continue trading via the neutral islands; but the French occupation nevertheless involved the loss of assets seized or destroyed in the course of the capture of the colony.[20] In the Bahamas, taken by the Spanish in 1782, there seem also to have been confiscations, despite the terms of the capitulation.[21] When the French destroyed the forts of the Hudson's Bay Company in August of the same year, the company's losses were computed at some £500,000.[22] In the rebel colonies, the property of King George's British and Irish subjects was of course even more exposed. Captain William Houghton of the Royal Artillery, for instance, lost the 2,000 acres he owned in Albany County, New York, when the new state decided to seize all British and loyalist possessions.[23] John Ewer & Sons, a London merchant house that owned an ironworks in Maryland, suffered when the company's American plant, equipment, and stocks were confiscated by the revolutionary authorities. Dr John Shuttleworth of Aylesbury, who had been granted land in the same colony by the governor in 1768, suffered similarly; as did

---

[16] *PH* xix. 709.

[17] NLW, Peniarth MS 416A, Journal of Elizabeth Baker, 18 Feb. 1780.

[18] John J. McCusker and Russell R. Menard, *The Economy of British America, 1607–1789* (Chapel Hill, NC, 1991 edn.), 362.

[19] Lancashire RO, Grundy Papers, DD X 207/32/1, Parsons & Prior to Cooke, Relph & Barnardeston, 14 Dec. 1782.

[20] See the letters sent to R. G. Bruce, relating to his estates on Dominica, NLW, Nassau Senior Papers, E 36–8, 41.

[21] *The Journal of the General Assembly of the Bahama Islands . . . 1779–1786* (Nassau, 1912), 1784 session, p. 7.

[22] David Macpherson, *Annals of Commerce* (4 vols., London, 1805), iii. 717.

[23] PRO, Audit Office Papers, Loyalist Claims Commission, AO 12/20, fos. 141–2.

Robert Taaffe of County Meath, who lost the landed estate—and rental income—that he had acquired in 1758 by marriage into a Baltimore family.[24]

Even in the British Isles themselves, property was not necessarily secure. Friendly armies can be as destructive as those of an enemy, and civilians regularly protested at losses experienced at the hands of British soldiers on the march or in camp. At Waterford in September 1776, soldiers of the Thirty-second Foot were said to be 'Stealing Linnen fruit Poultry &c' from local people.[25] In September 1779 a militia officer at Coxheath Camp in Kent noted that the farmers in the neighbourhood 'have for some time complained of a great deal of mischief being done them by the soldiers, I am afraid with too much truth'.[26] A year later, Sir Francis Buller wrote from Devon that the Fiftieth Foot was 'an intolerable Grievance to the Country . . . Hardly a Night passes that some Felony is not committed by them, they have broken open several Houses, committed Highway Robberies, stolen four sheep from one man & three from another, stripped a third of all his poultry, & robbed Orchards & Gardens without End & to a considerable Value'.[27] The problem was particularly acute in southern England, which experienced considerable military activity from 1778 as the country braced itself for an invasion. Owners of land used for encampments were paid for its hire,[28] but the damage to their property could be considerable: after part of his estate had been occupied in this way, Henry Penton of Winchester reckoned that his losses—through fences destroyed, crops trampled, and other causes—amounted to more than £862.[29]

Taxation and Public Borrowing

Many more Britons were affected, of course, by the taxation required to fund the war. At the local level, property-owners in England and Wales were obliged to foot the bill for the dependants of militiamen, either through parish poor rates, or, if necessary, a

---

[24] Ibid., AO 12/8, fos. 127, 171, 212.
[25] NLI, MS 3750, Order-book, 32nd Foot, 19 Sept. 1776.
[26] BL, Althorp Papers, F. 8, Lord Althorp to Lady Spencer, 21 Sept. 1779.
[27] WO 1/1007, p. 259.
[28] Hampshire RO, Jervoise Collection, 44 M69 E86, Daniel Paterson to Tristram Huddleston Jervoise, 4 Apr. 1780.   [29] WO 4/104, pp. 324–5.

special county rate. In Hampshire concern was expressed at 'the great Charge' to the county, which rose from £383 in 1778 to £533 the following year.[30] In Cambridgeshire it amounted to more than £700 in 1779, while in Shropshire the costs associated with militiamen's dependants almost certainly contributed to the increases in the county rate in 1780 and 1781.[31] Some of the justices in Hertfordshire were sufficiently alarmed to try to put impediments in the way of claimants.[32] Parish poor rates bore the brunt, however. In November 1778 Sir Roger Newdigate complained of 'the heavy burthens on parishes' in Warwickshire, owing in part to their responsibility to feed 'the militia families'.[33] It was not inevitably and universally a bad time for local taxpayers: in some cases parish rates were probably eased by the recruitment of many of the able-bodied unemployed.[34] But relief in this respect was often more than counterbalanced when the families of absent soldiers and sailors became a charge on the parish. The deputy mayor of King's Lynn wrote in 1781 that 'The Poor rates are very exorbitant', which he attributed to the depression in trade '& the very many familys that are left upon the parish by the impress'd sailors, a very large number [of whom] are now on board His Majesties Ships'.[35] We can surmise that something similar might have been happening at Ovenden, near Halifax, where the unusually large sum of £141 was expended on poor relief in 1775, when recruiting had hardly started, and the woollen industry was still trying to adjust to colonial boycotts, but even more—in excess of £185—in 1780, by which time the demands of the army and navy would surely have soaked up most of the able-bodied men with no employment.[36]

---

[30] Hampshire RO, Jervoise Collection, 44 M69 030; Quarter Session Order-book, 1777–83, fos. 62, 103.

[31] J. R. Western, *The English Militia in the Eighteenth Century* (London, 1965), 289; in R. L. Kenyon and O. Wakeman (eds.), *Abstracts of the Orders of the Shropshire Quarter Sessions* (Salop County Records, vols. xiv-xvii, Shrewsbury, n.d.), 251–4.

[32] William Le Hardy (ed.), *Notes and Extracts from the Sessions Records of the Liberty of St. Alban Division 1770 to 1840* (Hertford County Records, vol. iv, Hertford, 1923), 15.

[33] *The Correspondence of Sir Roger Newdigate*, ed. A. W. A. White (Dugdale Society Publications, vol. xxxvii, Hertford, 1995), 220.

[34] For an instance of declining poor rates, see Berkshire RO, Downshire Papers, D/ED F106, Sandys Account-book. [35] WO 1/1013, p. 29.

[36] Calderdale Archives, Ovenden Parish Records, HAS 208 and 204. Fluctuations might, of course, be attributable to other causes: there is no obvious explanation, e.g. to the pattern of disbursements in Newick, Sussex, during the war: East Sussex RO, Add. MS 5554.

But much more important than increases in local taxation was the growth in the demands sanctioned by the British and Irish Parliaments. There were, admittedly, all manner of local and private initiatives that reduced the potential charge on the central state. Public subscriptions covered the cost of recruiting several new regiments, or subsidized bounties for entrants into the old corps; loyal corporations paid bounties to naval recruits; the East India Company spent considerable sums on British soldiers sent to India; and West Indian merchants and planters helped to raise a regiment and contributed to the costs of transporting troops to the Caribbean.[37] Nor was parliamentary taxation the only way in which the government tried to increase its income. Efforts were made to maximize crown revenues, though sometimes with politically disastrous consequences. An attempt to squeeze income from crown lands in Wales, by collecting arrears and acting against encroachments, caused a storm of protest and cost Lord North the support of several Welsh MPs.[38]

The bulk of new revenue, however, had to come from increased taxation. Even in Ireland, which was generally accepted to be much less prosperous than Britain and therefore less able to bear tax rises, duties were increased to cover wartime costs. In Britain, the government's revenues rose by about 30% between 1774, the last full year of peace, and 1782, when the total collected in tax was just under £13 million, or about 11% of estimated national income.[39] At first, Lord North was confident that he could confine the extra burden to those who were comfortably off, and that he could minimize the impact on trade, industry, and the poor. The land tax, a crude form of property taxation, was increased in 1775 to its normal wartime rate of four shillings in the pound. In 1776 carriage duty was extended to stagecoaches and hackney carriages, and stamp duties were increased on deeds and other legal documents, newspapers, cards, and dice, the last two of which, North told the Commons, 'were matters of real luxury and ought therefore to be taxed'.[40] The following year he pursued the same policy of concentrating the burden on those best able to bear it: the 1777 budget increased

---

[37] See below, Ch. 4, for the political conflict caused by some of these contributions.

[38] P. D. G. Thomas, 'A Welsh Political Storm: The Treasury Warrant of 1778 Concerning Crown Lands in Wales', *Welsh History Review*, 18 (1997), 430–49.

[39] P. K. O'Brien and P. A. Hunt, 'The Rise of a Fiscal State in England, 1485–1815', *Historical Research*, 66 (1993), 175 (table 4).   [40] *PH* xviii. 1319.

stamp duties and excises on glass, while introducing a tax on male servants (except those involved in trade or business) and another on auctioneers and the goods that they sold. In 1778 new taxes took the form of a house tax, with those valued at less than £5 per annum rental exempted, and an increase in the duties on imported wines.

Further stamp duties were imposed in later wartime budgets, but as the cost of the conflict mounted it became increasingly difficult for North to avoid more generally applicable taxes.[41] He had already pointed out in 1777 that it might in future be necessary for taxation to 'reach the body of the people, who are the great consumers'.[42] From 1779 this is what happened. First came a general increase of 5% on customs and excises. Still reluctant to abandon his established position, North excluded beer from this general surcharge on the ground that it was 'a great article of consumption of the lower orders'.[43] Soap, candles, and leather were also exempted. But coal, an undoubted necessity for many people, bore the full 5% increase, and malt and hops duties rose, which had the effect of putting upward pressure on beer prices despite North's apparent concern for beer drinkers. Further malt duties followed in 1780, together with a duty of 10d. per bushel on salt, which North conceded 'was a necessary of life, and equally so to the poor and the rich'.[44] In 1781 another 5% surcharge was added to customs and excises, with certain exemptions again, and North regretfully imposed duties on sugar and tobacco, both of which were items of popular consumption. North's last budget, delivered only days before he fell from power in March 1782, demonstrated the extent to which he had been forced to give up the fine intentions of the first years of the war. Not only were duties increased again on tobacco and salt, and imposed on beer and soap, but commerce was further hindered by a new tax on the carriage of goods, whether by waggon, canal, or coastal vessel.[45]

---

[41] We should also note that some of his earlier taxes had failed to produce the anticipated yield: see John Chartres, 'English Landed Society and the Servants Tax of 1777', in Negley Harte and Roland Quinault (eds.), *Land and Society in Britain, 1700–1914: Essays in Honour of F. M. L. Thompson* (Manchester, 1996), 34–56, esp. 35.

[42] *PH* xix. 243.   [43] *PH* xx. 166.   [44] *PH* xxi. 168.

[45] See *Aris's Birmingham Gazette*, 18 Mar., 13 Apr. 1782, for the protest of Birmingham merchants and manufactures against so 'very injurious' a tax. See also NLW, Bodrhyddan MSS, Bishop of St Asaph to William Shipley, dean of St Asaph, 11 Mar. [1782]: 'you will see the new Taxes in ye Papers that upon ye Inland Carriage is very heavy & very unequal & will certainly be opposd'.

By the end of the war the proportion of per capita income taken in taxation stood at 23%[46]—higher than in any previous conflict, and higher, it seems, than in any other of the belligerents.[47] The effects of this reduction of spending power on individual patterns of purchasing are difficult to gauge. In some cases tax increases seem to have had a minimal impact. Matthew Flinders, a Lincolnshire surgeon, avoided the 'new heavy Tax on Male Servants' because his servants were deemed 'instrumental towards their Masters Business'. Although he was obliged to pay an extra 2s. 6d. a year from 1779 by virtue of the house tax, he had already more than covered this by reducing his liability for the window tax by 3s. 4d. by blocking in two of his windows. His account book suggests that he was far from overburdened by direct taxes.[48] A similar impression is conveyed by the wartime day-book of James Lister, a cloth merchant and landowner in Yorkshire and Lincolnshire.[49] Others, however, believed that taxes were 'squeezing our Purses',[50] and moaned 'most confoundedly at the increasing load of taxes wch. we all labour under'.[51] The perception that the tax burden had increased markedly may well have been enough to induce more caution in expenditure. Tax increases hit some trades particularly hard. After the budget of 1779 increased malt and hops duties, brewers complained of a fall in demand for their beers. Henry Thrale produced 86,000 barrels in 1777–8; this slipped to 76,000 in 1778–9, and only 60,000 in 1780—'so horribly is the consumption lessened by the war', Mrs Thrale lamented.[52] In this case a general trade depression was perhaps as important as higher taxes on malt and hops; but in other areas we can be fairly confident that the impact of tax increases was deleterious. The construction trade, which experienced a boom in the early years of the war, was badly affected by the introduction of higher duties on glass and wallpaper in 1777. Bankruptcies in this

---

[46] John Brewer, *The Sinews of Power: War, Money and the English State, 1688–1783* (London, 1989), 91.

[47] Ibid. 89–91. See also Peter Mathias and Patrick O'Brien, 'Taxation in Britain and France, 1715–1810', *Journal of European Economic History*, 5 (1976), 601–50.

[48] Lincolnshire Archives Office, Diary and Account-book of Matthew Flinders the Elder, fos. 29, 30, 36.

[49] Brotherton Library, R. V. Mariner Ltd. Papers, James Lister Day-book, 1776–83.

[50] Leeds Archives, Ramsden Papers, Rockingham Letters, vol. 3b, Revd William Palgrave to William Waddell, 31 Mar. [1780].

[51] Dr Williams's Library, Wodrow-Kenrick Correspondence, MS 24157 (69).

[52] Peter Mathias, *The Brewing Industry in England 1700–1830* (Cambridge, 1959), 270.

sector rose from an average of fifteen per year in 1772–7 to thirty in 1777 itself and fifty-eight in 1778.[53]

Increased government borrowing seems also to have had a noticeable effect on the economy. Tax increases covered less than 20% of the extra expenditure required,[54] and borrowing made up the difference. North proposed to Parliament a loan of £2 million in his 1776 budget; £5.5 million for 1777–8; £6 million for 1778–9; £7 million for 1779–80; £12 million for 1780–1; another £12 million for 1781–2; and, in his last budget, £13.5 million. His successor as chancellor of the exchequer, Lord John Cavendish, proposed a further loan of £12 million in 1783. Inducements to creditors in the form of free annuities or lottery tickets added to the debt. But this was not the full extent of public borrowing. Interest-bearing exchequer bills were produced to raise short-term loans, and various government departments—such as the navy, ordnance, and victualling boards—issued their own bills to cover everyday costs. Between 1775 and 1783 the unfunded debt, as these bills were collectively termed, rose from £3.1 million to £19 million. At the end of the war this was incorporated into the national debt proper, which climbed from £127 million at the start of the conflict to £232 million at its close.

It could be argued that this system of public credit, based on confidence in reliable and regular taxation which paid the interest charges on the funded debt, enabled Britain to finance its war effort more easily than either the French or the Americans.[55] But the strain imposed on the system itself, and the effect this strain had on the wider economy, should not be ignored. Trust in government funds slipped; on 1 May 1775 the consolidated three per cents stood at eighty-nine and a quarter, they steadily fell over the next two years, then slumped to sixty and three-quarters in May 1778, and by May 1781 were down to fifty-eight and five-eighths.[56] This lack of confidence meant that, as the war dragged on, it became more and more difficult for government to raise the necessary loans. In 1779,

---

[53] Julian Hoppit, *Risk and Failure in English Business* (Cambridge, 1987), 125.

[54] Patrick O'Brien, 'The Political Economy of British Taxation, 1660–1815', *Economic History Review*, 2nd ser. 41 (1988), 4 (table 3).

[55] See Peter Mathias, 'The Finances of Freedom', in id., *The Transformation of England* (London, 1979), 286–94, for a comparison of British and American war finances.

[56] James E. Thorold, *A History of Agriculture and Prices in England* (7 vols., London, 1866–1902), vii. 919–26.

for instance, North told the Commons of his labours in negotiating 'owing to the very high terms that had been insisted upon by the monied people'; while in 1781 he 'lamented exceedingly, that he should be obliged to come down and propose so large an addition to the debt of the empire, where we were obliged to borrow on such disadvantageous terms'.[57] To attract savings, the government had no choice but to offer the substantial inducements mentioned earlier.

Historians differ as to the impact of government borrowing during the next great war against revolutionary and Napoleonic France. Jeffrey Williamson argues that the demands of the state for money effectively diverted investment from the private sector, not least because the usury laws restricted the interest on private transactions to a maximum of 5%, while the state was able to offer higher rates.[58] Carol Heim and Philip Mirowski counter that interest rates were not the vital factor in determining investment patterns, and they point out that the rates on government stock were often no higher than those to be found on other issues. In 1793, for instance, the nominal yield on government consols was 3.9 %, while the nominal yield on India stock was 4.04%. India stock, however, was hardly representative of stocks in general—it was not subject to the usury laws. More significant, surely, is that Heim and Mirowski's data shows wartime pressure to have lifted rates on the consols above 5% on a regular basis; and this seems to have been true in the American war as well as in the long conflict of 1793–1815. In 1781 the yield on consols was 5.33%, and in 1782 it was 5.25%.[59]

There is also ample anecdotal evidence to suggest that in the American war there was a diversion of investment. Bankers saw their stocks steadily decline in the face of competition from government: Hoare's lost nearly a sixth of its deposits between 1777 and 1780, and in such circumstances the company had little choice but to reduce its lendings.[60] In July 1778 an Edinburgh lawyer wrote of 'the universal Stagnation of Credit & Want of Money'.[61] The

---

[57] *PH* xx. 157; xxi. 1330. [58] Williamson, 'Why was British Growth So Slow?'.

[59] C. E. Heim and P. Mirowski, 'Interest Rates and Crowding Out during Britain's Industrial Revolution', *Journal of Economic History*, 47 (1987), 117–39, esp. 120.

[60] D. M. Joslin, 'London Bankers in Wartime, 1739–1784', in L. S. Presnell (ed.), *Studies in the Industrial Revolution Presented to T. S. Ashton* (London, 1960), 172–3.

[61] Hull University Library, Maxwell-Constable Papers, DD EV/60/20B, John Syme to William Haggerston Maxwell Constable, 10 July 1778. Using almost identical language, John Lloyd wrote to his mother from London on 2 July 1778 of 'this universal Scarcity of Money': NLW, Wigfair Papers, MS 12423C.

following year a pamphleteer was making much the same point: 'the quantity of circulating cash in the hands of our merchants, manufacturers, builders, improvers, is remarkably diminished'.[62] A London merchant handling the investments of a Yorkshire clergyman put the matter plainly: 'the Interest on Government Securitys is indeed now very tempting . . . I see no Trade now equall to the Government funds'.[63] As a petition to the king explained in December 1781: 'Private credit has been almost wholly annihilated by the enormous Interest given in the public loans superior to that which is allowed by Law in any private Contract.'[64]

We should note, too, that there was a noticeable decline in enclosure activity. In Nottinghamshire, for instance, the number of parliamentary enclosures fell from six in 1775 to four in 1776 and 1777, and two in 1778. In the next year it went up again to three, but thereafter there were no enclosures until 1786.[65] In England and Wales as a whole, the number of bills relating to land—mainly enclosure bills—coming before Parliament fell from 111 in the 1776–7 session to fifty in 1779–80, thirty-seven in 1780–1, thirty in 1781–2, and thirty-one in 1782–3.[66] There may, of course, be a variety of explanations for this trend. Uncertainty was probably in itself a good reason to be hesitant about investing. Experts on enclosure have pointed out that some eighteenth-century troughs in enclosure activity can be related to falling cereal prices. But the very limited enclosure legislation of 1781–3 coincided with a period of *rising* cereal prices, following a series of poor harvests. What this suggests is that the mounting financial demands of the war were the major contributory factor, encouraging those with capital to spare to purchase government stock rather than run the risk of pouring money into a longer-term investment such as agricultural improvement.[67]

---

[62] Cited in Joslin, 'London Bankers in Wartime', 175.

[63] Hull University Library, Sykes Papers, DD SY/10/50, Joseph Denison to Revd Mark Sykes, 6 Mar. 1779.

[64] BL, Minutes of the Westminster Committee of Association, Add. MS 38594, fo. 22.

[65] William Edward Tate, *Parliamentary Enclosures in the County of Nottinghamshire* (Thoroton Society Record Series, vol. v, Nottingham, 1935), 53–69.

[66] There was no significant revival until 1792–3, and the trough was in 1784 (only 14). I owe this information to my colleague Julian Hoppit, who has recently completed a study of 18th-cent. legislation. Some of his findings are analysed in 'Patterns of Parliamentary Legislation, 1660–1800', *Historical Journal*, 39 (1996), 109–31.

[67] See Michael Turner, *Enclosures in Britain 1750–1830* (London, 1984), ch. 3, for an assessment of the various factors involved in the decision to enclose land.

Land prices themselves also fell,[68] again almost certainly partly due to the unattractiveness of land as an investment at a time when government stocks were selling at significant discounts and offering tempting interest payments. In July 1779 a Norfolk landowner explained to the Earl of Buckinghamshire: 'The fact is I cannot let my farm now in hand to its value and unfortunately my great farm comes out of lease at Michs. 1780, for which I have not yet been bid near its value'.[69] Canal construction was hit, too; work was suspended on the Oxford Canal in 1779 for want of funds, and the Leeds and Liverpool Canal suffered the same fate.[70] Turnpike trusts were obliged to increase their borrowing rates up to the 5% limit, but unable to go further they soon found it difficult to raise the necessary money.[71] Housebuilding, which was badly affected, as we have just seen, by increased indirect taxation, also seems to have suffered as a result of the flight of investment to the public funds. The West End of London was undergoing much development in the first years of the conflict, but by 1782 a visitor was able to comment that many of the buildings in Westminster were 'unfinished & falling to pieces from the bankruptcy of their owners—Portland Place, Stratford Place, Harley Street, Wimpole Street furnish ample proof of this'. In Manchester Square 'the Duke's own Mansion [was] in the centre of the West side standing alone surrounded with rubbish & pits of water'.[72]

Ireland experienced similar difficulties. Government borrowing increased, partly as a result of the resistance of the Irish Parliament to higher taxes, but mainly due to a fall in consumption of dutiable articles: in 1777–9 Irish government revenues were more than 20% lower than in 1775–7; as a result, nearly £486,000 had to be borrowed.[73] The high rates of interest that the government was obliged to pay attracted surplus capital, pushed up interest rates generally,

---

[68] See Christopher Clay, 'The Price of Freehold Land in the Later Seventeenth and Eighteenth Centuries', *Economic History Review*, 2nd ser. 27 (1974), 174 (table 1).

[69] HMC, *Lothian MSS* (London, 1905), 354.

[70] J. R. Ward, *The Finance of Canal Building in Eighteenth-Century England* (Oxford, 1974), 31–3, 102, 168. See also Christine Richardson and Philip Riden (eds.), *Minutes of the Chesterfield Canal Company 1771–1780* (Derbyshire Record Society, vol. xxiv, Chesterfield, 1996), 207, 216.

[71] William Albert, *The Turnpike Road System in England 1663–1840* (Cambridge, 1972), 129, 131.

[72] *The Diary of Sylas Neville, 1767–1788*, ed. Basil Cozens-Hardy (Oxford, 1950), 291.

[73] HMC, *Stopford Sackville MSS* (2 vols., London, 1904–10), i. 265–6.

and made it much more difficult for private individuals and companies to borrow. The consequences, inevitably, were bankruptcies among merchants, unemployment, a fall in the price of many commodities, unsold agricultural produce, and difficulties for landowners.[74] Lady Louisa Conolly was writing in May 1778 of terrible poverty in Ireland, and attributing the distress to 'The high interest that Government pay for their loans'.[75] Her husband's agent at Ballyshannon, County Donegal, sent exceedingly gloomy reports in that year of rent arrears, which he attributed to money shortages and poor markets for cattle and linen yarn. The next summer rents were still nearly impossible to collect, 'occasioned by an extraordinary Scarcity of Money'.[76]

Overseas Trade

The root cause of the Irish credit crisis was the decline in linen exports, which led to a general reduction in the purchase of goods bearing excises, and therefore a shortfall in government revenue.[77] Linen exports slipped because of the collapse of the American market and a cut in British consumption; from 1778 the disruption of European trade exacerbated the difficulties. In October 1775 John Moore, Arthur Annesley's land agent in County Down, was writing that linens sent to Dublin market 'do not sell at all' due to the 'loss of the American trade'. In April 1778 the situation was no better: 'thanks to our American War' linen prices were depressed. The following June he was reporting that 'Our yarn and linen have absolutely fallen 50 percent in our own markets'.[78] Irish linen exports in 1780–1 were at their lowest level, in terms of millions of yards, since 1764–5.[79]

The decline in linen exports was part of a more general pattern of trade contraction affecting many parts of the British Isles. Smuggling, admittedly, might have increased during the war, with the

---

[74] See e.g. *The Letters of Charles O'Conor of Belanagare*, ed. Catherine Coogan Ward and Robert E. Ward (2 vols., Ann Arbor, 1980), ii. 121, 122, 129; HMC, *Lothian MSS*, 316–17, 354.

[75] *Correspondence of Emily, Duchess of Leinster*, ed. Brian Fitzgerald (3 vols., Dublin, 1949–57), iii. 285.

[76] Trinity College Dublin, Conolly Papers, MS 3997/522, 542, 581.

[77] L. M. Cullen, *An Economic History of Ireland since 1660* (London, 1972), 75.

[78] W. H. Crawford (ed.), *Letters from an Ulster Land Agent 1774–1785* (Belfast, 1976), 5, 22, 23.

[79] Conrad Gill, *The Rise of the Irish Linen Industry* (Oxford, 1924), 180, 342.

attention of the navy distracted from customs enforcement and duties increased on many items of popular consumption. An informed source argued in early 1783 that smuggling had led to a shortfall of about 40% in the revenue from excise duties.[80] On the other hand, the concentration of naval vessels in home waters and the stationing of regular troops and militia along the coast to repulse any invasion attempt could well have meant that opportunities were reduced.[81] By the very nature of smuggling, we shall never know the full picture. But it is clear that legitimate external commerce markedly diminished. War against the American colonies was bound to have a profound effect on the British economy. Before the conflict began, the thirteen colonies that were to break away to form the United States produced important staples that freed Britain from reliance on foreign supply, and contributed to a lucrative trade in re-exports. Large quantities of tobacco from Virginia and Maryland, in particular, were consumed in northern Europe, but not before they had contributed to British public revenue through customs duties and to the profits of merchants in entrepôts such as Glasgow, Bristol, and London. With its rapidly growing population—around 2.5 million people on the eve of independence—North America was also a valuable market for British manufactures. About a quarter of British exports, measured in monetary terms, went to the British North American colonies in 1772–3.

In the first years of the war, there was a near cessation of trade with the rebel colonies. The value of British goods sent to the thirteen colonies had stood at more than £2.5 million in 1774; by 1776 it had fallen almost to nothing. Commodities continued to enter British-held enclaves like New York City, and hopes were frequently expressed that British military success would soon make inland markets accessible again. But such hopes proved illusory. 'All prospect of the Countrys opening is now at an end for this Campaign', Frederick Rhinelander, a New York merchant,

---

[80] Langford, *Polite and Commercial People*, 633–4; Arthur Lyon Cross (ed.), *Eighteenth-Century Documents relating to the Royal Forests, the Sheriffs and Smuggling* (New York, 1928), 289, 291. See also 306.

[81] In the summer of 1782 a company of the Sussex militia based at Horsham was on anti-smuggling duty: see Horsham Museum, Medwin Papers, MS 331/2 and 3. Without the war, the militia would not have been embodied, and would therefore have been unavailable for such a service. See also Cornwall RO, DDJ 2245, Journal of Thomas Hawkins, who in 1782 was serving in Sussex on anti-smuggling duties with the 10th Dragoons.

told a British supplier; to another he explained: 'When we sent you this order we certainly presumed on a Conclusion of this unhappy Contest and of course an open Country'.[82] The textile industry seems to have been a major casualty: in 1772 the official value of woollen exports to the thirteen colonies had been more than £900,000; in other words, woollens accounted for nearly 30% of pre-war British exports to North America. In the West Riding of Yorkshire, output of wool products did not consistently return to the level of 1773 until the end of the war. While some commentators put on a brave face ('our trade & Manufactures are as good & brisk as ever they were known to be'),[83] John Wesley, visiting Leeds in 1775, was decidedly gloomy. 'I had appointed to dine at a merchant's; but before I came, the bailiffs were in possession of the house. Upon my saying "I thought Mr. —— had been in good circumstances" I was answered. "He was so: but the American war has ruined him."'[84] The situation was, if anything, even worse in the other textile-producing regions. Joseph Savill, who made bays at Bocking in Essex, wrote in 1780: 'I have now unsold more than 1050 bays and no prospect of selling . . . trade never worse'.[85] This naturally had an impact on the price of raw wool: Savill noted in the same lament that wool had never been cheaper. Indeed, such was the fall in wool prices that sheep farmers, especially in Lincolnshire, petitioned Parliament in 1780 and 1781 for the suspension of ancient legislation prohibiting the export of raw wool. They were unsuccessful—the woollen textile producers were of course fearful that wool exports would help their European competitors, and Parliament was disinclined to undermine Britain's major industry. Even so, the wool-growers' petitions are a clear indication that the American war was having a damaging impact.[86]

---

[82] New-York Historical Society, Rhinelander Papers, Letter-book 1774–83, Rhinelander to Rawlinson & Chorley, 12 Nov. 1777, to Smith, Son & Russell, 29 Jan. 1778.

[83] Calderdale Archives, Lister of Shibden Hall MSS, SH 7/JL/49, James Lister to Jeremy Lister, 9 Nov. 1775.

[84] HMC, *Dartmouth MSS* (3 vols., London, 1887–96), iii. 220.

[85] A. F. J. Brown (ed.), *Essex People 1750–1900 from their Diaries, Memoirs and Letters* (Chelmsford, 1972), 45.

[86] See Richard Wilson, 'Newspapers and Industry: The Export of Wool Controversy in the 1780s', in Michael Harris and Alan Lee (eds.), *The Press in English Society from the Seventeenth to the Nineteenth Centuries* (London, 1986), 80–104. See also *The Sheep and Wool Correspondence of Sir Joseph Banks*, ed. Harold B. Carter (Norwich, 1979), 43–76; *The Oakes Diaries*, ed. Jane Fisk, i (Suffolk Record Society, vol. xxxii, Woodbridge, 1990), 224; John Gascoigne, *Science in the Service of Empire: Joseph Banks, the British State and the Uses of Science in the Age of Revolution* (Cambridge, 1998), 71–81.

The metalworking trades of the West Midlands also felt the consequences of the loss of most of the American market. As early as July 1775 a Worcestershire businessman was writing of the war's 'baleful effects in the iron manufacture particularly nails'.[87] Although in the following year Andrew Oliver, an American loyalist refugee, could still wondrously describe Birmingham as 'a perfect Beehive',[88] by November 1778 a subscription had been opened in the town to help 'many of our industrious and deserving Artificers' who were out of work and 'in great Distress'.[89] In October 1781 the staunchly pro-American Sylas Neville was recording in his diary that Birmingham's Soho Works had employed 1,000 operatives before the war, but now had work for only half that number. 'This is a confirmation', he added sarcastically, 'of what we are told by our worthy governors & their tools that Birmingham & Sheffield are not in the least affected by the American troubles.'[90]

But the collapse of the American market was only part of the explanation for a general decline in exports and all the ills that came in its wake. In Ireland, an embargo on the export of provisions was laid by the government at Dublin Castle in February 1776; only exports to Britain and the loyal colonies were exempted. The intention, it seems, was to prevent provisions, especially salted beef, reaching the French navy, and to ensure a sufficient supply for the British armed forces and the British Caribbean islands.[91] From the perspective of many Irish commentators, however, the embargo was an intolerable burden, which threatened to destroy a trade that benefited not only the mercantile and processing interests in Cork, Waterford, and Limerick, but also countless farmers throughout the island. The French, it was argued, were now purchasing from new north European sources at competitive prices: 'if our [provisioning] trade does not speedily return into its former Channel, it will be totally lost, & entirely engrossed by the Merchants of the Baltick, particularly the Danes', John Forbes, an opposition MP, told the Irish Commons in December 1777.[92] A few months later David Connel of Cork wrote despairingly that 'A very valuable branch of

---

[87] Dr Williams's Library, Wodrow-Kenrick Correspondence, MS 24157 (51).
[88] BL, Egerton MS 2672, p. 184.   [89] *Aris's Birmingham Gazette*, 2 Nov. 1778.
[90] *Diary of Sylas Neville*, ed. Cozens-Hardy, 280.
[91] *The Harcourt Papers*, ed. E. W. Harcourt (14 vols., Oxford, 1880–1905), x. 90.
[92] *An Edition of the Cavendish Irish Parliamentary Diary 1776–1778*, ed. Anthony R. Black (3 vols., Delavan, Wis., 1984), iii. 377.

trade is upon the verge of being lost for ever to us'.[93] But the principal grievance concerned the so-called small beef, 'which the French & Spaniards particularly the French mostly took from us before the Embargo'.[94] The British government shunned small beef in favour of heavier Ox beef, with the result that Irish graziers and merchants were left with unsold stocks.[95]

Ill feeling generated by the embargo contributed to mounting Irish hostility to British commercial and political restrictions, and one of the manifestations of Irish discontent added to the problems facing British exporters. Ireland had been an important consumer of British products before the war, but events in America, as we shall see, inspired the Irish to press for redress of their own grievances by pledging to suspend the purchase of British goods and consuming more home-produced items.[96] British exports to Ireland, which had been valued at £1.2 million in 1775 and nearly £1.4 million in 1776, slid to £958,000 in 1778 and £843,000 the following year. The worst affected areas seem to have been those which had protested most loudly when commercial concessions to Ireland were first proposed in April 1778. Lancashire, having led the petitioning against the lifting of restrictions on Irish trade, was specifically mentioned in many of the Irish non-importation agreements. Josiah Wedgwood, writing in October 1779, noted a sharp increase in local unemployment in Bolton, which he attributed to Irish economic retaliation.[97]

More important from the British perspective was the entry of France and Spain into the war. There was not, it must be said, a total suspension of commercial relations. In January 1779, many months after France and Britain had become formal enemies, a French businessman visited the Birmingham Soho Works to discuss with James Watt and Matthew Boulton a scheme for raising water to supply Paris.[98] But the expansion of the war did in effect close many continental markets, or at best made them less accessible. In October 1778 Richard Price, a radical critic of the American conflict, told the Earl of Shelburne that in Norwich there was much distress 'in

---

[93] NLI, O'Hara Papers, MS 20395, Connel to Charles O'Hara, 16 Mar. 1778.

[94] Ibid., Stephen Roches to O'Hara, 13 Mar. 1778.

[95] Ibid., NLI, Shannon Papers, MS 13301, Great Smyth to Lord Shannon, 24 Oct. 1777.   [96] See below, Ch. 6.

[97] *The Selected Letters of Josiah Wedgwood*, ed. Ann Finer and George Savage (London, 1965), 241.

[98] Birmingham City Archives, James Watt Papers, JWP C3/4, Watt's Journal, 5 Jan. 1779.

consequence chiefly of the loss of the trade to the Mediterranean'.[99]
John Wilson, a Leeds linen manufacturer whose political views were
less pronounced, confirmed Price's message: 'The war with Spain
am afraid will putt a damp upon Trade for some time', he wrote in
1779.[100] Indeed, for many sectors of the economy serious problems
were encountered only from the time of the outbreak of the Bourbon
war, not from 1775. Exeter's exports of serge cloth to Spain were
worth about £150,000 in 1778. In the next two years they dwindled
almost to nothing. Similarly, the city's trade with the Italian states
fell by over 70% between 1775 and 1780, most of the decline coming
with the interruption of Mediterranean commerce once France and
Spain entered the war.[101] In 1779 British exports to southern
Europe were worth only half as much as in 1774, and they continued
to decline until 1782.

Further afield, war with France and Spain meant still more
interference with Caribbean trade. The sugar islands were already
suffering from the cutting-off of their supplies from the mainland
North American colonies, which led to the deaths of many slaves and
falling output; and as more land had to be turned over to the
cultivation of foodstuffs for the labour force, output of export
staples, particularly sugar, fell still more. But with the entry into
the conflict of the Bourbon powers the difficulties experienced by
the British islands became even more acute. The threat from enemy
privateers and naval vessels increased greatly, some of the islands
themselves were taken by the French—Dominica in 1778, St Vincent and Grenada in 1779, Tobago in 1781, and St Kitts and Nevis
in 1782—and Jamaica, the most important of the British islands,
was frequently seen as under threat. In these circumstances, the
West Indian interest in London lobbied persistently for greater naval
and military protection.[102] But, hardly surprisingly, British imports
from the Caribbean, which had been worth £3.4 million in 1772,
dipped below £2 million in 1781. The picture was equally bleak in
Asia. British imports from the region had been worth £2.4 million in

[99] *The Correspondence of Richard Price*, ed. W. Bernard Peach and D. O. Thomas (3
vols., Durham, NC, 1983–94), ii. 28.
[100] Leeds Archives, John Wilson Papers, W/3/8, Letter-book, Apr. 1779–Feb. 1780,
Wilson to Robert Gillies & Son, 8 July 1779.
[101] W. G. Hoskins, *Industry, Trade and People in Exeter* (Manchester, 1935), 81.
[102] Andrew J. O'Shaughnessy, 'The Formation of a Commercial Lobby: The West
Indian Interest, British Colonial Policy and the American Revolution', *Historical Journal*,
40 (1997), 95–8.

1772; they were higher in 1781, but in 1779 and 1780 they fell below £1 million, and in 1782 to only £626,000. The presence in the Indian Ocean of a significant French naval force from 1778, and especially from the beginning of 1782 when it came under the command of the energetic and enterprising de Suffren, must surely explain at least part of this decline. But the main problem was that the East India Company was obliged to spend vast sums of money on military operations and maintaining British forces in India; money that would ordinarily have been employed in trade. As one of the company's officials at Calcutta concluded dolefully at the end of 1782; 'War is a dear Hobby Horse and Soldiers expensive Play things'.[103]

Besides these local and specific problems, there were general difficulties. Uncertainty undermined the confidence of many merchants and made them keen to restrict the scope for loss. John Wilson followed closely the events of the war, and regularly urged caution on his correspondents: 'at present we think it will be more prudent to defer purchasing for a few weeks' (19 December 1777); 'we think it not prudent to lay in too large a Stock at present, as our National Affairs appear here with a very indifferent Aspect' (20 June 1778); 'I am at present desiring my friend to buy with caution & sparingly, waiting the great Events of the present Struggle' (24 November 1781).[104] Nor did increased customs duties help to promote international trade. In April 1782 Wilson bluntly informed one of his overseas suppliers that 'The additional Duties lately laid on all dry Goods imported . . . render them much dearer than I can purchase the like Articles for here'.[105] Higher insurance rates, mentioned by Wilson in the same letter, must surely have had an impact too. Pre-war insurance rates for the transatlantic routes varied from 2% to 2.5%. By February 1778—that is before the French entered the war—they had more than doubled for vessels in convoy, and were as high as 15% for vessels sailing without the protection of other ships.[106] Another impediment was created by the requirement of the navy board and other government departments for shipping to transport troops and provisions to the different theatres of operation. Large numbers of vessels were taken out of mercantile service

---

[103] Lincolnshire Archives Office, Stubton Papers, II D/3, George Foley to Sir Richard Heron, 10 Dec. 1782.
[104] Leeds Archives, John Wilson Papers, Letter-books W/3/6 and 10.
[105] Ibid., W/3/11.   [106] PH xix. 709.

to meet this demand; by December 1781 more than 113,000 tons of shipping was under hire to the navy board alone—the equivalent of about one-seventh of all pre-war British tonnage.[107] And a further and still more important contribution to trade contraction was the capture by Britain's enemies of an estimated 3,386 merchant vessels in the course of the war.[108]

There was, admittedly, a more positive side. If the British merchant marine suffered at the hands of enemy naval vessels and privateers, British merchant ships acting as privateers made their own captures.[109] Bristol had about 203 vessels commissioned as privateers between 1777 and 1783; Liverpool, 390; and London, 719. The prospect of war with the Dutch sent Portsmouth into a frenzy of excitement: the town was reported to be 'full of people from London, come down to buy ships for privateers'.[110] 'The merchants and adventurers', the Earl of Camden wrote contemptuously of the situation in London, 'are in raptures with the idea of possessing all the wealth of this commercial republic, and embrace the event as a general license to plunder. All the ships are brought up, and the attorneys have hardly time to draw up articles of partnership.'[111] At the same time, Philip Mayow, a Cornish naval chaplain, wished that he had £1,000 to fit out a privateer at Fowey. 'It wd. return better interest than the Stocks', he told his sister.[112] Such expectations were often wildly over-optimistic. The Royal Navy took a good number of the prizes, and the American war saw a 'productivity rate' for privateers of only 0.5 prizes per vessel. Worse still, some of the prizes were not sufficiently valuable to compensate for the cost of fitting and maintaining a privateer. But even in these circumstances the benefit to the local economy—through work for shipwrights and sailmakers, for instance—could

---

[107] Cf. David Syrett, *Shipping and the American War* (London, 1970), 250; Ralph Davis, *The Rise of the English Shipping Industry in the Seventeenth and Eighteenth Centuries* (Newton Abbot, 1972), 27; and Gordon Jackson, 'Scottish Shipping, 1775–1805', in P. L. Cottrell and D. H. Aldcroft (eds.), *Shipping, Trade and Commerce* (Leicester, 1981), 126 (table 16). [108] Davis, *Rise of the English Shipping Industry*, 318.

[109] The information in this paragraph, unless otherwise indicated, is from David J. Starkey, *British Privateering Enterprise in the Eighteenth Century* (Exeter, 1990), 200, 221, 279.

[110] Cited in id., 'British Privateering against the Dutch in the American Revolutionary War', in H. E. Stephen Fisher (ed.), *Studies in British Privateering, Trading Enterprise and Seaman's Welfare* (Exeter, 1987), 11.

[111] West Suffolk RO, Grafton Papers, Ac 423/78.

[112] Cornwall RO, Wynell-Mayow Papers, DDWM 552.

be some compensation for the contraction of conventional overseas trade. And there were certainly individual triumphs. The *Snap Dragon*, a forty-ton vessel from Dartmouth in Devon, cost £157 10s. to put to sea, but made a net profit of £21,088 3s. 5d. when it captured a Dutch West Indiaman. In some cases, furthermore, individual success could aggregate into regional benefit. The Channel Islands were notable in this regard: their 223 commissioned vessels took 435 prizes.[113]

Vessels hired out to the navy board and other service departments reduced the number available for normal mercantile purposes, but the owners were able to earn a decent profit—at least until the later stages of the war, when some found themselves locked into contracts that offered them rates which failed to take account of cost inflation. Ralph Elliot, owner of the *Polly*, hired to the board for thirty-three months of the war, ended up spending in maintenance costs and wages in excess of £1,000 more than he received in freight allowances. But other owners, who hired out their ships at the beginning of the war, or for shorter periods, seem to have emerged as winners rather than losers.[114] Moreover, shipowners who hired their vessels to the victualling board, or to the ordnance board, made a clear profit throughout the war, because these boards required fewer vessels than the navy board and could therefore afford to offer higher freight rates to owners.[115] Nor should it be assumed that every ship taken into government service necessarily meant a ship less was available for the movement of goods in the private sector. Some of the gap was filled by the vessels of foreign powers. In 1782 the overseas trade of Weymouth was said to be much diminished by the war, but it was able to continue in 'neutral bottoms'.[116]

We should also note that, despite the narrowing of opportunities

---

[113] But for a cautious note about privateering's impact on the Channel Islands see Peter L. Wickens, 'The Economics of Privateering: Capital Dispersal in the American War of Independence', *Journal of European Economic History*, 13 (1984), 375–95. Wickens's argument is endorsed in A. G. Jameson, 'The Return to Privateering: Channel Island Privateers, 1739–1783', in id. (ed.), *A People of the Sea: The Maritime History of the Channel Islands* (London, 1986), 172.

[114] David Syrett, 'The Navy Board and Merchant Shipowners during the American War, 1776–1783', *American Neptune*, 47 (1987), 12.

[115] David Syrett has written two helpful essays on this: 'The Victualling Board Charters Shipping, 1775–1782', *Historical Research*, 68 (1995), 212–24; and 'Procurement of Shipping by the Board of Ordnance during the American War, 1775–1782', *Mariner's Mirror*, 81 (1995), 409–16.

[116] *The Torrington Diaries*, ed. C. Bruyn Andrews (4 vols., London, 1934–8), i. 94.

in the rebel colonies, the American market at least partly recovered as the war dragged on. The British army and navy operating in the thirteen colonies and the population of the port towns that it occupied were important customers for British manufacturers and merchants. The presence of large numbers of troops, and the hard cash at the army's disposal, ensured that prices were high in the British enclaves.[117] Shortly after the British army took Philadelphia, Thomas Clifford Jnr., a local merchant, told a London contact that although some types of goods could be sold only when the country as a whole was open to trade, in the meantime 'there are many particular Articles, which will be wanted & appear safe to speculate in'.[118] At the same time, Colborn Barrell, a New York merchant, was busy conveying ship loads of goods, many of them British manufactures, to newly captured Philadelphia. His local agent, Tench Coxe, reported that the city was now 'one of the Best if not the Best [market] upon the Continent' for such goods.[119]

There was, indeed, a dramatic rise in the official value of British exports to America in the last years of the war, from a mere £38,000 in 1778, to £351,000 in 1779, £829,000 in 1780 and £855,000 in 1781 (see Fig. 2.1). In part this was a result of the growth in the population of New York. On the eve of the war, the city had some 25,000 residents. The number fell to only about 5,000 at the time of the British occupation in September 1776, but thereafter steadily climbed as loyalists flocked in to seek protection. As a British army surgeon remarked in April 1780, the troops were 'crowded with refugees from all parts of the Continent'.[120] By 1781 New York's population, not counting military and naval personnel, was back at around 25,000.[121] On the other hand, many of the loyalists who came into New York were hardly in a position to consume significant quantities of British goods: they had left their homes and lost much

---

[117] See Julian Gwyn, 'The Impact of British Military Spending on the Colonial American Money Markets, 1760–1783', Canadian Historical Association, *Historical Papers / Communications historiques* (1980), 77–99.

[118] Historical Society of Pennsylvania, Clifford Papers, vol. 29, Clifford to Thomas Franks, 27 Dec. 1777.

[119] Library of Congress, Stephen Collins & Son Collection, vol. 142, Barrell's Invoice-books, 20 Nov., 23 Dec. 1777; vol. 21, Coxe to Barrell, 22 Oct. 1777.

[120] PRO, Documents of Unknown Ownership, 30/39/1, Richard Hope to Mrs Rogers, 10 Apr. 1780.

[121] Oscar T. Barck, *New York City during the War for Independence* (New York, 1931), 75–8.

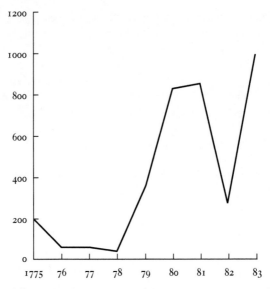

Fig. 2.1. British exports (including re-exports) to the thirteen colonies/United States, 1775–1783 (in £000s)

Source: Mitchell, *British Historical Statistics*, 494

of their property. Some were so destitute that they had to be supported from the public purse.[122] The capture in 1780 of Charleston, South Carolina, may well have been more important. For a brief period, the tidewater area of the province was under British control, and much of the interior too. British goods seem to have flooded into the city in expectation of the restoration of pre-war trading conditions. William Smith, a London merchant, sailed with a cargo said to be worth about £40,000 as soon as he heard of the fall of Charleston, and his partner, John Schoolbred, sent out further shipments thereafter.[123] The theory that South Carolina was responsible for a good portion of the growth in British exports is supported by the sharp fall of 1782 (down to £267,000), which could be explained by the contraction of the area under British control during the second half of 1781, and then by the evacuation of Charleston itself at the end of 1782. But even this interpretation is not wholly

[122] See e.g. William L. Clements Library, Mackenzie Papers, 'A list of the Names of Persons . . . Who . . . Are allowed . . . the Sums, opposite their Names', 24 Dec. 1779.
[123] PRO, Audit Office Papers, AO 12/50, fos. 174–7.

satisfactory. Proper account must be taken of the significant quantities of British imports that were reaching Americans outside the areas occupied by the British army. There is abundant evidence that by the last years of the war, British goods were penetrating deep into the revolutionary hinterland. In Connecticut the authorities were worried that the state might be drained of specie to pay for British goods at New York.[124]

Even before 1780, however, the reduction in exports to the thirteen colonies was probably not as sharp as the official figures would suggest. The Americans almost certainly continued to import British goods indirectly, especially via their continental and island neighbours. British exports to Canada rose noticeably, and remained well above pre-war levels throughout the conflict. To some extent the reinforcement of the British army in Canada was responsible: the inflated export figures for 1777 (£1.6 million, compared with £830,000 in 1776) almost certainly reflect purchasing for General Burgoyne's ill-fated expedition. But the increase in British exports started in 1775, when the British garrison, which had been depleted to strengthen the main army at Boston, was in fact smaller than in 1774. This suggests that, just as in earlier wars, the border between Canada and the old British North American colonies was a far from impenetrable barrier to the movement of goods.[125] The same pattern is discernible elsewhere. The sparsely populated Floridas, on the southern flank of the rebel colonies, started to receive more British goods: the value more than trebled between 1773–4 and 1775–6.[126]

Increased trade with other areas also offered some compensation for the shrinkage of the American market. In August 1775 Richard Champion, a Bristol merchant, noted that 'Trade in general is tolerably good', and attributed this 'somewhat surprising' development, considering the 'entire Stop put to the American Trade', in part to increased sales to Poland and Russia.[127] The value of Exeter's serge exports to Flanders rose from £58,000 in 1775 to £270,000 in

[124] Richard Buel Jnr., 'Time: Friend or Foe of the Revolution?', in Don Higginbotham (ed.), *Reconsiderations on the Revolutionary War: Selected Essays* (Westport, Conn., 1978), 140–3. This was happening on a smaller scale earlier in the war: see Library of Congress, Stephen Collins & Son Collection, vol. 21, Coxe to Barrell, 28 Dec. 1777.

[125] McCusker and Menard, *Economy of British America*, 115–16, 190.

[126] Macpherson, *Annals of Commerce*, iii. 564, 673.

[127] G. H. Guttridge (ed.), *The American Correspondence of a Bristol Merchant* (Berkeley and Los Angeles, 1934), 60. See also *The Correspondence of Edmund Burke*, ed. Thomas W. Copeland et al. (10 vols., Cambridge, 1958–78), iii. 187.

1780,[128] and at the end of 1782 the people of the Austrian Netherlands were said to be most distressed at the prospect of peace and the return to pre-war trading patterns.[129] Indeed, although British exports to northern Europe as a whole dipped in 1781, the first full year of the war with the Dutch, they remained remarkably steady for most of the conflict, the annual average for 1775–83 being only marginally less than for 1772–4.

But, qualifications and caveats notwithstanding, the American war was very damaging to British trade. Earlier eighteenth-century conflicts had seen fluctuations in the country's trade figures, particularly the War of Austrian Succession, when imports slipped in 1744 and exports in 1744 and 1745. But the pattern was for imports and exports to rise during the course of hostilities. In the Seven Years War there was a more or less uninterrupted growth in trade until 1762. In 1760 the total value of imports, exports, and re-exports was nearly 19% higher than in 1756. Much the same happened in the War of Spanish Succession at the beginning of the century. The aggregated value of English trade increased by 27% between 1702 and 1711. The situation was very different in the American war. In 1778 the total value of overseas trade was 26% less than in 1774. There was no real improvement until 1782. Indeed, for the years 1778–81 average annual imports were worth nearly £2.6 million less than in 1774 (an 18% fall), exports just under £2.4 million less (or minus 24%), and re-exports £2.1 million less (down a swinging 32%).

Pay and Prices

The contraction of overseas commerce was not necessarily disastrous for the overall health of the economy. Although exports fell noticeably as a proportion of national output—they stood at an estimated 9.4% in 1780, compared with 14.6% in 1760 and 15.7% in 1801[130]—industrial production in England has been estimated to have fallen by only about 1.4% between 1775 and 1780.[131] Part of

---

[128] Hoskins, *Industry, Trade and People*, 81.
[129] Leicestershire RO, Turville Constable Maxwell MSS, 1122.
[130] N. F. R. Crafts, *British Economic Growth during the Industrial Revolution* (Oxford, 1985), 131 (table 6.6).
[131] W. A. Cole, 'Factors in Demand', in Roderick Floud and Donald McCloskey (eds.), *The Economic History of Britain since 1700* (2 vols., Cambridge, 1981), i. 40 (table 3.1).

the explanation for the limited nature of this slip must be import substitution. Expansion of the iron industry was certainly aided by the disruption of American and Scandinavian iron inflows. But at least some of the war years seem also to have witnessed a growth in domestic demand that helped to compensate for the decline in exports. This was connected, no doubt, with a markedly favourable balance of trade, particularly in the worst years of trade depression, which would have provided more money for the purchase of domestically produced goods and services. In 1779 and 1780 the value of exports (including re-exports) exceeded the value of imports by around £2 million a year. This compares with a much smaller favourable balance in 1777 (some £847,000) and a deficit in 1781 (−£1,392,000). A rise in consumption within Britain could also be linked to an increase in family incomes. As more men went into the armed forces, particularly from 1778, women's employment opportunities probably increased.[132] In at least some families, where the male wage-earners were still present and the women and even children were able to take up new paid work, this would have meant a greater disposable income and so more demand for goods and services.[133] We should also note that wage levels for men seem in some cases to have risen. Granted, wages in certain occupations and in certain parts of the country remained static or even fell: in 1778 framework-knitters could earn no more than seven shillings a week, much less than before the war;[134] and, as we have seen, there was certainly unemployment in some industries, which usually has the effect of holding wages steady or driving them down. But wages certainly rose in many areas and in many sectors of the economy. Labourers in north Staffordshire experienced a rise in their daily wage rate from 1s. 4d. between 1775 and 1777 to 1s. 6d. in 1778 and 1779.[135] Labourers in Maidstone saw their daily pay increase by 11% between 1775 and 1780. It slipped back fractionally in 1781,

---

[132] See below, Ch. 3.

[133] For emphasis on the household as a unit of consumption, and the vital role played by female and child earnings in increasing consumption, see Jan de Vries, 'Between Purchasing Power and the World of Goods: Understanding Household Economy in Early Modern Europe', in John Brewer and Roy Porter (eds.), *Consumption and the World of Goods* (London, 1993), 85–132.

[134] John Rule, *The Experience of Labour in Eighteenth-Century Industry* (London, 1981), 69. See also, below, Ch. 3.

[135] F. W. Botham and E. H. Hunt, 'Wages in Britain during the Industrial Revolution', *Economic History Review*, 2nd ser. 40 (1987), 389 (table 3).

but stabilized at this rate for the rest of the war. Craftsmen's wages in Guildford in Surrey followed a similar pattern. They climbed steadily from 2s. 2d. in 1774 to 2s. 3d. in 1776, to 2s. 5d. in 1777, and reached a wartime peak of 3s. in 1778. They remained at this level until the conclusion of the peace in 1783, when they dropped to 2s. 5d.[136]

Increases of this kind probably owed something to local and contingent factors. In north Staffordshire the rise in wage rates in 1778 was followed by a fall in 1780 and only a gradual and slight recovery thereafter, a pattern that admits of no ready explanation.[137] In the case of Maidstone, we can speculate that the establishment of a very large camp for the militia and regulars at Coxheath, only a short distance away, might well have had an impact on the demand for labour in the town. It seems highly likely, however, that in general terms the manpower demands of the armed forces made an important contribution to wage rises. In Guildford there was certainly a local perception of considerable strain on manpower resources. In 1782 the corporation felt unable to respond positively to the government's proposals for a new popular militia on the grounds that there were too few 'Persons fit to bear Arms' remaining in the town.[138] This seems to have been a widely experienced problem. The need for more soldiers and sailors, and the embodying of the militia from 1778, took significant numbers of men out of the labour market—and not just the unemployed and readily dispensable: farmers felt the loss of men at harvest time in particular, and called for militiamen to be released to help bring in their crops,[139] while masters regularly complained at the enlistment of apprentices, who were supposed to be exempted by law from recruitment.[140] In the Scottish Highlands, where many men joined the new regiments, male servants became a rarity as early as the spring

---

[136] E. W. Gilboy, *Wages in Eighteenth-Century England* (Cambridge, Mass., 1934), 260, 263-4.   [137] Botham and Hunt, 'Wages in Britain', 389 (table 3).
[138] Surrey RO, Guildford Muniment Room, Borough Records, BR/OC/2/9/1/(4). For the new militia proposals of 1782, see below, Ch. 4.
[139] See WO 1/1000, Capt. Edward Meux Worsley to Barrington, 21 July 1778.
[140] e.g. ADM 1/2390, Capt. Robert Roddam to Philip Stephens; WO 4/95, p. 424; WO 4/96, p. 266; WO 4/102, p. 351; WO 4/103, p. 92; WO 4/112, p. 337. For an apprentice found guilty of fraud for enlisting see Worcestershire RO, Quarter Sessions Order-book, vol. v, fo. 87.

of 1778.[141] In 1781 a Jamaica planter who was keen to recruit a plumber, a blacksmith, and a coppersmith in Bristol was told by a merchant in the city that such skilled workers were in short supply because 'the Navy & Army take all the young and unsettled people'.[142]

Nor should we forget that the state employed a growing number of civilians to service the armed forces. For generations, civilians had been paid to repair and build ships in the royal dockyards and to drive supply wagons and artillery trains; but with the wartime expansion of the army and navy, and the embodying of the militia, the demand for civilian labour correspondingly rose. True enough, the civil branch of the ordnance took on only a handful of extra clerks and labourers,[143] and the dockyard labour force expanded only slightly—at Portsmouth, for instance, from 2,089 in 1774 to 2,471 in 1783—because the navy preferred to contract out work to private yards rather than try to recruit many more workers of its own.[144] But the victualling board increased its payroll at Chatham by 31% between 1775 and 1782.[145] It was even found necessary to send some British civilian employees abroad, notwithstanding the normal practice was to hire local labour.[146] Fifty civilian drivers were sent out to help the Royal Artillery in North America in 1776, after the ordnance board had received reports that local drivers were un-reliable;[147] and shipwrights based at Portsmouth dockyard went to Nova Scotia.[148]

In one occupation there can be no doubt of the impact of mobilization on wages: those merchant seamen who escaped the attention of the press-gangs saw a spectacular growth in their monthly pay. As

[141] John Malcolm Bulloch, *Territorial Soldiering in the North-East of Scotland during 1759–1814* (Aberdeen, 1914), 87–90. For the heavy recruitment in the Highlands see also Robert Clyde, *From Rebel to Hero: The Image of the Highlander 1745–1830* (Edinburgh, 1995), 150, 156–9, and Andrew Mackillop, *'More Fruitful than the Soil': Army, Empire and the Scottish Highlands 1715–1815* (East Linton, 1999).

[142] Kenneth Morgan (ed.), *Calendar of Correspondence from William Miles . . . to John Tharp* (Bristol Record Society Publications, vol. xxxvii, Bristol, 1985), 96.

[143] See the estimates for 1775 and 1783 in WO 54/215 and 216.

[144] R. J. B. Knight (ed.), *Portsmouth Dockyard Papers 1774–1783* (Portsmouth Record Series, Portsmouth, 1987), 157; Bernard Pool, *Navy Board Contracts 1660–1832* (London, 1966), 90–1.   [145] Cf. ADM 113/17 and 19.

[146] e.g. William L. Clements Library, Wray Papers, vols. 3 and 4, muster rolls of the civil branch of the ordnance at Rhode Island, 1779, and Charleston, 1780.

[147] WO 55/1537, fos. 51, 53, 57, 77, 138.

[148] R. J. B. Knight (ed.), *Portsmouth Dockyard Papers*, 50.

early as September 1776, sailors at Cork were reported to be paid £3 a month 'and ship provisions; before the american war, 28s'.[149] In February 1778 the House of Lords was told that seamen's wages had risen from 25–28s. a month to 55–65s.[150] Another source suggests more cautiously that the increase was from £1. 10s. in 1776 to £3. 5s. in 1783.[151] But whatever the precise figures, the overall pattern is clear: labour shortages, brought on primarily by the demands of the Royal Navy, had a dramatic effect on levels of remuneration.

More money makes little difference, of course, unless it increases purchasing power. If prices are rising as fast—or faster—there will be no beneficial effect on levels of domestic demand. For much of the war, this seems to have been the case. Inflation outstripped many of the wage rises. In parts of the country the presence of significant bodies of soldiers, militiamen, or sailors had the effect of pushing up prices. The mayor of Norwich complained in the summer of 1780 that the quantity of dragoon horses stabled in the city had greatly increased the price of hay—an essential commodity in an age when the horse was responsible for landward movement of nearly all goods.[152] Three years earlier, a visitor to Plymouth noted that it would 'not do for a Traveller to stay here long without a full Purse; for there are so many military and marine Residents here, that Provisions are very dear'.[153] More generally, we have already seen that higher customs and excise duties started to have an effect even on items of popular consumption from 1778; most people—including those on low incomes—would have found themselves obliged to pay more for soap, sugar, salt, and tobacco. Coal purchased in London, where it was vital for heating, was about 15% more expensive in 1781 than in 1775, partly as a result of the new duties imposed in 1778 and 1781 but also because of the increased costs of transporting it by sea from the north-east of England. Carriage duties, introduced in North's last budget, would presumably have

---

[149] Arthur Young, *A Tour in Ireland* (London, 1780), pt. i, p. 276.

[150] *PH* xix. 709.

[151] T. S. Ashton, *An Economic History of England: The Eighteenth Century* (London, 1955), 226.

[152] WO 1/1007, p. 789. See also BL, Liverpool Papers, Add. MS 38212, fo. 136, where the innkeepers of Bury St Edmunds complain that they are not able 'to Support the expence of procuring Forrage for a Regiment of Horse, besides what is wanted for our usual consumption, the Camp last year, and this, haveing taken off the greatest part of the Old Hay in the neighbourhood, and but little have been grown this Summer'.

[153] Oliver's Journal, BL, Egerton MS 2672, p. 304.

increased the cost of nearly all items moved by land or water. The decline in imports would also have contributed to upward pressure on prices. Potash, which was purchased from the American colonies in large volumes before the war and was vital for textile bleaching, was said to have tripled in price by April 1779.[154] Likewise, sugar prices, a House of Commons committee was told in 1782, had trebled 'since the Commencement of the war', partly due to recent import duties, but mainly as a result of a reduction in the quantity of Caribbean sugar reaching the British market.[155]

But in 1778–80 the trend was for prices to fall. There is some evidence of a rise in real wages in these years. For craftsmen in southern England real wages were 8% higher in 1780 than they had been in 1777. The wages of labourers in Lancashire were worth 12% more in 1779 than in 1777; those of labourers in London, 17% more. The financial crisis that started to become acute in 1778 no doubt played a part in depressing prices, but the major cause of the improvement in living standards, it would appear, was a run of good harvests—especially in 1779 ('grain the cheapest it has been for many years')[156] and 1780—which led to a considerable fall in bread prices. Average annual wheat prices in England and Wales were £2. 2s. a quarter in 1775–7 and £1. 18s. a quarter in 1778–80. Bread sold in London cost 17% less in 1779 than in 1777; in Dublin 11% less. This fall seems to have been sufficient to counteract the inflationary pressures in the economy. A rough cost of living index, based on goods in southern England, suggests that prices were more than 10% lower in 1779 than in 1777.[157] By a stroke of good fortune, cheap bread (together with a rise in money wages) seems to have increased the spending power of domestic consumers just at the time when the decline in overseas trade was at its most acute.

The final years of the war saw this situation inverted. The revival of British and Irish exports coincided with a sharp reduction in domestic spending power caused by the poor harvests of 1782 and 1783 ('remarkable bad weather . . . the corn not yet cut and in a

[154] PRONI, Downshire Papers, D/607/B/77.
[155] Sheila Lambert (ed.), *House of Commons Sessional Papers of the Eighteenth Century* (145 vols., Wilmington, Del., 1975), xxxvii. 84.
[156] *The Weather Journals of a Rutland Squire: Thomas Barker of Lyndon Hall*, ed. John Kington (Rutland Record Series, vol. ii, Oakham, 1988), 84.
[157] In north Staffordshire they were about 8% lower: see Botham and Hunt, 'Wages in Britain', 388 (table 2).

wretched condition').[158] Almost every part of the British Isles felt the pinch. The poor in the neighbourhood of Stourbridge, Worcestershire, were said to be living on 'Hips and Haws, which they gather from the Hedges'.[159] But the Highlands of Scotland suffered particularly badly. 'The harvest is so terrible and the crops so scarce . . . servants calling for bread and none to give them', Lord Fife's mother wrote in October 1782.[160] Ireland, too, experienced dreadful distress. Bread prices went up by more than 50% in Dublin (compared with 22% in London). Potato prices across Ireland have been calculated to have risen by a staggering 71% in 1782–3.[161] The Irish economy, already under severe pressure from wartime developments, went into a severe crisis from which it did not begin to emerge until the autumn of 1784.[162]

Government Spending

If there was a rise in domestic demand that helped to offset the decline in overseas trade in 1778–81, a vital ingredient still needs to be considered. We have seen that the state took money out of the economy through taxation and borrowing; but the other side of the coin, of course, was greatly increased public expenditure. This was particularly beneficial because the growth in spending took off when the French entered the war, just as overseas trade was going into recession (see Fig. 2.2). Rather than overheating an already-buoyant economy, increased military and naval expenditure was able to provide an important stimulus at a time of sluggishness.[163] British government spending on the armed forces rose from £3.8 million

---

[158] 'The Diary of Nicholas Brown', *Surtees Society Publications*, 118 (1910), 245.

[159] *Aris's Birmingham Gazette*, 16 Dec. 1782.

[160] Alistair and Henrietta Tayler (eds.), *Lord Fife and his Factor* (London, 1925), 145. T. C. Smout, 'Famine and Famine Relief in Scotland', in L. M. Cullen and T. C. Smout (eds.), *Comparative Aspects of Scottish and Irish Economic and Social History 1600–1900* (Edinburgh, n.d.), 26, refers to 'a regional mortality crisis' in the Highlands in 1782.

[161] Liam Kennedy and Martin W. Dowling, 'Prices and Wages in Ireland, 1700–1850', *Irish Economic and Social History*, 24 (1997), 101–2.

[162] Ray Refaussé, 'The Economic Crisis in Ireland in the Early 1780s', University of Dublin Ph.D. Diss., 1982; James Kelly, 'Scarcity and Poor Relief in Eighteenth-Century Ireland: the Subsistence Crisis of 1782–1784', *Irish Historical Studies*, 28 (1992–3), 38–62.

[163] If spending had dramatically increased in 1775—which it did not—it would have had a rather different impact, for in 1775 the British economy was in a relatively robust state, having recovered strongly from the trade depression of 1772–3. Continuing

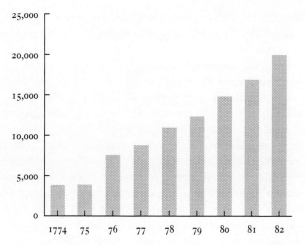

Fig. 2.2. Government expenditure on the armed forces, 1774–1782 (in £000s)
Source: Mitchell, British Historical Statistics, 579

in 1774 to over £20 million in 1782, with a surge coming in 1778 and 1779, when it reached just under £12.5 million. Some of this money, of course, was used abroad: the British Parliament authorized the expenditure of £19.3 million on the armed forces in North America during the conflict.[164] But much of even this money was spent in the British Isles rather than the rebel colonies. Indeed, the vast majority of the £108 million devoted to military and naval spending between 1775 and 1783 found its way back into British and Irish pockets, and helped to stimulate British and Irish industry and agriculture, either through government contracts or the innumerable more modest transactions of individual officers, soldiers, sailors, and militiamen with a multitude of different kinds of traders.

The armed forces, it must be said, were not always ideal customers. Rebecca Howell of Chatham had to wait eighteen months to receive the money due to her from a lieutenant who had embarked for North America;[165] while other creditors, such as John Mason, an

increases in war-related spending in 1782 and 1783, when exports were picking up strongly, might well have had an inflationary effect, though this would have been dampened, no doubt, by the fall in domestic consumption related to the sharp rise in food prices following poor harvests, especially in 1782 and 1783.

[164] Gwyn, 'Impact of British Military Spending', 77.
[165] WO 4/100, p. 491; WO 4/104, p. 19; WO 4/106, pp. 92, 93, 182, 349.

innkeeper of Newcastle-under-Lyme, were given very little assistance by the authorities in pursuing military debts.[166] Publicans, indeed, often had cause to complain of their ill-treatment, not least because they felt aggrieved at having to accommodate soldiers for only a modest recompense and turn away customers who might have paid more handsomely. The alehouse-keepers of Twyford in Hampshire resented the recruiting party of the Fourth Foot that they were obliged to put up, and pressed for their speedy removal.[167] The innkeepers of Whitehaven secured the services of an influential local landowner to press for relief from the large number of militiamen quartered on them;[168] while Penryn magistrates wrote to one of the town's MPs asking him to help the 'poor distressed Innkeepers, & Victuallers' who were having to cope with quartering the East Kent militia.[169]

But, despite problems such as these, considerable sums could be made. As the navy expanded, pressure on the royal docks meant that private yards took on more work. Buckler's Hard, the Duke of Montagu's shipyard in Hampshire, was one of the beneficiaries of the wartime shipbuilding programme. It launched eleven naval vessels between 1771 and 1774, but six in 1779 alone.[170] At the end of 1774 the navy envisaged spending £17,574 in merchant yards in the following year; by 1783 the estimates presented to the House of Commons were pointing to planned expenditure of £770,100. In all, Parliament agreed to spending of more than £2.6 million in private yards during the war, and navy bills might well have added significantly to this sum.[171]

The manufacturers of small metal goods, so badly hit by the shrinkage of overseas markets, won some consolation prizes in the form of orders to provide equipment for the expanded army and embodied militia. When, for example, hardware merchant Thomas Stiff of Covent Garden received an order for 700 pairs of copper clasps for the Staffordshire militia, the manufacturers of the clasps shared in his good fortune.[172] Boulton & Fothergill, a Birmingham

---

[166] WO 4/109, pp. 196, 202.

[167] Hampshire RO, Banbury Papers, 1 M44/66, Letter-book, 1775–7, fos. 18–19.

[168] WO 1/1009, p. 367.

[169] North Yorkshire RO, Chaytor Papers, Z2H 11/2/175.

[170] Beaulieu, Montagu Estate Papers, 'Ships built for Government at Bucklers Hard from Septr. 1743 to January 1791'.

[171] *Journals of the House of Commons*, xxxv. 56–7, 434–5, xxxvi. 38–9, 590, xxxvii. 34–5, 550–1, xxxviii. 88–9, 634–5, xxxix. 167–8.

[172] Staffordshire RO, Paget Papers, D 603/0/2/3, bill of 25 Oct. 1779.

company, likewise benefited when various militia and regular corps required buttons, breast-belt plates, muskets, and cartouche boxes.[173] For the great ironmasters even more of a boost was provided by the increased demand for artillery pieces. Anthony Bacon, an MP with a bewildering array of commercial and manufacturing interests, secured contracts to supply nearly 1,000 cannons to the ordnance board between 1775 and 1779; he appears to have made sufficient money from his dealings with the board and other government departments to be able to retire from business at the end of the war.[174] Samuel Walker's Rotherham ironworks were reported to have 1,000 employees in 1777,[175] and the firm doubled its capital between 1775 and 1782, thanks largely to profits from the manufacture of artillery pieces.[176]

While brewers might complain about falling domestic and overseas consumption, those who contracted to supply the armed forces could make good all or part of the losses on conventional trade. The special naval breweries established to service the fleet in peacetime were unable to cope with the demands of a vastly expanded navy, and contract breweries in London, Chatham, Portsmouth, and Plymouth provided the shortfall. In 1778 alone Whitbreads supplied the navy with 3,000 barrels of porter; Calverts, 3,300.[177] Indeed, with an official naval ration of a gallon of beer a day per man, and with over 100,000 sailors and marines serving at the end of the war, the overall demand for beer would probably have increased, even given problems with domestic demand and the disruption of overseas trade that reduced exports. Benjamin Wilson's brewery in Burton upon Trent sent about 1,095 barrels of ale to the Baltic in 1776–7, but only 558 in 1777–8 and 664 in 1779–80.[178] We can be reasonably confident that this decline was part of a general pattern. Yet official figures for beer on which duty was charged in England and Wales show a steady increase in production from 5.5 million barrels in 1775

---

[173] Birmingham City Archives, Matthew Boulton Papers, MBP 141, pp. 485, 529–30, 542–3, 546–7, 555, 556–7, 564, 568–9, 579, 582–3, 609–10, 627, 633, 635; MBP 142, pp. 460, 481, 493, 528, 550, 584, 686, 702.

[174] Sir Lewis Namier, 'Anthony Bacon MP, an Eighteenth-Century Merchant', in W. E. Minchinton (ed.), *Industrial South Wales 1750–1914* (London, 1969), 83–4.

[175] Oliver's Journal, BL, Egerton MS 2673, p. 400.

[176] A. H. John (ed.), *The Walker Family: Ironfounders and Lead Manufacturers, 1741–1893* (London, 1951), 11–19.   [177] Mathias, *Brewing Industry*, 199.

[178] C. C. Owen, *The Development of Industry in Burton upon Trent* (Chichester, 1978), 203 (app. 8).

to 6.4 million in 1782, followed by a fall to 5.7 million in 1783.[179] The most likely explanation for this wartime trajectory would seem to be increased consumption by the expanded armed forces.

Farmers and merchants also benefited from increased demand for certain types of provisions. Before the war, the British garrison in America had mainly been supplied from colonial sources. Once hostilities commenced, the greatly enlarged British army in America (and its German and American loyalist auxiliaries) had to rely heavily on provisions purchased in the British Isles and shipped 3,000 miles across the Atlantic.[180] There were also, of course, substantial regular and militia forces to be provisioned in the British Isles themselves, not forgetting the Royal Navy. The quantities involved were very substantial, given the enormously increased size of the armed forces and the generosity (by contemporary civilian standards) of the official army and navy rations. The weekly allowance for each of the 35,000 men 'to be victualled in North America' for 1779–80 included seven pounds of beef or two of pork, together with seven pounds of bread and variable quantities of butter, cheese, peas, and oatmeal.[181] Producers and sellers of provisions in Ireland, such as Joseph Jacob of Waterford, seem to have benefited particularly. In August 1779 Jacob was looking forward to 'a handsome Share' in naval contracts; by November he was reporting having 'already Salted near 5000 Barrs Beef & Pork'.[182] The embargo, which was not relaxed until 1779, was no doubt a strong countervailing force—in the middle of 1777 the merchants and traders of Cork complained that several thousand barrels of beef and pork remained on hand, over and above those supplied to the army, navy, and East India Company service.[183] But in the first years of the war, when government contractors were making substantial meat purchases in Ireland, the cost of beef rose, despite the embargo. In October 1776 'good prices' were given at Limerick 'for Beefe Hide & Tallow';[184] and the month before beef was fetching 21s. per

[179] Mathias, *Brewing Industry*, 543.

[180] R. A. Bowler, *Logistics and the Failure of the British Army in North America* (Princeton, 1975), chs. 3 and 4; Norman Baker, *Government and Contractors* (London, 1970), ch. 3.

[181] Library of Congress, Colebrooke, Nesbitt, Colebrooke and Franks Papers, 'Corke Contract 1779'.   [182] PRONI, Greer Papers, D 1044/552, 572.

[183] HMC, *Lothian MSS*, 316–17.

[184] Limerick City Archives, Vere Hunt Papers, Thomas Browne to Hunt, 22 Oct. 1776 (microfilm in NLI).

hundredweight in Cork, 'never so high by 2s. 6d.', while pork, which had never been more than 18s. 6d., cost 30s. These inflated prices, Arthur Young stated authoritatively, were 'owing to the army demand'.[185]

If the Irish provision trade provided vast quantities of foodstuffs for the army in America, and for much of the navy as well, British producers and retailers were not excluded. Ireland was principally important for the supply of 'wet provisions', that is meat and dairy produce. The bread, oats, peas, and other 'dry provisions' sent across the Atlantic mainly came from British sources. East Anglia, in particular, was an important area for this branch of the provision trade. Great Yarmouth merchants purchased some of their cereals from abroad, but the bulk were taken from the port's own agricultural hinterland.[186] The demands of the forces at home were met by a wide range of suppliers. When military camps were established across southern England from 1778, a host of local merchants and farmers put in tenders to supply such items as bread, oats, hay, straw, and wood.[187] And if the army and militia were important customers, the navy was no less so. Its requirement for long-lasting foodstuffs was immense, and could only be met by dispersing considerable sums of money amongst an array of producers. Elizabeth Buck, a London biscuit-maker, was paid £1,000 between 29 Decemeber 1775 and 18 March 1776 alone;[188] while in 1782 Thomas Bell received nearly £9,000 for butter and cheese.[189]

Government contracts even seem to have helped certain sectors of the textile industry to overcome the difficulties created by the loss of overseas markets. Thomas Langton, a Lancashire flax merchant, was able to secure orders to supply the navy with sail cloth; his 1780 contract was worth £2,400.[190] And if the armed forces needed to be fed, they also needed to be clothed. There was no uniform for naval ratings at this time, but in 1756 the navy had established an office for the bulk purchase of seamen's apparel, and all the army's soldiers and the militia were issued with regulation clothing. More sailors,

---

[185] Young, *Tour of Ireland*, pt. i, p. 276. See also Raymond D. Crotty, *Irish Agricultural Production: Its Value and Structure* (Cork, 1966), 21 (table 4); Thomas M. Truxes, *Irish-American Trade, 1660–1783* (Cambridge, 1988), 238–9.

[186] Baker, *Government and Contractors*, 64–84.

[187] e.g. T 1/543, fos. 12, 64; T 1/545, fos. 9, 389, 391, 430; T 1/547, fo. 210.

[188] ADM 112/162.   [189] ADM 112/168.

[190] *The Letters of Thomas Langton*, ed. Joan Wilkinson (Chetham Society, Manchester, 1994), 21.

soldiers, and militiamen meant more orders. In the six years 1769–74 Richard Lowe, a London clothing contractor, earned an average of £8,425 per year from supplying uniforms to the marines; in the first six years of the American war this annual average went up to £22,068. In 1782 he received £35,125. 10s.[191] James Wadham of Southwark earned some £79,000 in 1780–2 for the 612,914 items of naval clothing that he delivered to government storehouses.[192] Even smaller-scale transactions could be profitable. John Hetherington, another London tradesman, was paid £1,237. 6s. 9d. in May 1781 for supplying clothing to the Twenty-second Light Dragoons, one of the newly raised regiments.[193] And such purchases, of course, were no less welcome to the textile manufacturers who provided the likes of Lowe, Wadham, and Hetherington with their raw materials. On the eve of the war, Henry Hindley of Mere, Wiltshire, was hoping that army orders would make up for the loss of the market in the rebel colonies ('will not the red cloths sell for clothing the Army going to America[?]').[194] Likewise, when in 1776 a Leeds clothing house was reported by the local press to have received orders from government for 60,000 yards of coarse broadcloth 'to be dyed black, for Spatterdashes, for the Use of the Army in America', we can speculate that hopes were high that such orders would provide some recompense for the closure of most of the American market.[195] Nor do these hopes seem to have been unrealistic. It seems likely that military and naval orders help to explain why even in 1779, a year of dreadful depression in overseas trade, output of woollen textiles in West Yorkshire was higher than in 1770.[196]

For the Irish linen industry, demand for army clothing, and particularly for soldiers' shirts, certainly appears to have offered some compensation for the problems encountered in overseas trade.[197] In Scotland, the clothing of the Highland corps in tartans

---

[191] D. J. Smith, 'Army Clothing Contractors and the Textile Industries in the 18th Century', *Textile History*, 14 (1983), 159 (table 4).

[192] Beverly Lemire, *Dress, Culture and Commerce: The English Clothing Trade before the Factory, 1660–1800* (London, 1997), 21–2.

[193] East Sussex RO, Sheffield Papers, A 2714/265.

[194] Julia De L. Mann (ed.), *Documents Illustrating the Wiltshire Textile Trades in the Eighteenth Century* (Wiltshire Archaeological and Natural History Society, Records Branch, vol. xix, Devizes, 1964), 153. [195] *York Courant*, 24 Sept. 1776.

[196] H. Heaton, *Yorkshire Woollen and Worsted Industries from the Earliest Times up to the Industrial Revolution* (2nd edn., Oxford, 1965), 278.

[197] Truxes, *Irish-American Trade*, 242.

also provided new opportunities at a difficult time. John Stevenson of Stirling and Charles Rattray of Bannockburn contracted with government in 1775 to supply plaids and hose to the Royal Highland Emigrants, an American loyalist regiment later taken on to the British establishment.[198] The expansion of the army had an obviously beneficial impact on William Wilson and Son, based, like Rattray, in Bannockburn. Wilsons produced a variety of woollen textiles—carpets and tartans in particular. The records of the company go back to 1765, though by repute the family started the business in 1724. But it was the raising of large numbers of troops in the Scottish Highlands during the American war that was to be the making of Wilsons. From 1778 the company sold vast quantities of plaid, kilts, and hose to merchants supplying the newly raised Highland regiments. A surviving company day-book reveals the importance of this wartime trade. Sales of military clothing were worth £94 in December 1778; £119 in February 1779 and £109 in May; £182 in February 1780, £100 in March, £553 in May, and £120 in June.[199] These sums appear to have exceeded any received for non-military orders either before or during the war. Indeed, the company was so busy catering for the requirements of the army that it was obliged to turn away other customers: 'since we left your place', Alexander Fraser, a merchant of Forres was told on 9 November 1778, 'we have Engaged in the Cloathing for some of the Highland regts. which puts it out of our power to get your order ansrd. at this time'.[200] Wilsons made sufficient money to branch out and establish a trading sideline with the West Indies in 1780, importing cotton, logwood, and mahogany in exchange for their textiles. Towards the end of the war, Wilsons diversified further by buying from another supplier Highland bonnets to sell to the army, together with the company's own range of products.[201] The firm was well prepared when the next conflict—with revolutionary and Napoleonic France—saw an even greater mobilization of Scottish manpower; the foundations of a highly profitable business had been securely laid.[202]

---

[198] Alastair J. Durie (ed.), *The British Linen Company 1745–1775* (Scottish History Society, 5th ser. vol. ix, Edinburgh, 1996), 223–4.

[199] NLS, William Wilson Papers, MS 9672, fos. 138, 142, 172, 174, 178–9, 180.

[200] Ibid., MS 9670, fo. 12.   [201] Ibid., fo. 43.

[202] See ibid., MSS 9667–9699.

If we return to the macroeconomic overview, a conclusion that could be drawn from this survey is that the American war had much less of an impact on the vitality of the economy than might be expected. Despite the buffeting, there appears to have been no lasting harm. Exports of Irish linen picked up dramatically once the conflict ended, resuming their steady upward trajectory.[203] In 1792 the value of all British imports was 26% higher than in 1772, and of exports 40% higher. During the war itself, the potentially catastrophic collapse of exports and re-exports was to a considerable extent offset by a rise in domestic demand which owed much to the stimulation provided by the great increase in public expenditure associated with the equipping, feeding, and clothing of the substantially augmented armed forces. Industrial output seems to have fallen, but only slightly. Yet if disaster was averted, we should recognize that the war caused enormous turmoil and compelled often considerable adjustments and adaptations. In many years of the conflict, national product per head probably marked time or even declined rather than increased. Only with the close of the war was sustained growth resumed.

[203] Gill, *Rise of the Irish Linen Industry*, 339.

3

The War, Society, and Culture

SURVIVING DIARIES AND journals can suggest that the American war had a minimal impact on the texture and structures of everyday life in the British Isles, or even that it made no difference at all. Continuity is often the dominant impression. Mary Shackleton, a young Irish Quaker, left a detailed diary, which is dominated by routine, trivia, reflections, and meetings. Were it not for occasional references to troop movements and the volunteers we could easily overlook the fact that she penned many of her entries during the American conflict.[1] Judging by his diary, Jonathan Adams, a Baptist minister living in Salisbury, regarded the armed struggle with an almost complete lack of interest. It interrupted his crudely written lists of births, marriages, and deaths but once, when, on learning of Admiral Rodney's victory at the battle of the Saints, 'we illuminated [our windows] at night'.[2] The impression of remoteness from the conflict is similarly conveyed by the diary of William Dunne, a Worcestershire schoolmaster. Wartime fast days are mentioned, and the presence of the Franco-Spanish fleet in the Channel off Plymouth merits a few words in August 1779, but much more excitement seems to have been generated by the defeat of a canal project that would have profoundly affected Dunne's village, which welcomed the news with 'great Ringing and Illumination'. For the most part, his diary is focused on local events and the weather.[3]

Sources such as these serve as a useful reminder of the capacity of many people to concentrate on their routine even when events are occurring that engross the attention of decision-makers, the political

[1] NLI, MSS 9300–8, Diaries of Mary Shackleton, 1775–1782. For an analysis of her diaries see Kevin O'Neill, '"Almost a Gentlewoman": Gender and Adolescence in the Diary of Mary Shackleton', in Mary O'Dowd and Sabine Wichert (eds.), *Chattel, Servant or Citizen: Women's Status in Church, State and Society* (Historical Studies, vol. xix, Belfast, 1995), 91–102.
[2] Wiltshire RO, 547/1, Diary of Jonathan Adams, 27 May 1782.
[3] Bodleian Library, MS Don. c. 76, fos. 101, 117, 128, 142.

cognoscenti, and later historians. In many respects, life simply goes on—has to go on—even in momentous times. But this obvious truth should not be allowed to obscure the very different picture that emerges from other sources, and even from a careful reading of at least some of those sources that appear at first to point to continuity. For Mary Shackleton to display a distinctly un-Quaker-like interest in artillery pieces on the move to Clonmel camp, or to comment on seeing the volunteers exercise, surely suggests that the war *was* impinging on her life; just as it was intruding on the well-regulated affairs of Jonathan Adams and even William Dunne's absorption in local matters. The war, in short, made its mark. In some instances, as we shall see, this was merely ephemeral: the conflict, like a boat on a quietly flowing river, disturbed the surface of the water for just a few moments before the normal unhurried current was restored. But in certain areas change was more profound and long-lasting.

The War and Women

The impact of the American conflict on women in the rebel colonies has attracted the interest of historians,[4] but little has been written on the ways in which it affected their British and Irish counterparts.[5] There are some grounds for thinking that the war might have enhanced the status of women. Recent scholarship has stressed the vital role many eighteenth-century women played as wage earners in poor families.[6] It seems probable that more women were employed, or employed more extensively and in different capacities, as men left the labour market for military or naval service.[7] While there is no evidence of women substituting for men in all-male preserves like the merchant marine, it seems that in some places such substitution

---

[4] e.g. Mary Beth Norton, *Liberty's Daughters* (Boston, 1980); Linda K. Kerber, *Women of the Republic* (Chapel Hill, NC, 1980); Joy Day Buel and Richard Buel Jnr., *The Way of Duty: A Woman and Her Family in Revolutionary America* (New York, 1984).

[5] There are, however, wider considerations of British women and war in the 18th cent., notably Linda Colley, *Britons: Forging the Nation 1707–1837* (New Haven, 1992), ch. 6.

[6] See e.g. R. W. Malcolmson, *Life and Labour in England 1700–1780* (London, 1981); Maxine Berg, *The Age of Manufactures* (London, 1985), 100, 121, 132, 135, 137–8; Bridget Hill, *Women, Work and Sexual Politics in Eighteenth-Century England* (Oxford, 1989); Duncan Bythell, 'Women in the Workforce', in Patrick O'Brien and Ronald Quinault (eds.), *The Industrial Revolution and British Society* (Cambridge, 1993), 31–53.

[7] See above, Ch. 2.

took place amongst agricultural workers. On Steventon Farm in Berkshire, female labour was often used in the spring, but in 1780 four women were paid for reaping, an altogether more strenuous task, and one which in the immediately preceding years had apparently been carried out exclusively by men.[8] If this were more than an isolated case, then it would seem that the American war, like the struggle against revolutionary and Napoleonic France that followed it, reversed, if only temporarily, the trend for women to be squeezed out of harvest work, a trend associated with the introduction of heavier scythes.[9] It seems likely that such new responsibilities, even if acquired for just a few years, changed relations within families; but, in the absence of direct testimony from those involved, this must, of course, remain speculation.

We can be more certain about women of a higher social standing. There are some interesting indications of a new assertiveness. Just as in previous periods of crisis, the deep political divisions engendered by the conflict encouraged some aristocratic females to reflect on matters that they had hitherto considered beyond their competence. The letters of Lady Sarah Bunbury are liberally sprinkled with references to the war. She began by expressing her '*incapability* in polliticks', and apparent desire to 'talk of things more suited to me', but before long such remarks were dropped and she commented freely on her opposition to 'so *vile* a war'. 'I grow a greater rebel every day upon principle', she wrote in December 1777; and in the following August proclaimed herself 'an American in my heart as to the *cause*'. By April 1779 she was reading with evident approval the new oppositionist weekly paper the *Englishman*.[10] Lady Wallingford, who adopted a rather different attitude, told her nephew in February 1778 that she was 'no politician', yet went on to wish 'for the good of the nation that we would not be at war within our Selves but all unite for the general good'.[11] This was hardly an original sentiment, and suggests that she believed less

---

[8] Reading University Library, BER. 16/1/1.

[9] K. D. M. Snell, *Annals of the Labouring Poor: Social Change and Agrarian England 1660–1900* (Cambridge, 1985), 21–2, 40, 45, 49–50; R. A. Houston, 'Women in the Economy and Society of Scotland, 1500–1800', in id. and I. D. Whyte (eds.), *Scottish Society 1500–1800* (Cambridge, 1989), 121.

[10] *Life and Letters of Lady Sarah Lennox*, ed. Countess of Ilchester and Lord Stavordale (2 vols., London, 1901), i. 234, 247, 252, 263, 275, 297.

[11] Hampshire RO, Banbury Papers, 1M 44/7/25(b).

politics was required not more; but her observation was itself a sign that she was becoming politicized.

Politicization, moreover, could go beyond merely commenting on current events. Women sometimes contributed to the public subscriptions designed to cover the costs of raising troops or sailors: Mary Ann Leslie, for instance, gave £200 towards the recruiting of the Eighty-second Foot, of which her father was the newly appointed colonel.[12] At Bath, leading female inhabitants went further, and established their own subscription to augment the bounty money offered to volunteers entering a regiment of light dragoons 'about to be raised in that city and neighbourhood'. That women were organizing the subscription was novel enough to attract the curiosity of the London press, but at the same time their endeavours brought forth the acknowledgement that women could be as patriotic as men.[13] Another example of the female desire to lower the barriers segregating the sexes was cross-dressing, the wearing by women of clothes that aped masculine styles. This started before the war, but became particularly fashionable during its course. Lady Louisa Lennox, who had accompanied her soldier husband to Minorca several years earlier, had worn a riding dress based on the uniform of his regiment during the early 1770s.[14] It was only when she returned to Britain, however, that her outlandish attire attracted public attention. While her husband's troops were based at Romsey in the spring of 1776, she caused quite a stir. According to a witness, Lady Louisa was 'the principal feature of the Show, at the Evening Parades'.[15] She set the trend that others followed. Georgiana, Duchess of Devonshire, was with her husband at Warley camp in 1778, when the Duke was serving with the Derbyshire militia. Like Lady Louisa before her, the Duchess wore a kind of uniform, and she organized the wives of other officers, similarly dressed, into their own pseudo-military unit.[16]

[12] *Glasgow Mercury*, 29 Jan. 1778.

[13] *Morning Post, and Daily Advertiser*, 6 Aug. 1779. For more on this subscription see *Bath Chronicle*, 12 and 19 Aug. 1779.

[14] See the painting reproduced in David Chandler and Ian Beckett (eds.), *The Oxford Illustrated History of the British Army* (Oxford, 1994), facing p. 111.

[15] Huntington Library, MS HM 54457, vol. 6, Diary of John Marsh, 6 May 1776 (microfilm in West Sussex RO).

[16] Amanda Foreman, 'A Politician's Politician: Georgiana, Duchess of Devonshire and the Whig Party', in Hannah Barker and Elaine Chalus (eds.), *Gender in Eighteenth-Century England* (London, 1997), 182.

Nor was this style of clothing confined to camps and garrisons. The next year, Elizabeth Montagu, the author and artistic patron, commented that many young women were 'striding about the walks at Tunbridge with their arms akimbo dressed in martial uniform'.[17] Perhaps it was no coincidence that the war years saw the publication of a number of literary works that gave prominence to the female perspective, notably William Alexander's *History of Women*, which appeared in two volumes in 1779, and that during the conflict there was a great growth in women's involvement in the debating societies that proliferated in the capital.[18]

But the importance of these developments can easily be exaggerated. They need to be set against the ways in which the war—like earlier and later conflicts—bolstered traditional attitudes. With invasion a real possibility, it was all too easy for women to be cast as weak and in need of male protection from libidinous enemy troops. Indeed, recruiters seem to have sought to appeal to male pride by emphasizing female vulnerability. A song composed to stimulate enlistment in the Twenty-second Light Dragoons, raised in 1779 by John Baker Holroyd, declares[19]

> No Spaniard nor Frenchman our women need fear,
> While Holroyd's Dragoons in their cause will appear.

Wartime crises, moreover, added another dimension to this reassertion of gender distinctions by provoking considerable reflection on the way in which the nation had lost its manly virtues and grown soft. 'Effeminacy' was widely identified as the root cause of the problem, and the recovery of masculinity as the obvious solution. So, William Cowper's poem 'Table Talk', published in 1782, pronounces that 'effeminacy' tends naturally to 'Enervate and enfeeble' a nation, inviting the contempt of its enemies; only with repentance would power be renewed.[20] Similarly, Henry Wansey, a Wiltshire clothier, hoping for a national revival in the autumn of 1779, wrote that 'almost all the Vices of the present Age spring from the same

---

[17] HMC, *Bath MSS* (4 vols., London, 1904–68), i. 345–6.
[18] Donna T. Andrew, 'Popular Culture and Public Debate: London 1780', *Historical Journal*, 39 (1996), 410, 412–14.
[19] East Sussex RO, Sheffield Papers, A2714/265, 'Song in Honour of the 22d Light Dragoons'.
[20] *The Poems of William Cowper*, ed. John D. Baird and Charles Ryskamp (3 vols., Oxford, 1980–95), i. 252.

pernicious Source. Effeminacy of Manners'.[21] The same theme was addressed in more jocular form in Richard Brinsley Sheridan's musical comedy *The Camp*, first performed in 1778. One of the characters, Sir Harry Bouquet, is derided by the females of his social circle for 'not being in the Militia' and for being 'so finical' that 'he ran a risk of being mistaken for another Female Chevalier'—an allusion to a notorious contemporary male cross-dresser.[22] In this atmosphere of assertive gender distinction, women wearing masculine-style clothing became increasingly suspect. Initially, as Dror Wahrman has pointed out, female cross-dressing was regarded with some interest and even amused indulgence. But as the war failed to produce British victory, such female encroachments into male spheres came to be seen as one of the 'unnatural' symptoms of all the ills befalling Britain.[23] Contemporary cartoons mercilessly pilloried the new style of female clothing, and the role reversal it seemed to involve. 'An Officer of the Light Infantry driven by his Lady to Cox-Heath' depicts a woman in military-style clothing, standing up as she drives a chaise: her husband is sitting asleep by her side.[24] Women themselves could be as critical as men. Mrs Montagu complained that 'many of our modern dames want the modesty of women'. She disapproved the vogue for military-style female clothing, and hoped 'whenever we are so happy as to have a peace, the Ladies' regiment will be reformed, as is the phrase. In quiet times gentle Miss Molly appears more amiable than blustering Captain Moll'.[25]

Nor was the mobilization of a significant portion of the available manpower necessarily to the advantage of women. In many areas of the British Isles, the presence of large numbers of armed men posed a considerable threat. A servant maid in Salisbury, to give just one

[21] Wiltshire RO, Wansey Papers, 314/4/2, Wansey to Richard Laurence, 1 Oct. 1779.

[22] *The Dramatic Works of Richard Brinsley Sheridan*, ed. Cecil Price (2 vols., Oxford, 1973), ii. 744.

[23] Dror Wahrman, '*Percy*'s Prologue: From Gender Play to Gender Panic in Eighteenth-Century England', *Past & Present*, 159 (1998), 113–60. Wahrman goes so far as to suggest that the shift from a positive view of women who attempted to cross gender boundaries to a distinctly negative one, is attributable to the 'major historical quake' that was the American war.

[24] Printed in Colley, *Britons*, 243, where it is dated 'c.1770'. Internal evidence suggests that it was drawn during the American war, sometime between 1778 and 1783. See also BM 5600 and 5601, 'The Three Graces of Cox-heath' and 'The Coxheath race for £100, No Crossing nor Jostling, Won by Miss Tittup agt Tumbling Jenny', both dated 1779.

[25] HMC, *Bath MSS*, i. 346.

example, was sexually assaulted by a dragoon from the nearby encampment; when the civil authorities arrested the trooper, several of his regimental colleagues rescued him from gaol.[26] Such things had happened before the war, of course; but with more men detached from the restraints of their own home communities, and deposited in the largely masculine environment of the armed forces, the danger must surely have increased. And even women who were not themselves attacked could be put into frightening situations as a result of the more legitimate military activity going on around them. Dorothea Herbert, the daughter of an Anglican clergyman at Carrick-on-Suir, County Tipperary, could still remember many years later the upset caused by an attempt by a party of the Twelfth Dragoons to impress the family's horses and carts when a French landing was expected.[27]

For the women whose menfolk were away serving in the armed forces, there were also problems of a rather different nature. Separation from loved ones could cause considerable dismay. Captain William Congreve, serving with the Royal Artillery in North America, was told how much his wife was 'affected by yr. Leaving her'.[28] Lady Louisa Conolly wrote that General Howe's wife was 'in such a miserable state of anxiety that I tremble for her continually'.[29] For Martha Hudd, the wife of a private in the marines, the consequences were more dramatic. In November 1775 she was apprehended in Westbury, Wiltshire, categorized as a rogue and vagabond, and subsequently removed to her husband's native parish of Bradford-on-Avon.[30] Separation, to be sure, was not inevitable in all cases. We have seen that aristocratic women like the Duchess of Devonshire and Lady Louisa Lennox accompanied their husbands on service. Women of more lowly status did the same. Indeed, the number of women wishing to follow their menfolk abroad caused some difficulties for the military authorities: in March 1776 Lord Barrington admonished the colonel of the Thirty-first Foot for allowing his regiment to embark across the Atlantic with forty-five

---

[26] WO 1/1006, pp. 521–4; WO 4/105, pp. 452–3.
[27] *Retrospections of Dorothea Herbert* (2 vols., London, 1929–30), i. 88.
[28] Staffordshire RO, Congreve Papers, D 1057/M/F/26.
[29] *Correspondence of Emily, Duchess of Leinster*, ed. Brian Fitzgerald (3 vols., Dublin, 1949–57), iii. 226.
[30] Phyllis Hembry (ed.), *Calendar of Bradford-on-Avon Settlement Examinations and Removal Orders 1725–1798* (Wiltshire Record Society, vol. xlvi, Trowbridge, 1990), 43.

women more than the regulation quota of sixty, and forty-seven children too. 'The great number of Soldiers Wives & Children already in America', Barrington wrote, 'are very inconvenient to the regiments there'.[31] Women followed their husbands around Britain as well; women such as the thirty-four wives of the Staffordshire militia identified in July 1778 as 'Willing to Assist the Taylors';[32] and Mary Raynes, Mary Parker, Mary Butcher, and Phebe Valethart, who were encamped with their menfolk on Warley Common in the summer of 1778.[33] But even women who followed their husbands might be parted from them. Martha Spooner, the wife of a trooper in the Tenth Dragoons, went with her husband as he moved with his regiment from quarter to quarter around the country, only to be taken up by the authorities in Northampton when she was found 'Wandering' in the town with her two children. The family, minus the father, was promptly packed off to Trooper Spooner's original parish of settlement, Northchapel in Sussex.[34]

And, of course, separation could be permanent. Many men did not return—they died in action, or more often of disease, or fled from the service and started a new life elsewhere, or simply failed to come home when discharged at the end of the war. Indeed, in some instances enlistment seems to have been motivated, in part at least, by a desire to escape from family entanglements or an unhappy marriage. In most cases, nothing underlined the subordinate and dependent status of women more than the loss of a male partner. For the vast majority of women, bereavement or permanent separation meant acute hardship. The widows or deserted wives of common soldiers or sailors frequently ended up in the poorhouse,[35] and even the partners of officers could find themselves in difficulties. Elizabeth Fulton, for instance, who was the mistress of Captain John Ridley of the Twenty-eighth Foot for nine years, was described as 'left with two helpless Infants, without a possibility of supporting them' when Ridley died at New York in December 1776.[36]

Government support for the widows of officers, and the subsidies

---

[31] WO 4/96, p. 364.
[32] Staffordshire RO, Paget Papers, D 603/O/2/4.
[33] Essex RO, St Thomas of Canterbury, Brentwood, Parish Records, D/P 362/1/2.
[34] West Sussex RO, Northchapel Parish Records, 142/32/4/1.
[35] See D. A. Kent, '"Gone for a Soldier": Family Breakdown and the Demography of Desertion in a London Parish, 1750–1791', *Local Population Studies*, 45 (1990), 27–42.
[36] Northumberland RO, Ridley of Blagdon MSS, ZR1 30/4a.

paid by parishes and counties to the wives and children of militia-men on service,[37] while no doubt welcome, furthered the image of helpless womanhood. It was as if the central and local agencies of the state were surrogate husbands and fathers. Such assistance, more-over, provided the opportunity for the authorities to distinguish between 'worthy' and 'unworthy' women, and to distribute largesse accordingly. Thus the respectable and dutifully suppliant Elizabeth Hall, the penniless widow of an officer in the Westmorland militia, could reasonably expect some relief when she applied to the secre-tary at war.[38] By contrast, women who deviated from the accepted norm, while often no less desperate, received no such favours. Ann Griswell and Ann Melow, charged in 1780 by an officer of the East Yorkshire militia 'with being common prostitutes, wandering abroad, infecting the said regt.', could expect nothing but punish-ment at a time when, with large bodies of soldiers in camp or on the march, prostitution was seen as particularly dangerous.[39] In this sense, the war merely further entrenched the deep-seated male view of women as saints or harlots.

Social Mobility, Social Status, and Social Conflict

There is movement up and down the social ladder at all times, but twentieth-century experience has emphasized the extent to which war accelerates the process. There is every reason to believe that the American conflict had the same effect, albeit on a smaller scale. We have seen that the war led to a major credit crisis, increased the rate of bankruptcy, and caused unemployment in certain trades. We have seen, too, that it provided opportunities for gain, particularly to those who supplied goods and services to the expanded armed forces. The loss or acquisition of money does not, of course, neces-sarily alter social circumstances; but there can be little doubt that the American war was the cause of such a change for a far from negli-gible number of George III's British and Irish subjects. Perhaps the most conspicuous victims in this regard so far as the historian is concerned are the bankrupts whose plight was exposed to public

[37] See above, Ch. 1.
[38] BL, Liverpool Papers, Add. MS 38343, fo. 290.
[39] Bedfordshire County Records, *Notes and Extracts from the . . . Quarter Sessions Rolls* (Bedford, n.d.), 50.

view in listings in newspapers and periodicals; unfortunates such as John Harris, a London 'money-scrivener'; John Wilson and Jonathan Lockwood, brandy merchants of Gosport; William Kiss, a Birmingham button-maker; and Thomas Howard, a Lancashire cotton-manufacturer.[40] There were nearly twice as many bankruptcies in England in 1778 as in 1775.[41] To be sure, some of these people would probably have failed without a war; but we can be confident that a good number were hit by the contraction and disruption of overseas trade attributable to the conflict, and that most of them were detrimentally affected by the liquidity crisis which was caused by wartime government borrowing. Among others who sank down the social scale were the widows or deserted wives of servicemen, mentioned earlier, who often had no choice but to rely on poor relief.

But if many contemporaries were aware of increasing poverty—or at least of rising poor rates—and were concerned by the number of bankruptcies, upward social mobility seems to have been more of a preoccupation, especially in elite circles. Unease or even hostility to the arrival of 'new men' owed much to assumptions dating back to the long wars of 1689–1713, when the creation of a new system of public credit and wartime taxation was seen as the cause of redistribution of wealth, power, and status from land to money.[42] In 1773 Lord Fife, echoing the language of sixty or seventy years before, could still write of 'Stock jobers, Jews and Contractors' as the only beneficiaries of war, and the landed classes as those who were 'out of pocket'.[43] But criticism of nouveaux riches tended to be much more focused by the time of the American war, not least because the national debt was no longer an innovation but an established institution which attracted the savings of numerous country gentlemen. The targets were now particular types of 'new men'. Stockholders were generally immune from attack, for the reason just mentioned. East Anglian grain farmers who had done well out of supplying the armed forces were also unlikely to provoke the ire of landed MPs. Nor were the relatively modest gains of businessmen providing uniforms and suchlike a matter of great concern; and windfalls from privateering caused no more than the occasional

---

[40] *Gentleman's Magazine*, 48 (1778), 95, 336; 49 (1779), 272; 50 (1780), 448.
[41] Julian Hoppit, *Risk and Failure in English Business* (Cambridge, 1987), 183.
[42] Geoffrey Holmes, *British Politics in the Age of Anne* (rev. edn., London, 1987), ch. 5.
[43] Alistair and Henrietta Taylor (eds.), *Lord Fife and his Factor* (London, 1925), 78.

expression of patrician disdain.[44] What excited the anger of the landed elite were the allegedly bloated profits of the leading government contractors and the dubious practices of the army's quartermasters, commissaries, barrack-masters, and other ancillary staff, who were believed to be swallowing up much of the public money spent in America. On this narrow front, the prejudices prevalent in Queen Anne's day lived on. Landed MPs still tended to assume that contractors came from a lower social strata and had made their money—and acquired their power—illegitimately, while the wealth and influence of the gentry and aristocracy was taken to be 'natural'.[45] Anthony Bacon, one of the targets of this kind of snobbery, was so hurt that he 'could not conceive why contractors should be treated in so unbecoming, nay, contemptuous a manner— as if they were monsters, and not fit for human society'.[46] The staff of the army's service departments were likewise subjected to considerable upper-class scorn. Earl Percy, the heir to the dukedom of Northumberland, resigned his command in America partly because he believed that General Howe preferred the word of a commissary to his own; to be trusted less than a commissary was more than the aristocratic Percy could bear.[47]

In reality, most of the major beneficiaries of government contracts between 1775 and 1783 were already well-established merchants or industrialists, who had long since acquired their own landed estates and entered elite society. Bacon might have appeared a suitable candidate for the animus of landed MPs; an army provision contractor and supplier of cannons to the ordnance, he was able to retire on his profits in 1782. But even Bacon was not quite the 'new man' that he seemed. He had been a contractor since the Seven Years War; he held vast acres of land in South Wales; and he had been MP for Aylesbury since 1764. Thomas Harley, who profited enormously during the war from government contracts to supply clothing and remit money to the army in North America, was still more remote from the stereotypical parvenu. His father was the third Earl of

---

[44] See the comments of the Earl of Camden, above, p. 65.
[45] Burke, writing in Apr. 1780, argued that country gentlemen MPs 'have a natural antipathy to inordinate gain in any Body and they are more disposed to the censure of abuses among Trading people than of those among any other description of Men'. *The Correspondence of Edmund Burke*, ed. Thomas W. Copeland et al. (10 vols., Cambridge, 1958–78), iv. 219.   [46] *PH* xix. 1091.
[47] Alnwick Castle, Percy Papers, vol. xlix, pt. A, pp. 13, 18, 24–5, 30, pt. B, pp. 12–13.

Oxford and his family was already very influential in Herefordshire, where Harley bought an estate and built a mansion.[48] In these and other similar instances, contracts benefited established and well-connected businessmen, rather than propelled new faces into the limelight. Much the same point, *mutatis mutandis*, could be made about some of those in the army service departments who made a lot of money. One of the biggest beneficiaries was Sir William Erskine, a Scottish baronet, who as quartermaster-general from 1776 to 1779, was able to send home at least £13,000 in 1777 alone.[49] Similarly, Thomas Aston Coffin, a deputy quartermaster, was from a well-established Massachusetts mercantile dynasty and used his profits to recoup losses made by his family as a result of their loyalty.[50]

All the same, the American war did facilitate the social progress of some of those in receipt of government money. Three contractors became baronets during the conflict, though one of them had been in line for this elevation since 1765. Another, Laurence Cox, received his title a few years later, but his service to government during the war certainly contributed to his advancement.[51] And by no means all the beneficiaries in the army's service departments were already well placed. Archibald Robertson, an engineer who served as a deputy quartermaster, had risen very slowly through the officer ranks before the American conflict, languishing as a lieutenant for twelve years from the end of the Seven Years War, which suggests that he had neither money nor connections to help him on his way. Yet when he retired in 1783 he was able to spend £35,000 on a 20,000-acre estate in Ayreshire. The similarly obscure William Shirreff, another deputy quartermaster, seems to have done just as well, purchasing an estate at Old Alresford, Hampshire, at the close of the war; while his colleague Henry Bruen became a landowner in County Carlow.[52]

[48] Sir Lewis Namier and John Brooke, *The History of Parliament: The House of Commons 1754–1790* (3 vols., London, 1964), ii. 586–7.

[49] NLS, Halkett Papers, MS 6410, fos. 26, 31, 37, 77.

[50] Massachusetts Historical Society, Coffin Family Papers, vol i, Coffin to his mother, 5 Nov. 1777; 8 Jan., 8 Feb., 9 Nov. 1778; 14 Nov., 17 Dec. 1779; 23 Oct. 1781. We might also note that those nobles and landed gentlemen who raised regiments and became their colonels were often able to make considerable sums of money. For the entrepreneurial side of the raising of Highland regiments see Andrew Mackillop, *'More Fruitful than the Soil': Army, Empire and the Scottish Highlands 1715–1815* (East Linton, 1999).

[51] Norman Baker, *Government and Contractors* (London, 1971), 237.

[52] R. A. Bowler, *Logistics and the Failure of the British Army in North America* (Princeton, 1975), 196.

Seen from an instrumental rather than a censorial perspective, what was happening in the ancillary departments was perhaps only an extreme version of what was happening in the armed forces as a whole. The war speeded up promotion in the officer ranks, as resignations, retirements, casualties, and the expansion of both the army and the navy introduced much greater fluidity into the system.[53] Frederick Mackenzie, a poorly connected Irishman who was a 37-year-old lieutenant in the Royal Welch Fusiliers when the conflict began—his first commission was dated 1756—had managed to climb to be the regiment's major by August 1780.[54] James Robertson, already a lieutenant-colonel in America in 1775, rose still more spectacularly. He had progressed during the previous conflict but stagnated in the peace that followed. Once the American war broke out, he moved forward rapidly. By its end he was a lieutenant-general. No doubt as a result of the social prestige that attached itself to high military rank, he was able to marry his daughter to the son of a Scottish baronet; and after the war he found himself exerting an influence in the narrowly exclusive world of Scottish electoral politics—no mean achievement for a poor boy from Newbiggin, Fife, who was said to have started his army career as a common soldier.[55]

Robertson obtained his first commission during the War of Austrian Succession, when the growth of the army facilitated the entry into the officer ranks of men from non-elite backgrounds. The same process was observed in the Seven Years War, and indeed provoked some adverse comment from those who feared dilution of the officer corps.[56] Nonetheless, it happened again in the American war, and, as the army became larger than ever before, we can be reasonably confident that an even greater number of officers came from beyond the traditional social catchment. Samuel Bradford was not exactly promoted from the ranks; but the fact that his father, an Irish linen draper, had sent most of his other sons to serve as

[53] William Braco Gordon e.g. could barely conceal his delight after Bunker Hill: 'By the affair of the 17th of June, I got five Steps, which brings me within three of being Eldest Lieut: I am in great spirits, and expectations of getting a Company before matters can possibly be concluded' (Aberdeen University Library, Duff of Braco Muniments, MS 2727/1/181).

[54] William L. Clements Library, Gage Papers, vol. 132, Mackenzie's memorials, [July 1775]; WO 27/51.

[55] For Robertson's humble origins see Thomas Jones, *History of New York*, ed. E. E. DeLancey (2 vols., New York 1879), i. 162.

[56] See 'An Officer', *A New System . . . for the Army* (London, 1775), 29.

common soldiers seems to have been responsible for Samuel's gaining a commission as ensign in the Ninety-second Foot. He was given
this opportunity, it seems, to encourage recruiting in his father's
neighbourhood.[57] Young Bradford's good fortune was tragically
brief: later that same year his regiment was ordered to the West
Indies, where on 25 December 1780 he was mustered with the rest of
his company at Spanish Town, Jamaica; but thereafter he disappears
from the official record, a victim, in all probability, of one of the
deadly diseases prevalent in the Caribbean.[58] David McFall, another
Irishman, was a sergeant in the Twenty-sixth Foot in 1775. The next
year he was appointed a lieutenant in Ebenezer Jessop's American
loyalist corps. In August 1777 he transferred to another loyalist unit
with the rank of captain. Shortly afterwards, he was captured at the
battle of Bennington, and in August 1780 he claimed £557. 10s. in
arrears of pay. Whether McFall was successful in his claim is
unclear; but it would surely have been most unlikely that he would
even have dreamed of such a sum while he remained a sergeant.[59] James
Green went still further. He joined the Sixty-second Foot as a private in
1772, and worked his way up through the non-commissioned officer
ranks to sergeant-major. This was as far as he could reasonably
expect to go in peacetime. But then in 1777, when his regiment
was short of officers following heavy casualties at the battle of Freeman's Farm on the Burgoyne expedition, Green was made an
ensign. Two years later he transferred to the Twenty-sixth Foot as
a lieutenant, drawing extra pay as the regimental adjutant. He
impressed his superiors sufficiently to be appointed a deputy judge
advocate in America. We can surmise that life was not always easy for
Green. For several years the officially produced *Army List* seemed
determined to highlight his humble origins by refusing to acknowledge that he had a Christian name. In due course, however, he
became indistinguishable—at least in print—from his regimental
colleagues, and rose by steps so that by 1803 he was a lieutenant-
colonel.[60] Similar examples could be produced for the navy, in
which, as we have seen, wartime promotion of long-serving seamen
of humble origins was far from unusual, especially in the last years of
the conflict, when the navy was expanding rapidly. Most of these

[57] BL, Liverpool Papers, Add. MS 38212, fo. 81.   [58] WO 12/9320.
[59] BL, Haldimand Papers, Add. MS 21827, fos. 98, 205.
[60] National Army Museum, 7201-36-1.

officers were already middle-aged when they received their lieutenant's commission, and consequently advanced no further. But there
were at least a few who became senior officers. Robert Watson was 35
when he became a lieutenant, and had spent eleven years at sea,
serving on a variety of ships as able seaman and warrant officer. He
remained in the navy at the peace, and went on to become a
commander in 1787. In the war against Napoleonic France he rose
to vice admiral.[61]

Needless to say, those who remained common seamen or soldiers
tended to have fewer opportunities to make money or to advance
socially. Indeed, we should not forget that enlistment was often itself
part of a process of downward social mobility. Whatever the role
played by patriotism, the pressure of social superiors, or family
circumstances, immediate financial need must surely have accounted
for many men's taking the king's shilling. In Belfast, for instance, it
was reported in April 1778 that 'The Linen & every branch of
Business are as low as Possible, a Scarcety of Money & Prices of
provisions very High—which obliges the Manufacturers to Enlist in
great Numbers'.[62] Joining the colours was perhaps more obviously a
step down for some recruits. This was certainly the case for James
Hamilton, a young merchant from Lanark who became a private in
the Third Foot Guards;[63] for Charles Flood, a schoolmaster from
Naas, County Kildare, who entered the Forty-sixth Foot with the
same rank in January 1776;[64] and for Patrick Quin, a former Catholic
priest educated at the University of Paris who had converted to
Protestantism, been robbed in London, and joined the Thirty-fifth
Foot in a moment of despair. For such men the army can hardly have
seemed to be a means by which they could move up in the world:
Quin, for one, begged to be released from his position as a private,
'which bears so great incongruity with his former Rank and
vocation'.[65]

But even ordinary soldiers and naval ratings could see their
fortunes improve. Pay in the army was unlikely to have been
much of a help in itself—common soldiers were supposed to receive
a mere sixpence a day, and even this meagre wage was subject to

---

[61] ADM 107/7, p. 72. See above, Ch. 1.
[62] PRONI, Downshire Papers, D 607/B/21.
[63] BL, Loudoun Papers, Add. MS 44084, fo. 231.
[64] WO 1/992, 'List of recruits Rais'd for the 46th Regiment', 9 Feb. 1776.
[65] William L. Clements Library, Clinton Papers, Quin's petition, 26 July 1777.

deductions for all manner of purposes.[66] In the navy it was rather better, with able seamen receiving, after deductions, the equivalent of about ninepence a day, and ordinary seamen seven and a half pence (they were paid every twenty-eight days).[67] But in wartime, when large numbers of seamen were pressed into the navy, pay rates for merchant seaman soared, making remuneration levels in the Royal Navy very unattractive to trained mariners.[68] Bounty money, paid to entrants into the army and navy, could be more helpful, especially when it was augmented by public subscriptions or contributions from loyal corporations. But it was prize money, derived from the capture of enemy property, that offered the best opportunity for financial gain. The precious metals of South and Central America continued to cast their spell: a Spanish war, a marine officer wrote in June 1779, 'is always agreeable to the Jack Tars of Britain';[69] and even recruiters for the army conjured up the image of opportunities to 'pillage the Don'.[70] In truth, for the private soldier the chance of making a great deal of money was limited. An expedition to Virginia in 1780 netted more than £6,500 for the military participants; but each private pocketed less than ten shillings.[71] For the navy's ratings, however, prize money tended to be a larger and more frequent bonus. A seaman on the *Perseus* recorded no less than twenty-five captures between 2 November 1776 and 9 January 1777; while in October 1778 John Kirby, a sailor on the *Unicorn*, told his father that since the ship's arrival in American waters, the crew had taken 'abought 50. Saile of Vessels'.[72] Such a rate of success could lead to the accumulation of handsome sums, even by those who occupied the lower decks.

The acquisition of money was not the only way in which a soldier or seaman could find his situation improved. To encourage enlistment into the army, the 1779 Recruiting Act, as we have seen,

[66] Sylvia R. Frey, *The British Soldier in America: A Social History of Military Life in the Revolutionary Period* (Austin, Tex., 1981), 54.

[67] N. A. M. Rodger, *The Wooden World: An Anatomy of the Georgian Navy* (London, 1986), 125.   [68] See above, Ch. 2.

[69] SRO, Logan Home of Edrom Muniments, GD 1/384/6/10. See also *Belfast News-letter*, 9–13 July 1779, for an advert encouraging local men to join the navy: 'the Seamen belonging to some of his Majesty's Ships in the late War with Spain shared 750*l.* each for the capture of one Ship only, and many others shared 200*l.*'.

[70] East Sussex RO, Sheffield Papers, A 2714/265, 'Song in Honour of the 22d Light Dragoons'.   [71] Liverpool RO, Parker Papers, PA 3–3, 'State of the Case'.

[72] E. Arnot Robertson (ed.), *The Spanish Town Papers* (London, 1959), 21–2; SRO, Lindsay of Dowhill Muniments, GD 254/1055.

offered artisans, craftsmen, and retailers who joined the colours the opportunity, on their discharge, to practise their trade in any parish, town, or city in the kingdom.[73] Local authorities might dispute the claims of former soldiers, but the rights of the ex-servicemen seem to have been upheld.[74] The number of young artisans joining the army might indicate that a temporary period of service was being used in much the same way as a period of apprenticeship or indentured servitude—as a means of gaining mobility and opening up new possibilities. And at a time when the North American colonies themselves were difficult to access, perhaps the army seemed to provide an alternative route to opportunity.[75] It could even have been viewed as a means by which emigration could continue. At the close of the Seven Years War, the troops in the regular regiments employed in North America had been offered land and been given encouragement to settle, particularly in the newly conquered territories.[76] We can surmise that at least some of those men who joined the colours during the American war hoped that similar opportunities would be presented by British victory. It was surely no coincidence that the Scottish Highlands, which had provided many of the pre-war emigrants to North America, provided many soldiers once hostilities commenced.[77]

Nor should we forget that the armed services could, in certain circumstances, act as a means of social rehabilitation. For convicts or those charged with offences the army or navy could provide an opportunity for a fresh start. This is not to deny the capacity of the armed forces to be schools for crime, which we will consider

---

[73] See above, Ch. 1.

[74] See M. G. Hobson (ed.), *Oxford Council Acts 1752–1801* (Oxford Historical Society, NS, vol. xv, Oxford, 1962), 144–5.

[75] For pre-war migration to North America, particularly amongst artisans and craftsmen, see Bernard Bailyn, *The Peopling of British North America: An Introduction* (London, 1987), 9, 11, 63–4.

[76] Some of these disbanded soldiers, who benefited from the royal proclamation of 7 Oct. 1763, show up in the papers of the Loyalist Claims Commission after the American war. After having become American landowners they joined various loyalist corps during the conflict: see e.g. PRO, Audit Office Papers, AO 12/21, fos. 194–5; AO 12/32, fos. 29, 72–4.

[77] For the Scottish, and esp. Highland, contribution, see below, Ch. 5, and, more generally, Mackillop, *'More Fruitful than the Soil'*. Both migration and recruitment can also been seen as the consequences of changes in Highland society and economic structure after the 'Forty-Five Rebellion. Joining a Highland regiment might have appeared to Highlanders who were conscious of the decline of their traditional culture as a way of preserving and celebrating that culture.

later; nor to claim that they converted every malefactor who came within their reach: Richard Slater, who was allowed to join the Thirty-first Foot as an alternative to punishment, was able to return to his native parish and continued to be 'Very troublesome & disorderly', much to the annoyance of those who thought that they had seen the last of him.[78] But there were cases where reformation seems the appropriate term. We can only guess whether Edward Kitson flourished in the post-war years, but the war itself certainly helped him. In August 1776 he was enlisted in Shrewsbury gaol by Lieutenant John Ridout of the Forty-sixth Foot. Within a year of joining the regiment in America, Kitson had become a corporal. In due course he was promoted to sergeant, and he continued to hold that rank until he was released from service on 4 April 1783 after a period 'On furlough'—a sure sign that he was regarded by his officers as trustworthy.[79] A spell in the army had transformed Kitson, it seems, from a lowly prisoner to a respected veteran.

Service with a volunteer corps could also improve one's social standing. Laurence Cox, the merchant and contractor who was given a baronetcy after the war, found that the leading role he had played in the volunteers kept him in the mind of those with favours to bestow.[80] But the volunteers did not always meet with government approval, as we have seen, and so volunteering was not an obvious route to official reward. More importantly, volunteering allowed the 'middling sort'—who provided the bulk of the officers and men— to assert their claims to recognition. Many of the volunteer companies were based on agreements drawn up by the participants which specified their duties and responsibilities. In the case of the Irish volunteers, these were often political in character: the First Newry Volunteers, to give an example, agreed that their object was 'to defend our Country against Enemies, foreign or domestic, open or Concealed'.[81] In England, however, such political aims were not usually mentioned—even if they sometimes lurked in the background[82]—and the military role the volunteers envisaged for themselves was usually strictly limited; they were generally unwilling to serve outside their own immediate locality. In Lyme Regis the 130 volunteers agreed 'under the direction of the first Magistrate to

---

[78] WO 1/1010, [John] Daniell to [Charles Jenkinson?], 28 Aug. 1781.
[79] WO 12/5797, fos. 16, 42, 44, 57.   [80] SP 41/33, fo. 312.
[81] PRONI, T 3202/1A, Minute-book of the First Newry Volunteers, 1 Aug. 1780.
[82] See below, Ch. 6.

defend the Town against the Incursions of a small body of men from Privateers & smuggling vessels'; while in Great Yarmouth the 'voluntary association' of merchants and tradesmen confined itself 'to the local defence of the Town in Case of an attack by the Enemy'.[83] By remaining within their communities, volunteers ensured that their service was conspicuous. Their drill sessions, held on Sundays or on weekday evenings, attracted a good deal of interest.[84] The progress of the volunteers, moreover, was often reported in newspapers that carried their reputations to neighbouring towns, or even across the county. The readers of the *York Courant* were regaled with information on the 'genteel uniforms' of the volunteers of Bradford; the purchase of firearms from Birmingham (at no expense to government) by the Scarborough volunteers; and the field day of the company at Kirkby Moorside.[85] For those who served in such corps volunteering was as much a matter of proving local worth and gaining wider celebrity—for oneself and one's community—as it was a form of patriotic duty.[86]

If the American conflict witnessed a growing confidence among the 'middling sort', this occasionally manifested itself not simply in claims to recognition but also in a more critical attitude towards the traditional landed elite. Aristocratic opponents of the war were criticized almost as strongly as aristocratic supporters of Lord North. The Rockingham Whigs, as we shall see later, were regarded with considerable suspicion when they tried, unsuccessfully, to hijack the protest movement inaugurated by the formation of the Yorkshire Association in December 1779.[87] But if complaints about the dominance of the aristocracy came from the rural squires, some elements of the urban 'middling sort' were also expressing resentment. This was not in itself novel; Gerald Newman and

---

[83] HO 42/205, fos. 132, 186.

[84] e.g. *Mary Hardy's Diary*, ed. Basil Cozens-Hardy (Norfolk Record Society Publications, vol. xxxvii, Norwich, 1968), 43; *Leeds Intelligencer*, 31 Dec. 1782.

[85] *York Courant*, 31 Aug., 26 Oct., 9 Nov. 1779.

[86] See R. J. Morris, 'Voluntary Societies and British Urban Elites, 1780–1850: An Analysis', *Historical Journal*, 26 (1983), 95–118; J. E. Cookson, 'The English Volunteer Movement of the French Wars, 1793–1815: Some Contexts', *Historical Journal*, 32 (1989), 867–91, and *The British Armed Nation, 1793–1815* (Oxford, 1997), 10, 91–2. See also Jonathan Barry, 'Bourgeois Collectivism? Urban Association and the Middling Sort', in id. and Christopher Brooks (eds.), *The Middling Sort of People: Culture, Society and Politics in England, 1550–1800* (London, 1994), 84–112. For the social dimension of Irish volunteering see A. T. Q. Stewart, *A Deeper Silence: The Hidden Roots of the United Irish Movement* (London, 1993), 20–1.   [87] Below, Ch. 6.

Kathleen Wilson have shown that anti-aristocratic sentiment was emerging much earlier, and that it was particularly noticeable during the Seven Years War.[88] But we should not be surprised that the American conflict added to the tensions. After all, the war—at least in its American aspect—could easily be portrayed as a struggle between an essentially aristocratic society at home and a more egalitarian society in the colonies. At a time when the Americans were rejecting the hereditary principle, it was only to be expected that some of their sympathizers and supporters in the British Isles should adopt a more sharply anti-aristocratic tone.[89] Care should be taken, of course, not to anticipate nineteenth-century developments. A middle-class consciousness was far from fully formed. Even so, there were some interesting pointers to the future. A contemporary cartoon, emphasizing the patriotism of plain and simple Englishmen, used one of its characters to cast doubt on the patriotism of effete lords, whose culture, so heavily influenced by the French, could easily be seen as cosmopolitan rather than national ('Dont Talk to me of your Dukes & your Lords, I'm a true Born Englishman').[90] More directly, Samuel Kenrick, a Dissenting manufacturer of Bewdley, Worcestershire, and a determined critic of the conflict with America, referred scathingly to 'a parcel of useless idle beings, called gentlemen's youngest sons' who obtained commissions in the army and, if they survived the war, would then be 'maintained afterwards on half pay' at public expense.[91] The words could have come from the lips of Cobden and Bright sixty or seventy years later, in one of their tirades against the landed classes and their vested interest in war.

Similarly, we can see that the American struggle increased friction between entrepreneurs of the 'middling sort' and their labour forces, adumbrating the bitter social conflicts of the next century. The

[88] Gerald Newman, *The Rise of English Nationalism: A Cultural History 1740–1830* (London, 1997 edn.); Kathleen Wilson, *The Sense of the People: Politics, Culture and Imperialism in England, 1715–1785* (Cambridge, 1995).

[89] See John Cannon, 'The British Nobility, 1660–1800', in *The European Nobilities in the Seventeenth and Eighteenth Centuries*, i. *Western Europe*, ed. H. M. Scott (London, 1995), 76.

[90] BM 5614, 'Apothecaries—Taylors &c. Conquering France and Spain', 1779. For the influence of France on the aristocracy see Newman, *Rise of English Nationalism*, ch. 1; Robin Eagles, 'Beguiled by France? The English Aristocracy, 1748–1848', in Laurence Brockliss and David Eastwood (eds.), *A Union of Multiple Identities: The British Isles, c.1750–1850* (Manchester, 1997), 60–77.

[91] Dr Williams's Library, Wodrow-Kenrick Correspondence, MS 24157 (59).

tensions visible in the war period were essentially the fruits of long-term change, and particularly mechanization of traditional production processes. But the war added to the pressure by increasing the cost of living for working people (apart from in the period autumn 1778 to the summer of 1781, when good harvests led to cheaper food prices) and disrupting overseas trade, which made employers especially concerned about the need to keep costs down to remain competitive. In January 1778 framework-knitters petitioned Parliament for the regulation of their wages to arrest a decline that made bare subsistence a struggle for their families. The employers responded with a counter-petition asking for no regulation of wages, on the ground that wage flexibility was vital to their survival; legislative interference, they argued, would lead to the loss of a valuable branch of overseas trade. In the course of examination of witnesses by MPs, it was said that 'the Troubles in America' had contributed to the marked decline in the glove and mit industry.[92] The following year, widespread machine-breaking affected the infant Lancashire cotton industry. The militia was deployed to combat nocturnal attacks on mills;[93] and local weavers petitioned for regulation of wages. Again, technical innovation can be seen as the long-term problem, but wartime disruption of supplies of raw cotton from the Caribbean and the Levant, and effective closure of many overseas markets, created unemployment which the introduction of machinery threatened to make worse. Josiah Wedgwood had no hesitation in attributing the disorders to the lost jobs caused by trade depression; the Irish non-importation agreements were seen as the primary problem.[94] Two years later, in 1781, while overseas commerce was still slack, weavers in Oldham returned to the theme of regulation of the trade, and a lengthy strike occurred as labour relations remained strained.[95]

Social tensions were not confined to those areas where textile production was the dominant economic activity. The war had the

---

[92] *Journals of the House of Commons*, xxxvi. 633, 728, 740–2. When Parliament voted down a bill for wage regulation, Nottingham stockingers smashed the windows of the town's master hosiers. See Charles Tilly, *Popular Contention in Great Britain 1758–1834* (Cambridge, Mass., 1995), 189–90.

[93] HMC, 15th Report, app., pt. v, *Foljambe MSS* (London, 1897), 152.

[94] *The Selected Letters of Josiah Wedgwood*, ed. Ann Finer and George Savage (London, 1965), 241.

[95] John Rule, *The Experience of Labour in Eighteenth-Century Industry* (London, 1981), 168.

general effect of widening the gulf between those on low incomes and the comfortably-off. The rise in food prices that characterized all but the middle years of the conflict, was mainly connected, of course, with deficient harvests; but wartime taxation, though criticized by the upper and middling ranks of society, hit the 'lower sort' hardest. Despite the laudable intentions of Lord North, wartime budgets accentuated the regressive nature of the tax system, with excises and other duties on items of popular consumption rising sharply. The annual yield from customs and excises was £1.5 million higher at the end of the war than at the beginning, while assessed taxes produced less than £1 million more in 1782 than in 1775. Much of the tax raised was used to pay interest on loans—the annual debt charge was more than £8 million in 1783, compared with only £4.7 million in 1775. With increasingly generous discounts, loan issues attracted the savings of many of those with money to spare. Landowners, clergymen, professionals, and even successful farmers were able to invest heavily in government stock. As a London merchant succinctly explained in May 1779: 'it is a fine time for buying into our Funds'.[96] The overall effect of war finance, then, was mildly redistributive, taking wealth from the poor and less well-off and giving it to those with enough money to invest in the national debt.

This does not, on the whole, seem to have generated immediate and overt social conflict. Most of the crowd action of the war years was an expression of localized and distinctly ephemeral hostility to perceived violations of the 'moral economy', a set of widely held assumptions about what constituted fair trading behaviour,[97] rather than part of a broader protest against changes in the social system. So in Staffordshire in the autumn of 1782, when food prices were high, colliers attacked the mill at Bescot and obliged the miller to part with his wheat at well below the current rate; it was then sold at Walsall market at this lower price for the benefit of local people.[98] The following March, food riots took place in the potteries, with a barge of corn being seized and the contents again sold at below the market rate.[99] On this occasion, the militia was called in to restore

---

[96] Berkshire RO, Barrett and Belson Family Papers, D/EBt F140/6.
[97] See E. P. Thompson, 'The Moral Economy of the English Crowd in the Eighteenth Century', *Past & Present*, 90 (1971), 76–136.
[98] *Aris's Birmingham Gazette*, 21 Oct. 1782.
[99] *Selected Letters of Wedgwood*, ed. Finer and Savage, 267–8.

order and calm the nerves of local property-owners,[100] but the aims of the rioters were confined to food distribution; there was no general threat to the social order.

Once in a while, however, it appears that the 'lower sort' demonstrated their hostility to changing patterns of wealth and power, and we can glimpse what looks like class resentment bubbling to the surface. The Gordon Riots which shook London in 1780 can be viewed in this way. True, the riots were primarily an expression of popular anti-Catholicism, inspired by wartime reforms designed to give Catholics limited relief from some of the legislative burdens imposed on them.[101] Even so, the most thorough study of the victims of the rioters argues that there was a class element to the disorders. The principal targets were Catholic chapels attached to foreign embassies, the homes of politicians associated with the 1778 Catholic Relief Act, and assorted symbols of authority and law, including the Fleet, Newgate, Bridewell, and King's Bench prisons. But shops, distilleries, warehouses, and—perhaps most significantly—the Bank of England were attacked in incidents where anti-popery seems to have been blended with animus against the financial system, property, affluence, and a consumer culture inaccessible to the metropolitan poor.[102]

None of this, of course, undermines the generally accepted view that it was the social, economic and political tensions created by the long conflict with revolutionary and Napoleonic France, combined with the problems of increasing industrialization, that led to the emergence of class-consciousness among artisans and semi-skilled

---

[100] Staffordshire RO, Dartmouth MSS, D(W) 1778 v. 731.

[101] See below, Ch. 7. Colin Haydon, *Anti-Catholicism in Eighteenth-Century England, c.1714–1780: A Political and Social Study* (Manchester, 1993), 220–44, argues that the riots should be seen simply as an outburst of popular anti-Catholicism, not as an expression of social rebellion.

[102] George Rudé, 'The Gordon Riots: A Study of the Rioters and their Victims', *Transactions of the Royal Historical Society*, 5th ser. 6 (1956), 93–114. Nicholas Rogers, 'Crowd and People in the Gordon Riots', in Eckhart Hellmuth (ed.), *The Transformation of Political Culture: England and Germany in the Late Eighteenth Century* (Oxford, 1990), 52, notes that in the final stages of the riots, the rioters directed their anger against pawnshops, crimping houses, spunging houses, and the toll houses of Blackfriars Bridge—'the petty oppressors of the poor'. He is reluctant, however, to endorse Rudé's view that the riots were directed at the rich. In his latest look at the riots, Rogers argues that 'they were directed at the most visible and influential members of the Catholic community, and at the cosmopolitan quality who believed in a qualified toleration for the rejuvenated Catholic Church'. *Crowds, Culture and Politics in Georgian Britain* (Oxford, 1998), 175.

workers.[103] What it does suggest, however, is that the developments after 1793 were not simply a response to immediate pressures, but rather the coming to fruition of a process of class identification that had been moving fitfully forward over many years and was given some impetus by the experiences of the American war.

Crime

Despite the machine-breaking and associated disturbances in the industrial districts and the destruction wrought by the Gordon Riots, the American war years appear to have seen a fall in the number of criminal prosecutions. This was in line with a general eighteenth-century pattern. Studies of Surrey and Staffordshire suggest that indictments diminished during hostilities, and then rose sharply at the end of wars as the armed forces shed men to slim down to their new peacetime establishments.[104] The figures for Hertfordshire vary less dramatically, but follow the same trajectory. There was a 7% fall in the average number of persons per year indicted for property offences between midsummer 1775 and midsummer 1782, compared with the previous seven years of peace. From Michaelmas 1782 to Michaelmas 1784 the annual figure for this kind of indictment was on average 45% higher than during the war.[105]

Does the decline in the number of indictments mean that the war years saw less crime? Not necessarily. We have seen that soldiers in camp or on the march were accused of all manner of thefts—from filching orchard fruit and poaching game to highway robbery. Indeed, military service could be seen as a training for criminality: one officer noted how men who had been in North America were accustomed to taking what they wanted in the way of extra food; once they returned to Britain they continued to behave in the same

---

[103] The classical exposition is E. P. Thompson, *The Making of the English Working Class* (London, 1963). For a recent endorsement see Douglas Hay and Nicholas Rogers, *Eighteenth-Century English Society* (Oxford, 1997).

[104] Douglas Hay, 'War, Dearth and Theft in the Eighteenth Century: The Record of the English Courts', *Past & Present*, 95 (1982), 117–60; John Beattie, *Crime and the Courts in England 1660–1800* (Princeton, 1986), ch. 5.

[105] William Le Hardy (ed.), *Calendar to the Sessions Books, Sessions Minute Books and Other Sessions Records . . . 1752 to 1799* (Hertfordshire County Records, vol. iii, Hertford, 1935), 146–332.

way.[106] Even militia service was regarded by some contemporaries as subversive. While the militia was not sent abroad and exposed to the temptations of a war zone, militia service in theory involved a new set of men every few years, and so spread the contagion widely. According to Samuel Kenrick, 'The Militia of England has been the utter destruction of the morals of our country people . . . thefts, robberies & debauchery are diffused through the whole of the lower class'.[107] Nor was the problem confined to property offences. Violent clashes between recruiting parties and local people, or between soldiers in garrison towns and their unwilling hosts, were far from unusual. In Dublin, for instance, a riot involving soldiers of the Nineteenth Foot and 'a Number of Carmen' occurred in September 1780,[108] while two years later officers of the Leicestershire militia appear to have attacked the town watch in Newcastle.[109] Military offenders could be brought before civilian magistrates;[110] but minor offences, particularly, tended to be dealt with by the military's own tribunals. At Warley Camp in September 1778 several soldiers in the Sixth Foot were punished by a court martial for crimes affecting local people.[111] In November 1780 a regimental court martial found three soldiers of the Pembrokeshire militia guilty of stealing food from the public house in which they were quartered; the principal offender was sentenced to 300 lashes. Nearly two years later, two soldiers in the Warwickshire militia based at Coxheath were brought before a court martial and 'found Guilty of Moroding'.[112] And many more military delinquents than civilian ones probably eluded any kind of justice because they were far from home and could rely on the anonymity of a redcoat to protect them from detection: the exhortatory tone of orders issued by the military authorities certainly suggests that they were fighting a losing battle.[113] The net result was a good deal of criminal activity over and above that

---

[106] *The Journal of Gen. Martin Hunter*, ed. Ann Hunter and Elizabeth Bell (Edinburgh, 1894), 45.
[107] Dr Williams's Library, Wodrow-Kenrick Correspondence, MS 24157 (59).
[108] SP 63/471, fo. 67.
[109] HMC, *Rutland MSS* (4 vols., London, 1888–1905), iii. 62.
[110] e.g. Essex RO, Quarter Sessions Book, Q/SMg 23, 11 Jan. 1780.
[111] C. A. Markham, *The History of the Northamptonshire and Rutland Militia* (London, 1924), 21.
[112] NLW, Spence Colby Papers, B, Pembrokeshire militia documents: regimental court martial proceedings, 14 Nov. 1780; Orderly-book, Capt. Thomas Tucker's Company, 18 July 1782.   [113] e.g. Kent Archives Office, Amherst MSS, U 1350 O88/2.

represented by the wartime indictments. A fall in the number of prosecutions at quarter sessions and assizes might, then, be no guide to the number of offences committed—it might mask a crime rate that remained static or even rose. Perhaps, indeed, the propertied classes fooled themselves into believing that crime was less of a problem. As they saw unemployed young men absorbed into the expanded armed forces, and as magistrates gleefully identified local ne'er-do-wells as suitable objects for enlistment,[114] perhaps the fear of crime diminished and so the propensity to prosecute lessened also. Though industrial disorders and, of course, the Gordon Riots led to much disquiet, there was nothing akin to the 'moral panic' about crime that gripped the propertied mind in the post-war years.

Yet, for all this, it seems entirely probable that fewer offences were perpetrated during the war. If the army and militia themselves contributed to the level of crime, volunteer forces—usually made up, we should recall, of the propertied middling sort—had an important public-order function which helped to combat lawlessness. This role was particularly clear in Ireland. Indeed, the first Irish volunteer companies of the American war period appear to have been formed in 1775 and 1776 to counter the Whiteboy agrarian terrorists.[115] And once the volunteers proper came into being from 1778, this aspect of their activities remained prominent. James Hamilton, agent of the absentee Earl of Abercorn, was 'by no means an advocate for volunteers', yet even he had to admit 'it's certain that they have put an end in this Country very much to house brakers and robbers'.[116] In Dublin the volunteers patrolled the streets to deter thefts, and on occasion apprehended burglars.[117] In London, too, some of the military associations formed in 1779–80 played a role in combating the Gordon rioters, and continued to perform a police function for some years after.[118] There is also a more generally applicable reason for believing that the level of criminal activity dropped. Quite simply, the propertied classes were right to feel more secure: recruitment did take a good many

---

[114] See e.g. WO 1/992, Revd J. Vashony to Barrington, 26 July 1776.

[115] *The Harcourt Papers*, ed. E. W. Harcourt (14 vols., Oxford, 1880–1905), x. 197; Maurice J. Bric, 'The Whiteboy Movement in Tipperary, 1760–80', in William Nolan and Thomas G. McGrath (eds.), *Tipperary: History and Society* (Dublin, 1985), 166.

[116] PRONI, Abercorn Papers, D/623/A/44/29.

[117] See Dublin's *General Evening Post*, 22 Jan., 16 Feb., 12 Mar. 1782.

[118] Rogers, 'Crowd and People in the Gordon Riots', 53.

potential miscreants out of circulation. Some, as was just noted, remained within the British Isles and went on to commit offences while wearing redcoats; but we should remember that a significant proportion of the army served abroad, and that the navy's ratings— even if they were on ships stationed in home waters—were often removed from their areas of recruitment for months or even years at a time. We should note, too, that large-scale enlistment had the effect in some trades of pushing up the wages of those who were left behind.[119] While wage increases were not always sufficient to counteract a rising cost of living, it seems reasonable to suppose that at least in the low-food-price years 1778–81 the economic pressure to slide into criminality was somewhat diminished.

Nor should we be surprised that the close of the war saw a sharp upturn in the number of prosecutions. With the end of the fighting, the army and navy were dramatically slimmed down to their pre-war strengths and the militia was disembodied. This meant that about 200,000 men were no longer required. The problems caused by a demobilization on this scale can readily be imagined. For many ex-servicemen the first difficulty was returning home. In August 1783 discharged marines at Portsmouth petitioned for a passage to Ireland, while the authorities at Bristol complained of the large number of former soldiers and sailors who were gathering in the city seeking a ship to take them across St George's Channel.[120] Even if they reached home, employment opportunities were likely to be very limited in an overstocked labour market. Unable to find work, many ex-servicemen took to wandering about and begging: in the summer of 1783 Hertfordshire magistrates were obliged to recompense their conveyor of vagrants for her extraordinary expenses, mainly occasioned, it seems, by the demobilization.[121] There was a general fear amongst property-owners—as there had been in 1748– 9 and 1763–4—that ex-servicemen, in the absence of work to occupy them, would become a threat.[122] 'Lord have mercy on us', Lord Fife wrote in January 1783. 'What shall we do with all the

---

[119] See above, Ch. 2.

[120] ADM 1/5118/20, fo. 83; E. E. Butcher (ed.), *Bristol Corporation of the Poor: Selected Records 1696–1834* (Bristol Record Society, vol. iii, Bristol, 1932), 120.

[121] William Le Hardy (ed.), *Notes and Extracts from the Sessions Records of the Liberty of St Alban Division 1770 to 1840* (Hertfordshire County Records, vol. iv, Hertford, 1923), 20.

[122] For still earlier problems see John Childs, 'War, Crime Waves and the English Army in the Late Seventeenth Century', *War & Society*, 15 (1997), 1–17.

Army set a Drift at once without employment[?]'[123] Some commentators, as we have seen, were also fearful of the bad habits that
the army, navy, and militia were thought to inculcate. The services
were said to be brutalizing, a school for crime, and, because of the
long spells of inactivity that characterized military life, to destroy the
desire for work, making labourers and artisans lazy and unfit to
resume their former stations. As the *Salisbury Journal* explained:
'a great number of disbanded militia-men, who are too idle to return
to their farming business, are robbing all parts of the country'.[124]
Anxiety begat crime-prevention initiatives. Societies for the prosecution of felons proliferated. In England, according to a recent
calculation, six such societies were formed in 1783, seven in 1784,
and five in 1785. This compares with an average of less than two a
year in the period 1763–82.[125] The post-war years also saw various
schemes progressed by Parliament to encourage forestry and fishing,
with the need to provide employment for ex-servicemen one of the
considerations in mind.[126]

Social Reform

If the war influenced the crime rate, it also created conditions that
enabled the ideas of penal reformers to gain wider acceptance.[127]
Before the outbreak of hostilities, it was standard practice to transport felons to the American colonies for seven or fourteen years, the
bulk going to Maryland and Virginia. An estimated 30,000 convicts
made this journey across the Atlantic between 1718, when transportation was first given parliamentary approval, and the outbreak of
the American war.[128] With the closure of the rebel colonies to this
trade, new means of dealing with the convicts had to be found. The

---

[123] Alistair and Henrietta Taylor (eds.), *Lord Fife and his Factor*, 148; see also 150.

[124] Beattie, *Crime and the Courts*, 228.

[125] David Philips, 'Good Men to Associate and Bad Man to Conspire: Associations for
the Prosecution of Felons in England 1760–1860', in Douglas Hay and Francis Snyder
(eds.), *Policing and Prosecution in Britain 1750–1850* (Oxford, 1989), 161–2.

[126] Joanna Innes, 'The Domestic Face of the Military-Fiscal State: Government and
Society in Eighteenth-Century Britain', in Lawrence Stone (ed.), *An Imperial State at
War: Britain from 1689 to 1815* (London, 1994), 116–17.

[127] The following account is heavily indebted to Beattie, *Crime and the Courts*, 560–82.

[128] A. Roger Ekirch, *Bound for America: The Transportation of British Convicts to the
Colonies* (Oxford, 1987), 23.

problem was given added urgency by the poor state of the prisons in Britain. Most were in bad repair, unhealthy, and far from escape-proof. Lengthy imprisonment in such buildings was hardly a viable option; yet once transportation to America ceased, hard-pressed members of the judiciary, in the absence of any obvious alternative, were compelled to confine convicts to the gaols, which soon began to fill up at an alarming rate. In London, the numbers were so great by January 1776 'that it became necessary in order to avoid pestilential Disorders to remove near 140 aboard a Vessel in the River'.[129] Some male offenders and suspects were packed off to the army, navy, or East India Company Service, which were all in desperate need of recruits. But, as we have seen, even in the face of an acute manpower crisis, the military authorities were reluctant to take convicts, and their scruples were shared, it seems, by many recruiting officers, who simply refused to accept such men as appropriate additions to their corps.[130] To tackle the problem of convict disposal, then, the government was obliged to legislate without delay. An act was passed in May 1776, and renewed in 1778 and 1779, establishing hard labour on the Thames and detention in hulks moored on the river as a temporary alternative to transportation. William Eden, the under-secretary responsible for the original act, was himself a penal reformer,[131] and the new legislation marked a shift from the disposal of offenders—by execution or transportation—to custodial sentences and reformation: it was confidently claimed that hard labour would improve the character of the offender, making him or her fit for return to society.

It would be easy to exaggerate the importance of this change. Once the war ended, transportation recommenced—first to the West African coast and then, from 1787, to Australia. Indeed, the development of New South Wales as a convict colony breathed fresh life into the old system, much to the chagrin of penal reformers.[132] Even so, imprisonment came to be seen by a growing body of opinion as an appropriate alternative at least partly because the practice of

---

[129] BL, Auckland Papers, Add. MS 34413, fo. 11. See also Lord Suffolk's enquiries about the situation in Scotland: HO 104/1, p. 154.   [130] See above, Ch. 1.

[131] He was the author of *Principles of Penal Law* (London, 1771).

[132] Jeremy Bentham, in particular, was bitterly opposed to New South Wales. See his *Letter to Lord Pelham* and *Second Letter to Lord Pelham* of 1802, and *A Plea for the Constitution*, printed in 1803. These works were published together in 1812, with the first *Letter* re-entitled *Panopticon versus New South Wales*.

imprisonment, more or less forced on the authorities by the collapse of the transportation system during the war, brought the theories of the reformers into prominence. Detention and forced labour in the hulks added much strength to the arguments of those who had long advocated the redeeming qualities of incarceration and disciplined work—reformers like Jonas Hanway and John Howard, who now found their ideas gaining ground. It was no coincidence, surely, that in 1779 Parliament passed the Penitentiary Act. This envisaged the building of a series of new-style prisons, the inmates of which would be subjected to a rigorous regime of hard labour, religious instruction, and solitary confinement at night. The Act itself was never put into effect, but it encouraged Jeremy Bentham to spend many years pursuing his ultimately unsuccessful Panopticon scheme,[133] and, more positively, brought forth local emulation in the form of the penitentiary-building initiatives of the Duke of Richmond in Sussex and Sir George Onesiphorus Paul in Gloucestershire. While it would be too much to say that the American war transformed British penal policy, it certainly gave a great boost to the reformers whose ideas finally bore fruit in the next century.

In similar fashion, wartime conditions created an appropriate environment for the reform of the poor laws of England and Wales.[134] Thomas Gilbert, the most celebrated advocate of change, had been arguing since 1764, when he unveiled his first scheme, for the grouping together of parishes to build workhouses and the sanctioning of outdoor relief. A bill drafted by Gilbert passed the

---

[133] See Janet Semple, *Bentham's Prison: The Panopticon Penitentiary* (Oxford, 1992).

[134] The situation was very different in the other parts of the British Isles. The Scottish Poor Law was at this time generally deemed to confine relief to those who were unable to work and was based on voluntary contributions collected by the kirk. See R. A. Cage, *The Scottish Poor Law 1745–1845* (Edinburgh, 1981). In Ireland a statute of 1772 had established corporate bodies for the levying of poor rates, but for the most part the poor were similarly assisted by voluntary subscriptions. Richard Woodward, a prominent Irish churchman, continued to campaign for improvements (see his *Address to the Public on the Expediency of a Regular Plan for the Maintenance and Government of the Poor* (Dublin, 1775)), but there remained strong opposition to the introduction of any system on the English model: see *An Edition of the Cavendish Irish Parliamentary Diary 1776–1778*, ed. Anthony R. Black (3 vols., Delavan, Wis., 1984), ii. 227. Indeed, the experience of the American war years—or, more precisely, the poor harvests and accompanying hardship at its end—may well have breathed fresh life into the Irish system. A recent account suggests that the avoidance of large-scale starvation in 1782–4 was taken by many propertied Irishmen as proof that the Irish Poor Laws were working adequately. See James Kelly, 'Scarcity and Poor Relief in Eighteenth-Century Ireland: The Subsistence Crisis of 1782–1784', *Irish Historical Studies*, 28 (1992–3), 38–62.

Commons in April 1765, only to be thrown out by the Lords. There was a good deal of sympathy amongst the propertied classes for Gilbert's aims, not least because his proposals promised to save money. A pamphlet written in 1770 referred to 'a very great increase in the poors-rate of late years . . . a fact too notorious to be denied';[135] while the *Gentleman's Magazine* was similarly alarmed by 'this increasing evil' and praised Gilbert's efforts to find a remedy.[136] Even so, it was not until 1782 that he was finally successful.

The timing, it could be argued, was coincidental. A parliamentary committee had considered the poor laws early in 1775 and resolved that they were 'defective, and the good Purposes intended by them in many Respects prevented'. The committee in essence adopted the Gilbertian position that the parochial basis of the system of relief was the nub of the problem, and recommended that the poor should be maintained by a county-based system; this, it was confidently predicted, would reduce costs by cutting the number of expensive disputes between parishes about responsibility for particular paupers.[137] The next year saw the House of Commons order all parishes to send in details of their relief expenditure, and the publication of abstracts of the data.[138] There was, then, a head of steam building up in favour of reform before the war; the 1782 legislation can be viewed as its corollary. It might be added that Gilbert's Act was less about innovation than confirmation. Outdoor relief, while for the first time given legislative approval, was already widely practised. There is evidence of various forms of outdoor relief in Warwickshire as early as 1727, in Bedfordshire from 1734, and throughout Berkshire by the early 1770s.[139]

Nonetheless, the American conflict may well have contributed significantly to Gilbert's legislative triumph. The sanctioning of outdoor relief was perhaps no more than a belated recognition of historical practice in some parts of England, but could it be that it seemed acceptable to the legislature in 1782 because at that time

---

[135] 'A Kentishman', *Thoughts on the Present State of the Poor* (London, 1776), 5.

[136] *Gentleman's Magazine*, 46 (1776), 176.

[137] Sheila Lambert (ed.), *House of Commons Sessional Papers of the Eighteenth Century* (145 vols., Wilmington, Del., 1975), xxxi. 1–9.

[138] *Journals of the House of Commons*, xxxv. 694. See also 699, 708, 722, 730–1, 792–3, 800, 804.

[139] George R. Boyer, *An Economic History of the English Poor Law 1750–1850* (Cambridge, 1990), 24; Paul Slack, *The English Poor Law 1531–1782* (Basingstoke, 1990), 43–4.

most local authorities were paying for the maintenance of militia-men's families? Here was a form of outdoor relief—an allowance system calibrated to reflect family size—operating in nearly every parish in England and Wales.[140] Less speculatively, we can say that the war made the issue of costs seem all the more urgent. Poor rates in many parishes rose steeply during the conflict, fuelling the desire for retrenchment. Other imposts increased as well, adding to the feeling among the propertied that incomes were being squeezed. Cost-consciousness, in short, was heightened. As Gilbert himself explained in 1781: 'I hold Oeconomy essentially necessary at all Times, but more so under our present national Calamities, and the pressure of so many heavy Taxes.'[141] With concern about public expenditure at fever pitch, any bill that was said to provide the means by which the burden on local taxpayers could be reduced was almost bound to be received favourably by Parliament.

The conflict led to reform in many other areas, too. Wartime crisis and defeat convinced many of the religiously committed that national degeneracy was the root cause of all the ills of the age. 'As to our national affairs', the Revd Richard Elliot told his brother at the height of the invasion scare in July 1779, 'I say nothing, but rejoice to believe that the *Lord still reigneth*, and doth all things well, and for the *best*—God never sends the *pestilence, famine,* or *sword* upon a Land, or people, but when their enormous inequities make it necessary'.[142] Beilby Porteus, the bishop of Chester, was more fulsome about the nature of the 'inequities' in question, referring to 'that deluge of impiety and irreligion, of dissipation and extravagance which has overspread this land' and 'by provoking the anger of an offended God, has, I am convinced, been the principal, the radical cause of our present misfortunes'.[143] Supporters and opponents of the Americans could unite on this issue: Joshua Toulmin, a Dissenting critic of coercion of the colonists, reminded his congregation that 'War is a *Judgment of God*', and went on to condemn 'The dissipation and luxury of the age; the increase of all places of diversion and amuse-ment throughout the kingdom, and the excessive spirit of gaming';[144]

---

[140] Innes, 'Domestic Face of the Military-Fiscal State', 111–12, suggests a link between militiamen's family support and the extension of outdoor relief in the 1790s.

[141] *Plan for the Better Relief and Employment of the Poor* (London, 1781), 11.

[142] Reading University Library, Elliot Family Papers, DEV. 3/1/50A/53.

[143] *A Charge Delivered to the Clergy of the Diocese of Chester* (Chester, 1779), 26.

[144] *The American War Lamented* (London, 1776), 12, 14.

while James Scott, the ultra-loyal rector of Simonburn, similarly attacked the 'Gaming, swearing and Blasphemy' that had helped to bring forth God's wrath.[145] The remedy, so this line of thinking went, was an urgent and general change in personal conduct.

One of the fruits of this desire for moral regeneration was the Sabbatarian Act of 1781, introduced into the House of Lords by Bishop Porteus. It found its full flowering, however, in the post-war movement for the reform of manners, to which the king himself was easily persuaded to lend his weight. A royal proclamation against vice, profaneness, and immorality was issued in 1787.[146] The emphasis of those involved in this moral crusade was the need for a more zealous application of the laws, particularly those laws controlling popular behaviour. 'The licentiousness designed to be obviated by the Proclamation', a Surrey justice wrote, 'hath its source in a want of attention to the conduct of the lower degree of people'.[147] The tightening-up of the licensing of public houses and prosecution of hitherto condoned misdemeanours were seen as vital social reforms in themselves—certainly more important than any tinkering with the poor laws.[148] And the impetus for this movement, it seems clear, was provided by the shock of national defeat.

The same commitment to moral regeneration, often evangelical in tone, can be seen in a host of other reforming endeavours of the period. The widely supported campaign for 'economical reform', financial retrenchment, and administrative efficiency during and after the war owed its strength to this general mood of reformation; so did the less well-supported cry for changes in parliamentary representation.[149] For our present purposes, however, the main aspect to highlight is the campaign for the abolition of the slave trade and slavery itself. There had, of course, been condemnation of slavery before the American conflict; but, perhaps because it was

---

[145] *A Sermon Preached at York on 21ˢᵗ of February, 1781* (York, [1781]), 21.

[146] See Joanna Innes, 'Politics and Morals: The Reformation of Manners Movement in Later Eighteenth-Century England', in Hellmuth (ed.), *Transformation of Political Culture*, 57–118.

[147] William Man Godshall, *A General Plan of Parochial and Provincial Police* (London, 1787), p. viii.

[148] One of the leading lights in the Reformation of Manners movement was the Revd Henry Zouch, who had earlier declared the poor laws to be 'the noblest, the most perfect system, in the world'. *Remarks upon the Late Resolutions of the House of Commons, Respecting the Proposed Changes of the Poor Laws* (Leeds, [1776]), 54.

[149] See below, Ch. 6.

acknowledged as a major source of national prosperity, it was not seriously challenged. In the aftermath of defeat the slave trade looked less defensible, not least because national prosperity—or at least the 'luxury' that it generated—appeared to many as part of the problem. If slavery, which was productive of so much profit and luxury, had played a significant part in bringing divine disfavour on Britain, then the time had come for it to be abandoned.[150] It was no coincidence, surely, that the first petition to Parliament on the subject was presented in 1783.

'Quite a Military Rage'

Britain has been portrayed as one of the least militaristic countries in eighteenth-century Europe;[151] and there is contemporary testimony that would seem to sustain the claim. In the Seven Years War, the Revd John Brown published an influential work which argued that, under the influence of a Francophile aristocracy, the nation was growing soft and effeminate and losing the manly virtues that produced military strength.[152] The British experience in the American war, however, hardly bears out Brown's picture of a fading martial tradition. The war, as we shall see, divided British and Irish political opinion, and the issues surrounding military and naval mobilization were hotly contested;[153] yet even opponents of the American aspect of the conflict, who often feared the growth of the regular army, the professionalization of the militia, and the rise of a military despotism, seem to have shared in what can only be described as a military mania. 'There is quite a military *rage* just now', Lady Louisa Conolly wrote in April 1778, 'and I believe one must go a little with the torrent'.[154]

This enthusiasm for things military was not particularly apparent in the early years of the war. Newspapers and periodicals carried, of course, accounts of military operations in America, often illustrated with maps and topographical drawings; but surviving diaries, journals, and letters suggest that it was not until the eve of the Bourbon

---

[150] Colley, *Britons*, 352–3.
[151] André Corvisier, *Armies and Societies in Europe 1494–1789* (Bloomington, Ind., 1979), ch. 6.
[152] *An Estimate of the Manners and Principles of the Times* (2 vols., London, 1757).
[153] See below, Ch. 4.   [154] *Correspondence of Leinster*, ed. Fitzgerald, iii. 273.

war, and invasion threatened, that military matters captured the public's imagination. The Revd Gilbert White, author of *The Natural History of Selbourne*, kept a journal devoted mainly to weather conditions and observations on local flora and fauna. Between the outbreak of the fighting and May 1778, he made no reference to the war. Thereafter it features regularly, with entries covering the royal inspection of the navy at Spithead; Rodney's defeat of the Spanish fleet in January 1780; Spanish prisoners at Winton; Cornwallis's victory at Guilford Court House; the 'bloody & obstinate engagement' between the British and the Dutch off Dogger bank; Cornwallis's surrender at Yorktown; naval operations in the West Indies; and the siege of Gibraltar.[155] On a more practical level, the Duke of Richmond, though determinedly hostile to conflict with the Americans, showed great enthusiasm in 1778 for his duties as colonel of the Sussex militia,[156] and in 1779 he led the way in forming volunteer companies throughout the county.[157] Even William Jones, the noted oriental scholar and lawyer, and another critic of the coercion of the rebel colonists, expressed his willingness in 1778 to exchange his lawyer's clothes for a redcoat should the need arise; two years later he went further, and formed his own volunteer company from amongst the barristers and students of his Inn of Court.[158]

Indeed, the embodying of the militia in England and Wales, and the formation of fencible regiments in Scotland and then volunteer corps throughout the British Isles, were important stimulants to this new enthusiasm. Not only did this mobilization of part-time and amateur soldiers put many more Britons and Irishmen into uniform, it also excited considerable interest among the wider public. In May 1778, when the newly embodied Northamptonshire militia was inspected, Lord Althorp noted the 'great number of people who notwithstanding the rain came to see the review'.[159] Scottish minister James Wodrow was himself a witness to the intensive training of the fenciblemen stationed near the Clyde estuary that September, and he wrote admiringly of the way in which they had been kept 'in

[155] *Journals of Gilbert White*, ed. Walter Johnson (London, 1982 edn.), 140, 156, 158, 164, 171, 177, 182, 187, 190, 198–9.
[156] *The Letters of Edward Gibbon*, ed. J. E. Norton (3 vols., London, 1956), ii. 187.
[157] HO 42/205, fos. 156–8.
[158] *The Letters of Sir William Jones*, ed. Garland Cannon (2 vols., Oxford, 1970), i. 264, 408.   [159] BL, Althorp Papers, F8, Althorp to Lady Spencer, 22 May 1778.

the field for 8 hours every day for many weeks past'.[160] The following year, when a volunteer corps was formed in Bath, George
Wansey applauded 'this Military Spirit' and looked forward to its
being 'once again well established in the Land'.[161] By 1782 John
Mells, a customs officer in Lincolnshire, was filling his journal or
day-book with extracts from newspapers relating to even the most
trivial military happening, such as the loading of equipment and
stores into wagons at the Tower of London 'for the use of the several
regiments going into Camp next Month'.[162]

The camps created across southern and eastern England between
1778 and 1782, when invasion, or at least an enemy landing, seemed
a distinct possibility, became, in fact, one of the main focuses of
public interest in things military.[163] The first camps were set up to
protect the vital naval bases at Portsmouth, Plymouth, and Chatham;
inland at Winchester, Salisbury, and West Stowe, near Bury St
Edmunds, from where troops, especially cavalry, could move as
required; and at Coxheath, near Maidstone, and Warley Common,
close to Brentwood, to block any advance on London from either the
south or the east. In 1779 further camps were formed at Cavenham
Heath, near Newmarket, and Westfield, near Hastings. The next
year saw the establishment of several camps in and around London
as a result of the Gordon Riots, and of more along the south coast
(Gosport, Brixham, and Playden Heights, close to Rye) or further to
defend the approaches to the capital (Waterdown, near Tunbridge
Wells, and Tiptree Heath and Danbury in Essex). In 1781 Lenham
Heath, in Kent, was added to the list, and in 1782 camps appeared
near Yarmouth and Beccles in Suffolk in response to the Dutch
entry into the war.[164]

The larger camps, in particular, proved a great attraction. Coxheath
drew large crowds: in August 1779 the review of the Somerset militia
was watched by 'a vast concourse of spectators'.[165] Richard Hayes, a
farmer from Cobham in Kent, was as keen as anyone to see the

---

[160] Dr Williams's Library, Wodrow-Kenrick Correspondence, MS 24157 (65).
[161] Wiltshire RO, Wansey Papers, 314/4/2, Wansey to Laurence, 1 Oct. 1779.
[162] Lincolnshire Archives Office, Misc. Don. 681/1, Journal of John Mells, 13 Apr.
1782.
[163] The Irish camps also attracted some interest, though not as much, it seems, as those
in England. See *Caledonian Mercury*, 9 Sept. 1778, for an account of the mock battle at
Clonmel Camp.
[164] John Houlding, *Fit for Service: The Training of the British Army, 1715–1795*
(Oxford, 1981), 330.   [165] *Morning Post, and Daily Advertiser*, 12 Aug. 1779.

encampment, even though he was opposed to the war against the Americans. Climbing a neighbouring hill, he and a companion could 'see it with ye naked eye very plain', but by using 'long spy glasses' they could pick out details of the layout, which the fascinated Hayes proceeded to record in his diary.[166] An inspection by an eminent figure naturally added to public interest. In October 1778 'almost all Sarum [Salisbury] & its neighbourhood sallied forth' to enjoy the spectacle of the 'Grand review' of the troops by Lord Amherst, the commander-in-chief. 'It was . . . a glorious day for the Turnpike', one observer noted, 'as I believe the cavalcade of Coaches Chaises Waggons, Carts, Horses &c extended near 2 Miles'.[167]

Even those who did not themselves visit the tented towns could fall prey to this version of camp fever. Newspapers both stimulated and catered for public interest by running regular items of 'Camp Intelligence'. These reports, it should be added, were not usually narrowly focused on news of local militia regiments; they presented readers with every scrap of information and gossip. In August 1779, for example, a Chester newspaper carried a report on the large number of sutlers and shopkeepers servicing Coxheath, while a York paper told its readers all about the reviews at Warley and Winchester.[168] Even Scottish and Irish papers carried items on the main camps in England.[169] The London and provincial stage, furthermore, put on entertainments inspired by Warley and Coxheath. A musical comedy, *The Camp*, written by Richard Brinsley Sheridan, with music by Thomas Linley, opened at Drury Lane on 15 October 1778 and was performed fifty-seven times that season. It appeared in Bristol as well.[170] At Sadler's Wells in July 1779 an entertainment was presented 'consisting of singing, dancing, and decorations, called A Trip to Coxheath, with a distant view of the Camp'. The following month, the performance of *Romeo and Juliet* at the Theatre Royal, Richmond Green, was supplemented by 'the New Pantomime Entertainment, call'd Harlequin Volunteer; Or,

---

[166] Reading University Library, KEN 3/1/1, Diary of Richard Hayes, 21 June 1778.
[167] Huntington Library, MS HM 54457, vol. 6, Diary of John Marsh, 1 Oct. 1778.
[168] *Adams's Weekly Courant*, 10 Aug. 1779; *York Courant*, 27 Oct. 1778.
[169] e.g. *Caledonian Mercury*, 10 Aug., 9, 21, 28, 30 Sept. 1778; 11, 25 Aug., 27 Oct. 1779; *Belfast News-letter*, 14–18, 25–8 Aug., 28 Aug.–1 Sept., 1–4, 4–8 Sept. 1778; 24–7 Aug., 10–14, 24–8 Sept., 26–9 Oct. 1779.
[170] Philip H. Highfill, Jr., et al., *A Biographical Dictionary of Actors, Actresses, Dancers, Managers and Other Stage Personnel in London, 1660–1800* (16 vols., Carbondale, Ill., 1973–93), xiii. 310.

a trip to Coxheath', which included 'new Scenes and Machinery, particularly a perspective of the Camp at Coxheath'.[171] Other forms of artistic endeavour likewise owed their origins to the camps. Philippe de Loutherbourg, who designed and painted the scenery for Sheridan's musical comedy, produced a series of magnificent pictures of George III's visit to Warley, including the review and mock battle. At a less distinguished level, cartoons were published celebrating the attractions of Coxheath, the very name of which gave ample scope for sexual allusion.[172] In literary terms, the camps brought forth in 1779 the novel *Coxheath Camp*, produced by 'A Lady'; together with satires such as the anonymous *Camp Guide* and George Huddesford's *Warley*, both published in 1778. Even William Tasker's *Ode to the Warlike Genius of Great Britain* highlighted the role of the camps.[173]

Literature and the Arts

These responses to the camps were, of course, merely one aspect of the way in which the war affected literature and the arts. The American conflict did not, it must be said, bring forth any new artistic genre. There was no equivalent of the First World War poetry of Wilfred Owen, Rupert Brooke, and Siegfried Sassoon, nor of the Second World War 'real life' documentary films of Humphrey Jennings and Roy Boulting. There was not even anything comparable to the flood of narratives from humble participants that came in and after the Napoleonic Wars (interestingly, one of the few common soldiers to pen an account of the American war published it during this later struggle).[174]

Yet the American war made its mark. Unsurprisingly, given the expansion of the regular armed forces, the embodying of the militia, and the creation of volunteer corps, it led to the publication of much technical literature—treatises on infantry and cavalry tactics and

---

[171] *Morning Post, and Daily Advertiser*, 26 July, 11 Aug. 1779.
[172] e.g. BM 5523, 'A Trip to Cocks Heath'.
[173] [William Tasker], *Ode to the Warlike Genius of Great Britain* (London, 1778), 18, 19; see also 7, 12. For more on the cultural impact of the camps see Gillian Russell, *The Theatre of War: Performance, Politics and Society, 1793–1815* (Oxford, 1995), 33–46.
[174] Roger Lamb, *An Original and Authentic Journal* (Dublin, 1809); id., *Memoir* (Dublin, 1811).

organization; advice for young officers; and manuals on courts martial and military finance.[175] Reforming tracts also appeared, recom-
mending changes in the pay and recruitment of the army,[176] or the
greater use of tourniquets to save the lives of wounded sailors.[177]
Nor was there any shortage of narratives of the conflict intended for
a general readership, even if they were produced by officers rather
than the rank and file. William Carter, a subaltern in the Fortieth
Foot in the early stages of the war in America, produced an account
of the siege of Boston and operations at New York, apparently based
on letters that he had written at the time.[178] Banastre Tarleton, who
contested Liverpool in the 1784 election, published in 1787 a narrative of his services in the southern campaigns in the rebel colonies,
which provoked an angry response from a fellow officer and then
brought forth a defence by a former colleague.[179] John Graves
Simcoe, a British officer appointed to lead the American loyalist
Queen's Rangers, published his journal of the war in 1787,[180] while
the siege of Gibraltar was responsible for a crop of accounts, the
most famous of which was by John Drinkwater, who had been a
captain in the Manchester Regiment.[181] These officer narratives
were often politically motivated—Tarleton's *History* was probably
designed to support his parliamentary ambitions; the subtext of
some of the Gibraltar journals was that the Rock should never be

[175] e.g. Benet Cuthbertson, *System for the Complete Interior Management and Oeconomy
of a Battalion of Infantry* (London, 1776); Richard Hinde, *Discipline of the Light-Horse*
(London, 1778); Robert Donkin, *Military Collections and Remarks* (New York, 1777);
Thomas Simes, *Military Guide for Young Officers* (London, 1776); Stephen Payne Ayde,
Treatise on Courts Martial (London, 1778); John Williamson, *Treatise of Military Finance*
(London, 1782).

[176] Thomas Erskine, *Observations on the Prevailing Abuses in the British Army* (London,
1775); anon., *New System for the Establishment, Cloathing, Provisions . . . of the Army*
(London, 1775).

[177] James Rymer, *Observations and Remarks Respecting the More Effectual Means of
Preservation of Wounded Seamen and Marines* (London, 1780).

[178] William Carter, *A Genuine Detail of the Several Engagements, Positions and Movements of the Royal and American Armies, during the Years 1775 and 1776* (London, 1784).

[179] Banastre Tarleton, *History of the Campaigns of 1780 and 1781, in the Southern
Provinces of North America* (London, 1787); Roderick Mackenzie, *Strictures on Lt. Col.
Tarleton's History* (London, 1787); George Hanger, *An Address to the Army in Reply to
Strictures, by Roderick Mackenzie* (London, 1789).

[180] J. G. Simcoe, *A Journal of the Operations of the Queen's Rangers* (Exeter, 1787).

[181] *A Description of Gibraltar, with an Account of . . . Every Thing Remarkable . . . Since
the Commencement of the Spanish War* (London, 1782); *An Authentic and Accurate Journal
of the Late Siege of Gibraltar* (London, n.d.); John Drinkwater, *A History of the Late Siege
of Gibraltar* (London, 1785).

given up—but at least some of the authors had literary as well as political pretensions.

Beyond this type of output, there was a good deal of other material that bore the imprint of the war. This, of course, was only to be expected. Then as now, artists and writers sought to reflect topical concerns in their work, as well as comment on eternal themes. An obvious *pièce d'occasion* was the *New Naval Ode* for 1780 by James Hook, the resident organist and composer at Vauxhall Gardens, where it was sung before a large and socially mixed audience.[182] Musical comedies were also prone to capitalize on the interests of the moment: hence Edward Neville's *Plymouth in an Uproar* of 1779 and Frederick Pilon's *The Invasion, or a Trip to Brighthelmstone* (1778), *The Liverpool Prize* (1779), and *The Siege of Gibraltar* (1780), all of which were performed at Covent Garden. But more elevated forms of artistic endeavour were not slow to draw on the war. The *Gentleman's Magazine* regularly carried new poetic offerings, and between 1775 and 1783 a significant proportion was directly inspired by the conflict. Amongst the more eye-catching were the piece to the memory of a subaltern killed at Bunker Hill; an ode, addressed to General Gage, entitled 'Lord Ch[atha]m's Prophecy'; another on 'The Genius of Britain to Gen. Howe, the Night before the battle of Long Island'; verses on the appearance of the combined fleet off Plymouth, in Latin and English translation; and a celebration of the thwarting of the besiegers of Gibraltar.[183] These works were anonymous, or by little-known poets; but the more famous also seized the opportunities presented by the dramatic events of the war. George Crabbe included references to the conflict in his poems *The Candidate* (1780) and *The Village* (1782), while in *The Library* (1781), his musings on history and the rise and fall of nations is surely influenced by Britain's contemporary difficulties ('And foes join foes to triumph in her fall').[184] William Cowper was more explicit, writing verses on 'The Trial of Admiral Keppel', 'An Address to the Mob on Occasion of the Late Riot at the House of Sir Hugh Palliser', and 'On the Victory gained by Sir George Rodney

---

[182] *London Chronicle*, 18–20 May 1780.

[183] *Gentleman's Magazine*, 45 (1775), 396; 46 (1776), 228; 47 (1777), 80; 49 (1779), 463; 52 (1782), 495, 542.

[184] George Crabbe, *Poems*, ed. Adolphus William Ward (3 vols., Cambridge, 1905–7), i. 84, 113, 132–5.

over the Spanish Fleet off Gibraltar in 1780'. His *Table Talk* of 1782 included criticism of

> Gen'rals who will not conquer when they may
> Firm friends to peace, to pleasure, and good pay

which was presumably directed at Howe and Clinton; while his poem 'The Modern Patriot' was a scathing attack on those who encouraged and abetted rebellion in America and wished 't'would come . . . A little nearer home'. In the loss of the *Royal George*, with most of its crew, including the much-admired Admiral Kempenfelt, Cowper perhaps found the most suitable subject for his melancholic turn of mind.[185] Anna Seward, the Lichfield poetess, published in 1781 a *Monody on Major André*, condemning the execution of one of her friends by the Americans;[186] Thomas Day, once part of the same literary circle, wrote *The Desolation of America*, which sought to persuade its readers of the particular horror of a contest against fellow subjects;[187] and Dr Johnson, a staunch supporter of coercion, made scathing references to prominent opponents of the war in his *Temple of Fashion*.[188]

Prose writing was affected by the war as well. William Robertson had apparently decided to bring out his multi-volume *History of America* only once he had completed the whole work, but the great public interest in the colonies stimulated by the conflict encouraged him to publish the first two volumes in 1777.[189] Moreover, when the war ended unsuccessfully for Britain, he concluded that he must drop the project altogether: 'alas America is lost to the Empire and to me', he wrote in 1784, 'and what would have been a good introduction to the settlement of the British Colonies, will suit very ill the establishment of Independent States'.[190] On another level, we can see that Fanny Burney's *Evelina* (1778), though based on

---

[185] *Poems of Cowper*, ed. Baird and Ryskamp, i. 211–12, 221, 246, 408, ii. 17. Vincent Newey, *Cowper's Poetry: A Critical Study and Reassessment* (Liverpool, 1982), 39, emphasizes Cowper's topicality.

[186] *Monody on Major André* (Lichfield, 1781). See below, Ch. 8.

[187] *The Desolation of America: A Poem* (London, 1777).

[188] *The Temple of Fashion: A Poem in Five Parts* (Shrewsbury, 1781), 19, 35, 36.

[189] *Memoirs and Correspondence . . . of Sir Robert Murray Keith*, ed. Mrs Gillespie Smyth (2 vols., London, 1849), ii. 60–1.

[190] Quoted in David Armitage, 'The New World and British Historical Thought: From Richard Hakluyt to William Robertson', in Karen Ordahl Kupperman (ed.), *America in European Consciousness, 1493–1750* (Chapel Hill, NC, 1995), 70.

well-rehearsed criticism of the corrupting influence of sophisticated French culture, and the superiority of plain, sincere Englishness,[191] owed some of its popularity to the intense gallophobia generated by the conflict. More directly, the war influenced the content of some contemporary novels. Samuel Jackson Pratt's *Emma Corbett*, published at Dublin in 1780, is an obvious example. Set during the war, it milked to the full the sentimentality associated with a family divided by the conflict.

Contemporary painting likewise reflected the importance of the struggle. Art historians are inclined to highlight the significance of the Seven Years War rather than the American conflict, not least because the first gave rise to a new style of history and neo-contemporary narrative painting, in which the characters were depicted in modern dress, as in Benjamin West's famous *The Death of General Wolfe*.[192] But the American war played an important part in developing this style of composition. Besides de Loutherbourg's canvases on Warley Camp, there were John Singleton Copley's striking *Death of Major Peirson* (1783), a patriotic tribute to one of Britain's war heroes, killed while expelling a French invasion force from Jersey; the same artist's commemoration of the repulse of the Spanish floating batteries at Gibraltar, commissioned by the Corporation of London; and Joseph Wright of Derby's depiction of the same victory, displayed at Robins's Rooms, Covent Garden, in 1785. Even Benjamin West produced the *Battle of La Hogue* in 1778; the entry of France into the war clearly inspiring this rendition of an earlier triumph over the ancient foe. In Ireland, too, wartime developments provided artistic opportunities. Francis Wheatley produced two impressive canvases in the historical painting style: *View of College Green, with a Meeting of the Volunteers, on 4th November, 1779* and *The Irish House of Commons, 1780*. The first depicted a decisive moment in the struggle for the lifting of restrictions on Irish trade, and the second was in effect a collective portrait of the membership of the Irish legislature, notable for the large number of military uniforms on display, most of them belonging to officers in the various volunteer corps.[193] There were also the numerous

---

[191] See Newman, *Rise of English Nationalism*, 136–9.
[192] See e.g. Albert Boime, *Art in an Age of Revolution 1750–1800* (Chicago, 1987), ch. 2; David H. Solkin, *Painting for Money: The Visual Arts and the Public Sphere in Eighteenth-Century England* (New Haven, 1993), 191–213.
[193] For Irish developments, see below, Ch. 6.

portraits by Reynolds, Romney, Gainsborough, and others of notable figures such as Tarleton, Lord Rawdon, and General Cornwallis.

Engravings brought many contemporary paintings to a wider audience. Reynolds's rendering of Admiral Samuel Barrington, for instance, was engraved by Richard Earlom in 1780; while Tilly Kettle's full-length portrait of Kempenfelt was reproduced both by Earlom and by Robert Pollard in 1782. Pollard, one of the leading London engravers and print-sellers, in the same year also brought out his own version of Nathaniel Hone's picture of George Augustus Elliot, the governor of Gibraltar. William Woollet produced an engraving of West's *Battle of La Hogue* in 1781; John Emes published an etching of James Jeffreys's *The Scene before Gibraltar on the Morning of 14th of September 1782*; and Thomas Stothard's *Death of Lord Robert Manners*, who was killed at the victory at the Saintes, was engraved by John Sherwin in 1786.[194] Cartoons by the likes of Matthew Darly and the young James Gillray similarly highlighted topical themes, such as the alleged rapacity of the Hessian auxiliary troops; the activities of the press-gang; and the British seizure of Omoa from the Spaniards.[195] Equally well pitched to cater for popular taste were the cheap mementoes mass-produced to celebrate events like the acquittal of Admiral Keppel. The potter Josiah Wedgwood, one of the shrewdest businessmen of the age, churned out ceramic heads of the popular naval hero, while at the same time bitterly regretting that he had not been quick enough to profit to an even greater extent from public enthusiasm.[196] Irish linen manufacturers likewise seem to have seized the opportunity to boost their sales by depicting a national hero on their products: a surviving fabric illustrates Lord Charlemont's review of the volunteers at Dublin in 1782.[197]

We can say with some confidence, then, that the war affected many aspects of society and culture in the British Isles. Gender distinctions, while in some respects challenged, were ultimately reinforced

[194] Timothy Clayton, *The English Print 1688–1802* (New Haven, 1997), 240–3.

[195] See BM 5483, 'A Hessian Grenadier'; BM 5609, 'The Liberty of the Subject'; BM 5623, 'The British Tar at Omoa'.

[196] Neil McKendrick, 'Josiah Wedgwood and the Commercialization of the Potteries', in id., John Brewer, and J. H. Plumb, *The Birth of a Consumer Society* (London, 1982), 122.

[197] *1776: The British Story of the American Revolution* [catalogue of the 1776 Exhibition, National Maritime Museum, Greenwich, 14 Apr.–2 Oct. 1976] (London, 1976), 99.

by the conflict. Social mobility, both upward and downward, was observable as the war created opportunities and brought personal disasters. Service in the volunteers had an important social function, improving the social standing of sections of the middling sort within their localities. Social conflict was also a feature of the war years; criticism of the aristocracy and its influence became more vocal, and tensions between manufacturers and their workforces were in some cases exacerbated by wartime conditions. Criminal activity probably declined during the conflict, only to become a cause for great concern amongst property-owners with the demobilization of a large portion of the armed forces at the coming of the peace. Penal policy was influenced by the war, in as much as transportation to the American colonies was no longer an option and an alternative means of punishment had to be found. Reform of the poor laws in England and Wales, encouraged by the desire for public economy, which was itself a consequence of the war, was perhaps linked to the wartime payment of allowances to militiamen's families. Reform in other areas seems likewise to have been stimulated by the experience or outcome of the conflict; defeat caused much introspective reflection, leading to a campaign for moral regeneration and increasing criticism of the slave trade. British and Irish society was militarized, not just in the sense that large numbers of adult males went into uniform, but also in that military events fascinated the public. The camps established in southern England to repel an enemy landing were a particular focus of interest. In 1778–9, when invasion fears were at their height, there was a veritable camp mania, with newspapers carrying regular features on the camps and even the London and provincial stage putting on entertainments based on camp life. Artistic endeavour generally seems to have been influenced by the struggle. The war provided a subject for prose and poetry, for paintings and engravings, and for mass-produced artefacts. The impact of the war in these widely varying areas was itself clearly varied, but in all of them it made its mark, further reinforcing the impression that the American conflict, far from being a limited affair that impinged very little on life within the British Isles, was a deeply intrusive event.

4
Divisions within the Whole

'THERE DOES NOT perhaps occur in the annals of Britain a single instance of a war more popular at its commencement than that which fatally took place between Great Britain and her colonies.'[1] This assessment, while published long after the events described, accords well with the views of many of those contemporary politicians at Westminster who opposed the war. They had no doubt that they were in a decided minority. 'We are not only *patriots out of place*', Sir George Savile told the Marquis of Rockingham in January 1777, 'but patriots out *of the opinion of the public.*'[2] Rockingham himself was equally gloomy: 'This Country is altogether as determined as the Ministers, to continue the Pursuit of measures which must end fatally'; nothing could be achieved, he wrote, 'till the Publick are actually convinced of the calamitous State we are in'.[3] Only when the Yorkshire Association tapped into a rich vein of discontent at the very end of 1779 and early 1780 did members of the parliamentary opposition sense that the tide was turning.[4] The 1780 British general election was a complicated affair, with the opposition parties experiencing both gains and losses; but in those constituencies where public opinion counted—namely the counties and larger boroughs—government candidates fared badly. With the surrender of Cornwallis at Yorktown the public and parliamentary clamour for an end to the fighting across the Atlantic became irresistible. As an opposition MP wrote on 13 December 1781, 'every Body seems really sick of carrying on ye American War'.[5]

---

[1] Thomas Somerville, *My Own Life and Times 1741–1814*, ed. Richard B. Sher (Bristol, 1996), 187.
[2] *Memoirs of the Marquis of Rockingham*, ed. Earl of Albemarle (2 vols., London, 1852), ii. 305.
[3] Nottingham University Library, Portland Papers, PWF 9109 and 9117.
[4] See below, Ch. 7.
[5] Leeds Archives, Ramsden Papers, Rockingham Letters, vol. 2c, William Weddell to Rockingham, 13 Dec. 1781.

Until recently, historians readily accepted this interpretation of public attitudes.[6] The emphasis was on change brought about by wartime developments, rather than an ongoing struggle between two diametrically opposed viewpoints. It was assumed that the conflict was generally supported at its outset, and that public opinion began to shift after Saratoga and then dramatically turned against continuing the struggle in America after Yorktown. Only when a long and expensive war produced British defeats and humiliations instead of the anticipated victory, in other words, did the attempt to subdue the American rebellion become unpopular. But the work of James Bradley has made it clear that even in the early stages of the war there was considerable opposition to the use of military force against the colonists. Bradley analysed the anti-war petitions and pro-war addresses sent in by many boroughs, counties, and corporate bodies in 1775 and 1776, and found that the number of signatures against the war exceeded those in its favour.[7] This, to be sure, is an inexact guide to the state of public opinion, but at the very least it suggests that the parliamentary opponents of the conflict were unduly pessimistic about the strength of their support in the country at large. Kathleen Wilson's research has similarly revealed strong and consistent opposition to the war in several urban centres, particularly her two case studies, Newcastle and Norwich.[8]

These new findings do not, of course, mean that we should now assume that public opinion as a whole was at all times more inclined to conciliation and peace with America than to coercion and war against the colonies. John Wilkes, like many radical opponents of the war, was much more confident than the Rockinghamites of public support, but when he claimed in March 1776 that parliamentary reform was plainly necessary because an unrepresentative House of Commons was allowing the ministry to pursue the war against the wishes of the people, he could offer no evidence to sustain this assertion.[9] Given the patchy information available to us, it will surely never be possible to provide any definitive verdict on the relative strengths of the pro- and anti-war parties. What emerges

---

[6] See e.g. Dora Mae Clark, *British Opinion and the American Revolution* (New Haven, 1930); Charles R. Ritcheson, *British Politics and the American Revolution* (Norman, Okla., 1954), esp. 227–9.

[7] James E. Bradley, *Popular Politics and the American Revolution in England* (Macon, Ga., 1986), 65–9, 137. See also id., *Religion, Revolution and English Radicalism* (Cambridge, 1990), ch. 9.

[8] Kathleen Wilson, *The Sense of the People: Politics, Culture and Imperialism in England, 1715–1785* (Cambridge, 1995).   [9] See below, Ch. 6.

most clearly from recent scholarship is not the preponderance of one side or the other, but the deep division over the justice and necessity of the conflict. It might legitimately be said that at the level of high politics this division was sometimes less bitter and disruptive than it appeared. Differences over America did not stop Lord North's beleaguered ministry putting out feelers to the opposition in 1779 and 1780 with a view to broadening the basis of the administration. And it was quite possible for the Earl of Pembroke and the Earl of Denbigh, who adopted diametrically opposed opinions on the American war, to maintain a friendly, even occasionally light-hearted, correspondence on the subject.[10] But the polite forms of aristocratic exchange should not obscure the very real hostility generated within the British Isles by the conflict with the colonists. Negotiations between the Rockingham opposition and North broke down in 1780 precisely because Rockingham's terms exposed the irreconcilable gap between the two parties. He demanded the removal of the ministers most closely associated with the conduct of the war, and the acknowledgement of American Independence— neither of which North could be expected to accept.[11] Denbigh, moreover, while perfectly polite in his dealings with Pembroke, was rather less restrained when he argued that imprisoning a few oppo-sition peers in the Tower for treason would do more to quell the rebellion than a defeat of the American army.[12] At the level of popular politics similarly violent language was used. In July 1779, at a dinner for the Enniskillen volunteers, one of the toasts was 'May the King's evil counsellors be speedily brought to the block'.[13] And on occasion the temperature reached boiling point. 'My father', Abigail Frost of Nottingham wrote in her diary for 1777, 'had a dispute with Mr Robert Denison at the Exchange hall about giving "General Washington" for a toast, Sep 29; my father got upon the table, crossed it, and leaned on Mr. R. Denison's shoulder and crushed him down to the floor.'[14] The following December a

[10] See Marion Balderston and David Syrett (eds.), *The Lost War: Letters from British Officers during the American Revolution* (New York, 1975), 203–5.

[11] Ian R. Christie, 'The Marquis of Rockingham and Lord North's Offer of a Coalition, June–July 1780', *English Historical Review*, 69 (1954), 388–407; Frank O'Gorman, *The Rise of Party in England: The Rockingham Whigs 1760–1782* (London, 1975), 423–4.

[12] HMC, *Denbigh MSS* (London, 1911), 298.

[13] *Belfast News-letter*, 27–30 July 1779.

[14] *The Diary of Abigail Gawthern*, ed. Adrian Henstock (Thoroton Society Record Series, vol. xxxiii, Nottingham, 1980), 33.

'considerable clothier' in the West Riding of Yorkshire was tarred and feathered 'for drinking Gen. Washington's health in a public company'.[15] The purpose of this chapter is to analyse this division within Britain and Ireland, looking first to see whether a geographical pattern can be discerned, and then examining the political, social, and religious backgrounds of the two sides. Once these matters have been considered, attention can then be turned to the issues of contention themselves.

National and Regional Variations

Contemporary opponents of the conflict with the Americans sometimes called it 'a *Scots* war'.[16] The purpose of this jibe was to highlight the part played by the Scots and their enthusiasm for the government's line. The claim, while exaggerated and therefore misleading, was not without substance. Of all the countries and regions of the British Isles, Scotland perhaps came the nearest to unanimity on the American issue. To a considerable extent, it seems, Scottish opinion supported the war. Loyal addresses flooded in from the Scottish counties and burghs—more than seventy in all between September 1775 and February 1776. Scotland, in other words, produced as many addresses in favour of the war as England, and this at a time when England's population was about five times as large.[17] And while there were many English petitions calling for reconciliation, and condemning the war, there was none from Scotland.[18] True, the Scottish addresses carried very few signatures, and so cannot be taken as infallible guides to Scottish opinion. There was certainly Scottish opposition to the war. James Boswell, Dr Johnson's biographer, for instance, who described himself as 'more & more an American' in August 1775, thought North's government 'mad in undertaking this desperate war';[19] and at one stage it seemed that a petition opposing the conflict might be drawn up in Glasgow.[20] The Church of Scotland was more divided than the loyal messages emanating

---

[15] *Leeds Intelligencer*, 16 Dec. 1777.   [16] *Caledonian Mercury*, 7 Jan. 1778.

[17] Linda Colley, *Britons: Forging the Nation 1707–1837* (New Haven, 1992), 140.

[18] None, that is, once the war had started. For Glasgow's conciliatory petition of Jan. 1775 see below, Ch. 8.

[19] *The Correspondence of James Boswell and William Johnson Temple*, i, ed. Thomas Crawford (Edinburgh, 1997), 394.   [20] See below, Ch. 8.

from its synodical meetings suggested, with the evangelical Popular Party inclining towards opposition to the war against the Americans.[21] Scotland's Presbyterian Seceders tended also to be critical of coercion of the colonists. In October 1779 General James Adolphus Oughton, the commander-in-chief in North Britain, reported that 'a great number of the dissenting ministers and several of the established clergy are avowedly republicans and Americans'.[22] But most of the available evidence tends to strengthen the case for considering the Scots as very largely in favour of coercion of the colonists. James Wodrow, Church of Scotland minister at Stevenston, Ayrshire, claimed in August 1775 that, having travelled extensively throughout the Lowlands that summer, 'I do not think there is one in a hundred of us who has not espoused the side of Govt. or ventures to speak in favour of the Americans'. Two years later his fraction was different, but the message was essentially the same: 'In Scotland I am sure nineteen twentyeth parts . . . of the people are on the side of Govt. in the present unhappy Quarrel'.[23] As William Drennan, an Ulster Presbyterian opponent of the conflict wrote from Edinburgh in January 1778: 'Every order of Men from the highest to the Lowest, are emptying their Pockets . . . in the support of the war'.[24]

In Ireland the Protestant population for the most part took the opposite view. Expressions of hostility to the conflict came from Protestants in Dublin, Belfast, and Cork in 1775 and 1776; the petition to the king from the freeholders, freemen, and merchants of Dublin carried 3,000 signatures.[25] But in Ireland opinion was by no means so heavily weighted on one side as in Scotland. There was a significant number of Protestants who favoured coercion. A petition against the war might have emanated from Cork in the summer of 1776, but the city's leading lights had drawn up a loyal address, 'declaring our abhorrence of the American rebellion', only a few months earlier.[26] In the Dublin Parliament a two-to-one majority of MPs rejected an attempt to insert an anti-war passage in the loyal

---

[21] See Robert Kent Donovan, 'The Popular Party of the Church of Scotland and the American Revolution', in R. B. Sher and J. R. Smitten (eds.), *Scotland and America in the Age of the Enlightenment* (Edinburgh, 1990), 81–99.   [22] SP 54/47, fos. 342–3.
[23] Dr Williams's Library, Wodrow-Kenrick Correspondence, MS 24157(52) and (58).
[24] PRONI, Drennan Letters, T 765/1/20.
[25] R. B. McDowell, *Ireland in the Age of Imperialism and Revolution 1760–1801* (Oxford, 1979), 242–3.
[26] Richard Caulfield (ed.), *The Council Book of the Corporation of the City of Cork* (Guildford, 1876), 906.

address at the opening of the new session in October 1775.[27] Two years later, Lieutenant-Colonel Arthur Browne, MP for County Mayo, spoke for a sizeable—if fluctuating—body of Protestant opinion when he declared that Irishmen should 'strain every Nerve to reduce them [the Americans] to a proper submission'.[28] Catholic Ireland, moreover, seems largely to have been inclined to loyalty. Admittedly, as in the Protestant community, there was division: some members of the Catholic ecclesiastical hierarchy were doubtful about the extent to which the church should associate itself with the state authorities in Dublin and London.[29] But addresses in support of the war, and offering material assistance, were submitted by leading members of the Catholic community at regular intervals. The Catholic Committee, for instance, drew up a loyal address in July 1779, when invasion threatened; another in December 1780, on the outbreak of the Dutch war; and a further one in April 1782, when the arrival of a new lord-lieutenant provided the opportunity for a fresh profession 'of inviolable attachment to our most gracious sovereign, his family and government, and our unabating zeal for the success of his majestys arms'.[30]

Wales was likewise divided. There were some notable and well-known champions of the American cause. Richard Price, David Williams, and William Jones come readily to mind. All three published works supporting the colonists and opposing the war—Price's *Observations on the Nature of Civil Liberty* (1776), Williams's *Letters on Political Liberty* (1782), and Jones's *Letter to a Patriot Senator* (1783). But the temptation to see this trio as representative of a broadly based Welsh sympathy for the Americans should be resisted. They were living in London during the war, not in Wales. The evidence from Wales itself is more mixed. The North administration's attempts to squeeze additional revenue from the crown's lands in the principality, as we have seen, provoked fierce resistance.[31] John Lloyd railed against 'our diabolical, cursed Ministers, God damn them all'.[32] But this was not necessarily an indication of

---

[27] *Journals of the House of Commons . . . of Ireland*, xvii. 10.
[28] *An Edition of the Cavendish Irish Parliamentary Diary 1776–1778*, ed. Anthony R. Black (3 vols., Delavan, Wis., 1984), ii. 201.
[29] Eamon O'Flaherty, 'Ecclesiastical Politics and the Dismantling of the Penal Laws in Ireland, 1774–1782', *Irish Historical Studies*, 26 (1988–9), 33–50.
[30] R. Dudley Edwards, (ed.), 'Minute Book of the Catholic Committee, 1773–1792', *Archivium Hibernicum*, 9 (1942), 39, 41, 55, 68.   [31] See above, Ch. 2.
[32] NLW, Wigfair MS 12423C, Lloyd to his mother, 5 Dec. 1778.

widespread pro-Americanism. There were Welsh ballads published at this time that opposed the war;[33] but others were sharply critical of the Americans: William Williams, for instance, attacked their materialism and use of slave labour, while Dafydd Samwell urged ancient Britons to draw their swords in support of the crown.[34] In truth, Wales, though divided, was perhaps less excited by the conflict than any other country in the British Isles. A roll of freemen in Llantrisant, Glamorgan, annotated in 1778 for the electoral use of the borough's patron, Lord Mountstuart, identifies just one freeman with views on the American war ('zealously in the interest of the Americans, furious railer against his king and country & as far a rebel as a man can be that has not actually taken up arms against his Prince'); the remaining 114 are simply described in terms of their local connections and obligations.[35] More generally, it should be noted that only three formal expressions of Welsh opinion were sent to the crown in the course of the war, half the number that the principality's population might lead one to expect, if a comparison is made with England.[36]

England was the scene of great activity. Bradley has calculated that more than 44,000 Englishmen were directly involved in petitioning or addressing the crown on America between 1775 and 1778.[37] The northern counties tended to be behind the government. Lancashire, in particular, displayed considerable enthusiasm for the war. Nearly 6,500 Lancastrians signed the county's address, and in Bolton 1,600 of the inhabitants put their names to the town's loyal submission. East Anglia, by contrast, was something of a stronghold of the opponents of the American aspect of the war. True, coercive addresses as well as conciliatory petitions were submitted by Great Yarmouth, Colchester, and Cambridge, and Sudbury produced a loyal address only. But when the Norfolk gentry stirred themselves, they were able to secure 5,400 signatures on their anti-war petition of 1778, a substantial demonstration of the feelings of the county.[38]

[33] J. H. Davies, *A Bibliography of Welsh Ballads Printed in the Eighteenth Century* (London, 1911), pp. xvii and 100–1.

[34] Geraint H. Jenkins, *The Foundations of Modern Wales 1642–1780* (Oxford, 1987), 321–2.

[35] J. Barry Davies, *The Freemen and Ancient Borough of Llantrisant* (Gloucester, 1989), 111. The annotated roll is now NLW, Bute MS 2505.

[36] For the reported indifference of the Welsh to the American war see below, Ch. 5.

[37] Bradley, *Religion, Revolution and English Radicalism*, 319.

[38] For the background to this petition see below, p. 156.

In most regions of England, however, the picture was much more complicated and defies easy categorization. Five counties and twenty-one boroughs submitted both anti-war petitions and pro-war addresses—a clear indication that many communities were divided within themselves. Even in Lancashire a conciliatory petition was signed by around 4,000 inhabitants.[39] A geographical approach, then, takes us only so far. To understand more about the nature of the great divide over America, we need to consider how far it reflected pre-war fault lines. The political, social, and religious backgrounds of the antagonists need to be explored.

The War and Existing Divisions

At the level of high politics, the split over the American war was based on the existing divisions between government and opposition parties. There were, to be sure, some changes of allegiance that can be attributed to the conflict across the Atlantic. Lord North's government lost the support of the Duke of Grafton, the lord privy seal, who resigned in October 1775. According to the bishop of Worcester, Grafton justified himself by arguing that it was now too late to crush the rebellion because 'the Americans [were] too strong' and all the colonies in arms. The government, in Grafton's view, now had no choice but to 'repeal all the Acts they complain of, & restore everything to the state it was in, in 1762'.[40] Several of Grafton's close friends and associates defected to the opposition at the same time: John Crewe, MP for Cheshire; Hugo Meynell, MP for Stafford; Richard Hopkins, MP for Dartmouth; and Charles Fitzroy Scudamore, MP for Thetford. The following month the Earl of Upper Ossory, MP for Bedfordshire, and his brother the Hon. Richard Fitzpatrick, MP for Tavistock, also joined the opposition.[41]

---

[39] Bradley, *Religion, Revolution and English Radicalism*, 319, 334.

[40] Bodleian Library, North MS d. 25, fo. 47.

[41] Ossory was greatly relieved to be freed from a situation where he was obliged 'to support measures which I totally disapproved' (Bedfordshire RO, Grantham Papers, L30/14). Fitzpatrick, an officer in the Guards, served in America, though he remained opposed to the government's policy; 'having been a witness to all the horrors of this war has made me ten times more violent than ever against it, and I hate the Ministry more cordially than ever for having obliged me to become a sort of instrument (though a feeble one indeed) of injustice, barbarity, and oppression' (Library of Congress, Misc. MSS, Fitzpatrick to his brother, 31 Jan. 1778).

In Ireland, Thomas Conolly, a ministerial supporter on most issues and related by marriage to the Earl of Buckinghamshire, lord-lieutenant from 1776 to 1780, was an outspoken critic of the American conflict.[42] But, for the most part, the war merely intensified an existing party struggle rather than cut across established battle lines. Rockingham argued in November 1777 that his party's opposition to the American war was part and parcel of its opposition to 'the fatal Change of Principles in government, which this reign has introduced'.[43] Similarly, the 'Patriot' opposition in the Irish Parliament, which had much in common with the opposition in Britain, readily saw the colonial crisis as related to their own long-running struggle against the executive power of the administration at Dublin Castle and the British government.[44]

Beyond the two parliaments, the dispute over the war also reflected existing political divisions. Bradley's work has revealed that a significant number of those involved in petitioning for peace in 1775 and 1776 had been involved in the petitioning movement in favour of Wilkes during the Middlesex election dispute in 1769. Just as importantly, we can see that the quarrels over the American war built on long-running tussles for power in many boroughs. In Colchester, for instance, the contest between the corporation and the anti-corporation parties had been a feature of local politics for many years. When the American dispute flared up into armed conflict the corporation sent in an address supporting the government and the anti-corporation party responded by organizing a counter-petition for peace.[45] In Coventry, where the corporation came out in favour of the Americans, supporters of the war denounced the mayor as motivated by the same rebellious principles as the colonists; but if the American issue seemed to polarize local opinion it probably did no more than entrench and embitter the established struggle between the corporation and its critics.[46] The

---

[42] See e.g. *Cavendish Irish Parliamentary Diary*, ed. Black, iii. 270–2.

[43] Nottingham University Library, Portland Papers, PWF 9117. Rockingham may well have exaggerated the consistency of his party. A recent study of the pre-war Rockinghams traces their movement from a court-centred group to a party with a reform programme: W. M. Elofson, *The Rockingham Connection and the Second Founding of the Whig Party, 1768–1773* (Montreal, 1996).

[44] See David Lammey, 'The Growth of the "Patriot Opposition" in Ireland during the 1770s', *Parliamentary History*, 7 (1988), 257–81.

[45] Bradley, *Religion, Revolution and English Radicalism*, 350–1.

[46] John Money, *Experience and Identity: Birmingham and the West Midlands, 1760–1800* (Manchester, 1977), 188.

American war, it could be argued, merely provided new ammunition for the two sides to use against each other.

Was there a social and economic dimension to the division over the conflict with the colonies? Some contemporaries certainly thought that there was. In August 1775, Edmund Burke, a leading Rockinghamite spokesman, believed that most merchants supported the government's line because 'They all, or the greater Number of them, begin to snuff the cadaverous Haut Gout of a Lucrative War. War indeed is become a sort of substitute for Commerce.'[47] On the other side, Lord Suffolk, one of the secretaries of state, wrote from London in June 1775 that the efforts of the 'Americans on this side of the Atlantic' had failed to have any impact on 'the respectable part of the city'; while Lord Barrington, the secretary at war, seems to have believed that the insubordination in the colonies had spread to the common people in the mother country, amongst whom there was 'a very levelling spirit'.[48] Historians have been no less inclined to identify a social and economic aspect to the political division. Bradley points out that many struggles in local government essentially revolved around the attempts of wealthy corporation members to keep power in their own hands and the efforts of a wider, usually less wealthy, public to increase participation. Given that corporations overwhelmingly backed the government's stance over America, while anti-corporation parties tended to be in favour of peace and conciliation, he argues that it could be said that pro- and anti-war attitudes were related to social and economic status. Indeed, Bradley maintains that the strongest support for coercion came from the elite, especially those defined as gentlemen or professionals, 'whereas shopkeepers and artisans provided the bulk of support for peaceful concessions'.[49] John Sainsbury, having analysed the occupations of the addressers and petitioners in London, came to much the same conclusion: the division was 'to a large extent' socio-economic.[50] Peter Marshall's study of Manchester also suggests that

[47] *The Correspondence of Edmund Burke*, ed. Thomas W. Copeland et al. (10 vols., Cambridge, 1958–78), iii. 191.

[48] HMC, *Stopford Sackville MSS* (2 vols., London, 1904–10), ii. 1; Shute Barrington, *The Political Life of William Wildman Viscount Barrington* (London, 1814), 156.

[49] Bradley, *Religion, Revolution and English Radicalism*, 372.

[50] John A. Sainsbury, *Disaffected Patriots: London Supporters of Revolutionary America* (Kingston, 1987), 119.

social and economic background was an important determinant of support for or opposition to the war.[51]

All of this work, based on comparisons between the signatures on petitions and addresses and entries in directories, poll books, and other local sources, tells us much about the nature of the division within many towns. But increasingly important as urban centres were in the eighteenth-century British Isles, the countryside was still where most of the British and Irish lived and worked. So was the socio-economic pattern discernible in the towns replicated, *mutatis mutandis*, in the rural areas? Not so clearly. There is, to be sure, some anecdotal evidence to suggest that many of the 'middling sort' in the country, as in the towns, were against the war. When a leading clergyman proposed to the Lincolnshire county meeting in August 1779 that a subscription be established 'to strengthen the hands of Government', he was said to have been 'hissed by many of the middling class', which in this context presumably means small freeholders as well as traders and shopkeepers.[52] But Dora Mae Clark's claim that the 'country gentlemen' supported the war at its outset, and turned against it only when it went wrong, is no longer a convincing summary.[53] While the squirearchy undoubtedly became more hostile to the conflict as it began to become ruinously expensive and yet productive of no good results, a significant portion of the rural elite opposed the government's American war from the start. Hampshire's petition for peace carried many more signatures than the county's loyal address.[54] In Berkshire, as we shall see later, prominent landowners were in the forefront of local opposition to coercion, and stress was even laid on the lower social status of many of the loyal addressers.[55] Nor should we forget that the opposition in both the Westminster and Dublin Parliaments included some of the most substantial landowners in Britain and Ireland. The Cavendishes, just to cite one family group in the Rockingham party, owned many thousands of acres in Derbyshire, Lancashire, and Yorkshire.

Opinions on the American war were influenced in many cases by religious affiliation, though care should be taken not to adopt a

---

[51] Peter Marshall, 'Manchester and the American Revolution', *Bulletin of the John Rylands University Library of Manchester*, 62 (1979), 173.

[52] HMC, 15th Report, app. pt. v, *Foljambe MSS* (London, 1897), 151.

[53] Clark, *British Opinion*, esp. 133–5, 141.

[54] Bradley, *Popular Politics and the American Revolution in England*, table 3.3.

[55] See below, Ch. 8.

simplistic religious determinism—tendencies are readily observable, but no religious denomination seems to have been unanimous in its views on the conflict. In Ireland, as we have seen, leading Catholics sought to demonstrate their loyalty, the church hierarchy proclaiming the need to preach fast-day sermons for the success of the British war effort. There were, it must be said, members of the Irish Catholic clergy who were less than fully cooperative, and the mass of the Catholic peasantry were probably nowhere near as enthusiastic about military service as were their social superiors; but this owed more to hostility towards the British as an occupying force than to any sympathy with the Americans. For those Catholics in Ireland who thought about the war in ideological terms, identification with the rebel colonists was unthinkable: they were, as Bishop Troy told the papal nuncio in October 1777, 'calvinistical and republican'; their downfall was therefore an event devoutly to be wished.[56] British Catholics seem to have recognized as clearly as their Irish brethren that the conflict offered an opportunity to prove their attachment to the state and reliability as loyal subjects. William Haggerston Maxwell Constable was keen to ensure that the petition for the relief of Scottish Catholics included a clause 'beging leave for R.C. to be admitted Officers in ye Army or Navy';[57] while Richard Whyte, who offered to form a regiment, pointed to the assistance he expected from 'Roman Catholick Gentlemen of great landed Property in Lancashire & Yorkshire, where I last War raised so many Men, and who now seem very desirous of shewing their Zeal'.[58]

Protestant Dissenters were largely opposed to the conflict. The Independent congregation at Isleham, Cambridgeshire, agreed at its meeting on 19 October 1775 to ask the Lord 'if it is his heavenly will to put an end to this bloody and unnatural war'.[59] Dissenting efforts, however, went beyond prayer. Bradley has shown that throughout England Dissenters played a leading role in promoting petitions in 1775–6.[60] They seem also to have been instrumental in preventing

---

[56] Quoted in Thomas Bartlett, '"A Weapon of War yet Untried": Irish Catholics and the Armed Forces of the Crown, 1760–1830', in T. G. Fraser and Keith Jeffery (eds.), *Men, Women and War* (Historical Studies, vol. xviii, Dublin, 1993), 71.

[57] Hull University Library, Maxwell-Constable Papers, DD EV/60/20B, draft of Constable to ——, 8 Oct. 1778.

[58] BL, Liverpool Papers, Add. MS 38211, fo. 167.

[59] Kenneth A. C. Parsons (ed.), *The Church Book of the Independent Church . . . Isleham 1693–1805* (Cambridgeshire Antiquarian Records Society, vol. vi, Cambridge, 1984), 97–8.

[60] Bradley, *Religion, Revolution and English Radicalism*, esp. 389–95.

the drawing-up and submission of loyal addresses: the town clerk of Tiverton in Devon believed an address might have attracted a large number of signatures had not some of the local Dissenters offered violent opposition and threatened a 'counter-Address'.[61] In Scotland, as we have seen, Presbyterian Seceders were inclined to sympathy with the colonists and to opposition to the American aspect of the war. In Ireland, the Presbyterians were said to be very averse to war against a people who included many co-religionists of Ulster birth.[62] In 1775 the lord-lieutenant described the Ulster Presbyterians as 'in their hearts . . . Americans'.[63] At the beginning of 1778, his successor suggested that the troops in a corps proposed to be raised in Ulster would have to 'be sent on any service rather [than] the American as they would make admirable recruits for Washington'.[64] In June 1782, the Synod of Ulster, the governing body of the Presbyterian Church in the province, sent an address to the king expressing 'gladness' at the recent change of ministry and rejoicing at the 'pleasing prospect' of peace with the Americans.[65] And if Dissenters were conspicuous opponents of the war, Rational Dissenters were perhaps the most outspoken. Richard Price, as we have seen, published his arguments in support of the Americans; Sylas Neville, a young medical student at Edinburgh, hoped fervently for the defeat of British arms;[66] while William Drennan, in a letter to his sister, congratulated the people of Belfast on Burgoyne's surrender.[67]

But there were some notable exceptions to the general rule. Samuel Kenrick, a Worcestershire Dissenter, was convinced that most of his co-religionists were, as a result of their preference for religious liberty, naturally inclined to political liberty. It followed, he argued, that they were opposed to the war against the Americans. Kenrick acknowledged, however, that on this matter 'the protestant dissenters are far from unanimous'. As evidence he cited his 'old

---

[61] *Georgian Tiverton: The Political Memoranda of Beavis Wood*, ed. John Bourne (Devon & Cornwall Record Society, NS, vol. xxix, Torquay, 1986), 29.

[62] See W. H. Crawford (ed.), *Letters from an Ulster Land Agent* (Belfast, 1976), 5.

[63] *The Harcourt Papers*, ed. E. W. Harcourt (14 vols., Oxford, 1880–1905), ix. 363.

[64] NLI, Heron Papers, MS 13036, Buckinghamshire to Heron, 1 Jan. 1778.

[65] Synod of Ulster, *Records of the Synod of Ulster* (3 vols., Belfast, 1890–8), iii. 46.

[66] *The Diary of Sylas Neville*, ed. Basil Cozens-Hardy (Oxford, 1950), 246.

[67] PRONI, Drennan Letters, T 765/1/17. See also Ian McBride, 'William Drennan and the Dissenting Tradition', in David Dickson, Daire Keogh, and Kevin Whelan (eds.), *The United Irishmen: Republicanism, Radicalism and Rebellion* (Dublin, 1993), 48–61.

friend' Job Orton, a Dissenter 'most violently ministerial'.[68] Orton himself was contradictory about the views of Dissenters in general. He claimed on one occasion that Dissenting ministers, apart from those 'in *London, Bristol* and some other populous places', were supportive of the government and critical of the Americans. Yet shortly afterwards he accepted that his own attempts to 'promote loyalty' had made him very unpopular amongst fellow Dissenters.[69] Quakers, on the whole, tried to steer clear of involvement on either side, though their pacifist inclinations made most of them lean towards conciliation. Quakers, we should note, were amongst the Lancashire petitioners of 1775.[70] But the Quaker experience in America could propel their brethren in the British Isles in the opposite direction. Isaac Fletcher of Cumberland expressed sharp criticism of the Americans in his diary, describing them as 'the enemy' and one of their army commanders as 'the rebell general'. His hostility, it seems, was based at least partly on the treatment meted out to the Quakers in seventeenth-century New England, where they had been mercilessly persecuted. In December 1778 Fletcher was reading George Bishop's *New England Judged by the Spirit of the Lord*, first published in 1661. He concluded that the New Englanders were a 'wicked people', and hoped that they would feel the full force of God's wrath.[71]

We should not be surprised to find clergymen of the established churches supporting the government's line. The General Assembly of the Church of Scotland, controlled by the Moderate party, submitted loyal addresses on an annual basis, and those of the American war years strongly backed the measures of the North ministry.[72] Church of Ireland bishops supported the administration's policies in the Irish House of Lords; even the somewhat eccentric and disingenuous bishop of Derry, who pressed for legislative relief for both Catholics and Protestant Dissenters, looked forward to Catholic troops raised in Ireland helping with 'the speedy reduction of America'.[73] Lower

---

[68] Dr Williams's Library, Wodrow-Kenrick Correspondence, MS 24157(69).

[69] *Letters from the Rev. Job Orton* (2 vols., Shrewsbury, 1800), i. 219, 244.

[70] Colley, *Britons*, 138.

[71] *The Diary of Isaac Fletcher*, ed. Angus J. L. Winchester (Cumberland and Westmorland Antiquarian and Archaeological Society, extra ser., vol. xxvii, Kendal, 1994), 340, 351–2, 358, 363, 392.

[72] Church of Scotland, *Acts of the General Assembly of the Church of Scotland* (Edinburgh, 1843), 790–1, 794–5, 798, 800–1, 806–7, 808–9.

[73] HMC, *Stopford Sackville MSS* (2 vols., London, 1904–10), ii. 140.

down the clerical hierarchy, the Revd Philip Skelton attacked the Americans for what he believed to be their ungrateful and dishonest conduct.[74] Some of the clergy of the Church of England were still more critical of the colonists: 'If they were all put to the Sword, I will not condemn the Severity', wrote the Revd John Butler.[75] There were, to be sure, Anglican clergymen who took a very different view. Three bishops—Peterborough, Exeter, and St Asaph—opposed coercion. Richard Watson, Regius professor of divinity at Cambridge, supported the opposition and praised Rockingham's approach as likely 'to do you the highest credit with every unprejudiced man & sincere Christian'.[76] William Johnson Temple, rector of Mamhead, Devon, regarded the North government's treatment of the colonies as 'not only contrary to the plainest dictates of justice & humanity, but even to policy, foresight & common sense'.[77] But these clerical 'friends to America', as Paul Langford has written, 'were never more than a beleaguered minority'.[78] Not every supporter of the government's American policies adopted the extreme line of Butler, or of the archbishop of York, who was dubbed in one cartoon of the time as 'General Sanguinaire Mark-ham' for his advocacy of the most bloody means to put down the rebellion.[79] Indeed, many seem to have followed the lead of Beilby Porteus, bishop of Chester, who reminded his clergy of the need for moderation in political controversies.[80] But whether their language was measured or not, the underlying assumption of most Anglican clergymen seems to have been that the Americans were in the wrong.

---

[74] McDowell, *Ireland*, 241.

[75] Surrey RO, Guildford Muniment Room, Onslow MSS, 173/2/1/114.

[76] Leeds Archives, Ramsden Papers, Rockingham Letters, vol. 2a, Watson to Rockingham, 10 Dec. 1778.

[77] *Correspondence of Boswell and Temple*, ed. Crawford, i. 390.

[78] 'The English Clergy and the American Revolution', in Eckhart Hellmuth (ed.), *The Transformation of Political Culture: England and Germany in the Late Eighteenth Century* (Oxford, 1990), 277.

[79] BM 5400. See also BM 5492, 'Review of the York Regiment', and BM 5631, 'The Allies—Par Nobile Fratrum!'

[80] *A Charge Delivered to the Clergy of the Diocese of Chester* (Chester, 1779), 24–5. F. C. Mather has pointed out in a somewhat different context that moderately conservative divines like Porteus were more typical of the Church than extreme latitudinarians like Watson: 'Georgian Churchmanship Reconsidered: Some Variations in Anglican Public Worship, 1714–1830', *Journal of Ecclesiastical History*, 36 (1985), 282–3.

They were condemned routinely as 'rebellious Colonists' engaged in an 'unnatural Proceeding'.[81]

Anglican laymen, however, appear to have been more evenly divided. A good many no doubt followed the line preached by their clergy. At the beginning of the war, at least, fast-day sermons, invoking the Lord's assistance for British arms, seem to have been well attended. On 13 December 1776, for instance, the Revd James Woodforde, vicar of Weston Longeville in Norfolk, wrote in his diary: 'I had as full a congregation present as I have in an afternoon on a Sunday, very few that did not come'.[82] But there were significant numbers of lay Anglicans who opposed the conflict across the Atlantic. The parliamentary opposition in Britain and Ireland, at a time when membership of the House of Commons in both kingdoms was formally closed to Catholics and Protestant Dissenters, was made up almost exclusively of Anglicans, many of whom were strongly committed to their church. And beyond the parliaments hostility to the war was expressed by Anglicans as well as Dissenters. Dublin's Protestant petitioners for peace included many Anglicans, not least because Dissenters formed only a small minority of the Protestant part of the city's population.[83] And Bradley, while arguing that Dissenters often provided the dynamic leadership in the petitioning campaign of 1775–6, readily acknowledges that the majority of those signing anti-war petitions in England were Anglicans.[84] Perhaps representative of the conciliatory lay Anglicans was Kentish farmer and sometime churchwarden, Richard Hayes. His diary entry of 27 February 1778 sums up his position admirably: 'A general Fast. But we now begin to find we must restore peace to the Americans. I was not at Church. I do not like this War.'[85]

---

[81] James Scott, *A Sermon Preached at York on the 21st of February, 1781* (York, [1781]), 15; Staffordshire RO, Hanbury Parish Records, D 1528/1/4, memo. by the vicar, 1 Jan. 1777.

[82] John Beresford (ed.), *The Diary of a Country Parson* (5 vols., Oxford, 1924–31), i. 194.

[83] In 1792 some 90% of Dublin's Protestants were Anglicans. See David Dickson, '"Centres of Motion": Irish Cities and the Origins of Popular Politics', in Louis Bergeron and L.M. Cullen (eds.), *Culture et practiques politiques en France et Irlande XVI–XVIIIᵉ siècles* (Paris, 1991), 105–16.

[84] Bradley, *Religion, Revolution and English Radicalism*, 390 (table 10.2), 404–5.

[85] Reading University Library, KEN 3/1/1.

The Issues of Contention

Now that we have looked briefly at the geographical, political, social, and religious backgrounds of the antagonists, we can turn to the substance of the division. The purpose here is first to establish the general position of the two sides, and then to explore their attitudes to specific issues thrown up by the progress of the war. On a general level, opponents of the conflict with the Americans, from Richard Price to Edmund Burke, saw it as a civil war within the British empire. This internecine struggle, they argued, had been caused by the aggression of Lord North's ministry towards 'fellow subjects' in America, or 'our brethren and best friends'.[86] The colonists, in this view, were merely defending the rights and liberties of Englishmen everywhere against the claims of a ministry with dangerously authoritarian tendencies. 'The cause of America', David Hartley told his constituents, 'is the cause of the British nation'.[87] If the government succeeded in 'making slaves' of the colonists, opponents of the war said, then the British people themselves would be the next victims.[88] On the eve of the conflict, Price regarded the Massachusetts Government and Quebec Acts of 1774, both of which reinforced executive power, as a clear sign of what was to come: 'By the government which our ministers *endeavour* to establish in *New-*England, and that which they *have* established in . . . *Canada*, we see what sort of Government they wish for in this country; and as far as they can succeed in America, their way will be paved for success here'.[89] Or as Rockingham wrote in June 1775, British victory was greatly to be feared: 'If an arbitrary Military Force is to govern one part of this large Empire, . . . it will not be long before the whole of this Empire will be brought under a similar Thraldom'.[90] Most of those who sympathized with the colonists were dismayed by American independence. Their aim was to keep the empire intact by appropriate concessions, not least because they recognized the great benefits, economically, fiscally, and strategically, that Britain derived from the American colonies. The aim of the Rockinghams,

---

[86] *The Selected Letters of Josiah Wedgwood*, ed. Ann Finer and George Savage (London, 1965), 217.   [87] *Letters on the American War* (London, 1778), 71.
[88] *Diary of Sylas Neville*, ed. Cozens-Hardy, 245–6.
[89] *The Correspondence of Richard Price*, ed. W. Bernard Peach and D. O. Thomas (3 vols., Durham, NC, 1983–94), i. 189.
[90] Sheffield Archives, Rockingham MSS, R 1/1569.

the Marquis himself explained, had 'always been to try to preserve a friendly union between the Colonies and the Mother Country'.[91] Only gradually did they embrace the policy of recognizing the reality of separation, and the Chathamites, the other main element in the parliamentary opposition, harboured hopes right until the end that a constitutional relationship with the former colonies might be reconstructed.[92]

Supporters of the war saw it as the only means of maintaining an imperial system that underpinned Britain's prosperity and power. They shared with most of the opponents of the conflict the assumption that without the trade, revenues, and naval strength that the colonies generated, Britain would be no match for its great rival, France. But while the anti-war party believed that concessions were the key to securing the continuance of the benefits of empire, ministers and their supporters held that the Americans had to be compelled to accept the authority of the British crown and Parliament or the colonies would inevitably go their own way. As Charles Jenkinson wrote in October 1775, 'If the King's authority is not on this occasion to be supported, there is an end of the British Empire'.[93] Armed force, then, was regarded as the only way to suppress an 'unnatural Rebellion' against the legitimate dispensation.[94] The defence of legally constituted authority in the colonies united many of those who shared in the exercise of power in the British Isles, from government ministers to borough councillors and aldermen.[95] Nothing but military defeat of the American insurgents, the corporation of Leicester argued in its loyal address, could restore to them 'that invaluable blessing of Law without which the thing called Liberty is nothing but Licentiousness'.[96] The colonists, according to this line of thinking, were bent on the destruction of the balanced constitution and the establishment of an unchecked

---

[91] *Correspondence of Burke*, ed. Copeland et al., iii. 295.

[92] See the comments of the Earl of Camden in *Autobiography and Political Correspondence of Augustus Henry Third Duke of Grafton*, ed. Sir William R. Anson (London, 1898), 288–9. For the efforts of the Earl of Shelburne to revive a constitutional connection at the time of the signing of the peace treaties see H. M. Scott, *British Foreign Policy in the Age of the American Revolution* (Oxford, 1990), 327–8.

[93] HMC, 12th Report, app. pt. ix, *Donoughmore MSS* (London, 1891), 284.

[94] John Warren, bishop of St Davids, *A Sermon Preached before the Lords Spiritual and Temporal . . . on Friday, February 4, 1780* (London, 1780), 16.

[95] Bradley, *Religion, Revolution and English Radicalism*, p. 394.

[96] Mary Bateson, Helen Stocks, and G. A. Chinnery (eds.), *Records of the Borough of Leicester* (7 vols., London, Cambridge, and Leicester, 1899–1974), v. 240.

democracy. Those who aided, abetted, and sustained American resistance, were stigmatized as part of a transatlantic plot to topple legal authority. The corporation of Beverley was just one of many loyal bodies to offer its support to the king 'against the dangerous designs of all his factious and seditious subjects both at home and abroad'.[97] Or, as the Revd John Butler put it in October 1776: 'The Cause is decided between the Constitution on one part and Doctor Franklyn, Price, Watson &c. on the other.'[98]

The specific areas of dispute were many and varied. It is not the intention here to provide a chronological narrative of the political debates related to the American conflict, but to focus on the issues created by the war and their impact on the struggle between the two sides. The cost of the war was an ongoing cause of complaint for opponents of the conflict. In the Berkshire by-election of February 1776, supporters of the opposition candidate emphasized that the expense associated with the military subjection of the Americans was enormous. 'To Carry on this War, an Additional Tax of 1s. in the Pound is already laid upon Land.—Another 1s. will probably be added next Year.—And Several Millions will be wanted besides'.[99] Matthew Robinson Morris made much the same point in an anti-war pamphlet. 'No one now has so much as a conception of war without borrowing. We set out this first year for a gentle beginning with five additional duties; but if we proceed thus adding debt to debt, funds to funds and taxes to taxes; how long for the love of heaven can possibly be left us not only any trade, but even any property itself?'[100] In the Commons, too, opposition speakers seized every opportunity to draw attention to the escalating costs of the war. In November 1775, when the land tax was increased to its normal wartime rate of four shillings in the pound, opposition speakers stressed the reasons for the rise. George Byng sarcastically 'congratulated the Country gentlemen on the additional shilling land-tax, as the first happy fruits of American measures'.[101] This approach was partly, no doubt, a consequence of the opposition's

---

[97] K. A. Macmahon (ed.), *Beverley Corporation Minute Books* (Yorkshire Archaelogical Society, record ser., vol. cxxii, Wakefield, 1958), 55.

[98] Surrey RO, Guildford Muniment Room, Onslow MSS, 173/2/1/126.

[99] Berkshire RO, Hartley Russell Papers, D/EHy O44, letter on W. H. Hartley's behalf, 15 Feb. 1776. For more on the by-election and the importance to it of the American war, see below, Ch. 8.   [100] *Peace the Best Policy* (2nd edn., London, 1777), 9.

[101] *PH* xviii. 937–8.

conviction that the country at large supported the government's line. In February 1777 the Duke of Richmond believed that concentrating on the expense of the conflict was 'our only chance'; 'I should . . . recommend the working this point almost alone'.[102] But emphasizing costs had other merits. Supporters of coercion, though by 1774–5 largely focused on defending the sovereign right of the British Parliament to legislate for the colonies, still professed to believe that it would be possible to extract a greater fiscal contribution from America to the costs of empire. Lord North said as much in the debate on the land tax in November 1775.[103] By stressing that the war was burdening British taxpayers rather than relieving them, the opposition hoped to undermine the government's case. The turning point would come, Sir George Savile predicted, when the people recognized that they 'had been promised Bread & had been given a stone: that we were to be tax'd & stamp'd our selves, instead of inflicting taxes & Stamps on others'.[104] Highlighting the costs also had the advantage, from the opposition perspective, of raising questions in the public's minds about where the money was going; as decisive victory over the colonists eluded the British forces, and the war dragged on, suspicions grew that the bloated tax income was being misappropriated to fund a system of corruption which was turning the House of Commons from an independent check on executive power into a rubber stamp for ministerial decisions.[105] Increased taxation, in short, could easily be linked with the opposition's central theme of the emergence of a dangerously authoritarian system of government.

The opposition also sought to criticize the administration's conduct of the war. Initially, of course, opponents of coercion of the colonists were inhibited by their hostility to the use of force. They could hardly attack the government directly for failing to defeat the Americans. So prior to French intervention, the emphasis was on the folly of ministers believing that it would be possible militarily to subdue the Americans. Thus, in February 1776, in a debate on Charles James Fox's motion for an inquiry into the causes of the 'ill success' of the British forces in America, Richard Fitzpatrick insisted that the 'whole American business, from the very beginning, had been planned in absurdity . . . and executed in a manner which

[102] *Memoirs of Rockingham*, ed. Albermarle, ii. 309.   [103] *PH* xviii. 940.
[104] Nottingham University Library, Portland Papers, PWF 8215.
[105] See below, Ch. 6, for more on the movement for economical reform and constitutional purification that sprung up in 1779–80.

evidenced the very excess of ignorance'.[106] Once the war broadened, there was more scope for detailed attacks on government incompetency, because the opposition was as committed as the ministry to the defeat of the Bourbon powers. Ministerial pamphleteers might try to deny this, and even suggest that the opposition was sympathetic to the French as well as to the Americans,[107] but so far as the conflict with the Bourbons was concerned the real issue was whether the government was prosecuting the war as effectively as it should be. Hence, in part, the great row that ensued after the naval action off Ushant in July 1778. Admiral Keppel, well connected with the parliamentary opposition, was against the American war. He was more than happy, however, to serve against the French. In this first major naval engagement of the conflict, the two fleets caused each other much damage, but neither side emerged as clear victor. Sir Hugh Palliser, Keppel's second in command, was attacked in the press for his part in the battle. He responded by accusing Keppel of failing to press home his advantage. A court martial at length acquitted Keppel of the charges brought against him. The opposition, unsurprisingly, made much of Palliser's links with the Earl of Sandwich, the first lord of the admiralty, and portrayed Keppel as the victim of a government smear campaign. For many months the navy, and much of the country, was bitterly divided, though the extensive and enthusiastic celebrations on Keppel's acquittal suggest that the opposition gained the upper hand.[108] The threat of invasion in 1778 and still more in 1779 gave opponents of the American aspect of the war many opportunities to parade their credentials for displacing the ministry. Richmond, both as colonel of the Sussex militia and as the leading light in the creation of volunteer corps in the county, was conspicuously involved in organizing defences in a particularly exposed part of the country. This gave added piquancy to his criticisms of government unpreparedness. In October 1778 he was lamenting the time lost in taking the necessary steps to repel a landing. 'Lord Amherst is asleep, or dares not act, & it looks as if the

---

[106] *PH* xviii. 1146.

[107] See esp. [James Macpherson,] *A Short History of the Opposition during the Last Session of Parliament* (London, 1779).

[108] See Wilson, *Sense of the People*, 253–9 and J. M. Broomfield, 'The Keppel-Palliser Affair', *Mariner's Mirror*, 47 (1961), 195–205. The popular dimension is examined in some detail in Nicholas Rogers, *Crowds, Culture and Politics in Georgian Britain* (Oxford, 1998), ch. 4.

same Man who has lost 13 provinces intended by equal bad management to risk the Loss of 3 Kingdoms'. The following year he was still more dismissive of ministerial efforts: 'we have every thing to fear', he told the Duke of Portland, 'from the sad mismanagement of our Rulers and Commanders in every Department, which daily proves worse and worse'.[109] When Plymouth was threatened by the combined Franco-Spanish fleet for several weeks in the summer of 1779, it was inevitable that the opposition should seek to exploit government embarrassment by forcing a debate on the poor state of the defences of Devon and Cornwall.[110]

Most of the issues of serious contention during the war were connected with military and naval mobilization; or, more particularly, with the form of mobilization pursued by the government. The use of foreign troops was a major cause of controversy. Besides hiring thousands of auxiliaries from German rulers to use directly in the rebel colonies, the government, as we have seen, borrowed a number of regiments from the king in his capacity as elector of Hanover. The Hanoverians did not themselves go to America, but they released for American service an equivalent number of British troops based in the Mediterranean garrisons of Gibraltar and Minorca. Similarly, the government hoped to use Hessians and Brunswickers to free for the war across the Atlantic some 4,000 British troops in Ireland. All of these expedients were of course condemned by opponents of the war against the Americans. In the Commons Lord John Cavendish criticized the treaties with the German princes as 'mortifying and humiliating' and an 'alarming consequence of the American war'.[111] Grafton drew up a memorial to the king against the use of German mercenaries.[112] And the Irish Commons, while agreeing to dispatch 4,000 troops to America, refused the offer of German replacements.[113] But the employment

---

[109] Nottingham University Library, Portland Papers, PWF 6321 and 6325. See also *The Pembroke Papers*, ed. Lord Herbert (2 vols., London, 1939–50), i. 202, where Lord Pembroke criticizes the creation of the cavalry camp near Bury St Edmunds ('They might as well be in Lapland') and depicts the general officers employed as political appointees 'who never oppose any Edict or any rogue, or fool'; 'one would really think the French Cabinet chose them'.   [110] *PH* xxi. 459–91 (25 Apr. 1780).

[111] *PH* xviii. 1168.   [112] West Suffolk RO, Grafton Papers, Ac 423/199.

[113] North had already feared that 'the name of foreign troops may furnish a handle to the Factious in Ireland'; when the proposal was voted down he expressed relief that money had been saved to British taxpayers, who would have footed the bill for the replacements. SP 63/437B, fos. 36–7, 39, 46.

of the Hanoverians sparked the fiercest argument, because it seemed to exemplify the high-handed approach of the government. The Irish Commons had been allowed to decide whether or not to accept German troops as part of Ireland's garrison; indeed, North showed himself to be most sensitive to Irish opinion on this issue. The treaties with the various German princes were likewise presented to the British Parliament for approval. The Hanoverian arrangements, however, were concluded without reference to the legislature. In the Lords the Duke of Manchester denounced what he believed to be a violation of the Bill of Rights; the king, he argued, had no authority to keep an army in any part of the dominions of the crown without the consent of Parliament. In the Commons opposition speakers drove the same message home: the government's actions, Sir James Lowther claimed, were 'contrary to law'; Serjeant Adair said they were a breach of the Act of Settlement; while Thomas Townshend pointed explicitly to the danger that 'an ill-designing prince [might] . . . fill all the exterior parts of the dominions with foreign mercenaries, and take opportunities to make them the means of overturning the constitution'.[114]

The expansion of the British armed forces was also a contested process. The growth of the navy, as we have seen, was initially very slow because, after some debate in government circles, the army was chosen as the principal instrument for the crushing of the American rebellion.[115] Only in October 1776 was impressment of mariners authorized by the cabinet, and not until early 1778, when conflict with France was seen as imminent, did full-scale naval mobilization begin. From this point onwards, however, every effort was made and the numbers taken into the navy rose dramatically. In part this was because impressment of sailors seems to have been pursued with a new urgency: Captain James Alms, sent to recruit in Sussex in December 1776, had raised 213 men by the end of 1777, only 66 (or 31%) of whom had been pressed; but two years later his tally of 570 included 243 pressed men (some 43%).[116] But an important contribution was also made by government supporters in many towns and counties throughout the British Isles. Loyal corporations sought to increase the rate of voluntary entry into the navy by offering bounties to seamen and landmen. In April 1778, for

---

[114] *PH* xviii. 799–801, 818, 831, 833.   [115] See above, Ch. 1.
[116] ADM 1/1445–6.

instance, the council at Youghal, County Cork, offered a bounty of two guineas for every able-bodied seaman and one guinea for every ordinary seaman joining the crew of the *Thunderer*, commanded by Captain Robert Boyle Walshingham; while Liverpool's corporation, having offered the same sums two years earlier, in 1779 increased its bounty to ten guineas for seamen and five for landmen.[117] In Middlesex and Westminster and in Surrey, general subscriptions to assist the government were designed to create a fund that could be used, among other things, to reward those who brought to the notice of the authorities any mariners eligible for naval service who were hiding from press-gangs.[118]

Naval expansion caused some difficulties for opponents of the American war. Until the French entered the struggle, members of the parliamentary opposition tended to argue against any increase in the size of the navy.[119] In November 1776 Sir George Yonge told the Commons that while he would not attempt to stop the augmentation proposed in the naval estimates for 1777, 'he must condemn the service for which the greatest part of the seamen were destined'.[120] The following year, when the estimates for 1778 were under consideration, Thomas Townshend was less restrained. He declared that 'he objected to the motion, on the simple principle that it was in support of a war that he detested and abhorred'.[121] But once the conflict broadened into war with France and Spain, the opposition changed its tune dramatically, and came to the support of the navy as a barrier to invasion. In 1779 Fox criticized the government for failing to have enough ships ready for the start of the war with France, and Sir Charles Bunbury used the desperate needs of the fleet for manpower as an argument against North's plans to double the size of the militia.[122]

But if opposition MPs changed tack in this respect, many of them consistently criticized the means by which the navy raised its recruits. Compulsion, in the form of the press-gang, met with strong disapproval. Temple Luttrell, a bitter opponent of North and Sandwich,

[117] Richard Caulfield (ed.), *The Council Book of the Corporation of Youghal* (Guildford, 1878), 499; Sir James A. Picton (ed.), *City of Liverpool: Municipal Archives and Records* (Liverpool, 1897), 181.

[118] *The Morning Post, and Daily Advertiser*, 19 July, 12 and 30 Aug. 1779.

[119] We should note, however, that Keppel in Nov. 1775 criticized the ministry's proposals for augmentation of the navy on the grounds that the expansion was inadequate for war and too large for peace. *Parliamentary Register*, ii. 268.   [120] *PH* xviii. 1449.

[121] *PH* xix. 457.   [122] *PH* xx. 204–39, 929–30.

argued that the press was ineffective, and recommended in its place a system of voluntary service with increased official bounties to encourage enlistment.[123] These practical considerations seem to have been less important, however, than the political objections, which went to the very heart of the opposition's claims about the ministry's intentions. When, at the height of the invasion scare of 1779, the government rushed legislation through Parliament allowing the impressment of hitherto exempt and protected categories of men employed at sea or in riverine activities, the opposition attacked the bill on libertarian grounds, stating that impressment was wrong in principle because it infringed the rights of the subject.[124] At a time when the opposition was regularly accusing the government of authoritarianism, the administration's bill was seen as yet another instance of such a disposition. Compulsion, though well established as a means of manning the navy in wartime, was particularly offensive to MPs who were inclined to suspect North and his colleagues of seeking to undermine long-cherished rights in both America and Britain. In these circumstances, an attempt to increase the scope of impressment was almost bound to be resisted, even at a time of national emergency.[125] And just as government supporters in Britain and Ireland did their best to promote naval recruitment, so extra-parliamentary opponents of the American war exerted themselves against impressment. In London, naval officers in charge of a press-gang were committed to trial by aldermen who opposed the coercion of the Americans.[126]

The army's expansion was a still greater matter of controversy. The government tried, of course, to encourage recruitment, first by reducing the term of service for new entrants to three years or the duration of the conflict,[127] then by increasing bounty money paid to enlistees. Tradesmen who joined the colours, as we have seen, were given the opportunity to establish themselves in business in any corporate town in England, irrespective of guild restrictions.[128]

---

[123] *PH* xix. 81–3. His proposals were based on Robert Tomlinson's *Plan for a Practicable . . . Method of Manning the Royal Navy . . . Without the Usual Mode of Impressing Seamen* (London, 1774).   [124] *PH* xx. 968.

[125] It should be added, however, that opposition members authorized the continued use of the press once they came into power in 1782. See Hull RO, Borough Records, BRL 1320.

[126] *Gentleman's Magazine*, 46 (1776), 576. See also Sainsbury, *Disaffected Patriots*, 28, 134–9; and, more generally, ADM 1/5117/9 and Rogers, *Crowds, Culture and Politics*, ch. 3.

[127] WO 26/29, p. 169.   [128] See above, Chs. 1 and 3.

The stick was used as well as the carrot. In January 1776 the privy council ordered the lord-lieutenants of the counties to issue warrants for the seizure of vagrants, who, under an Act of 1744, could in time of war be given the stark choice of enlistment or corporal punishment.[129] And as the need for manpower increased with the coming of the Bourbon war, the government turned to unadulterated compulsion. The 1778 and 1779 Recruiting Acts included clauses allowing the impressment of the unemployed and certain types of minor offenders.

Government supporters in the country offered every assistance. In the first years of the war, the army was helped by subscriptions established to provide the troops with comforts—such as blankets and winter coats—or to give financial aid to the families of soldiers killed or injured in North America.[130] From the end of 1777, however, when Bourbon intervention seemed inevitable, the emphasis changed. Subscriptions were used to help pay for the raising of new regiments in towns such as Manchester, Liverpool, Glasgow, and Edinburgh, or to augment bounty money for entrants into the old corps. Influential individuals also proved helpful. In Ireland, powerful landowners, such as the Earl of Shannon and the Earl of Bellamont, dipped into their pockets to encourage recruiting in their own localities.[131] Irish Catholic notables were also active, as we have seen. Lord Kenmare, the leading Catholic landowner in Ireland, offered to raise nearly 2,000 men in Kerry and Cork from amongst his tenantry and dependants.[132] In Scotland, regiments were raised by Highland landowners. In England loyal magistrates did all they could to assist the recruiting service. Thomas Woods Knollis, a Hampshire justice 'ever solicitous and attentive for the good of His majesty's service', played an active part in facilitating the enlistment of convicts,[133] and wrote proudly in June 1776 that the Twenty-fifth Foot had been 'very successful in recruiting and found

---

[129]   e.g. Cambridgeshire RO, Quarter Sessions Order-book, Q/S 07, pp. 453, 455.

[130]   e.g. Bateson, Stocks, and Chinnery (eds.), *Records of Leicester*, v. 238; Picton (ed.), *Liverpool: Municipal Archives*, 180; T 1/527, fo. 303; *York Courant*, 5 Dec. 1775.

[131]   *The Correspondence of King George III*, ed. Sir John Fortescue (6 vols., London, 1927–8), iii. 257.

[132]   Robert E. Burns, 'The Catholic Relief Act in Ireland, 1778', *Church History*, 32 (1963), 183. Kenmare does not seem to have succeeded in raising the men offered; but for the efforts of Sir Boyle Roche see BL, Abergavenny MS 76.

[133]   WO 1/992, Knollis to Barrington, 12 Mar. 1776.

me very useful in many particulars for that and other Regts. I have attested near 100 since last Christmas'.[134]

At least some opposition MPs made it clear that they could not accept any attempt to raise extra troops. Sir Charles Bunbury intervened in the debate on the Recruiting Bill of 1779 to object most strongly to the whole proceeding. 'He did not by any means approve the principle of the Bill', he told the Commons, 'which was confessedly calculated to recruit our armies for the purpose of carrying on a ruinous, offensive war in America; a war which, in his opinion, ought for every reason of policy and humanity to be abandoned.'[135] But not all opponents of the American war took such a negative view of the Recruiting Acts. Isaac Barré, a Chathamite with a well-established reputation as a firm friend to the colonies, gave his blessing to the 1779 Act on the basis that it included provisions for short-term enlistment, a change that Barré—a former soldier—wished to see extended to the army as a whole.[136] Given that the French had entered the struggle by this stage, and posed a considerable threat to the British Isles themselves, we should not be surprised at Barré's reaction. Indeed, Bunbury's fundamentalist approach was far from typical. For the most part, the parliamentary opposition was much more discriminating in its criticism. Burke appears to have had no objection to the expansion of the army as such; he concentrated his fire on the mode. The raising of new corps, he argued, was less effective than the augmentation of the old regiments—exactly the line, curiously enough, that the king had taken when trying to fend off applications to raise new corps in the first years of the war.[137] Other opposition MPs and peers attacked the new corps on another front, claiming that the government had shown great partiality in the offers that it accepted. Several proposals submitted by individuals associated with the opposition had been rejected without good reason.[138] Special favour, on the other hand, had been given to ultra-loyal local authorities, like Manchester, Liverpool, Edinburgh, and Glasgow, and to Highland chiefs whose families had been involved in the Jacobite uprising of 1745.[139] The alleged favouritism shown to the Scots rankled particularly, and was taken as further proof of a desire on the ministry's part to resurrect

---

[134] Hampshire RO, Banbury Papers, 1 M44/66, fo. 32.   [135] *PH* xx. 114.
[136] Ibid. 114, 148.   [137] *PH* xix. 618. Cf. Ch. 1, above.   [138] *PH* xxi. 339.
[139] *PH* xix. 621, 626, 633.

Stuart tyranny, or, in the shorthand of the day, 'Scotch government'.[140] That the new corps were, in many cases, to be supported by public subscriptions added to the opposition's ire. So did the use of such subscriptions to increase the bounty money offered to recruits entering the old regiments. In both cases, the subscriptions were denounced as 'unconstitutional', and interpreted as another symptom of the slide into Stuart-style despotism. In the Commons, Sir Philip Jennings Clerk, a Rockinghamite, announced that he 'could never persuade himself to think, there was a power in the crown to raise an army in the country, to any extent it pleased, without the previous assent of parliament'.[141] In the Lords, the Earl of Abingdon produced an advert for a London subscription and declared it analogous to Charles I's attempt to secure an extra-parliamentary income. 'My Lords, if this be not unconstitutional, I know not what is. In my poor opinion, it is not only the most notorious violation of the rights of parliament that has happened since the levying of Ship-money, but when I compare the cases together, . . . I can see no difference between them.'[142]

These arguments were picked up and pursued beyond Parliament by opponents of the American aspect of the war. A Leeds newspaper supportive of the government noted that a local subscription to raise men for the army was progressing well, 'notwithstanding all the efforts of the tools of the patriotic party to overturn it'.[143] In Norfolk, a county meeting provided an opportunity for a public contest between the two sides. In January 1778, the young William Windham, keen to prepare the ground for his election to Parliament as an opponent of North's ministry, led opposition to an attempt to establish a subscription to add money to the bounties given to men recruited in the county. Windham was successful, and he followed up his triumph by securing 5,400 signatures on a petition to the Commons decrying the raising of troops without the consent of Parliament and criticizing the war with America.[144] Other disruptive tactics were employed, too, especially before the broadening of the war in 1778. Radical cartoons vividly depicted the disadvantages of army life, highlighting poor pay, danger, and separation from loved ones.[145]

---

[140] *PH* xix. 688, 689; xxi. 339. See also, below, Ch. 5.   [141] *PH* xix. 685.
[142] Ibid. 631.   [143] *Leeds Mercury*, 10 Feb. 1778.
[144] HMC, *Verulam MSS* (London, 1906), 124–5; *Windham Papers* (2 vols., London, 1913), i. 19–20; *PH* xix. 758–61; Wilson, *Sense of the People*, 419–20.
[145] e.g. BM 5295, 'Six-Pence a Day'; BM 5403, 'Head Quarters'; BM 5471, 'An Exact representation of the Manchester Recruits'.

Protestant Dissenters were identified as the primary cause of the problems experienced in recruiting soldiers. In October 1775 Edward Gibbon, the historian and government supporter, accused the Dissenters in England and Ireland of impeding the growth of the army.[146] Nottingham, where Protestant Dissenters dominated the corporation, gained a reputation as 'the most disloyal [town] in the kingdom', and one in which the local authorities 'do all in their power to hinder the service by preventing as much as possible the enlistment of soldiers'.[147]

The role of the militia was also a bone of contention. When, in 1775, the king obtained parliamentary permission to call out the militia due to the rebellion in America, opposition MPs declared that this made it no more than an adjunct of the army, and amounted to a perversion of its original function. Burke, while claiming to be a friend to the militia, announced that from now onwards he would watch it with suspicion. Fox was bolder, arguing that 'he saw no difference between a standing army of regulars, and a standing army of militia, whom the king could call out as he pleased'.[148] An attempt in 1776 to create a Scottish militia was bitterly opposed by the opposition, and ran aground thanks to the fears of many independent English MPs.[149] The record of the English and Welsh militia from 1778, when it was called out for service—or 'embodied'—seemed to bear out the concerns of the opposition. The militia regiments served until the end of the war, not just on a temporary basis while the threat of invasion was at its height. They depended heavily on substitutes and were paid in the same way as the regulars; they were officered not just by the landed elite of the counties—as originally intended—but often by men of lesser means or even with no estate within the locality; and they trained alongside regular regiments in the camps established at such places as Coxheath and Warley.[150] So while

---

[146] *The Letters of Edward Gibbon*, ed. J. E. Norton (3 vols., London, 1956), ii. 89.

[147] *The Private Papers of John, Earl of Sandwich*, ed. G. R. Barnes and J. H. Owen (4 vols., London, 1932–8), i. 340. Nottingham's corporation had petitioned the king against the war in 1775, and in 1779 it made Admiral Keppel, the opposition hero, a freeman: Borough of Nottingham, *Records of the Borough of Nottingham* (9 vols., Nottingham, 1882–1956), vii. 137–9, 166–7. [148] *PH* xviii. 857, 863.

[149] For more on the Scottish militia controversy see John Robertson, *The Scottish Enlightenment and the Militia Issue* (Edinburgh, 1985), chs. 5 and 6; and below, Ch. 5.

[150] J. R. Western, *The English Militia in the Eighteenth Century* (London, 1965), 130, 255–64, 306–7, 309–14, 367–8; Paul Langford, *Public Life and the Propertied Englishman, 1689–1798* (Oxford, 1991), 298–9; above Ch. 1.

opposition MPs continued to pay lip service to the militia as an ideal—and, indeed, in many cases served as militia officers themselves[151]—they became increasingly uncertain about the reality. In 1779, when North wished to double the size of the militia, many opposition MPs were reluctant to support him. Even the cautious Burke, who was keen to reduce the scope for government attacks on his party, argued that while the Rockinghams could not openly oppose North's plans, nor could they 'be active in forwarding' the scheme.[152] North's plans foundered, partly because practical difficulties seemed to militate against such an ambitious expansion, but mainly as a result of divisions within the government on this issue. In the end, Parliament merely approved the adding of extra companies to the established militia by voluntary recruitment; but even this outcome caused unease for the opposition, not least because the additional companies were usually raised with the aid of public subscriptions.[153] The role of the militia in the Gordon Riots of 1780 added to opposition concern. The militia had served alongside the regulars in the suppression of the disorders, acting, the opposition protested, without the authority of local magistrates. Here was fresh proof that the militia had been debased into a mere extension of the army and could no longer be viewed as anything but an instrument of the government. The opposition pointed to the armed associations, or volunteer companies, as a more constitutional means of maintaining order,[154] and came to the conclusion that a new popular militia was the only solution to the professionalization of the established militia.

Even before the Gordon Riots, the issue of whether to arm the 'respectable' portion of the people had further divided supporters from opponents of the American aspect of the war. There was considerable reluctance in official circles to see arms put into the hands of those who were seen as beyond the control of government. The king, admittedly, toyed with the idea of distributing pikes to

---

[151]   Richmond e.g. was described as working 'like a Serjeant, a Clerk, and a pack-horse' on behalf of his beloved Sussex militia: *Letters of Gibbon*, ed. Norton, ii. 187. See also *The Life and Letters of Lady Sarah Lennox*, ed. Countess of Ilchester and Lord Stavordale (2 vols., London, 1901), i. 296.

[152]   *Correspondence of Burke*, ed. Copeland et al., iv. 91.

[153]   See e.g. *The Morning Post, and Daily Advertiser*, 18 Aug. 1779, for a subscription to raise volunteers to supplement the Northamptonshire militia, and *Jackson's Oxford Journal*, 10 July 1779, for similar efforts to add a company to the Oxfordshire militia.

[154]   *PH* xxi. 728, 733.

'the Country People' when invasion fears were at their height in 1779; and the previous year Lord North had favoured giving fire-arms to the coal miners of north-eastern England.[155] But there was much concern about this form of mobilization. It was feared that volunteer corps in certain areas would serve as tools of opposition leaders and would reinforce their local power. In September 1779 the king was distinctly unenthusiastic about proposals to raise twenty-four volunteer companies in Sussex. He believed that this would increase the patronage at the disposal of the Duke of Richmond, the county's lord-lieutenant and a strong opponent of the war against the Americans. The twenty-four companies, George told North, 'will enable him [Richmond] to bring forward his own Creatures'.[156] But beyond this concern about the composition of the corps, there seems to have been a larger worry about the use to which they might be put. The fear, usually only implied rather than openly discussed, was that armed bodies of the people might take the opportunity to exert pressure for reform of the constitution. Barrington wrote darkly of the strength of the Wilkite radicals in the metropolis in the early years of the war, and of the existence of significant numbers of the disloyal and the disaffected in other parts of the country.[157] The Association movement, which started in Yorkshire at the very end of 1779, greatly increased the uneasiness in government circles. In the resolutions adopted at some county meetings, references to the right to arm were included alongside demands for constitutional change.[158] Irish developments almost certainly influenced government thinking, too. The Irish volunteers, as we shall see later, were as much a political as a military force, and the way in which they worked in conjunction with the opposition in the Dublin Parliament to press for first commercial and then con-stitutional concessions from the British government ensured that they were regarded with much hostility by North and his collea-gues.[159] Any attempt to create a similar force in Britain itself was perhaps bound to be viewed with deep suspicion. Hence the govern-ment reaction when volunteer corps, 'like the Irish', were formed in various parts of Scotland in 1778 and 1779. The units met with the

---

[155] Kent Archives Office, Amherst Papers, U 1350 074/38, 39, 41.
[156] *Correspondence of George III*, ed. Fortescue, iv. 418.
[157] Barrington, *Life of Barrington*, 155–6.
[158] See Christopher Wyvill, *Political Papers* (6 vols., York, 1794–1802), i. 254–5. For more on the Association movement, see below, Ch. 7.   [159] See below, Ch. 6.

disapproval of the commander-in-chief in Scotland, and were disbanded on the instructions of Lord Suffolk, the secretary of state.[160] Aberdeen, where a corps had been established and then broken in 1778, tried again in 1781, following the Dutch entry into the war, and was this time given official blessing—though only after Lord Stormont, Suffolk's successor, had been assured of the loyalty of the town and the suitability of the proposed officers.[161] In England, too, volunteers were given no encouragement. Official approval—in the form of the distribution of arms from the royal arsenals—was given somewhat grudgingly, and only once the government had vetted the officers and given them royal commissions—a safeguard, in the government's eyes, for the reliability of a unit.[162] Nonetheless, as we saw earlier, volunteer corps appeared and remained in existence, even without government approval.[163]

Grass-roots supporters of the North ministry and the war against the colonists were not always opposed to the widespread diffusion of arms. A number of governing bodies of towns conspicuous for their loyalty, such as Hull and Liverpool, wanted to form volunteer corps in 1779, when an enemy landing seemed a real possibility.[164] Adam Ferguson, a warm supporter of coercion of the Americans and a steadfast adherent of the North administration, was convinced that British military success abroad would be more assured if home defence was entrusted to 'every Sober Landholder & householder'.[165] Likewise, James Wodrow, another Scottish supporter of the war against the Americans, dismissed as groundless fears about mass arming, and put the authoritarian case in favour: 'I apprehend the people accustomed to military subordination & discipline woud be much more orderly & manageable than they are at present'.[166] On the whole, however, Lord North's friends in the country at large tended to disapprove of arming the people. Lord Poulett, the lord-lieutenant of Devon, condemned the formation of volunteer companies in his county as arming 'a Devonshire Mob'. Even with the

---

[160] Dr Williams's Library, Wodrow-Kenrick Correspondence, MS 24157 (74); SP 54/47, fos. 74–5, 135, 137, 306–7.   [161] SP 54/48, fos. 103, 105, 107, 125, 127.
[162] See e.g. the commission given to John Challen, appointing him captain of a Sussex volunteer company: East Sussex RO, Add. MS 1023.   [163] See above, Ch. 1.
[164] Hull RO, Borough Records, BRL 1386/4; Picton (ed.), *Liverpool: Municipal Archives*, 183.
[165] *The Correspondence of Adam Ferguson*, ed. Vincenzo Merolle (2 vols., London, 1995), i. 218, 224, 228.
[166] Dr Williams's Library, Wodrow-Kenrick Correspondence, MS 24157 (74).

combined fleet lying threateningly off Plymouth, he expressed the view that 'if such men are to have arms put into their hands I should be much more afraid of em than I am at present of ye Enemy'.[167] Thomas Twining, a fiercely loyal Essex curate, disliked the associations that had sprung up during the war, and his condemnation seems to have encompassed the military associations, or volunteer bodies, as well as the more overtly political reform associations. 'I shou'd think myself much safer in the protection of the army', he wrote in July 1780, 'than of my *fellow-citizens*, considering the unaccountable spirit of sedition & political malignity that prevails among them.'[168] Similarly, Viscount Wentworth, a staunch supporter of Lord North and his American policy, was delighted when a county meeting in Leicestershire in 1782 rejected proposals for a reformed popular militia put forward by the new government. 'I think ye whole scheme both absurd & dangerous', Wentworth wrote.[169] Indeed, local authorities that had been strongly supportive of North's American measures were often distinctly lukewarm, or even downright hostile, to the new government's proposals. Glasgow and Hull rebuffed the suggestions of the ministry that a popular militia be instituted, as did Manchester, a town renowned for its loyalty to Lord North.[170] Huntingdon, a borough dominated by the Earl of Sandwich, was particularly dismissive of the planned reform, concluding that it 'could be attended with no good Consequences to the Publick, would be burthensome to the inhabitants and probably dangerous to the Peace and quiet of the neighbourhood in which we live'.[171]

The new government's proposals, presented in a circular letter from Shelburne, the home and colonial secretary, to all lord-lieutenants of counties and the governing bodies of the major towns of the kingdom, included the possibility of the local appointment of

---

[167] SP 41/33, fo. 72.

[168] *A Selection of Thomas Twining's Letters 1734–1804*, ed. Ralph S. Walker (2 vols., Lampeter, 1991), i. 183–5.

[169] *The Noels and the Milbankes*, ed. Malcolm Elwin (London, 1967), 198.

[170] Robert Renwick et al. (eds.), *Extracts from the Records of the Burgh of Glasgow* (11 vols., Glasgow, 1882–1916), viii. 46–50; HO 42/205, fos. 171, 206.

[171] HO 42/205, fo. 249. See also the comments of Sir John Sinclair, an independent-minded supporter of the American war and North's government, who pointed out what he saw as the dangers inherent in Shelburne's plan: *Considerations on Militias and Standing Armies* (London, 1782), 46–7.

officers.[172] Together with legislation to encourage the formation of volunteer corps,[173] the scheme was the logical outcome of a long-term commitment to popular military participation. When in opposition, Rockinghamite and Chathamite politicians had made clear their wish to see weapons widely diffused. The Irish volunteers were praised and encouraged: in 1779 Rockingham offered to supply muskets, bayonets, and money to a unit in County Wicklow.[174] Burke, while dismissing George III's interest in the distribution of pikes as inappropriate, condemned the government's refusal 'to put arms in the hands of the people at large whenever particular places have applied for them', and declared that 'we ought to be an armed Nation'.[175] Sir George Yonge likewise called for a return to the old practice of 'arming the whole country' when the danger of an enemy landing seemed particularly acute.[176]

Beyond Parliament, opponents of the American aspect of the war were no less enthusiastic. In London, though some government supporters favoured the forming of military associations,[177] radicals seem to have been much more committed. It was surely significant that the members of the Light Horse Volunteers, meeting on 5 July 1780, pledged themselves to support Alderman John Kirkman, a noted opponent of the war against the Americans, as a radical candidate for London at the forthcoming general election.[178] The Gordon Riots and their suppression were of course particularly important influences in the metropolis. The right to bear arms was boldly asserted by radicals—just as by the parliamentary opposition—as a more appropriate means of preserving order. But radicals were no less keen to point to the role of popular military associations as a security against both foreign invasion and domestic oppression. In the aftermath of the riots, William Jones was deeply concerned by the mounting evidence of a desire on the part of

---

[172] The second clause of the 'Heads of a Plan' sent by Shelburne referred to the appointment of officers 'either by Commission from His Majesty, or from the Lord Lieutenant of the County, upon the Recommendation of the Chief Magistrate of the Town in which the Corps are raised'. See e.g. Leicestershire RO, Lieutenancy Papers, LM 8/8/3. For the background, and the role of the new commander-in-chief, Gen. Henry Seymour Conway, see Western, *English Militia*, 217–19; John Norris, *Shelburne and Reform* (London, 1963), 162–3.   [173] 22 Geo. III, c. 79.

[174] Sheffield Archives, Rockingham MSS, R 1/1854a.

[175] *Correspondence of Burke*, ed. Copeland et al., iv. 122–3.   [176] *PH* xx. 928.

[177] WO 34/116, fos. 20–1; *Correspondence of George III*, ed. Fortescue, iv. 430.

[178] Handbill, 5 Sept. 1780, BL press mark 1850 c 10 fo. 115.

government to strengthen prerogative power. His conclusion was that the greatest safeguard for liberty of the subject was 'a firelock in the hands of every gentleman'.[179] The link between popular military and political participation was also emphasized by radicals. A few days before the Gordon Riots, a subcommittee of the Westminster Committee of Association referred to the large number of men involved in the defence of the country as an argument for widening the franchise.[180] A true militia, it was claimed in a tract published in 1781, must draw by rotation on all men able to bear arms, for without rotation militiamen 'gradually lose their *civil capacity*, and from *free citizens*, are apt to become mere *Sold-iers*'. Membership of such a properly constituted militia would be no hardship 'if each freeman that bears arms was allowed his *natural right* of suffrage in the state, his due share of legislative influence, to controul the commanders, and regulate the service'.[181]

In rural Norfolk the democratic implications of popular arming were made less explicit; but it was noticeable that in September 1782, when a Dutch descent on the east coast was feared, the county's leading opponents of the American war were conspicuous in coming forward to form volunteer units. Sir Edward Astley, a consistent critic of North on America, took command of one such corps.[182] Earlier that year, Shelburne's new popular militia proposals had also elicited a favourable response from many individuals and localities opposed to the coercion of America. Colchester's inhabitants were inclined to peace with the colonies in 1775; more than four times as many of them signed the town's conciliatory petition as put their names to its loyal address.[183] In 1782 Sir Robert Smyth, who had criticized the American conflict since he became one of the borough's MPs in 1780, appears to have had little difficulty in encouraging the town to offer to raise a volunteer corps.[184] In Lewes, Sussex, Lieutenant-Colonel Thomas Hay, a

---

[179] *The Letters of Sir William Jones*, ed. Garland Cannon (2 vols., Oxford, 1970), i. 408, 412. Jones published in 1780 *An Inquiry into the Legal Mode of Suppressing Riots.*

[180] BL, Westminster Committee Papers, Add. MS 38593, fo. 41.

[181] 'A General Militia, Acting by a Well-Regulated Rotation, is the Only Safe Means of Defending a Free People', 42, 47, in *Tracts, Concerning the Ancient and Only True Legal Means of National Defence, by a Free Militia* (London, 1781).

[182] Leeds Archives, Ramsden Papers, Rockingham Letters, vol. 3b, Revd William Palgrave to William Weddell, 2 Sept. [1782]. For the Norfolk volunteers, see above, Ch. 1.

[183] Bradley, *Religion, Revolution and English Radicalism*, 390 (table 10.2).

[184] Essex RO, Smyth Family Papers, D/DFg Z1, Shelburne to Smyth, 11 June 1782.

former MP for the borough and a consistent opponent of North and his American policy, seems to have played an important part in persuading a meeting in the town to increase the local volunteer force, if not to adopt Shelburne's proposals. According to one account, Hay 'strongly encouraged the Idea of arming & declared every man an Enemy to his Country who did not offer his Services on the present Occasion; a proposal for raising 400 men in the Town & neighbouring Parishes was unanimously agreed to'.[185]

The American war was clearly a divisive issue in British and Irish politics. At times opponents and supporters of the coercion of the colonists took their differences to the point of violence. And if the merits of the conflict were hotly debated, the process of mobilization of manpower to fight the war was also bitterly contested. Divisions over the extent and form of military and naval participation reflected and deepened the divisions over the justice and efficacy of the war itself. True, many of the means employed were hardly novel. Compulsion was certainly not new. Naval press-gangs and the forcible recruitment into the army of paupers and vagrants had been features of earlier wars. The hiring of German units was merely a continuation of an established practice. Scottish Highland regiments had been used for the first time in the War of Austrian Succession, and more extensively in the Seven Years War. Irish recruitment, though officially prohibited until 1771, had been an accepted practice during earlier eighteenth-century conflicts. But the American war saw a marked intensification of some of these earlier methods of mobilization, and an important change in the role assigned to foreign auxiliaries. These developments fanned the flames of party controversy. The broader definition of legitimate targets for the press-gangs, the use of German mercenaries against fellow subjects in America rather than foreign enemies in Europe, the greater reliance on Scottish troops, and the policy of actively encouraging Catholic recruitment in Ireland, all seemed to add weight to the opposition case that North's government was set on an authoritarian course. And if conscripted Englishmen, hired German auxiliaries, and all too willing Scottish Jacobites and Irish papists were the means

---

[185] BL, Pelham Papers, Add. MS 33128, fo. 79. See also V. Smith (ed.), *The Town Book of Lewes, 1702–1837* (Sussex Record Society, vol. lxix, Lewes, 1973), 68–9; HO 42/205, fos. 152–4.

chosen by the administration to crush the liberties of the Americans, what was to stop the ministry using these same instruments to establish despotism at home? North's attempts to augment the militia, now seen by many of his opponents as merely an adjunct of the army, and the reluctance of his ministry to allow large-scale arming of the people, further reinforced the impression of a slide into tyranny. In these circumstances it was more or less inevitable that opponents of North and the American aspect of the war should turn to mass arming and, ultimately, to a reformed popular militia, under local control, as a check on executive power.

5

Uniting the Nations?

THE AMERICAN WAR saw a redefining of Britishness. Prior to the war, as recent historians have emphasized, the Americans saw themselves as Britons, or even as Englishmen, imbued with the rights of Englishmen.[1] Their quarrels with the British Parliament and with successive British governments between 1764 and 1775 were based on their perception that they, as Britons in America, were not being treated in the same manner as Britons in Britain. There were many people in the British Isles who accepted the colonial perspective. The colonists were seen by their British and Irish sympathizers as part of the same political community, the same British nation. Once the fighting broke out, as we have seen, there was still a significant number of opponents of the use of military force against the Americans, who wished fervently to reunify the fractured British Atlantic community. Events, however, were to make an inclusive, Greater-Britain type of Britishness untenable. Even before the war began there were Britons who looked upon the colonists as fellow subjects but nonetheless as foreigners.[2] After the bloodshed at Lexington and Concord, the Americans seem to have been envisaged as foreigners by many more Britons. As the Americans themselves were unwilling to be reincorporated into the empire, a grievous blow was struck to the vision of the British as a transatlantic people. By January 1777 Sir George Savile was writing that 'The cause itself wears away by degrees from a question of right and wrong between subjects, to a war between us and a foreign nation . . . I see marks of

[1] See e.g. Jack P. Greene, 'Empire and Identity from the Glorious Revolution to the American Revolution', in *The Oxford History of the British Empire*, ii. *The Eighteenth Century*, ed. P. J. Marshall (Oxford, 1998), 208–30.

[2] P. J. Marshall, 'A Nation Defined by Empire, 1755–1776', in Alexander Grant and Keith J. Stringer (eds.), *Uniting the Kingdom? The Making of British History* (London, 1995), 220.

this everywhere, and in all ranks'.[3] But if the concept of Britishness was increasingly unable, from 1776, to accommodate the Americans, did it become more popular within the British Isles themselves?

Linda Colley has argued in her influential book *Britons* that eighteenth-century wars played a vital part in furthering the adoption of a British national identity. She attaches particular importance to conflicts with France, the great Catholic 'other' against which Protestants throughout Britain could unite.[4] Her work has been criticized, implicitly or explicitly, by a great variety of scholars. For some, Colley's timing is the problem. There are those who see the emergence of a sense of Britishness before the eighteenth century;[5] and, conversely, those who deny that it appeared until the French revolutionary crisis right at its end.[6] Other scholars question whether Britishness ever took hold of the popular imagination. Adrian Hastings argues that Englishness remained the dominant concept for the English long after the end of the eighteenth century;[7] while Douglas Hay and Nicholas Rogers, pursuing a very different line, maintain that any unifying effects provided by wars were insufficient to counterbalance their fissile impact: they prefer to emphasize the kind of social, economic, and political divisions explored elsewhere in this book.[8] J. E. Cookson, for his part, stresses the very varied and complex nature of wartime 'patriotism', which he sees as rather less than a wholehearted expression of loyalty to the nation, let alone to the British state.[9] Eliga Gould, with specific reference to the American war, has pointed to the cosmopolitan tone, with its stress on civilized and enlightened

---

[3] *Memoirs of the Marquis of Rockingham*, ed. Earl of Albemarle (2 vols., London, 1852), ii. 305.

[4] *Britons: Forging the Nation, 1707–1837* (New Haven, 1992), esp. 18, 53, 322, 364–8, 370–1. See also her 'The Reach of the State, the Appeal of the Nation', in Lawrence Stone (ed.), *An Imperial State at War: Britain from 1689 to 1815* (London, 1994), 165–84.

[5] See e.g. Brendan Bradshaw and Peter Roberts (eds.), *British Consciousness and Identity: The Making of Britain 1533–1707* (Cambridge, 1998).

[6] Murray G. H. Pittock, *Inventing and Resisting Britain: Cultural Identities in Britain and Ireland, 1685–1789* (London, 1997), esp. 173. As John M. MacKenzie has written: 'Is the forging of Britishness to be located in the sixteenth, seventeenth, eighteenth or nineteenth centuries?' ('Empire and National Identities: The Case of Scotland', *Transactions of the Royal Historical Society*, 6th ser., 8 (1998), 215).

[7] Adrian Hastings, *The Construction of Nationhood: Ethnicity, Religion and Nationalism* (Cambridge, 1997), 60–3.

[8] Douglas Hay and Nicholas Rogers, *Eighteenth-Century English Society* (Oxford, 1997), esp. 152–67.

[9] J. E. Cookson, *The British Armed Nation 1793–1815* (Oxford, 1997), introd.

European norms, adopted by some members of the British elite—a response that would seem to be very different from the aggressive and introverted Britishness identified by Colley.[10] Further challenges might be offered if consideration is given to the recognition and strengthening of localism that occurred during the American conflict, and to the separate patriotisms of the four nations of the British Isles that were in some respects brought into sharp relief by the war and would seem to suggest considerable limitations on the growth of a British identity.

But the experience of the American war could just as easily be said to support the Colley thesis, or even to imply that it might be pushed further.[11] Localism, as we shall see, was not necessarily incompatible with an overarching sense of Britishness. Nor was contemporary English, Welsh, Scottish, and even Irish patriotism. Identity was and is multifaceted; which facet is in the sunlight depends to a considerable degree on the circumstances of the moment. The American conflict created circumstances conducive to widespread identification with Britain among the peoples of the British Isles. Military service, both for those who participated personally and for the public at large, can be seen as a means by which the sense of a British nation gained ground; the fear of invasion—which Colley has shown to have been so important in the 1790s—operated strongly from 1778; and, with France, Spain, and the United Provinces joining the war between 1778 and 1780, Britain was faced with a multiplicity of enemies.

Provincialism

Local loyalty, it could be argued, provided a considerable counterweight to commitment to the nation, whether that nation was seen simply as England, Wales, Scotland, Ireland, or the broader but more remote Britain. If the eighteenth century saw the emergence

---

[10] Eliga H. Gould, 'American Independence and Britain's Counter-Revolution', *Past & Present*, 154 (1997), 107–41.

[11] Colley, *Britons*, 8, explicitly rejects the idea that the Irish were willing to subscribe to Britishness, and thereafter gives them little coverage. The evidence presented below tends to support the views of Sean Connolly, who sees the Irish in the 18th cent. in a very different light. See his 'Varieties of Britishness: Ireland, Scotland and Wales in the Hanoverian State', in Grant and Stringer (eds.), *Uniting the Kingdom?*, 193–207.

in all its glory of the 'fiscal-military state', geared to the successful prosecution of wars,[12] this does not necessarily mean that the central state was playing a more significant role in domestic government. Local authorities remained vigorous.[13] Indeed, historians have recently pointed out that local government took on more responsibilities at this time, and sought to increase its scope for action.[14] Local government, moreover, was far more visible and intrusive to most inhabitants of the British Isles than was central government. Clergymen of the established churches could perhaps be said to be instruments of the state who were permanently (or at least frequently) present at the local level; and assize judges, travelling around their circuits, were peripatetic representatives. But important as these figures of authority undoubtedly were, day-to-day government of the provinces depended on those local worthies who sat as justices in the quarter and petty sessions or their equivalents, as councillors in boroughs or burghs, or even as parish officers. Despite the broadening opportunities offered in many parts of the British Isles by improved communications, an increasingly integrated market, and urban growth, the county, town, or even parish remained the mental horizon for many of the people. In the Highlands of Scotland, clan loyalty, though weakened since the 'Forty-Five Rebellion, continued to be influential. When the Earl of Bute was urging the formation of a company of fenciblemen in the Western Isles in *1778*, it was noticeable that he appealed to tradition and locality. Mountstuart House, the Earl's ancestral home, was thought to be under threat from American privateers; if the threat

---

[12] See John Brewer, *The Sinews of Power: War, Money and the English State 1688–1783* (London, 1989).

[13] For the situation in Wales see P. D. G. Thomas, 'Society, Government and Politics', in Donald Moore (ed.), *Wales in the Eighteenth Century* (Swansea, 1976), 20–2; Melvin Humphreys, *The Crisis of Community: Montgomeryshire, 1680–1815* (Cardiff, 1996), 201–5, 212. For Scottish county government see Ann E. Whetstone, *Scottish County Government in the Eighteenth and Nineteenth Centuries* (Edinburgh, 1981), and for an indication of its vigorousness, R. Mitchison, 'North and South: the Development of the Gulf in Poor Law Practice', in R. A. Houston and I. D. Whyte (eds.), *Scottish Society 1500–1800* (Cambridge, 1989), 215–17.

[14] David Eastwood, *Government and Community in the English Provinces, 1700–1870* (London, 1997), 17–18. Joanna Innes has stressed, however, the role of parliament — a central institution — in enabling many local initiatives. See her essays on 'Parliament and the Shaping of Eighteenth-Century Social Policy', *Transactions of the Royal Historical Society*, 5th ser. 40 (1990), 63–92 and 'The Local Acts of a National Parliament: Parliament's Role in Sanctioning Local Acts in Eighteenth-Century Britain', *Parliamentary History*, 17 (1998), 23–47.

materialized, there was no doubt that 'the Bute people to a man would take up arms'.[15]

Indeed, far from weakening local identification, the American war might well have strengthened it. The mobilization of manpower reflected and gave due recognition to the persistence of provincial feeling. Volunteer corps in England, Wales, and Scotland (though not, as we shall see, in Ireland) were in almost every sense the negation of a national force. They were formed on local initiative and mainly for local purposes. Their agenda was to defend their own communities from attack and to help preserve order in their own areas.[16] As the government did not for the most part approve of the volunteer companies, no effort was made to persuade them to cooperate with each other and form larger, militarily more efficient units. But even in its handling of the official armed forces, the government respected the strength of localism. The acceptance of various offers from Highland chieftains to raise regiments is surely a reflection of this. The claims of the lairds to be able to fill their corps with rapidity were based on their continuing importance as land-lords and sources of local patronage, not on assertions of Highland loyalty to the British state.[17] In England and Wales, the militia was organized by county, with each hundred and parish required to provide a quota of men. Embodied militia regiments became for many people manifestations of the spirit of the shire. True, the militia did not excite universal enthusiasm. Riots took place in Sussex when the county's regiment was embodied;[18] and throughout England and Wales many eligible men took every possible step to avoid service.[19] As a result of this unwillingness, a good proportion of militiamen seem to have been substitutes hired from beyond county boundaries—such as Noah Keene of Kirdford in Sussex, who served in the Surrey militia, Thomas Clark of the Leicestershires, who was a Nottingham freeman, and the men from Oxfordshire who acted as

---

[15] *Papers of Peter May, Land Surveyor*, ed. Ian H. Adams (Scottish History Society, 4th ser. vol. xv, Edinburgh, 1979), 206.   [16] See above, Ch. 3.

[17] See e.g. BL, Hamilton and Greville Papers, Add. MS 42071, fo. 195: 'The Earl of Seaforth being sensible that from his Influence & property in the Highlands of Scotland he can be of effectual Service to his Majesty by raising expeditiously a Body of men . . .'. The reality, however, was rather different. See below, p. 190 and n. 122. Andrew Mackillop, *'More fruitful than the Soil': Army, Empire and the Scottish Highlands 1715–1815* (East Linton, 1999), stresses the thoroughly entrepreneurial side of the lairds rather than their feudal influence.   [18] Kent Archives Office, Amherst MSS, U 1350 076/9.

[19] See above, Ch. 1.

substitutes in the Berkshire regiment.[20] Even so, to many contemporaries the militia symbolized the county and was therefore viewed with a special sense of pride. In December 1778 the directors of York's Assembly Rooms decided to allow the North Yorkshire militia to use part of their premises as a guard house 'in Consideration of its being a Corps belonging to the County'.[21] To William Thomas, a Glamorgan schoolteacher, the death of 'Two of our Militia' while serving with the regiment at Preston in Lancashire was an event worthy of note in his diary.[22] Lady Sarah Lennox, whose brother was colonel of the Sussex regiment, explained that she and her local social circle were '*mighty* proud' of the corps, '& think it may be matched with any Militia in England'.[23] Competition, indeed, seems to have been a driving force for those who commanded the militia. When different regiments met in camp, they spent a good deal of time trying to outdo each other, with rivalry between their bands being particularly intense.[24] But one of the clearest indications of the way in which the militia acted as a focus for provincial sentiment is a curious episode in Staffordshire. In 1779 the local gentry responded to the urgent need for troops by agreeing to augment the bounty money given to recruits joining regular regiments. But when the committee organizing the subscription suggested that a particular regiment should be singled out for their largesse, and that it should henceforth be called the Staffordshire regiment, there was a storm of protest. Such a designation, it was argued by opponents of the scheme, would offend the militia, which was already regarded as the county's own corps.[25] In the end, with subscribers threatening to withdraw their money, it was agreed to drop the plan for associating

[20] West Sussex RO, Kirdford Parish Records, 116/36/1; *An Exact List of the Burgesses, of the Town and County of Nottingham, who Polled . . . for the Election of Two Burgesses* (Nottingham, 1780); Berkshire RO, Quarter Sessions Order-book, 1779–86, Q/SO 5, p. 50.

[21] York City Archives, York Assembly Rooms Papers, M23/2, Minute-book of Directors and General Meetings, 155.

[22] *The Diary of William Thomas of Michaelston-super-Ely, near St Fagans Glamorgan 1762–1795*, ed. R. T. W. Denning (Cardiff, 1995), 312.

[23] *The Life and Letters of Lady Sarah Lennox*, ed. Countess of Ilchester and Lord Stavordale (2 vols., London, 1901), i. 296.

[24] Paul Langford, *A Polite and Commercial People: A History of England 1727–1783* (Oxford, 1989), 628. This probably explains why militia regiments tried to recruit musicians from far beyond county boundaries. See e.g. NLW, Spence Colby Papers, B, Pembrokeshire Militia Documents, certificates of enrolment, 1782.

[25] Staffordshire RO, Dartmouth MSS, D(W) 1778/v. 734–5.

a specific army regiment with the county, and to extend the subscription to cover recruits entering any regular corps.[26]

On this occasion, the initial suggestion that an army regiment might
be allocated to a county came, it appears, from members of the county
elite themselves; but in 1782 the initiative came from the new government, which sought to make such county affiliation universal as a means
of promoting recruitment. The lord-lieutenant of Leicestershire, for
instance, was told on 19 July that the commanding officer of the Eighth
Foot wanted to attach his corps to the county 'and bear its name'; the
lord-lieutenant, for his part, was expected to provide all the necessary
support and encouragement for the association, so that the regiment
could be brought up to strength with all possible speed.[27] But if this
arrangement was willed by the government, it was, paradoxically, a
reflection of the continuing importance of provincialism; the assumption behind the scheme was that men would more readily enlist in a
corps that they could identify as their own.

Yet the underlying message here was surely that provincialism and
loyalty to the nation were not mutually exclusive. Local allegiance
and national identity can exist side by side, or operate on different
levels of consciousness. The first can even reinforce the second,
enabling the component parts to relate to the more abstract and
inaccessible whole. Local subscriptions exemplify this point. The
Staffordshire situation was not replicated across the country. While
some county subscriptions appear to have been directed towards the
manpower needs of several regular regiments, usually those already
recruiting in the area,[28] there are instances of county elites successfully adopting a single regiment as a means of linking local initiative
with the national war effort. In Warwickshire, the subscription
raised early in 1778 led to the forging of a connection with the
Sixth Foot, seemingly on the initiative of the local organizers.[29] And
several town elites, we should recall, even raised their own
regiments—such as the Manchester Volunteers (or Seventy-second
Foot), the Liverpool Blues (or Seventy-ninth Foot), and the

---

[26] BL, Liverpool Papers, Add. MS 38212, fos. 134, 174.

[27] Leicestershire RO, Lieutenancy Papers, LM 8/8/6.

[28] In Oxfordshire e.g. the county subscription was intended to offer enhanced bounties
to recruits entering any one of ten infantry battalions: *Jackson's Oxford Journal*, 11 Sept.
1779.

[29] *Aris's Birmingham Gazette*, 19 Jan. 1778. The 6th Foot had been recruiting in the
county since the beginning of the war: see Gloucestershire RO, Blathwayt Papers, D
1799/F69.

Edinburgh Regiment (the Eightieth Foot). Similarly, in the last year of the war, schemes were pursued to build warships associated with a particular county. In Suffolk the county meeting decided to cover the cost of a seventy-four-gun vessel 'by voluntary subscription'.[30] A similar plan was discussed at a county meeting in Cornwall.[31] In Essex a proposal was put forward 'for building a Ship of 90 Guns for the Protection of the County of Essex and Kingdom of Great Britain, by a voluntary Subscription of the County of Essex'. The ship was to be called 'the Essex Lion', but the connection between local pride and a wider allegiance was brought out very clearly. Now was the time, it was said, 'for National Exertion'. 'It is obvious that a Fleet raised by the Counties for home Service will give Administration a greater force to send abroad for the protection of Gibraltar, the Mediterranean, Levant, and Baltic trade, our West India Islands and other possessions'.[32]

Component Patriotisms

Wales had been administratively absorbed into England in Henry VIII's reign. While linguistically the Welsh remained separate and distinct, and there was something of a cultural revival in the eighteenth century,[33] there was no movement for national independence, or even pressure for greater autonomy. Indeed, given that Wales was predominantly an agricultural country, with a small and mainly scattered population, the temptation is to view it less as a nation and more as a collection of locally oriented and tradition-bound communities. The impression of an inward-looking people is certainly conveyed by the observations of an American Quaker visitor in 1776. The Welsh, he wrote, were not at all interested in the war across the Atlantic: 'they know as little as they care'.[34] Yet even in Wales, the 'least restive of the Celtic dependencies',[35] there

---

[30] *The Oakes Diaries*, ed. Jane Fisk, i (Suffolk Record Society, vol. xxxii, Woodbridge, 1990), 225, 226.   [31] Cornwall RO, Tremayne of Heligan Papers, DDT 1891.
[32] Essex RO, Quarter Sessions Records, Q/SBb 309, Oct. 1782.
[33] Prys Morgan, *A New History of Wales: The Eighteenth-Century Renaissance* (Llandybie, Dyfed, 1981); Geraint H. Jenkins, *The Foundations of Modern Wales 1642–1780* (Oxford, 1987), ch. 10.
[34] *An American Quaker in the British Isles: The Travel Journals of Jabez Maud Fisher*, ed. Kenneth Morgan (Oxford, 1992), 229.
[35] Connolly, 'Varieties of Britishness', 199.

was national sensitivity. Daines Barrington and James Hayes, having presided over the Great Sessions for Merionethshire in March 1777, gave the secretary of state an indication of the continuing need to respect a well-developed sense of Welshness. The two judges had wanted to allow the law to take its course when Robert Williams was convicted before them of horse-stealing. But political considerations convinced them of the need for Williams to be spared. The previous September John Manley had been found guilty at the Merioneth-shire sessions of the same offence and, after a petition had been presented by his neighbours, his execution had been respited. Williams was a Welshman and Manley an Englishman, from Market Drayton, Shropshire. To execute Williams but allow Manley to live, the judges advised, would lead it to be supposed 'in this part of the world' that 'the same law does not hold with regard to Englishmen & Welshmen'.[36]

If there was a Welsh patriotism that might have militated against British unity, there was a still stronger Scottish national feeling. Scotland had joined England and Wales in a legislative union only in 1707. The preservation of a separate Scottish legal system and church structure, together with the continued vitality of long-established institutions of higher learning, meant that many Scots still identified strongly with Scotland as a nation. As recently as 1745–6—within living memory when the American war began—a Jacobite uprising had acted as a vehicle for the expression of national grievances. And assertive Scottishness was still to be encountered at the time of the American conflict. The failure of attempts to create a Scottish militia during the war convinced many Scots that they were still not trusted by the English, and that they were considered as second-class subjects rather than equal partners.[37] The official disapproval of the volunteer corps formed in such places as Aberdeen, Campbeltown, and Ayr in 1778, leading to their disbandment, similarly raised Scottish hackles.[38] Resentment at the way in which English contractors had cornered the profits of clothing the army gave rise to an outburst of distinctly Scottish national feeling: 'if the people of Scotland behave with proper spirit', an Edinburgh news-

[36] SP 37/12, fo. 54.
[37] See John Robertson, *The Scottish Enlightenment and the Militia Issue* (Edinburgh, 1985), chs. 5 and 6.
[38] See Dr Williams's Library, Wodrow-Kenrick Correspondence, MS 24157(74); SP 54/47, fos. 135, 137, 151, 306–7.

paper told its readers, 'they will *insist* that the regiments raised there shall be clothed in Scots manufactures; for it is fully as reasonable that the profits arising from our subscriptions should be given to our poor labourers, as that they should go into the pockets of government contractors'.[39]

Scottish sensitivities were as nothing, however, compared to those of the Irish. Both the Protestant minority and the Catholic majority demonstrated a sturdy sense of separateness from Britain and the British. For the Protestants, as we shall see in more detail later, the American war underlined Ireland's subordinate status but at the same time offered an opportunity to redress grievances.[40] The result was the intensification of a form of Irish Protestant patriotism that had been manifesting itself increasingly since the accession of George III in 1760. In the Dublin Parliament and the press direct comparisons were made between the American and Irish positions. Thomas Conolly, an influential MP and great landowner, announced in November 1777 that 'we shall be treated in the same manner I much fear as the other Colonies, as they were called, on the other side of the Atlantick: and the best that can be said is, that this Country has not been thought of at all, except when there was anything that could be taken from us'.[41] To support the British Parliament's claim to 'have an unlimited right to tax internally every part of the British dominions', a letter in a Limerick paper maintained, undermined the rights of Ireland as 'a distinct nation' and 'annihilates every principle of national liberty'.[42] Defence of Irish rights merged with sympathy for the Americans particularly strongly in the case of the Presbyterians, many of whom had relatives living in the rebel colonies, and who were given added reason to feel dissatisfied by the Irish Test Act of 1704, which limited office-holding to Anglicans.[43]

The volunteer corps formed among the Protestant population when French invasion threatened were therefore viewed with some apprehension by both the British and Irish governments, with the Ulster companies, which contained many Presbyterians, causing particular concern. The political role of the volunteers will be

---

[39] *Caledonian Mercury*, 10 Jan. 1778.   [40] See below, Ch. 6.
[41] *An Edition of the Cavendish Irish Parliamentary Diary 1776–1778*, ed. Anthony R. Black (3 vols., Delavan, Ws., 1984), iii. 270.
[42] *Limerick Chronicle*, 12 Dec. 1776.
[43] For a fuller discussion of this, see below, Ch. 7.

discussed in the next chapter, but for the moment we should note that, unlike most of their British counterparts, they were willing to serve outside their immediate locality and to amalgamate with other units to form larger formations. In October 1779, for instance, a meeting of the Tyrone Ditches and Acton Volunteers passed a resolution expressing their wish to join with other companies to make a battalion. On their own they could do little, they concluded; but as part of a larger unit they could contribute effectively to the defence of their country.[44] The pattern, then, was for companies to come together in battalions, and battalions in regiments. By 1781 there was in effect a volunteer army, with Charlemont as its commander-in-chief. A Dublin newspaper described the volunteers as 'rightly considered as the palladium of Ireland';[45] and at least some of the volunteers saw themselves as having a greater claim to be regarded as the Irish national force than did the British army based in Ireland. In 1780 there was a symbolically significant and potentially explosive incident in Dublin when, according to a cavalry officer, 'a Detachment of Regulars met a larger body of these Volunteers in the Street, who would not give way, as usual, & most likely would have proceeded to violence had not the well-judged prudence of the Regular Comg: Officer prevented it by letting them pass'.[46]

But if the war appeared to widen the gap between Britain and Protestant Ireland, what about Catholic Ireland? The Anglican Revd Dr John Hotham, newly arrived in Dublin, was taken aback by the sullen demeanour of the 'lower sort', which, in effect, meant the Catholics. He painted a picture of an alienated and irreconcilable people: 'They are slothful, gloomy, obstinate, and ungrateful; and neither improved by benefits, nor sensible of kindness.'[47] Quartermaster Dundas was convinced that an invading French army would be joined by the Catholic peasantry,[48] and other observers were equally sure that no reliance could be placed on their loyalty: 'we ought to be more and more on our guard', wrote Sir Edward Newenham after a visit to Kilkenny. 'The tunes their pipes played and the toasts they gave, were as good evidence as if given under their hands. The declarations of the younger females, who have not

---

[44] HMC, 12th Report, app. pt. x, *Charlemont MSS*, i (London, 1891), 360.
[45] *General Evening Post*, 3 and 12 Jan. 1782.
[46] *The Pembroke Papers*, ed. Lord Herbert (2 vols., London, 1939–50), i. 434.
[47] HMC, *Stopford Sackville MSS* (2 vols., London, 1904–10), i. 248.
[48] 'Considerations with regard to the Invasion, and Defence of Ireland'.

as yet learned political hypocrisy, were as bold as in former times.'[49] Likewise, the Earl of Shannon, a great southern grandee, reminded the lord-lieutenant that the original purpose of many of the volunteer companies was to protect their families and properties 'from being violated and plundered in Case of the apprehended Risings of the lower Class of People': a Catholic insurrection to match the Great Rebellion of 1641 was apparently what many Protestants feared.[50] More significant, perhaps, than the reports and anxieties of nervous Protestants are the insights into Catholic attitudes provided by the actions of the Catholic 'lower sort' themselves. To many such Catholics the British army was clearly the enemy—an occupying force that should be undermined at every opportunity. Soldiers who tried to escape from the service were sheltered: in November 1782 the lord-lieutenant referred to 'an almost universal disposition of the lower Class of People to assist Deserters'.[51] Those troops who remained with the colours were in danger of attack. The rank and file of the Thirty-second Foot was ordered not to go alone into the environs of Waterford, but only in groups of four or five.[52] In September 1776 Harcourt submitted to North a list of 'some of the unfortunate soldiers who were inhumanely houghed [maimed] in the streets of Dublin'.[53]

The English perspective is also instructive. When they thought of the nation, the English often thought only of England. Matthew Flinders, a Lincolnshire surgeon, wrote in October 1778 of 'this critical & important Crisis of England';[54] 'Jack England', rather than a more encompassing British figure, was contrasted with an effete Frenchman in a cartoon published in 1779;[55] in September 1780 Sir Thomas Egerton invited men in Lancashire to join his fencible regiment 'For the Defence of Old England';[56] Philip Mayow, a naval chaplain from Cornwall, bewailed the fate of 'poor Old England' in

---

[49] HMC, *Dartmouth MSS* (3 vols., London, 1887–96), iii. 240.
[50] NLI, Heron Papers, MS 13038, Shannon to Buckinghamshire, 15 Aug. 1779. See also NLI, MS 14306, 'Irish Military Associations', another paper by Dundas, dated 2 Feb. 1780: 'every Man trembled for his property and family expecting that the hour of foreign descent, would be that of Domestic Insurrection and that all the horrors of the year 40 [*sic*] would be again renewed'.
[51] BL, Buckingham Papers, Add. MS 40178, fo. 29.
[52] NLI, MS 3750, Order-book, 32nd Foot, 28 Feb., 6 July 1776.
[53] *The Harcourt Papers*, ed. E. W. Harcourt (14 vols., Oxford, 1880–1905), x. 182.
[54] Lincolnshire Archives Office, Flinders's Diary and Account-book, 3 Oct. 1778.
[55] BM 5611 and 5612.
[56] East Sussex RO, Sheffield Papers, A 2714/265, printed broadsheet, 27 Sept. 1780.

June 1781;[57] and Admiral Keppel routinely referred to the 'English fleet'.[58] In some cases this Anglocentric usage no doubt reflected the complacent belief that Britain could be conceived merely as an extension of England; in others it seems likely that the word Britain was avoided for a more defensive reason—because it implied partnership with the Scots, and therefore Scottish access to places of profit and power in England.

Indeed, it could easily be argued that anti-Scottish and anti-Irish feeling in England was heightened by the war. Irish calls for commercial concessions met with determined opposition from many manufacturing and trading towns in England. Even Lichfield, which had little industry but produced some sailcloth, sent in a petition against Irish free trade, protesting that such a concession would 'deprive the manufacturers in several Branches of Trade in this Kingdom of Employment and reduce them and their familys to great distress'.[59] And if economic interest pitted Ireland against England, or even Britain, so did religious reform. The granting of limited relief for Catholics almost certainly helped to stimulate hostility to the Irish, as did the fear that the government might try to raise Catholic regiments to put down the rebellious Americans. That the war years saw a revival in the publication of anti-Irish cartoons in England was surely no coincidence. One such was 'Paddy on Horse-Back', a traditional attack on the Irish as opportunistic fortune-hunters, which appeared in March 1779.[60]

But it was the Scots who came in for the strongest criticism, probably because they were believed to be gaining most from wartime developments. Elizabeth Baker, an Englishwoman living in Wales, was robustly Scotophobic. In October 1779, for instance, she declared that the Scots peers Bute and Mansfield directed government and that 'Sandwich, Germain, & North, are no more than their puppets; yet all should be shorten'd as Traitors to England'. Shortly afterwards, commemorating the anniversary of the battle of Agincourt, she reflected that '*our* 5th Henry' had been blessed with counsellors who were not '*Scots*'. Only when Scottish influence was extinguished, she seemed to imply, would

---

[57] Cornwall RO, Wynell-Mayow Papers, DDWM 565.
[58] e.g. Nottingham University Library, Portland Papers, PWF 6104.
[59] Lichfield RO, Corporation Records, D77/5/2, Hall Book, vol. ii, fo. 192.
[60] BM 5605.

success come in the present war.[61] A cartoon of 1781 attacked the Scots as feeding on 'Old Englands Vitals';[62] while in 1779 there appeared 'Sawney in the Bog-House', a piece of lavatorial humour that imitated earlier versions published at the time of the 'Forty-Five Rebellion and again in 1762, at the height of English hysteria about the influence of Bute.[63] When the issue of a Scottish militia was debated in the Commons in March 1776, John Sawbridge, a Wilkite radical, vehemently opposed the proposal, arguing that the Scots 'were in general tinctured with notions of despotism; their laws and education inclined them that way'. He went on to say that they could not therefore be trusted with a militia, 'for when they once got arms in their hands, their dispositions uniting with their interests, might render them instruments in the hands of a treacherous, tyrannic and unprincipled administration'.[64] We have seen that the parliamentary opposition also attacked the government for relying so heavily on Scottish troops, and how this reliance was taken as proof of ministerial commitment to the same authoritarian principles that lay behind Jacobitism.[65] A letter addressed to Lord Barrington, the secretary at war, which was published in a leading periodical, pursued the same line still further, complaining about the preference given to the offers made by Scots to raise new corps and even commenting adversely on the large number of Scots officers in the army as a whole.[66] Henry Jackson, a middle-aged lieutenant hoping for promotion, made much the same point with regard to the navy: 'had I been a Scotchman', he told the Duke of Portland, 'I make no doubt but I should have been prefered'.[67] And on at least one occasion this kind of tension went beyond a war of words: in 1779 a duel was fought near Coxheath camp between an English lieutenant and a Scottish ensign in the Somerset militia; 'The difference arose', according to a report on the incident, 'on some reflections cast on the country of the latter.'[68]

Mutual hostility between the peoples of the British Isles would seem to cast doubt on the unifying effects of the American war. But look at another set of views, and a different impression is conveyed.

---

[61] NLW, Peniarth MS 416A, Journal of Elizabeth Baker, 10 and 25 Oct. 1779.
[62] BM 5831, 'The Junto, in a Bowl Dish'. [63] BM 5539.
[64] *PH* xviii. 1236. [65] See above, Ch. 4.
[66] *Gentleman's Magazine*, 47 (1777), 15–16.
[67] Nottingham University Library, Portland Papers, PWF 5788.
[68] *Gentleman's Magazine*, 49 (1779), 375.

Consider first the Welsh. Linguistically separate, they prided themselves on being 'Ancient Britons', a status that might be used to
emphasize their distinctive purity but could just as easily lead to a
ready appreciation of their role in a wider entity. In December 1777
several Welsh landowners proposed to raise a regiment to help the
war effort. This could be seen both as an expression of Welshness
and as a commitment to Britain. But what gave this episode a
particularly British flavour was their choice of commanding officer.
The gentlemen in question nominated Thomas Dundas, a Scotsman
with strong Yorkshire connections. The king wanted a Welshman to
command the proposed corps, but the Welsh gentlemen were
unwilling to proceed without Dundas.[69]

The English, as we have just seen, often seem to have displayed a
continuing reluctance to consider themselves as British, and there
were signs of a heightened hostility to the Scots and the Irish. But
this has to be set against the equally striking willingness of some of
the English to see themselves as part of a wider Britain. The
corporation of Leicester, addressing the king in 1775, emphasized
'the two british [not just English] Blessings of Law and Liberty';[70]
Richard Reeve, a customs officer, considered the war to be a struggle
between 'Great Britain' and 'the Colonies';[71] Edward Gibbon, the
historian and MP, referred in a private letter to 'the Naval strength
of Great Britain';[72] and John Mervin Nooth, a surgeon attached to
the army in America, when he wrote of 'the Nation' and 'our
Country', clearly meant not simply England but Britain ('we shall
soon see a reconciliation between Great Britain & her Colonies').[73]
Anti-Scottish feeling, it might be added, should not always be taken
too seriously; on some occasions, at least, it was ridiculed by
contemporary Englishmen. When Earl Percy wrote from besieged
Boston that Brigadier James Grant's hold over General Howe would
convince the English radicals that 'the Scotch influenced the
Cabinets here as well as at home', he was poking fun at the

---

[69] North Yorkshire RO, Zetland (Dundas) MSS, ZNK X1/2/320.
[70] Mary Bateson, Helen Stocks, and G. A. Chinnery (eds.), *Records of the Borough of
Leicester* (7 vols., London, Cambridge, and Leicester, 1899–1974), v. 240.
[71] Buckinghamshire RO, Howard-Vyse Deposit, D/HV B10/2, 8.
[72] *The Letters of Edward Gibbon*, ed. J. E. Norton (3 vols., London, 1956), ii. 156.
[73] Hertfordshire RO, Verulam MSS, D/EV F 25, Nooth to Lady Grimston, 23 Nov.
1779 and n.d. [but Oct. 1781]. Nooth, it should be added, had studied at Edinburgh
University, where he qualified as a doctor of medicine in 1766, which might help to
explain his willingness to adopt a British perspective.

Wilkites.[74] There was even the occasional pro-Scottish cartoon. In 1779 'The Present State of Great Britain' depicted a Highland soldier defending the traditional cap of liberty from the French— an allusion, presumably, to the number of Highland regiments that had been raised.[75]

Indeed, by the end of the war conspicuous Scottish military service might well have helped to soften remaining English prejudices. Memories of the 'Forty-Five and Scottish invasion could now be overlaid by more positive images of Scottish loyalty and service. Scottish politicians and lawyers who made their careers in England might still be resented, but there was no denying the contribution of Scottish soldiers and sailors to the British war effort. The staunch defence of Minorca by the Scottish General James Murray, and particularly his refusal to accept a bribe offered by the allied commander, marked him out as a true British hero. 'The prop of Britain's sinking name', was how Murray was described in a topical ode, 'The bulwark of her falling fame'. Indeed, Murray was even ranked alongside such seventeenth-century *English* heroes as John Hampden and Algernon Sidney, who had made their libertarian reputations by resisting arbitrary Stuart (and therefore Scottish) monarchs.[76] The attempt to introduce a Scottish militia in 1782 came much nearer to success than the proposal of 1776, partly, one suspects, because advocates of a militia were able to point to the conspicuous service of the Scots during the war: 'no men had proved themselves firmer supporters of the crown than the Scotch', Lord Maitland told the Commons.[77] A month later the Marquis of Graham was given leave to bring in a bill to allow the wearing of Highland dress, which had been prohibited by legislation passed in the aftermath of the 'Forty-Five Rebellion. Again, the central argument was that the Scots had amply demonstrated their loyalty through their service 'by sea and land'.[78] English MPs appear to have been sufficiently persuaded to allow the bill to proceed. Two years later the estates forfeited by leading Jacobites in 1746 were returned to their families. One important practical reason seems to have been the failure of the board established to administer the

---

[74] Boston Public Library, Letters of Hugh, Earl Percy, G.31.39.7, 7 Jan. 1776.
[75] BM 5579.   [76] *Ode on the Taking of Minorca* (London, 1782), 7.
[77] *PH*, xxiii. 15–16.   [78] Ibid. 113.

estates;[79] but in the debates on the issue the military role of the descendants of the Jacobite rebels was stressed, and it seems likely that it was generally accepted that the families had redeemed themselves by service during the war.[80]

Turn to the Scots themselves, and similar observations can be made. Clan loyalty and Scottish patriotism exerted an influence, but, like English and Welsh provincialism, they were not necessarily incompatible with a British national identity. Indeed, expressions of Scottish patriotism, as Colin Kidd has noted, were often products of commitment to Britain and not a rejection of Britishness. What the Scots wanted was to be treated in the same way as Englishmen. Denial of that status, as when the Scots were not allowed a militia, provoked outbursts of 'Scotocentric patriotism', but this was essentially consistent with loyalty to the union.[81] Even pride in the Scottish contribution to the war effort, especially through the Highland regiments, was ultimately the pride of partnership rather than an assertion of distinctiveness. In August 1778 Captain Charles Napier, on the naval impress service in Edinburgh, used Anglo-Scottish rivalry to promote a British end, namely the manning of the fleet. 'He hopes', Napier's advertisement ran, 'that the brave fellows of Scottish Seamen will speedily repair to him and not allow themselves to be outdone by the English'.[82] Nor is there any shortage of evidence that many Scots were fully prepared to think as Britons when circumstances encouraged such a self-perception. In the course of the debates on the 1776 Scottish militia bill, Sir Adam Ferguson, MP for Ayrshire, even argued that 'the treaty of Union had abolished the names of Englishman and Scotchman, and united them in that of Briton'.[83] In the aftermath of Lieutenant-Colonel Baillies's disastrous defeat in India, and the precipitous retirement of the main Madras army of the East India Company in the face of Haidar Ali's forces, a Highland officer serving in India was deeply upset by 'so Scandalous so Dishonourable a retreat Made by British Troops'.[84] In August 1779, when the combined Franco-Spanish fleet

---

[79] Annette M. Smith, 'The Administration of the Forfeited Annexed Estates, 1752–1784', in G. W. S. Barrow (ed.), *The Scottish Tradition: Essays in Honour of Ronald Gordon Cant* (Edinburgh, 1974), 198–210.   [80] *PH* xxiv. 1322, 1365, 1370.

[81] Colin Kidd, 'North Britishness and the Nature of Eighteenth-Century British Patriotisms', *Historical Journal*, 39 (1996), 361–82.

[82] *Caledonian Mercury*, 1 Aug. 1778.   [83] *PH* xviii. 1231.

[84] Centre of South Asian Studies, Cromartie Papers, Major James Mackenzie to ——, 3 Nov. 1780.

was lying off Plymouth, the Glasgow firm of Alexander Houston and Sons told one of its Caribbean correspondents that the enemy was 'now Lording it in the *British* Channell'. Houstons added the hope that Sir Charles Hardy's ships would 'render a good account of them, otherwise this nation seems to be undone'.[85] The nation in question, it hardly needs to be said, was Britain, not Scotland. Likewise, Archibald Douglas, an army officer, prayed in April 1782 that the new ministry would 'never Suffer the British Sourd to be Sheethed until Britannia has gaind a complete redress of all her grievances: for that desirable end may the almighty inspire our Great national councils with wisdom to direct & our officers & people with zeal and courage to doe their duty'.[86]

Even Irish patriotism could live alongside a commitment to Britain. For Protestants, whatever their sympathy for the Americans, hostilities with France brought them closer to the sister kingdom. A French war, John Beresford, a member of the Irish administration, predicted in March 1778, 'will have certainly the advantage of uniting these nations'. 'The zeal and spirit of this country is up', he continued, 'and, if proper measures are adopted, great support may be had'.[87] The measures Beresford had in mind were trade concessions by the British government. But even before such concessions were granted in December 1779, the Bourbon threat seems to have propelled Protestants noticeably nearer to acknowledging their ultimate commitment to Britain. It was perhaps hardly surprising that Lord Shannon, a government supporter, should regard the coming of the Spanish war in June 1779 as an opportunity for all the king's subjects to unite 'in their most strenuous Exertions for the Support of the British Empire'.[88] More notable is the fact that Keppel's acquittal encouraged the volunteers at Donaghadee, County Down, to celebrate in February 1779 with loyal tunes such as 'Britons strike home'.[89] And when concessions over trade eventually came, and then, more importantly, reform of the constitutional relationship between the two kingdoms, identification with Britain and Britishness increased still more. Once it could be claimed, with some degree of plausibility,

---

[85] NLS, Houston Papers, MS 8794, p. 231, emphasis added.
[86] Birmingham City Archives, Galton Papers, 245/1.
[87] *The Correspondence of the Right Hon. John Beresford*, ed. William Beresford (2 vols., London, 1854), i. 21–2.
[88] NLI Heron Papers, MS 13038, Shannon to Buckinghamshire, 26 June 1779.
[89] *Belfast News-letter*, 19–23 Feb. 1779.

that Ireland had been put in a position of near equality with Britain, then Irish Protestants paraded their loyalty and seemed to wish to be regarded as part of the wider British nation. In gratitude for the granting of legislative independence, the Irish Parliament voted money for the manning of the navy. The volunteers, even those in Ulster who had been viewed with the deepest suspicion by the Irish and British administrations, helped to recruit the mariners.[90] News of Rodney's victory at the Saintes, which came very shortly after the winning of legislative independence, was celebrated with as much enthusiasm as anywhere in England. In Dublin, according to a local newspaper, in one of the windows in Parliament Street was a banner bearing the words 'Ireland is free,—Rodney,—and may the British flag flourish all over the globe.' 'Now, henceforth, and for evermore', the report went on excitedly, 'may Irishmen have cause to rejoice at Britain's success and glory!'[91]

There are even some grounds for suggesting that Irish Catholics could identify with Britishness. Leading Catholic gentlemen and traders had been lobbying for mitigation of the penal laws since the formation of the Catholic Committee in 1759. The American war provided a golden opportunity to press their case. At a time when the British government was urgently seeking military manpower, the largely untapped potential of the Irish majority gave the Catholic elite the very bargaining counter that it had been lacking. In September 1775 the lord-lieutenant was presented with the tantalizing prospect of 'two millions of loyal, faithful, and affectionate hearts and hands, unarmed indeed, but zealous, ready, and desirous to exert themselves strenuously in defence of his Majesty's most sacred person and government, against all his enemies of what denomination soever, in any part of the world where they may be'.[92] Catholic expressions of loyalty, furthermore, contrasted sharply with the rebelliousness of the king's Protestant subjects across the Atlantic— and even, it might be added, with the doubtful allegiance of at least some Irish Protestants. Charles O'Conor, one of the principal Catholic spokesmen, looked forward to the defeat of the Americans

---

[90] Ibid. 5–9 July 1782.

[91] *General Evening Post*, 23 May 1782. The phrase 'may the British flag flourish all over the globe' came from Rodney's own account of his triumph, published in almost every newspaper at the time. The inhabitants of Rathfriland, County Down, celebrated by drinking a toast in the very same words. See the *Belfast News-letter*, 24–8 May 1872.

[92] *Harcourt Papers*, ed. Harcourt, ix. 358.

by the British army (or 'our army', as he revealingly called it) paving the way to a restoration of Maryland to the Catholics, who could then act as 'a bridle here-after on the Republican provinces north and south of them'. Maryland had been seized by 'Protestant Puritans' whose posterity 'are now in rebellion', O'Conor argued, whereas the Catholics had never forfeited their right to the province 'by sedition or disaffection'.[93]

But while Irish Catholics might plausibly be embraced by the British state as a conservative counterweight to the rebellious republicanism of the American Protestants, the entry of the French into the war made them more problematic supporters of constitutional order. If conflict with Catholic France curbed Irish Protestant disaffection, might it not, at the same time, cool Irish Catholic loyalty? The timing of the Catholic relief measures of 1778, passed by the Westminster and Dublin Parliaments on the eve of the war with France, was surely no coincidence.[94] But any lingering doubts on the part of the British and Irish governments were countered by the pledges of Catholic notables who were at pains to stress the continuing loyalty of their co-religionists. The lord-lieutenant was given 'fresh assurances' when Spain entered the conflict in June 1779 by 'several principal Roman Catholicks of their attachment to His majesty and their cordial disposition, if call'd upon, actively to assist him'.[95] The following August, with the Franco-Spanish fleet threatening Ireland and England, a meeting of the Catholics of County Limerick resolved to help with subscriptions to raise men for military service and, perhaps more significantly, to act against deserters.[96]

While many Protestants, as we have seen, remained unconvinced of Catholic loyalty, others seem to have believed that even poorer Catholics were no longer a threat, or at least that they could be relied upon if handled in the right way. In 1779 Theophilus Jones, MP for County Leitrim, was of the view that the Catholics in his neighbourhood would have 'acted Zealously & Steadily' with their Protestant countrymen if an enemy landing had occurred.[97] Lord Lucan was so

[93] *The Letters of Charles O'Conor of Belanagare*, ed. Catherine Coogan Ward and Robert E. Ward (2 vols., Ann Arbor, 1980), ii. 110, 114.
[94] See below, Ch. 7, for a fuller discussion of the background to the relief legislation.
[95] HMC, *Lothian MSS* (London, 1905), 352.
[96] NLI, Heron Papers, MS 13060, Minutes of the meeting, 20 Aug. 1779.
[97] PRONI, Downshire Papers, D 607/B/94.

confident of the 'fidelity & attachment' of the Catholics in County Mayo that he offered to enlist 'any number' for military service.[98] Indeed, while many Protestants were deeply disturbed by Catholic recruitment into the armed forces, it is important to note that others regarded it with equanimity. There was nothing to fear, they argued, so long as the Catholics served alongside Protestants, and not in their own special units, and provided they could be employed outside Ireland itself, where the temptation to desert was seemingly irresistible. Humphrey Minchin, an officer in the Hampshire militia but also an Irish landowner, put the case clearly in 1780 when he offered to raise a corps of marines in Ireland. 'Irish Roman Catholics', he wrote, 'incorporated with others, will make as faithfull Soldiers especially in this line of Service, as Men of any Persuasion whatsoever if brought immediately into this Country [that is, England]'.[99] Minchin, of course, had his own reasons for emphasizing the loyalty of the Irish Catholics; he wanted to command the corps of marines that he offered to recruit. But he surely was right to suggest that identity could depend on location.[100] Irish Catholics in Ireland saw themselves as Irish Catholics; outside Ireland, in a British regiment, or on a British warship, they could become Britons too.

Military and Naval Service

The experience of serving in the regular armed forces or even the militia may well have furthered a sense of Britishness for men from all parts of the British Isles. Both the composition of the forces and the nature of their duties were relevant in this regard. In the navy's ships, the geographical origins of crew members seem to have owed much to the background of the captain and other senior officers.[101] As we saw earlier, a quarter of the ship's company on the *Elizabeth* came from Fife, the county in which the estates of the captain, the

---

[98] NLI, Heron Papers, MS 13036, Lucan to Buckinghamshire, 31 Mar. 1778.

[99] BL, Liverpool Papers, Add. MS 38313, fos. 144–5.

[100] Nor was Minchin the only military officer to think in this way. Captain Alexander Duff of the 46th Foot said much the same when discussing his Irish recruits in 1776: 'when they are once out of their Country I believe they wou'd make very good Soldiers'. WO 1/991, Duff to [Barrington], 5 Feb. 1776.

[101] See N. A. M. Rodger, *The Wooden World: An Anatomy of the Georgian Navy* (London, 1986), 156–7.

Hon. Frederick Maitland, were located.[102] Likewise, when Captain Lord Longford was looking for men to fill his ship in 1778, it was natural that he should return to Ireland to recruit.[103] Even so, every naval vessel seems to have contained men from all parts of the British Isles. On the *Elizabeth* Scots predominated, but 26% of the crew was English, 12% Irish, and nearly 3% Welsh.[104] In other vessels, the proportions were of course different, but the principle of mixing was the same. On the *Prince George* early in 1778, 66% of the crew was English, but there were significant numbers of Scots (15%), Irish (10%), and even some Welsh as well as men from the Channel Islands and the Isle of Man.[105] Shortly afterwards, the new crew members of the *Cumberland* fell into the following national categories: English, 36%; Irish, 30%; Welsh, 15%; and Scots, 7%.[106]

Once at sea, a ship became an enclosed community, largely cut off from outside influences. This seaborne society was, of course, rigidly hierarchical, with a particularly fierce code of discipline, and it can readily be imagined that there would have been many tensions between crew members. But naval ships were ethnic melting pots, where the English, Scots, Welsh, and Irish were brought together and obliged to remain with each other for long periods. It seems far from fanciful to suggest that a common sense of identity must, in time, have bound the crews together. Perhaps, to be sure, that identity was above all shaped by the experience of the sea and seamanship. Yet it was not simply a matter of occupation. A warship, as opposed to a trading vessel, was an instrument of the British state. It was used to project British power beyond the home territory. Its crew was pitted against enemy ships. In these circumstances, the seamen would surely have come to regard themselves not merely as mariners but as 'British Tars'.

The army can also be seen as a hothouse of Britishness. Every country of the British Isles contributed. Even Wales, with its small population, raised a regiment, the Seventy-fifth, or Prince of Wales's

---

[102] See above, Ch. 1.

[103] *The Private Papers of John, Earl of Sandwich*, ed. G. R. Barnes and J. H. Owen (4 vols., London, 1932–8), ii. 79 and n. For a comment on the contribution of the Irish to the manning of the fleet in Jan. 1775, before the war had begun, see *The Inchiquin Manuscripts*, ed. John Ainsworth (Dublin, 1961), 219.   [104] ADM 36/8017.

[105] ADM 36/8205.   [106] ADM 36/9026.

Regiment of Foot,[107] besides providing men for several others.[108] All parts of England yielded men for the army (see Map 5.1) but the growing commercial and industrial centres of the north and midlands attracted the attention of large numbers of recruiting parties: it was no coincidence, for instance, that Ensign Richard Augustus Wyvill of the Thirty-eighth Foot was sent to enlist men at Wolverhampton;[109] or that the West Riding towns acted like a magnet for officers on the recruiting service.[110] Scotland made an even more impressive contribution than in previous eighteenth-century wars. In 1761, the last full year of military operations in the Seven Years War, five specifically Highland battalions were identified in the *Army List*; in 1782, the last full year of the American war, there were eleven, not counting two raised in America, as well as regiments recruited in Edinburgh and Glasgow. Indeed, we can be confident that the Scots, with only about 12% of the available manpower in the British Isles, provided a disproportionate number of men. The Highlands, in particular, gave up incredible quantities—Ross-shire, it was claimed in 1782, had sent no fewer than 4,000 men to the army, not to mention another 1,000 to the navy.[111] Large-scale recruitment of Irishmen was also a feature of the American war. True, there had been enlistment in Ireland in the Seven Years War,[112] but until 1771 the official position was that Irishmen— Protestants as well as Catholics—should not be recruited, because Catholics were unreliable and the Protestants had to be kept at home to help defend their communities in case of a Catholic uprising.[113]

---

[107] An inspection return of 1781 lists 90% of the men as English, but a check with the regiment's description-book shows that most of these 'Englishmen' bore Welsh surnames. Cf. WO 25/472, fo. 30 and WO 25/471. See also Marion Balderston and David Syrett (eds.), *The Lost War: Letters from British Officers during the American Revolution* (New York, 1975), 158–9, where Lord Feilding, appointed a captain in the regiment, is said to be 'Recruiting in Wales'.

[108] See e.g. NLI, MS 3750, Order-book, 32nd Foot, 20 Mar. 1776; WO 1/1010, p. 259; NLW, Tredegar MS 76/188.

[109] Library of Congress, Peter Force Collection, Wyvill's Journal, 12.

[110] See e.g. *Leeds Intelligencer*, 4 Nov. 1777, 14 Sept. and 5 Oct. 1779.

[111] HO 42/205, fo. 324.

[112] See Thomas Bartlett, '"A Weapon of War yet Untried": Irish Catholics and the Armed Forces of the Crown, 1760–1830', in T. G. Fraser and Keith Jeffery (eds.), *Men, Women and War* (Historical Studies, vol. xviii, Dublin, 1993), 69–70; Marshall, 'Nation Defined by Empire', 210–11.

[113] Thomas Bartlett, 'Army and Society in Eighteenth-Century Ireland', in W. A. Maguire (ed.), *Kings in Conflict: The Revolutionary War in Ireland and its Aftermath, 1689–1750* (Belfast, 1990), 175, 179–80.

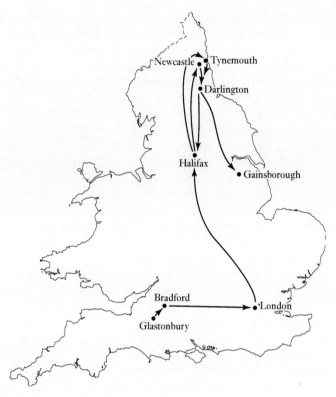

Map 5.1. Jeremy Lister's search for recruits for the Tenth Foot, 1776–1783

Source: Calderdale Archives, Lister of Sibden Hall MSS, SH7 JL/1, pp. 23–7

The cautious and limited permission to raise soldiers in Ireland in 1771 was reinforced by an Irish statute of 1774 that substituted an oath of allegiance for the former religious test.[114] And early in 1775, in anticipation of trouble in America, the lord-lieutenant was told to 'connive' at the use of Irish recruits to bring his regiments up to strength.[115] By 1781, even the infantry on the British establishment was heavily dependent on its Irish component, which amounted to more than a fifth of the total.[116] But if the army brought Englishmen, Welshmen, Scotsmen, and Irishmen together in the same

---

[114] A. J. Guy, 'The Irish Military Establishment, 1660–1776', in Thomas Bartlett and K. Jeffery (eds.) *A Military History of Ireland* (Cambridge, 1996), 229.

[115] *Harcourt Papers*, ed. Harcourt, ix. 303.   [116] WO 27/47.

institution, the most important perspective for our current purposes is not the macro-view of the army as a whole, but the situation within individual regiments, the micro-systems which were the military equivalents of the navy's warships.

As in naval vessels, so in many of the army's regiments, significant numbers of men from every country in the British Isles were to be found. The qualification is relevant because there were several corps with a strong regional or national base. The regiments of cavalry inspected in Ireland in 1775 were almost wholly Irish in composition; only 2.3% of the troopers came from other parts of the British Isles. The rank and file of the Royal Highland Regiment of Foot, reviewed at the same time, was reported to be 100% Scottish.[117] We have also seen that certain towns or counties recruited, or helped to recruit, particular regiments. But as the war went on, and the need for manpower increased, regiments were obliged to scour far and wide for new soldiers. The Glasgow Regiment, if deserter returns are any guide, contained significant numbers of Irishmen, some of whom were perhaps recent migrants to the town, while others were no doubt enlisted by one of the many recruiting parties sent across the Irish Sea to bring regiments on the British establishment up to strength.[118] The Ninety-eighth Foot, raised mainly in Derby, also topped up with men from Scotland and Ireland.[119] The Twenty-third Foot, or Royal Welsh Fusiliers, recruited successfully in Yorkshire;[120] the Royal Scots in Sussex.[121] Even Highland regiments became less than wholly Scottish, let alone Highland; the Seventy-eighth Foot, though supposed to be raised on the basis of the Earl of Seaforth's territorial influence, was in fact recruited in Ireland, the Isle of Man, and England as well as in other parts of Scotland, in order to preserve the Earl's estates.[122] If we look at the regiments that were not linked specifically with one of the countries,

---

[117] WO 27/35.

[118] *Glasgow Mercury*, 25 June 1778, lists thirty-three deserters from the regiment, nineteen of them Irish. The Irish commander-in-chief complained in 1778 of the difficulties of bringing the corps on the Irish establishment up to strength while regiments on the British establishment were using Ireland as a major source of recruits (HMC, *Lothian MSS*, 355), while one of his junior officers claimed that Ireland had been 'a good deal drained by the new Scotch & English Regts' (NLS, Fettercairn Papers, Box 5, Lt. George Urquart to Sir William Forbes, 3 Jan. 1780).

[119] BL, Liverpool Papers, Add. MS 38313, fo. 257.

[120] *York Courant*, 10 Mar. 1778.

[121] Horsham Museum, Medwin Papers, MS 288/41.

[122] BL, Hamilton and Greville Papers, Add. MS 42071, fo. 205.

regions, or towns of the British Isles, then the impression of mixing is still more striking. There were not many corps like the Forty-eighth Foot, which when it was inspected in October 1781 turned out to be 40% English and Welsh, 29% Scottish, and 31% Irish (see below, Fig. 5.1). But every infantry regiment on the British establishment inspected at this time seems to have contained significant Scottish and Irish minorities, with the Scots contributing between 4% and 13% and the Irish from 15% to 38%.[123]

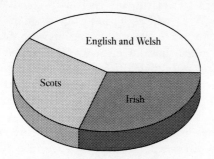

English and Welsh

Scots

Irish

Fig. 5.1. The military melting pot: The Forty-eighth Foot, 1781
Source: WO 27/47

Army regiments, then, like the king's ships, were communities in which Englishmen, Welshmen, Scotsmen, and Irishmen were brought together and could become Britons. But arguably the army blended and conditioned men even more thoroughly than the navy, as regiments often lived and worked in close proximity to other corps, while the crews of warships had less contact with each other. Even those Highland regiments that retained their Highland character usually found themselves serving alongside other regiments in which there were large numbers of Englishmen or Irishmen. In India, for instance, the Seventy-third Highlanders fought alongside corps raised largely in Ireland, while in America the Forty-second and Seventy-first Highlanders campaigned with regiments like the Fifteenth Foot, which in July 1775, before it left Ireland, had been reported to be 43% English, 23% Scots, and 34% Irish.[124]

---

[123] WO 27/47. See also the figures for the origins of recruits born in 1755–60 and 1760–5 in Roderick Floud, Kenneth Wachter, and Annabel Gregory, *Height, Health and History: Nutritional Status in the United Kingdom, 1750–1980* (Cambridge, 1990), 89 (table 3.2).   [124] WO 27/35.

The army in America, moreover, actively sought to emphasize its Britishness by celebrating all the days of the patron saints of the British Isles. On 23 April 1781, Scottish and Irish officers joined in the festivities for St George's Day at New York; on St David's Day in 1779 a Highland captain dined with the grenadier officers of the Royal Welch Fusiliers '& celebrated St. Taffy with a copious libation'; and at a large-scale dinner to celebrate St Andrew's Day on 30 November 1781 the toasts included 'our Brother Saints'— that is, St George, St David, and St Patrick—and 'May our Royal Master be serv'd, as well as he is lov'd, by all the Sons of those Saints we have given'.[125] Nor was contact between various regiments of the army limited, of course, to corps stationed overseas. The camps and garrisons in the British Isles brought regiments together and so increased the scope for the mixing of the English, Welsh, Scots, and Irish in the different corps. In November 1779 the Sixth, Fourteenth, Sixty-fifth, and Sixty-ninth Regiments were all under canvas at Coxheath in Kent, while the Eighteenth and Fifty-ninth were at Warley in Essex.[126]

Camps and garrisons also brought militia regiments into the military melting pot. These corps, as we have seen, were not recruited exclusively from the counties that bore their name. But the substitutes from beyond shire boundaries who played an important role in bringing militia regiments up to strength nearly all came from neighbouring counties rather than further afield, ensuring that the regional, if not county, character of the corps was preserved. Unlike the unofficial volunteer corps, the militia was expected to perform a national as opposed to a purely local defence function. Every militia unit, even if it spent time in its home county, was at some stage deployed elsewhere as part of a larger concentration of militiamen. So in 1782 the Leicestershire militia found itself with the East Yorkshire militia in garrison at Newcastle-upon-Tyne. Christopher Sykes, an officer in the East Yorkshires, recorded in his diary the occasions that summer when the officers of the two regiments dined together.[127] Garrisons provided less opportunity for mixing, however, than did the major camps. In the summer of 1779 Coxheath was the temporary home for militiamen from Devon,

---

[125] *John Peebles' American War: The Diary of a Scottish Grenadier, 1776–1782*, ed. Ira D. Gruber (Mechanicsburg, Penn., 1998), 251, 440, 497–8.
[126] BL, Liverpool Papers, Add. MS 38433, fos. 8, 10.
[127] Hull University Library, Sykes Papers, DD SY/102/13, 29 May, 10 June 1782.

Suffolk, Monmouthshire, Northamptonshire, Buckinghamshire, Norfolk, Somerset, Dorset, Gloucestershire, Warwickshire, Yorkshire, Lincolnshire, Rutland, Angelsey, and Carnarvon. At the same time, Warley camp included within its boundaries the militia of Berkshire, Cambridgeshire, Hertfordshire, Kent, Middlesex, Cheshire, Derbyshire, Pembrokeshire, and Radnorshire.[128] The members of these corps would have rubbed shoulders not simply with each other, of course, but also with the soldiers of the regular regiments encamped with them, which, as we have just seen, would all have contained significant numbers of Scots and Irishmen.

Passages in letters written from the camps suggest that contact between officers of the various militia and regular units was both frequent and largely amicable. Lieutenant-Colonel Thomas Watson Ward of the Cambridgeshires noted shortly after having arrived at Warley in the summer of 1779: 'The Berkshire on our Right is a Friendly and very agreeable Corps—we are well acquainted.'[129] Likewise, Captain Lord Althorp and his colleagues in the Northamptonshire regiment dined with the officers of the East Yorkshire militia, 'who seem in general to be a very good set'. A few weeks later, Althorp was mixing even more thoroughly—dining with Major the Hon. Thomas Stanley of the Seventy-ninth Foot and then taking the major with him to supper that evening in the combined mess of the Rutland and Monmouth militia.[130] Perhaps in some cases this kind of contact between officers did little to widen horizons. Some came from families which owned property in many different counties, and could therefore hardly be described as localist in outlook. Those who had attended distant schools or universities, like Althorp, or who had been on the Grand Tour of European cultural centres, like Lord Lewisham of the Staffordshire militia, were already well aware of life beyond their home county. A few, such as Lewisham and Captain Richard Aldworth Neville of the Berkshire militia, who served at Coxheath in 1778 and Warley in 1779, were MPs, and therefore part of an institution that was as self-consciously British as the army. But there were, as we have seen, a good number of militia officers from less elevated backgrounds—small landowners, and even tradesmen.[131] For some of them, at least,

---

[128] BL, Liverpool Papers, Add. MS 38343, fo. 344.
[129] BL, Hardwicke Papers, Add. MS 35660, fo. 182.
[130] BL, Althorp Papers, F.8, Althorp to his mother, 26 July–2 Aug., 20–3 Sept. 1778.
[131] See above, Ch. 1.

we can assume that life in the camps would have been an eye-opening experience, propelling them into contact with people from areas of the British Isles of which they had no knowledge. The same must surely have been the case for the bulk of the ordinary militiamen. In a few instances we can see that the camps brought Britons together quite literally: a Glamorganshire man married in July 1779 a woman that he had met at Warley the previous year when he was serving there as a militiaman.[132] But if for the most part we can only speculate, it seems probable that for men like John Gammon of the East Kent militia contact with soldiers such as John Butcher of the Seventy-ninth Foot, or Stephen Dann of the Twenty-fifth, would have increased awareness of involvement in a truly national enterprise.[133] Not every camp resident was uplifted, of course; one particularly disgruntled militia officer described Warley as 'damnation on earth'.[134] On the whole, however, it seems likely that the hardships of camp life—whether it was the damp and the cold in the autumn, or the poor quality of the bread ('the Contractors deserve to be hanged')[135]—did little to diminish a sense of solidarity; on the contrary, they probably gave it a great boost.

Military service, moreover, almost certainly had an impact on the wider public. Cartoons portrayed the armed forces as the embodiment of Britain. 'Rodneys triumph', published in March 1780 to commemorate his victory over the Spanish, carries an accompanying verse which reminds the enemy that 'To fight against Britons ye task is in vain'; while 'The Triumphant Britons', which appeared the next month, depicts a bayonet charge by British soldiers, under a prominent union flag, against the French and Spanish.[136] The camps also played a part in promoting a sense of the nation amongst civilians as well as soldiers and militiamen. We have already noted that the camps attracted large numbers of sightseers, particularly the

---

[132] *Diary of William Thomas*, ed. Denning, 290. Military marriages, of course, took place wherever troops were garrisoned or quartered for any length of time. In Falmouth e.g. local women married militiamen from the North and South Devon Regiments, the Hertfordshire Regiment and the East Kent Regiment, not to mention regular soldiers from as far away as Ireland and Scotland. See Susan Elizabeth Gay and Mrs Howard Fox (eds.), *The Register of Baptisms, Marriages and Burials of the Parish of Falmouth in the County of Cornwall 1663–1812* (Devon and Cornwall Record Society, Exeter, 1914), 58–70.

[133] All three had children born in the camp in Sept. 1778: see Essex RO, Parish Records of St. Thomas of Canterbury, Brentwood, D/P 362/1/2.

[134] HMC, *Du Cane MSS* (London, 1905), p. 239.

[135] Kent Archive Office, Amherst MSS, U 1350 086/9.   [136] BM 5648 and 5646.

larger ones like Warley and Coxheath.[137] Visitors to the camps were likely to have had a rather different perspective from the military residents; they were, after all, more spectators than participants. Even so, it seems probable that they were struck by the extent to which the camps were like Britain in microcosm. Indeed, the very layout of the camps furthered this impression. Each regiment had its own clearly defined portion of land, as though a piece of Warwickshire, or Yorkshire, or Anglesey, had sprung up in the midst of Kent or Essex. A spectator progressing through the camp would have come across successive patches of territory occupied by the different militias of the English and Welsh counties.[138] In Sheridan's musical comedy *The Camp*, we find the following dialogue:[139]

BLUARD. Ah! Monsieur Gauge, I am so very glad to find you, by Gar I was hunt you all over the Camp—I have been thro' Berkshire;—Cross Suffolk, and all over Yorkshire, and hear no word of you.

O'DAUB. Thro' Berkshire, and Suffolk, and Yorkshire!—What the devil does he mean?

GAUGE. Only thro' their Regiments.

Camps like Coxheath and Warley, which housed so many militia units, must have appeared like giant jigsaws, with all the separate pieces neatly joining together to form a coherent whole, much as the counties on the map of Britain interlocked to form the image of the country.

There are even grounds for believing that the camps were seen as loci of Britishness by those who never set eyes upon them, and were therefore probably unaware of the symbolism of their layout. Newspapers in London and the provinces—in fact newspapers the length and breadth of the British Isles—carried regular features on 'camp intelligence', especially during the campaigning seasons of 1778 and 1779, reflecting and helping to fuel the camp mania that was then at its height.[140] These reports, it should be added, were not narrowly focused on news of local militia regiments; on the contrary, they presented readers with every scrap of information and gossip coming from the camps, whatever the corps involved, and however

---

[137] See above, Ch. 3.

[138] See the detailed descriptions of Coxheath and Warley in BL, Hardwicke Papers, Add. MSS 35659, fos. 392–3 and 35660, fos. 4–5.

[139] *The Dramatic Works of Richard Brinsley Sheridan*, ed. Cecil Price (2 vols., Oxford, 1973), ii. 730.   [140] See above, Ch. 3.

trivial or inconsequential. The impact of this reporting is, of course, impossible to gauge. We can never even know how widely it was read; or, assuming that it was read, whether it had an impact that can be distinguished from that of the general reporting of the war. But it seems probable that, after having digested column upon column of 'camp intelligence', readers would have been left in no doubt that places like Coxheath and Warley were the focal points of national effort and determination to resist the invader—and, as such, veritable nerve centres of Britishness.

The Threat of Invasion

The camps were essentially products of the fear of invasion (see Map 5.2). This fear was perhaps the underlying spur to the development of a sense of Britishness in the American war. Apparently sneering dismissals of the French 'monsieurs', the Spanish 'Dons' or 'Diegos', and the Dutch 'Mynheers' should perhaps be seen not so much as expressions of confidence but rather as reflections of a deep concern that these enemies could mount a successful attack on the home territory. The French were particularly feared in this regard because their military potential was so awesome—the population of France was twice that of the British Isles—and because their proximity to the southern English and Irish coasts put them in in a good position to launch an invasion. In 1778 French troops were reported to be massing in Brittany and Normandy. On this occasion it turned out that the French were merely trying to ensure that the British navy remained concentrated in home waters; the invasion preparations were a feint to draw attention from Admiral d'Estaing's attempt to deliver a decisive blow at New York, the British headquarters in North America. The following year, however, the threat to the home territories was more serious. The Spanish had insisted on an attack on England as a condition of their entering the war— they wanted to bring the conflict to a rapid conclusion before their own far-flung and vulnerable empire became exposed—and the French, who were desperate to secure a Spanish alliance, readily agreed. From the British perspective, the Spanish junction with the French greatly increased the danger to southern England and Ireland, because it gave the combined Bourbon fleets a clear superiority. The Franco-Spanish naval force that appeared in the Channel

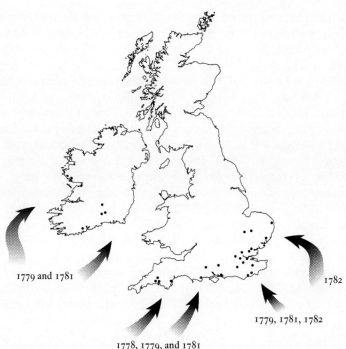

1779 and 1781

1782

1779, 1781, 1782

1778, 1779, and 1781

Map 5.2. The main military camps in the British Isles and the threat of invasion, 1778–1782

in the summer of 1779 comprised sixty-six ships of the line; Admiral Hardy's fleet had only thirty-nine comparable vessels and was deployed far to the west to defend the approaches to Ireland, which the British government had mistakenly assumed was the true object-ive of the enemy. For several weeks, there was no British naval presence in the Channel to impede a landing. Only sickness on board the enemy armada, together with increasing tensions between the allies, prevented the unthinkable from occurring. In the late summer and autumn of 1781 there was another crisis. The French and Spanish fleets once again threatened both England and Ireland, and for some time effectively blocked the western approaches. By this stage, the Dutch entry into the war had also opened up Britain's eastern flank, exposing the North Sea coast of England and Scotland to enemy incursions.

Now it is true that Dr Johnson believed any landing unlikely, and that Lord Barrington, the secretary at war, was also doubtful.[141] But for every Johnson and Barrington there seem to have been countless anxious people. 'Every body talks of an invasion', a marine officer wrote in June 1778;[142] 'every body's mind is fixed on Keppels fleet', Sir Richard Heron was told by a London correspondent a month later.[143] When the combined Franco-Spanish fleet appeared off Plymouth the following year, local inhabitants reeled with the 'Shock of the Enemy being at our gates';[144] 'I dont think of any thang else', a distressed Devonian wrote that August.[145] But fear and anxiety affected people far from the environs of Plymouth. A firm of London merchants reported to an Irish contact that the arrival of the combined fleet had 'thrown this Kingdom in to a Consternation never before experienced';[146] John Wesley, visiting Camarthen at this time, found 'the people here (as indeed in every place) under a deep consternation through the terrible reports which flew on every side';[147] and even the bishop of Bangor confessed that 'It intirely engrossed the mind, & absorbed all other recollections & considerations'.[148] John Kirkby, an officer in the Nottinghamshire militia based at Southsea camp, believed that the enemy had landed: at the end of August he took it for granted that Plymouth was already 'reduced to ashes. No doubt Portsmouth will be their next resort.'[149] A few days later, with Sir Charles Hardy's ships still not engaging the enemy, John Knill, a Cornish gentleman, expected a raid on Falmouth and then for the Franco-Spanish forces to 'ravage the neighbouring Country' in order to provoke the Royal Navy to attack the combined fleet.[150] In Ireland that October, when the immediate danger had passed, 'apprehensions of invasion continue[d] strong in the Minds of the People'.[151] Two years later, in 1781, when there was another Franco-Spanish fleet within striking distance, letters from Ireland again spoke of 'people here . . . greatly

---

[141] *The Letters of Samuel Johnson*, ed. Bruce Redford (5 vols., Oxford, 1992–4), iii. 180–1, 183; NLI, Heron Papers, MS 13036, Barrington to [Buckinghamshire], 21 April 1778.   [142] SRO, Logan Home of Edrom Muniments, GD 1/384/6/32.
[143] Lincolnshire Archives Office, Stubton Papers II D/1, J. Hankey to Heron, 25 July 1778.   [144] Devon RO, Drake of Buckland Abbey Papers, 346/F23.
[145] Cornwall RO, Tremayne of Heligan Papers, DDT 2126.
[146] PRONI, Greer Papers, D 1044/550.
[147] A. H. Williams (ed.), *John Wesley in Wales 1739–1790* (Cardiff, 1971), 102.
[148] BL, Blenheim Papers, Add. MS 61670, fo. 105.
[149] HMC, 15th Report, app., pt. v, *Foljambe MSS* (London, 1897), 151.
[150] Cornwall RO, Rogers of Penrose Papers, DDRP 37.
[151] NLI, Shannon Papers, MS 13301, Dr Richard Pigott to Shannon, 19 Oct. 1779.

allarmed'.[152] Even in 1782, when the east coast seemed to be menaced, the mayor of Hull was warned to prepare to repel an enemy landing and right up at the northern tip of the British Isles, at Lerwick in Shetland, batteries were erected 'to keep off the Dutch etc.'.[153]

Invasion fears of this kind seem to have engendered a sense of beleaguered Britishness, a grim determination to resist the enemy and pull together to defend the endangered national territory. After having discussed Keppel's action with d'Orvilliers, Richard Laurence, a young Oxford undergraduate, announced that 'The natural antipathy I believe we all have towards the French has rous'd the Britain [sic] in my soul.'[154] The press was full of prose and verse along the same lines. The *Morning Post, and Daily Advertiser* of 30 August 1779, for instance, produced the following little ditty for its readers:

> Tho' *Monsieur* and *Don* should combine,
> What have true *British* Heroes to fear?
> What are Frogs, and soup-meagre, and wine,
> To beef, and plumb-pudding, and beer?

Other forms of popular media likewise appealed to Britishness in this period of crisis. With the combined fleet lying off Plymouth, a cartoon entitled 'A Dance by the Virtue of British Oak' was published which showed a British sailor bravely resisting a Frenchman and a Spaniard.[155] A song composed to encourage recruitment into the Twenty-second Light Dragoons, raised in the same year by John Baker Holroyd, sought to play on this mood of defiance. The song opens with an appeal to 'All you who have spirit your Country to save', and proceeds to stress the need to repel marauding invaders ('And should they attempt for to land on our coast', 'We'll bring repentance to these Boasters of France').[156] Whether this kind of approach had the desired impact is difficult to say; but Holroyd's regiment was brought up to strength with remarkable speed.

[152] PRONI, Stewart of Killymoon Papers, D 3167/2/34.
[153] Hull RO, Borough Records, BRL 1386/154; *The Diary of the Reverend John Mill*, ed. Gilbert Goudie (Scottish History Society, vol. v, Edinburgh, 1889), 63.
[154] Wiltshire RO, Wansey Papers, 314/4/1, Laurence to George Wansey, 5 Aug. 1778.
[155] BM 5554.
[156] East Sussex RO, Sheffield Papers, A2714/265, 'Song in Honour of the 22d Light Dragoons'.

A Multiplicity of Enemies

The fear of invasion, though it lasted until 1782, was most intense in 1778 and especially 1779. But if apprehensions of a landing perhaps receded slightly in the last years of the war, British unity was given a boost by the feeling that the nation was fighting courageously against an array of enemies. The struggle against the Americans between 1775 and 1778 could hardly call forth the same emotional response because, however great the difficulties involved in trying to suppress a rebellion 3,000 miles away, there was a general and essentially correct assumption that Britain was the stronger of the two contending parties. Even while the British army was cooped up in Boston, and very much on the defensive, Lord Rawdon regarded the rebellious colonists with contempt: 'I hope that we shall soon have done with these scoundrels, for one only dirties one's fingers by meddling with them'.[157] Victory over the Americans could never bring true satisfaction to officers like Rawdon, not so much because the colonists were fellow subjects but because they were unworthy and ultimately unchallenging opponents. There were few laurels to be won in defeating such an enemy. The coming of the French war shifted the balance both militarily and psychologically. France was unquestionably a great power; no one suggested that to triumph over the French would be an easy matter, let alone that such a victory would reflect the obvious superiority of the strong over the weak. And when, in 1779, the Spanish joined the conflict, the balance tipped clearly in favour of Britain's enemies. The British could now see themselves as struggling gamely against a formidable coalition, rather than as using parental power to chastise their wayward colonial children. Opponents of the war against the Americans could unite with government supporters in their hostility to the French and the Spanish. Richard Watson, Regius professor of divinity at Cambridge, disapproved of the coercion of the colonists and condemned the methods used against them, yet he breathed fire and defiance at the House of Bourbon. 'Let her beware', he told his congregation in a fast day sermon in February 1780, 'she thinks we are divided, it may be so; but we are not divided in our disposition to punish her.'[158] But it was the declaration of war

---

[157] HMC, *Hastings MSS* (4 vols., London, 1928–47), iii. 167.
[158] Richard Watson, *A Sermon Preached before the University of Cambridge, on Friday, February 4th, 1780* (2nd edn., Cambridge, 1780), 6.

against the Dutch at the end of 1780 that appears to have been a particularly important stimulus to this growing sense of pride. While the Dutch could not be regarded as in themselves a strong enemy—indeed, there was some excited anticipation, as we have seen, of profit to be made at their expense[159]—their joining the coalition added to the number of powers ranged against the British. That the Dutch war should trigger fresh outpourings of patriotic sentiment may seem ironic; after all, this new dimension to the struggle was much regretted by many Britons who saw it as flying in the face of traditional alignments.[160] Yet it was perhaps this very sense of disappointment—a feeling that the 'perfidious' Dutch had betrayed a long friendship by aiding the Americans and the Bourbon powers—that gave added poignancy to the patriotism of the moment. A cartoon published on 17 January 1781, entitled 'The Ballance of Power', includes the verse:

> America, dup'd by a treacherous train
> Now finds she's a Tool both to France and to Spain;
> Yet all three united can't weigh down the Scale:
> So the Dutchmen jumps in with the hope to prevail,
> Yet Britain will boldly their efforts withstand,
> And bravely defy them by Sea and by Land.

Three days later, another print, though depicting 'Jack England' again, has the national hero 'Fighting the Four Confederates', and bears the inclusive motto 'To Arms you Brave Britons'.[161]

The euphoria with which news of Rodney's victory at the Saints was greeted in May 1782 becomes more readily understandable when this sense of struggling against the odds is appreciated. We have already seen something of the response in various parts of the British Isles; the celebrations in York, where 'ye City was generally illuminated, with bonfires, & fireworks', were typical.[162] Here was a triumph that was itself a source of great pride, and at the same time took off some of the pressure and began to make it look as though the war might not end disastrously. Lord Stormont, now out of office, observed to Rodney that his victory had restored his country

---

[159] See above, Ch. 2.

[160] The parliamentary opposition made much of the 'unnatural' nature of the Dutch war; but even government supporters felt uncomfortable. See e.g. *A Selection of William Twining's Letters 1734–1804*, ed. Ralph S. Walker (2 vols., Lampeter, 1991), i. 212.

[161] BM 5827 and 5828.

[162] York City Archives, Acc. 163, Diary of Dr William White, 21 May 1782.

'to such a Situation as will enable it to retrieve most of the Losses it has sustain'd'.[163] References to resurgent Britain were legion, alongside continued emphasis on the remarkable achievement of resisting the combined weight of 'Four Powers'.[164] 'The Spirit of the British Lion is at last roused', a Lincolnshire customs officer wrote in his day-book, 'and notwithstanding Great Britain has had to contend with the House of Bourbon America and Holland not one of these powers dare fairly meet her either on the Ocean or in the Field.'[165] The vicar of Hanbury, Staffordshire, was no less proud. On 1 January 1783, looking back over the last year, he decided to record his feelings in his church register.

To future ages it will appear to be an incredible Thing what however we know to be a Fact, that these Kingdoms shd. Maintain (as they have done) a glorious, but unequal, Conflict for several Years, with the most formidable & unprovoked Confederacy that could be formed against them; viz. France, Spain, the united Provinces of the Netherlands, & the 13 revolted Colonies of North-America.

In such circumstances, even eventual defeat might seem like a moral victory and be cause for national self-congratulation. And the vicar, we should note, regarded this as a truly British achievement: it was the effort of 'these Kingdoms' that was offered as a source of wonderment.[166]

[163] PRO, Rodney Papers, 30/20/21/2, fo. 75.

[164] See e.g. BM 6004, 'The British Lion Engaging Four Powers', 14 June 1782.

[165] Lincolnshire Archives Office, Misc. Don 681/1, Day-book of John Mells, 18 May 1782.

[166] Staffordshire RO, Hanbury Parish Records, D 1528/1/4.

6

Parliamentary Power and Parliamentary Reform

IN AUGUST 1775 George III, bracing himself for a full-scale conflict with the American colonies, declared that he was fighting 'the battle of the legislature'.[1] It is worth reminding ourselves that the American war, though it became a worldwide struggle for trade, empire, and even national survival, started as an extension and escalation of a long-running constitutional dispute over the authority of the Westminster Parliament in British North America. In that it ended with a British acknowledgement of the complete independence of thirteen of the old colonies, the outcome represented a total defeat for those British politicians who had believed it necessary to resort to force to maintain the claims of the British Parliament. If this were not a grievous enough blow to the imperial pretensions of the British legislature, a concession made in the course of the war left parliamentary authority still further circumscribed. In 1778, in a belated attempt to compromise with the rebels, the British Parliament formally relinquished its assumed right to tax British territories overseas. The Renunciation Act of that year, while offering too little too late to win back the American insurgents and prevent their junction with the French, was to have important repercussions for the post-war governance of Britain's remaining colonial possessions.[2]

These imperial developments might be regarded as beyond the scope of a work concerned with the impact of the American war on the British Isles. But American and domestic issues are not always neatly separable. The parallels with Ireland—which can be considered both as an imperial possession and as part of the metropolitan

---

[1] *The Correspondence of King George III*, ed. Sir John Fortescue (6 vols., London, 1927–8), iii. 256.
[2] See P. J. Marshall, 'Britain without America—A Second Empire?', in *The Oxford History of the British Empire*, ii. *The Eighteenth Century*, ed. P. J. Marshall (Oxford, 1998), 588.

core—are striking. The war that reduced the British Parliament's imperial authority in North America also saw a diminution in its control of Ireland, and a significant increase in the autonomy of the Irish Parliament. The American conflict provided a golden opportunity for Ireland's Anglican elite to press its claims for home rule. Distracted and overstretched, Lord North's government was not in a position to provide effective resistance to pressure for commercial concessions; and North's successors had committed themselves in opposition to redressing Irish grievances and so could do little but accept legislative independence for the Dublin Parliament in 1782–3.

The war, then, curbed the authority of the British Parliament and increased the importance of the Irish legislature. But both parliaments, during and immediately after the war, found themselves under attack from reformers who wanted to make them more representative. These British and Irish reform campaigns fed off each other to an extent that has only rarely been recognized. More importantly, they attracted a level of support never before experienced by advocates of change. Wartime conditions, while providing arguments for caution and delay, seem to have been conducive to a considerable broadening of the base of the reform constituency. Agitation for such causes as shorter parliaments, the redistribution of seats, extension of the franchise, and the secret ballot were, however, merely part of the story. If these and other such panaceas were more popular than in the past, still more contemporaries believed that national salvation lay through 'economical reform', a repackaging and sharpening of the old 'country' opposition programme of earlier in the eighteenth century, which incorporated administrative overhaul, financial retrenchment, and constitutional purification. The campaign for economical reform was probably the most significant of all the reform initiatives of this period, because it began to bear fruit in Britain as early as 1780, when a process was set in train that ultimately was to transform the whole political dispensation. By the middle of the nineteenth century, perhaps as early as by the late 1820s, patronage and peculation were no longer the cement of politics and administration. The old order had been replaced by a system associated more closely with party in its political aspects, and merit, probity, and public service in its administrative dimension; a system characterized above all by a general commitment to efficiency and 'cheap government'.

The Anglo-Irish Relationship

Before the American war, Ireland, as we have seen, while technically the 'sister kingdom', was in many senses in a state of dependency more restrictive than that of the colonies across the Atlantic. Ireland's overseas trade was tightly controlled. Access to the British North American and West Indian colonies was limited, and certain Irish manufactures were prevented from entering Britain. The government of Ireland was likewise directed from Britain. Poynings' Law of 1494 decreed that the Irish Parliament could not even meet until the bills to be introduced into it by the administration at Dublin Castle had been approved by the Privy Council in London. Any bills brought forward during a parliamentary session could be suppressed or amended by either the Irish or British Privy Council. All bills that passed through the Irish Commons and Lords could still be vetoed or amended by the British Privy Council. Bills so amended could only be accepted or rejected when they returned to the Irish Parliament; there was no opportunity for further amendments to be introduced by the Irish legislature, or for bills to be restored to their original form. And in 1720 the British Parliament, giving an early indication of its imperial pretensions, passed a Declaratory Act asserting its right to legislate for Ireland. This assumed right was not exercised frequently, but the Mutiny Act was a particularly offensive instance of such interference, taking control of the British army in Ireland out of the hands of the Dublin Parliament, even though the Irish legislature was expected to foot the bill for the British garrison. The Declaratory Act also stipulated that appeals from Irish courts should be heard in Britain. While British judges were removable only by the agreement of both houses of the British Parliament, Irish judges, like those in the colonies, were appointed and dismissible at royal pleasure. There was no Irish Habeas Corpus Act.

The denial of rights enjoyed by the king's subjects in Britain gave rise to considerable resentment amongst Ireland's Protestants—in much the same way as a similar denial offended the American colonists. A 'patriot' party emerged in the Dublin Parliament, keen to press for more equal treatment for Ireland, jealous of Ireland's remaining rights, and hostile to British encroachments.[3]

[3] J. L. McCracken, 'Protestant Ascendancy and the Rise of Colonial Nationalism, 1714–1760', in *A New History of Ireland*, iv. *Eighteenth-Century Ireland 1691–1800*, ed. T. W. Moody and W. E. Vaughan (Oxford, 1986), ch. 5.

In 1763 attempts were made to secure limitation on the duration of parliaments and to introduce 'good behaviour' tenure for judges. Criticism was also voiced of the 'mis-judged Jealousy of a Sister Nation, [which] precludes us from many commercial benefits, which we might otherwise share with her'.[4] Concern at Ireland's exclusion from much of Britain's colonial trade was no doubt heightened by the expansion of the empire that had occurred as a consequence of the Seven Years War; but the expression of discontent on a range of constitutional issues owed much to the accession of George III in 1760. The new reign raised expectations of change, not least because it brought an Irish general election—the first since George II's accession in 1727. But change, when it came, heightened rather than reduced resentment at British interference. Irish lord-lieutenants had only occasionally visited Dublin. They had left the day-to-day running of Irish affairs to Irish 'undertakers', leading politicians who through government patronage and their own influence managed the Dublin Parliament. From 1767, however, lord-lieutenants were resident and, with the assistance of a chief secretary who represented the administration in the Irish Commons, attempted to govern directly.[5] One of the fruits of this new approach was greater impositions on Ireland. Lord Townshend, the first of the resident lord-lieutenants, secured an increase in the Irish military establishment, paid for by the Irish Parliament, from 12,000 to 15,000 troops, the extra 3,000 to be available, when required, for overseas service.[6] In return, an Octennial Act was allowed to become law, providing for regular Irish general elections. This concession did little to quieten the opposition, partly due to the failure of the British government to deliver other promised reforms, including security of tenure for judges, but also because regular elections made the Irish Commons more responsive to public opinion and therefore strengthened the patriot party.

The end of the undertaker system, the arrival of resident lord-lieutenants, and Townshend's augmentation of the army can all be seen as symptoms of a new drive for greater British control. In this

---

[4] *Debates Relative to the Affairs of Ireland; in the Years 1763 and 1764* (2 vols., Dublin, 1766), i. 39–47, 292–6, ii. 613.

[5] For the background to the change see Martyn J. Powell, 'The Reform of the Undertaker System: Anglo-Irish Politics, 1750–1767', *Irish Historical Studies*, 31 (1998), 19–36.

[6] Thomas Bartlett, 'The Augmentation of the Army in Ireland, 1767–1769', *English Historical Review*, 96 (1981), 540–59.

sense, Irish developments parallelled the assault on colonial auto-nomy after the Seven Years War. The Irish patriots, it should be said, were not always prepared to accept the parallel. While they recognized certain similarities, and at times chose for tactical reasons to emphasize them, in a very real sense they saw Ireland's position as different from America's. Ireland, in their view, was a kingdom with rights and privileges that put it above a mere colony.[7] But if Irish patriots sought to distinguish themselves from the American colonists, British initiatives in America still caused some alarm in Ireland. The American Declaratory Act of 1766, modelled on the Irish Act of 1720, was viewed by many British politicians as an assertion of the right of the Westminster Parliament not simply to legislate for America but also to tax the colonies. If the British Parliament claimed this right, what was to stop it imposing taxes on Ireland on the basis of the legislative supremacy proclaimed in the 1720 Act?[8] Unsurprisingly, then, in 1771 Benjamin Franklin reported widespread support for America amongst Dublin patriots.[9]

The patriot cause, however, was at a low ebb in the years imme-diately prior to the American war. Three of the most talented patriot leaders were lost to patriot politics: Charles Lucas died in 1771, Edmund Sexton Pery was elected speaker of the Commons in the same year, and in 1774 Henry Flood accepted office.[10] Earl Harcourt, who succeeded Townshend as lord-lieutenant at the end of 1772, was able to construct a broadly based administration, and his chief secretary, Sir John Blaquiere, proved a capable manager of government business in the Irish Parliament. By the close of the 1773–4 parliamentary session the lord-lieutenant had made substan-tial progress towards improving Irish public finances. Votes in the Irish Commons indicated a strengthening rather than a weakening of the government's position.

The outbreak of fighting in the rebel colonies, then, did not so much intensify a process already underway as provide a great opportunity for the patriots to bring long-simmering discontent to

---

[7] Jacqueline Hill, *From Patriots to Unionists: Dublin Civic Politics and Irish Protestant Patriotism, 1660–1840* (Oxford, 1997), 142.

[8] Neil Longley York, 'The Impact of the American Revolution on Ireland', in H. T. Dickinson (ed.), *Britain and the American Revolution* (London, 1998), 211.

[9] David Noel Doyle, *Ireland, Irishmen and Revolutionary America, 1760–1820* (Dublin, 1981), 154.

[10] F. G. James, *Ireland in the Empire 1688–1770* (Cambridge, Mass., 1973), 272–3.

the boil. At first, it must be said, the situation was adroitly managed by Harcourt. By judicious use of patronage, Harcourt and Blaquiere ensured that the Irish Parliament remained responsive to the demands of the Castle. Opposition attempts to amend the address at the opening of the session in October 1775, as we have seen, were defeated by two-to-one majorities. Parliamentary approval of the dispatch of 4,000 troops to America, without replacements, was a considerable triumph for the lord-lieutenant, and one of which he was understandably proud.[11] But even the skilful Harcourt ran into trouble when he was obliged to impose the provisions embargo in February 1776. The embargo, as we have seen, caused an outcry. Its economic impact was probably exaggerated by contemporaries, but it almost certainly depressed trade in certain types of beef.[12] More importantly, it underscored Ireland's subordinate position. The embargo was imposed by the fiat of the lord-lieutenant, on instructions from London, in order to assist the British war effort. Irish interests were apparently of little account. Not surprisingly, the patriot opposition made much of the issue, recognizing and exploiting its symbolism as well the real difficulties that the embargo caused. Charles O'Hara assiduously gathered information from merchants throughout Ireland on the impact of the embargo;[13] and in December 1777 a fully fledged debate on the matter in the Irish Commons gave opposition speakers the opportunity to express the strongest criticisms and paint a bleak picture of the future of the Irish economy.[14]

The economic depression that afflicted Ireland at this time also brought longer-standing British restrictions on Irish overseas trade on to the political agenda. The removal of these restrictions, or 'free trade' in the language of the day, became the principal demand of the Irish patriots. Even government supporters regarded some commercial concessions as imperative: 'Great Britain must open her heart . . . and spontaneously offer us some essential objects of trade', John Beresford wrote in March 1778.[15] Initially, at least, there was some disposition on the part of both the British government and the

---

[11] *The Harcourt Papers*, ed. E. W. Harcourt (14 vols., Oxford, 1880–1905), x. 32–4.
[12] See above, Ch. 2.   [13] NLI, O'Hara Papers, MS 20395.
[14] *An Edition of the Cavendish Parliamentary Diary 1776–1778*, ed. Anthony R. Black (3 vols., Delavan, Wis., 1984), iii. 369–425.
[15] *The Correspondence of the Right Hon. John Beresford*, ed. William Beresford (2 vols., London, 1854), i. 22.

Westminster Parliament to accept the need for thoroughgoing change. In April 1778 a committee of the British Commons resolved that Ireland should be admitted to the colonial trade, with the exception only of the export of woollens and the import of tobacco, and that Irish sailcloth, cordage, and cotton yarn should be admitted into Britain. The resolutions were approved by the House and translated into four bills. But these attempts to give the Irish some commercial relief soon ran into determined resistance. The commercial and manufacturing towns of Britain lobbied vigorously against the bills, with Glasgow and Manchester leading the way. Thomas Conolly, who was both a British and an Irish MP, went over to London in the hope of seeing significant changes in the Anglo-Irish relationship, but was obliged to witness a government climbdown. The 'Lancashire Gentlemen', as he disdainfully described them, having been conspicuous in their support of the war, and having raised troops to prosecute it, were able to exert considerable leverage over Lord North.[16] Direct importation from the colonies was surrendered up in deference to the interests of British re-exporters, who looked to the Irish market as a vital prop in difficult times. Export to the colonies was retained, but the number of exempted articles was greatly increased. The scope for the export of Irish manufactures to Britain was much reduced.

The British government's retreat and the hostility towards the Irish displayed by the opponents of the bills, R. B. McDowell has written, 'had an electrifying effect on Irish opinion'.[17] The concessions were so much less generous than had originally been promised that resentment at British restrictions, rather than subsiding, reached fever pitch. Expectations had been raised only to be dashed. 'In short,' an Ulster land agent told his employer, '. . . we look on the whole transaction as an addition of insult to oppression.'[18] Calls from members of the opposition in the Irish Commons for the people to refuse to purchase manufactures from Glasgow or Manchester struck a chord. Over the following months all manner of public bodies and private associations decided to discourage the consumption of British products and to promote the use of Irish

[16] NLI, Heron Papers, MS 13049, Conolly to Buckinghamshire, 16 May 1778.
[17] R. B. McDowell, *Ireland in the Age of Imperialism and Revolution 1760–1801* (Oxford, 1979), 253.
[18] W. H. Crawford (ed.), *Letters from an Ulster Land Agent 1774–1785* (Belfast, 1976), 24.

substitutes.[19] Dublin's corporation, for instance, resolved not to use any goods sent from Britain 'until an enlightened policy founded upon principles of justice shall appear to actuate the inhabitants of certain manufacturing towns of Great Britain'.[20] While the tone of the non-consumption agreements varied greatly, at the most extreme end of the spectrum the threat of violence against anyone who transgressed was a reminder of how seriously they were regarded by many Irish people.[21]

Economic retaliation, as we have seen, had some impact on British manufacturers.[22] But more significant, in terms of mounting pressure for fuller concessions on trade, was the emergence in the spring of 1778 of the volunteers. We have already been introduced to the volunteers as a military force, as instruments of local law and order, as expressions of social ambition, and as a manifestation of Irish Protestant nationalism.[23] They need now to be considered more fully in a political light. At first, the lord-lieutenant, the Earl of Buckinghamshire, and his chief secretary, Sir Richard Heron, appeared unconcerned by the volunteers. In August 1778 Heron told Stewart Banks, the sovereign (or mayor) of Belfast, that the lord-lieutenant 'very much approves of the Spirit of the Inhabitants . . . who, have formed themselves, into Companies for the Defence of the Town'.[24] Indeed, in May Buckinghamshire expressed a preference for the volunteers over an Irish militia, which if chosen by ballot would be certain to contain 'disaffected Persons'.[25] In the summer of 1779 the governors of counties were permitted to distribute to the volunteer corps arms that had been kept in store for the militia. As the lord-lieutenant himself had written that May, 'Unpleasing as the Institution of those Corps may be in many respects, there can be no doubt, in case of a French Invasion, that most material utility might be deriv'd from them'.[26] Buckinghamshire's complacent acceptance of the volunteers was understandable. The Europeanization of the American war, and the failure of attempts to revive the militia, made the emergence of the volunteers more or less inevitable; and

---

[19] Hill, *From Patriots to Unionists*, 145, points out that this had been the response of the Irish in earlier economic crises.

[20] J. T. and R. M. Gilbert (eds.), *Calendar of Ancient Records of Dublin* (19 vols., Dublin, 1889–1944), xiii. 53.   [21] McDowell, *Ireland*, 253–4.

[22] See above, Ch. 2.   [23] See above, Chs. 1, 3, and 5.

[24] PRONI, Downshire Papers, D 607/B/29.

[25] PRO, Granville Papers, 30/29/3/9, fos. 835–6.

[26] PRONI, Downshire Papers, D 607/B/86.

while theoretically undesirable, they did not at first appear particularly menacing. Some volunteer officers were prepared to accept commissions from the lord-lieutenant, which would have regularized their status and turned their corps into a militia in all but name. Even by the autumn of 1779, by no means all the volunteers aspired to play a political as well as a military role. There was a distinction, Lord Hillsborough explained, between those corps that were republican and pro-American, the leaders of which preached principles 'little distant from high treason', and the majority raised by country gentlemen to defend the country and preserve order.[27]

All the same, the very internal organization of many of the corps suggests a politicized force. In all parts of Ireland, volunteers adopted a democratic system of regulation: admission was often by the vote of the existing members, officers were elected, discipline was enforced by fines and expulsions rather than corporal punishment.[28] And many of the corps were clearly political in their outlook. The First Newry Volunteers, as we have seen, declared their objectives to be defending their country from foreign and *domestic* enemies, 'to resist Usurpation and maintain The Constitution'; they ostentatiously paraded their independence by refusing to consider pay or commissions from government.[29] Nor was this political edge just to be found in Ulster. The Doneraile Rangers, in County Cork, decided at their inaugural meeting in July 1779 that their uniform should be of Irish manufacture only—a political statement, if ever there was one.[30] By October 1779 Beresford was referring alarmingly to the 'circumstances of no small danger' created by thousands of armed volunteers, beyond the control of the government, and often led by men who were opposed to the administration.[31] Even Buckinghamshire was becoming more apprehensive: 'the lyon walks abroad without his chain, and tho' he wags his tail, his fangs may prove dangerous'.[32]

When the Irish Parliament met in October 1779, the Dublin

[27] NLI, Heron Papers, MS 13038, Buckinghamshire to Heron, 9, 11 July 1779, Hillsborough to Buckinghamshire, 21 Sept. 1779.
[28] e.g. NLI, MS 838, Minutes of the Ennis Volunteers, 1778–82.
[29] PRONI, T 3202/1A, Minute-book of the First Newry Volunteers, original agreement of association, 22 Sept. 1778. See also above, Ch. 3.
[30] NLI, MS 12155, Minutes of the Doneraile Rangers, 1779–92.
[31] *Correspondence of Beresford*, ed. Beresford, i. 58.
[32] Hull University Library, Hotham Papers, DD HO 4/20, Buckinghamshire to Sir Charles Thompson, 12 Oct. 1779.

volunteers lined the streets. William Brownlow, an opposition MP and himself a volunteer officer in County Armagh, wrote with grim satisfaction that this military display would 'be the cause of some reflection on the other side of the water'.[33] Buckinghamshire, recognizing that the cry for 'free trade' was almost universal, and having put the economic case for it to British ministers, had been pressing for concessions from London during the recess. But none was forthcoming. The lord-lieutenant was therefore obliged to open the session with a speech that merely expressed the king's concern over Irish distress. The administration's discomfort was increased by the conduct of Walter Hussey Burgh, who had recently resigned as prime sergeant and effective leader of the Irish Commons. Burgh had promised to be as friendly to administration as circumstances would allow, but 'On the first day of the Session . . . no man was so violent, so inflammatory, or so perfectly hostile'.[34] On 4 November the Dublin volunteers assembled in College Green. In a piece of richly symbolic theatre, the base of King William's statue was decorated with the demand 'Free trade or else' and the 900 men on parade proceeded to demonstrate their military capacity by a display of disciplined musket-firing. In the Commons, an amendment to the lord-lieutenant's address, demanding free trade, was carried without a dissentient voice. In the absence of any sign of movement from London, the patriot opposition pressed for the adoption of fiscal sanctions against the Irish administration, which, in the feverish atmosphere of the time, was increasingly used, in A. P. W. Malcomson's words, as 'a whipping-boy' for North's government.[35] On 24 November a motion that it was inexpedient to vote any new taxes was carried by 170 to 47. The next day the House agreed to limit supplies to a period of only six months. As the Irish commander-in-chief wrote to his friend Germain, 'it is not possible to conceive a parliament more under the subjection of the people than this is'.[36]

Even in October Lord North had feared that Ireland was going

[33] HMC, 12th Report, app. pt. x, *Charlemont MSS* i (London, 1891), 359.

[34] HMC, 15th Report, app., pt. vi, *Carlisle MSS* (London, 1897), 516. Burgh's approach was not, perhaps, as mercurial as it appeared. In 1777 he had written of supporting Buckinghamshire's administration 'so far as is consistent with the true Interests of this Country' (Trinity College Dublin, Conolly Papers, MS 3976/488).

[35] A. P. W. Malcomson, *John Foster: The Politics of the Anglo-Irish Ascendancy* (Oxford, 1978), 38.

[36] HMC, *Stopford Sackville MSS* (2 vols., London, 1904–10), i. 263.

the same way as America.[37] A letter sent by Beresford to John Robinson, North's secretary to the treasury, the day after the College Green demonstration, painted a picture of Ireland on the verge of rebellion. 'There is not a moment to be lost', Beresford wrote. His recommendation was to grant free trade, or recall the lord-lieutenant and his secretary.[38] Buckinghamshire's position was far from secure. He was not the first choice as lord-lieutenant when Harcourt resigned, and he never felt that he had the confidence of North and his colleagues.[39] On 3 June 1779 he self-pityingly told Heron that he feared 'in England many think me both Indolent and inattentive'.[40] By the following November Lord Shannon, a prominent government supporter, was being informed that the British ministry believed the lord-lieutenant had become an Irish patriot and forgotten his duty.[41] But North kept Buckinghamshire and Heron in place, for the time being at least, and decided to give ground on Irish trade. In December, shortly after the opening of the British Parliament, he announced the kind of concessions that the Irish had sought in 1778. Direct trade with the British colonies was to be permitted, provided that the Irish Parliament imposed the same duties on colonial commerce as did the British, and restrictions on the export of Irish woollens and glass products were repealed.

North hoped that he had done enough to dampen down Irish agitation. The pressure for reform of the Anglo-Irish relationship did indeed slacken, but this probably owed as much to a reaction within Ireland against the political role of the volunteers as it did to North's efforts to avert an uprising. True, the Newry volunteers wasted no time in calling for legislative independence to protect the commercial settlement from British backsliding, and in January 1780 a pamphlet urged Lord North to grant this constitutional reform or risk seeing Ireland take it by force.[42] Over the next few months, furthermore, opposition MPs proposed amendments to Poynings' Law and introduced an Irish mutiny bill. In April 1780 Henry Grattan, in a great set-piece speech, called for legislative independence. Buckinghamshire worried about the defection of some

[37] HMC, *Dartmouth MSS* (3 vols., London, 1887–96), ii. 474.
[38] *Correspondence of Beresford*, ed. Beresford, i. 74.
[39] Staffordshire RO, Gower Papers, D 868/10/7.
[40] NLI, Heron Papers, MS 13038.
[41] NLI, Shannon Papers, MS 13301, Boyle Walshingham to Shannon, 15 Nov. 1779.
[42] Francis Dobbs, *A Letter to the Right Honourable Lord North* (Dublin, 1780).

members who had previously backed the Castle, complaining that 'several gentlemen who had . . . pledged themselves to support Government' had voted with Grattan.[43] But there was no immediate repetition of the victory over free trade. The patriots were unable to secure their desired objectives. This was partly because opposition leaders in Parliament, with the exception of Grattan, adopted the lofty position that they, not the volunteers, should be setting the political agenda. Burgh, Denis Daly, Barry Yelverton, Thomas Conolly, and the Duke of Leinster all condemned the raising of constitutional issues by armed men.[44] But this fastidiousness, which was conspicuous by its absence during the debates about free trade, should perhaps be seen merely as a symptom of a more general concern that the volunteers were becoming too powerful. In the aftermath of the College Green affair, Germain had hoped that 'this State of Anarchy and Confusion' would 'rouse the men of sense and property' to rally behind the Irish government.[45] The following January, North was likewise expressing the view that 'the principal persons of Ireland must see the danger of these irregular & independent Corps'.[46] There is some evidence that this is precisely what was happening. When the Rathfriland volunteers criticized the Irish Parliament for agreeing to a perpetual Mutiny Act, Lord Glenawly took back the muskets he had issued to the corps. The officers of the Coleraine volunteers, much to the disgust of the rank and file, effectively said that constitutional matters should be left to parliament to resolve.[47]

This conservative reaction meant that the Earl of Carlisle, who became lord-lieutenant in December 1780, was faced with a much less dangerous situation than that with which Buckinghamshire had struggled for much of his time in office. In January 1781, William Eden, Carlisle's chief secretary, wrote of a general conviction amongst 'men of the greatest weight and consequence in this kingdom' that the 'aristocratic part' of the constitution had been undermined by recent events, and that there was 'an evident necessity of

---

[43] HMC, *Lothian MSS* (London, 1905), 363.

[44] P. D. H. Smyth, 'The Volunteers and Parliament, 1779–1784', in Thomas Bartlett and D. W. Hayton (eds.), *Penal Era and Golden Age: Essays in Irish History, 1690–1800* (Belfast, 1979), 119–20.

[45] NLI, Heron Papers, MS 13052, Germain to Buckinghamshire, 20 Nov. 1779.

[46] Ibid., MS 13039, North to Buckinghamshire, 16 Jan. 1780.

[47] McDowell, *Ireland*, 271–2.

regaining from the people that power, which, if suffered to continue in their hands, must end in the general ruin of the whole'.[48] The volunteers, though they met in many reviews during the summer of 1781, were almost silent on political matters; only one volunteer gathering called for legislative independence at this time. Politically radical volunteers seem to have despaired of achieving anything either through the current Parliament or under the current administration.[49] The war situation also contributed to the relative absence of aggressive political agitation. The threat of invasion, which revived in the late summer and early autumn, had the effect of giving prominence to the volunteers' military functions. Carlisle reinforced the impression that this was their proper role by accepting their offers to cooperate with the army and by thanking them fulsomely for their services.[50] Meanwhile, Eden worked assiduously to build up a body of loyal supporters in the Commons for the new parliamentary session. 'As our political campaign approaches,' he wrote in August with regard to the allocation of army commissions, 'we become of course the more solicitous to content our friends.'[51] In November 1781 Carlisle was confident that he would achieve what had generally eluded Buckinghamshire—regular management of the Irish Parliament.[52] But this was not just a product of patronage. Carlisle and Eden shrewdly refrained from opposing constitutional reforms on Habeas Corpus and judicial tenure, and by allowing extensive discussion of Poynings' Law exposed a division in the ranks of the opposition. At the end of December 1781 Carlisle was looking forward to finishing the session 'with such attention to the chief subjects of popular ferment as may either allay men's spirits by shewing them their errors, or draw their gratitude by complying with their reasonable wishes'.[53]

But not even the skilful management of Carlisle and Eden could prevent Grattan bringing matters to a head in February 1782, when he moved in the Commons a declaration of Irish legislative independence. A motion by the attorney-general to postpone consideration of the matter was carried, but as Carlisle himself appreciated, there was almost universal support in the chamber

---

[48] SP 63/474, fo. 21.   [49] See below, Ch. 8.
[50] Eden explained to the Earl of Hillsborough that the offers from the volunteers should be interpreted as 'a very pleasing turn in the whole political state of Ireland, creditable and strengthening to His excellency's administration' (SP 63/476, fo. 108).
[51] Ibid., fo. 15.   [52] HMC, *Carlisle MSS*, 534.   [53] SP 63/480, fo. 10.

for the principle that Ireland was not bound by acts of the British Parliament. By the end of March the lord-lieutenant was again conjuring up the alarming spectacle of the volunteers: there were, he told Lord Gower,'thirty thousand men with the arms of government in their hands, who would take the field tomorrow' rather than submit to British claims of legislative supremacy.[54] But the major constitutional concessions of 1782, which in effect gave Ireland qualified legislative independence, were more a product of political change in Britain than a consequence of the revival of cooperation between the parliamentary opposition and the volunteers. This is not to deny that the volunteer convention at Dungannon in February 1782, which called for a package of measures to deliver legislative independence, started the process that culminated in the 'constitution of 1782'. Nor is it to minimize the role of Grattan, who, recognizing that the parliamentary opposition were making little progress on their own, played a significant part in reactivating the volunteers. The Dungannon resolutions can be seen as Grattan's bid to build up extra-parliamentary momentum to complement the efforts of the patriots in the Irish legislature. They certainly provided a lead for Irish opinion, and were soon adopted by volunteer conventions all over the country. As a Dublin newspaper remarked in March, after having reported the adoption by the Connacht volunteers of the Dungannon platform, 'It is now evident that the Ulster resolutions will become general'.[55] They were also embraced by meetings of grand juries and assemblies of constituents in the counties. In the face of such a mobilized public, Irish MPs, mindful of the proximity of the next general election, rallied behind the patriot leadership in the Dublin Parliament.

But the crucial ingredient was the change in administration in London and Dublin, which itself was a consequence of the war, or more precisely, British defeat in America. The fall of North brought Rockingham and Shelburne into office, and led to Carlisle's replacement by the Duke of Portland. The new ministers had supported the Irish demands in opposition, and had established close links with sections of the patriot party in the Irish Parliament. Not surprisingly, Grattan and his followers expected an immediate honouring of past pledges. Rockingham's ministry tried to delay concessions to

---

[54] PRO, Granville Papers, 30/29/1, Carlisle to Gower, 23 Mar. 1782.
[55] *General Evening Post*, 21 Mar. 1782.

secure a comprehensive settlement that would preserve the connection between Britain and Ireland. But the Irish patriots were impatient; they were not prepared to negotiate on matters that they considered Rockingham and his colleagues honour-bound to concede. With Grattan using the threat of the volunteers to back his demands, the British cabinet finally capitulated. In May 1782 the British Parliament was persuaded, though not without some difficulty, to back the government's line. The following year, a Renunciation Act, by which the British Parliament formally disavowed any intention to legislate for Ireland, seemed to put the seal on Irish legislative independence.

Recent scholarship tends to consider these changes in a less dramatic light. 'The reality of 1782', Roy Foster has written, 'was largely cosmetic'; the importance of the concessions was exaggerated 'by the retrospective idealizations of nineteenth-century nationalists'.[56] James Kelly similarly emphasizes the continuing and generally successful efforts of British governments to control Irish affairs after 1782: 'in practice, things changed remarkably little'.[57] But this revision, while no doubt necessary to correct some of the more dewy-eyed accounts of the past,[58] should not be allowed to blot out the feelings of euphoria with which many Protestants greeted the constitutional concessions. In April 1782 Lord Lucan declared that 'poor old Ireland is at the eve of being free and of accomplishing all her wishes'.[59] When the concessions finally came, notices were displayed in Dublin windows, as we have seen, announcing that 'Ireland is free'. In gratitude for what was regarded as the establishment of a more equal status under the crown, the Irish Parliament voted £100,000 to help man the fleet and the volunteers busied themselves in assisting with recruitment of mariners.[60] Perhaps these elated Protestants exaggerated the significance of what had occurred, and failed to appreciate that British governments would try to limit the effects of the concessions. But the very fact that British governments made such efforts to recover lost ground is

---

[56] R. F. Foster, *Modern Ireland 1600–1972* (London, 1988), 251.
[57] James Kelly, *Prelude to Union: Anglo-Irish Politics in the 1780s* (Cork, 1992), 1.
[58] And, to a lesser extent, the present. See Gerard O'Brien, *Anglo-Irish Politics in the Age of Grattan and Pitt* (Dublin, 1987).
[59] HMC, 14th Report, app., pt. ix, *Emly MSS* (London, 1895), 164.
[60] See above, Ch. 5.

surely an indication that they recognized that something meaningful had happened in May 1782.

Reform of the Representation

The British Parliament, while conceding its assumed authority over Ireland, came under pressure from a different direction at much the same time. The turmoil associated with the war brought into being a movement for reform of the representative system. There had, to be sure, been agitation for changes before the conflict began. In 1769, in the aftermath of the controversy surrounding the libertarian hero John Wilkes and his attempts to secure election for Middlesex, and at a time when ministerial treatment of the American colonists was causing concern in some quarters, metropolitan radicals had formed the Society of Supporters of the Bill of Rights. This body, as its name suggests, sought to defend long-cherished English liberties against what were seen as dangerously authoritarian tendencies on the part of government. But the Society went beyond this traditional position to draw up reform proposals on a wide range of issues, including the representative system. In their debates they called for shorter parliaments and action against bribery at elections, and considered the secret ballot and a redistribution of parliamentary seats to increase the number of MPs for the growing metropolis.[61] John Sawbridge, an MP and one of the Society's founder members, in 1771 asked the Commons to commit itself to shorter parliaments; he was to repeat the attempt year after year. The Society of Supporters of the Bill of Rights, however, soon broke up over the issue of Wilkes's debts, and on the eve of the American war only a small core of radicals was putting the case for parliamentary reform.

The galvanizing effects of the conflict were not immediately apparent. In March 1776 Wilkes himself put forward a motion in the Commons calling for a more equal representation of the people

[61] For Wilkes and the Wilkites see Ian R. Christie, *Wilkes, Wyvill and Reform* (London, 1962), chs. 1 and 2; John Cannon, *Parliamentary Reform, 1640–1832* (Cambridge, 1972), ch. 3; John Brewer, 'The Wilkites and the Law, 1763–1774', in id. and John Styles (eds.), *An Ungovernable People* (London, 1980), 128–71; H. T. Dickinson, 'Radicals and Reformers in the Age of Wilkes and Wyvill', in Jeremy Black (ed.), *British Politics and Society from Walpole to Pitt 1742–1789* (London, 1990), 123–46; Kathleen Wilson, *The Sense of the People: Politics, Culture and Imperialism in England, 1715–1785* (Cambridge, 1995), ch. 4; P. D. G. Thomas, *John Wilkes: A Friend to Liberty* (Oxford, 1996), esp. ch. 7.

in parliament. He urged the redistribution of seats from small 'rotten' boroughs to the counties and 'rich and populous manufacturing towns' such as Birmingham, Leeds, and Sheffield, and pointed to the need for a substantial extension of the franchise. Wilkes argued that the American war made this reformation imperative, because the war was so obviously the work of a 'ministerial junto' acting against the wishes of the people, whose views were not properly represented in parliament—a point that was to be made by numerous reformers during the course of the conflict.[62] Yet Wilkes's motion received no backing in the Commons, and there was no extra-parliamentary agitation for the measures he proposed. In the same year, John Cartwright, a Nottinghamshire landowner and militia officer, published an essay on parliamentary reform arguing for manhood suffrage on the basis that all males were taxpayers, either directly or indirectly.[63] Cartwright tried to persuade the Duke of Portland to take his ideas seriously,[64] but again there is no indication of a widespread interest in his scheme at this time. Richard Price, the Dissenting minister, might have agreed with Cartwright that 'The salvation of the kingdom indeed depends on a reformation of parliament',[65] but radical energies in the first years of the war seem to have been directed towards criticism of the North government's line on America; many of those who had been prominent in the Wilkite activities of the 1760s, as James Bradley has shown, played a leading part in the anti-coercion and anti-war petitions of 1775–6.[66]

Wartime developments, however, were to transform parliamentary reform from the preoccupation of a small band of enthusiasts to a mainstream issue. Increased taxes, a mounting national debt, trade dislocation, economic depression and a fall in land values began to persuade even normally conservative squires that all was not well, especially when victory continued to elude the British armed forces. Military failures and humiliations—culminating in the Combined Fleet's securing command of the Channel in the summer of 1779— added to widespread alarm and despondency. As Admiral Hardy's ships remained inactive, Sir William Meredith, once a supporter of

---

[62] *PH* xviii. 1287–97.   [63] *Take Your Choice!* (London, 1776), 19.
[64] Nottingham University Library, Portland Papers, PWF 2567.
[65] *The Correspondence of Richard Price*, ed. Bernard Peach and D. O. Thomas (3 vols., Durham, NC, 1983–94), i. 250.
[66] James E. Bradley, *Religion, Revolution and English Radicalism* (Cambridge, 1990), 344, 348.

Lord North but now an opposition MP, wrote gloomily of a 'fatal torpor which hangs like the night-mare over all the powers of this Country'.[67] And to those Britons who were dismayed and inclined to look critically at the political dispensation that had brought on all these woes, Ireland seemed to offer a lead. 'Was it love for Ireland that made Lord North so anxious to hurry the Irish bills thro' Parliament?', a speaker asked rhetorically at the Yorkshire county meeting on 30 December 1779 that gave rise to the Yorkshire Association. 'No—it was 64,000 bayonets pointed to his breast.'[68] Neither the Yorkshire Association nor any other reform organization of this period attempted to transform itself into an armed body— though Cartwright was keen to see the volunteer corps emerging in Britain play a similar 'service to the cause of freedom' as those in Ireland[69]—but the success of the Irish volunteers seemed to point unequivocally to the efficaciousness of well-applied extra-parliamentary pressure.

To the associators in Yorkshire and the other counties and boroughs that soon followed Yorkshire's lead, the root cause of the nation's problems was taken to be the unrepresentative nature of the House of Commons, which, rather than reflecting public opinion, had become a mere rubber stamp for ministerial decisions. This lamentable state of affairs had come to pass because ministers had been using their bloated wartime tax income to pay for a vast array of sinecures and pensions that effectively bought the continued support of a significant number of MPs; unchecked by an independent House of Commons, the ministers proceeded from blunder to blunder. One of the remedies was assumed to be economical reform. Central to this was a reduction in the number of places and pensions at the disposal of government, which it was thought would both cut public spending, allowing a reduction in taxation, and cleanse the Commons of corrupt elements and so restore it to its proper function as a check on executive power. 'The Civil List', wrote a prominent member of the Yorkshire

---

[67] BL, Miscellaneous Papers, Add. MS 46473, fo. 87.

[68] Christopher Wyvill, *Political Papers* (6 vols., York, 1794–1802), i. 12. See also Dr Williams's Library, Wodrow-Kenrick Correspondendce, MS 24157(69), where Samuel Kenrick, a Dissenting radical, writes in May 1780 that the Irish 'with undaunted resolution pointed 40,000 bayonets to their oppressors breast—the ultima ratio populi—wch. you see prevailed—& I hope will prevail yet to a much greater extent'.

[69] NLI, Dobbs Papers, MS 2251, Cartwright to Francis Dobbs, 12 Jan. 1780.

Association, 'is certainly the Banefull Source from which all Corruption Springs'.[70] But even at the beginning of the great campaign for economical reform there were those in the association movement who were calling for parliamentary reform as an essential complement.[71] The Revd Christopher Wyvill, the leading light in the Yorkshire Association, advocated both shorter parliaments and the creation of 100 new county seats. Wyvill and his allies believed that the first of these measures would help to further the aims of economical reform by making MPs less likely to accept government favours, because they would more frequently have to account for their conduct to the electorate. The creation of 100 new seats in the counties was intended to ensure a majority of MPs remained independent of government. County members, whose constituencies contained many voters and who were themselves required to meet a landed property qualification, were assumed to be the least likely to succumb to ministerial blandishment; if the benches of the House of Commons were filled by more independent country gentlemen then parliament would be better able to perform its proper constitutional role. The abolition of 'rotten' boroughs, initially thought too controversial a measure to advance as an avowed objective, was subsequently added to the programme of the association movement.[72]

Wyvill was supremely aware of the need to avoid alienating real and potential allies by too radical an approach; but if his parliamentary reform proposals could be portrayed as a logical extension of economical reform, the radicals who responded enthusiastically to Yorkshire's lead were much more extreme in their prescriptions, and seemed indeed to be moving in a very different direction. In February 1780 Nottingham's Committee of Association resolved that the legislature's independence from the executive could best be secured by manhood suffrage in the counties and the boroughs, equal-sized constituencies, the secret ballot, and annual parliaments.[73] In April a Society for Constitutional Information was established in London to propagandize for radical measures, distributing tracts by Cartwright and others calling in uncompromising

[70] North Yorkshire RO, Wyvill MSS, ZFW 7/2/4/33, Stephen Croft to Revd Christopher Wyvill, 20 Dec. 1779.
[71] e.g. ibid., ZFW 7/2/4/24, Sir James Norcliffe to Wyvill, 7 Dec. 1779.
[72] Wyvill, *Political Papers*, iv. 231.
[73] York City Archives, Yorkshire Association MSS, M 25/236.

terms for manhood suffrage.[74] In May, just two months after a meeting of county association delegates in London endorsed annual parliaments and 100 new county members, a subcommittee of the Westminster Committee of Association called for a programme of thoroughgoing democratic reform that incorporated the demands usually linked with the nineteenth-century Chartists—equal electoral districts, annual parliaments, the secret ballot, universal male suffrage, payment of MPs, and the abolition of property qualifications for MPs. One of the arguments advanced in support of this programme was the almost universal obligation of males to serve in the militia—a particularly pertinent point, of course, at a time when the militia was embodied on active service. If men were required to risk their lives in the defence of their country, surely they were entitled to a say in how their country was governed?[75]

This flurry of activity failed to produce any change in the representative system. In part this was because in 1780 economical reform was the primary objective; thirty-seven petitions from counties and boroughs submitted in this year concentrated on retrenchment in public expenditure. But there were other reasons why parliamentary reform failed at this point to become a major issue. The Gordon Riots of June 1780 were surely influential. Reformers naturally did their best to distance themselves from the destruction of property caused by the rioters, and even seized the opportunity provided by the controversial suppression of the riots to accuse the government of trying to create a military despotism,[76] but their task was made difficult by the involvement of metropolitan radicals in Lord George Gordon's Protestant Association.[77] Thomas Twining, a fiercely loyal Essex curate, noted with satisfaction in July 1780 that Essex's county association for constitutional reform 'has been silent & inactive of late. I hope', he continued, 'that *associating* spirit will be quenched by the terrible effect of the Protestant association. It must open the

[74] The Society distributed at least 88,000 copies of some thirty-three different publications between 1780 and 1783. See Edward Royle and James Walvin, *English Radicals and Reformers 1760–1848* (London, 1982), 30.

[75] BL, Minutes of the Westminster Committee, Add. MS 38593, fos. 40–4.

[76] See Nicholas Rogers, 'Crowd and People in the Gordon Riots', in Eckhart Hellmuth (ed.), *The Transformation of Political Culture: England and Germany in the Late Eighteenth Century* (Oxford, 1990), 39–55.

[77] For more on the Gordon Riots and the Protestant Association see below, Ch. 7.

eyes of many well-meaning people who had before joined in them.'[78] An upturn in British military fortunes also helped to reduce enthusiasm for change. If 1779 had, in many areas, been a disastrous and humiliating year for British arms, from the summer of 1780 the situation seemed markedly to improve. When news arrived of the surrender of Charleston to British forces, there seemed a real prospect of the recovery of the southern colonies. John Gibbons, a prebendary of St Paul's, wrote excitedly on 7 September of news 'that *All North America* has come in and submitted to the British Government';[79] while Richard Price, with no such enthusiasm, recorded a few days later that 'since the taking of *Charles=town* the common expectation has been that America will soon be ours again'.[80] By December Sir George Savile was telling Wyvill that the public had lost interest in parliamentary reform, and that without weighty external support advocates of reform within parliament were unlikely to be able to make much impression.[81]

Savile's characteristically downbeat assessment omitted to mention the very limited support for parliamentary reform in the Commons and Lords at this stage. Shelburne was sympathetic; indeed, he was a member of the Society for Constitutional Information. Amongst the Rockinghamites, Fox was a leading light in the Westminster Committee of Association, and sought to use his position to forge effective links between his party and the extra-parliamentary reformers: it was at this time that he established himself as a 'man of the people' and became indelibly linked with Westminster, which he represented in parliament from 1780 until the end of his life.[82] Richmond even presented a bill in the Lords in June 1780 calling for manhood suffrage, annual parliaments, and equal electoral districts.[83] But Rockingham himself was worried by what he called the more 'theoretical speculations' of the Yorkshire Association—by which he meant Wyvill's enthusiasm for shorter parliaments and 100 additional county members.[84] Burke, Rockingham's faithful lieutenant, was likewise unhappy in April 1780 that the activists

[78] *A Selection of Thomas Twining's Letters 1734–1804*, ed. Ralph S. Walker (2 vols., Lampeter, 1991), i. 184–5.
[79] Birmingham City Archives, Galton Papers, 248/2.
[80] *Correspondence of Price*, ed. Thomas and Peach, ii. 79.
[81] Wyvill, *Political Papers*, iii. 236.
[82] L. G. Mitchell, *Charles James Fox* (Oxford, 1992), 34–7.
[83] *PH* xxi. 686–8.
[84] Sheffield Archives, Rockingham MSS, R1–1062.

in the association movement 'had turned their thoughts towards a change in the Constitution, rather than towards a correction of it in the form in which it now stands'.[85] Lord John Cavendish, Rockinghamite MP for York, refused to sign the county's association, on the grounds that while he supported economical reform, he was much less keen on extra county members and shorter parliaments, which he foresaw would create all manner of difficulties.[86] In truth, economical reform was probably as far as most Rockinghamites were willing to go. It should be added that throughout 1780 relations between the opposition and the extra-parliamentary agitators were not close enough to provide the necessary momentum. This was partly attributable to the suspicions of the reformers outside parliament, who feared that the Rockinghams, in particular, wanted to take over the association movement and use it for their own ends.[87] There was also a feeling amongst some associators that aristocratic power was as much a danger as executive authority. In Yorkshire, for instance, Jeremiah Batley of Halifax argued that 100 new county MPs would inevitably boost the influence of peers and other great landed families, while Gamaliel Lloyd of Leeds hoped that no one should be chosen as a committee member who was 'a friend to Aristocratical Power'.[88]

The following years were to be more productive for the parliamentary reformers. Scotland, which had remained silent on economical reform in 1780, began to stir over parliamentary reform in 1782. Both in the counties and the burghs there was agitation for change. But neither the county nor the burgh reformers established durable links with their English counterparts. Despite Wyvill's best endeavours, the Scots appear to have regarded the Yorkshire Association's plans as too radical; accordingly, they determined to remain aloof and pursue their own course.[89] More promisingly, William Pitt, first as a supporter of Shelburne and finally as prime minister, introduced a series of reform proposals to the Commons, all of which secured a respectable level of support. Pitt's first effort, a motion on 7 May 1782 for an inquiry into a reform of parliament,

---

[85] *The Correspondence of Edmund Burke*, ed. Thomas W. Copeland et al. (10 vols., Cambridge, 1958–78), iv. 220.   [86] Wyvill, *Political Papers*, i. 160.

[87] See e.g. the views of the Revd William Mason: *Harcourt Papers*, ed. Harcourt, vii. 68.

[88] York City Archives, Yorkshire Association MSS, M25/256, 269.

[89] E. W. McFarland, *Ireland and Scotland in the Age of Revolution* (Edinburgh, 1994), 53–5.

was criticized by opponents as an unfortunate diversion from the needs of the moment (one MP said that it 'would not assist government in a ship, a man or a guinea towards carrying on the war with vigour, or towards establishing that much wished for object, peace').[90] But even though supporters of the new ministry were divided over the issue (it was 'friend against friend', according to General Burgoyne),[91] Pitt failed by only twenty votes (161 to 141). The closeness of this result buoyed up the reformers outside parliament. Shortly afterwards, preparations commenced for a petitioning campaign in the country at large. Reformers were also excited by Shelburne's becoming first minister in July 1782. His resolution to 'promote a fair & just representation of the people' was to Henry Wansey, a Wiltshire clothier, 'highly pleasing'.[92] By the autumn of 1782 the petitioning campaign was getting into full swing, and in February 1783 Yorkshire's petition was submitted, carrying 10,000 signatures—more than on the petition for economical reform in 1780. But when Pitt tried again to persuade the Commons to adopt a motion on reform, on 6 May 1783, he was back in opposition. Pitt invoked the war in his speech, arguing the by-now familiar line that the disasters of the conflict and the heavy taxes occasioned by it had persuaded the people to look for 'the internal sources of foreign fatalities'.[93] The close of hostilities, and the loss of America, might have been expected to make these arguments compelling; but Pitt was this time defeated decisively—by 293 to 149. This was largely because the impression of the state of parliamentary opinion conveyed by the 1782 vote had been deceptive. North's conservatively inclined supporters had been absent following North's recent resignation. But in May 1783 North was again a minister—in the somewhat improbable Fox–North Coalition—and his following was present in force to see off Pitt's motion. In April 1785, Pitt made one last attempt. Again Wyvill tried to stimulate a widespread petitioning campaign; but this time the response outside Yorkshire was very disappointing. Even prime ministerial authority failed to give Pitt much advantage: the result—defeat by 248 votes to 174— was only a modest improvement on the outcome in 1783. Pitt's defeat persuaded the Scottish reformers, who had been awaiting

---

[90] *PH* xxii. 1422.   [91] BL, Fitzpatrick Papers, Add. MS 47582, fo. 74.
[92] Wiltshire RO, Wansey Papers, 314/4/2, Wansey to —— Baker, n.d., but 1782.
[93] *PH* xxiii. 828–9.

the outcome of his efforts before bringing forward their own bill, to concentrate instead on burgh reform, though even on this restricted front nothing was achieved.[94]

Attempts to produce parliamentary reform were also made in Ireland at this time, influenced in part by British developments, but also building on the agitation for legislative independence. There were pre-war roots to this movement, just as in England. Striking continuities were observable, at least in some areas, between the independent interests, hostile to aristocratic management, that emerged in a number of boroughs and counties in the 1750s and 1760s, and the volunteers of the 1770s and 1780s.[95] It should also be pointed out that in the 1760s Dublin had experienced crowd activities similar to the contemporaneous Wilkite disturbances in London.[96] In the 1776 Irish general election the issue of parliamentary reform had been important in a few constituencies. It was the American war, however, that gave reformers their chance. This was not at first obvious, because concentration on free trade and legislative independence ensured that changes in the representative system remained a secondary concern for the next few years. But the agitation for changes in the Anglo-Irish relationship stimulated the growth of pressure for parliamentary reform insofar as the inability of the patriot opposition to secure parliamentary majorities for legislative independence in 1780 and 1781, by highlighting the obstructiveness of a significant segment of Irish MPs, was taken as proof of the corrupt and unrepresentative nature of the legislature. Once legislative independence was conceded, the concern was that a venal Irish Parliament, controlled and directed by the Castle and the British government, would gradually give back what had been gained.[97] But these external preoccupations were matched by internal considerations. Volunteering, Ian McBride tells us, entered deep into the culture of Protestant Ireland, and of Ulster in particular, with volunteer events punctuating the social calendar and artefacts celebrating the volunteers appearing in considerable numbers.

---

[94] *PH* xxviii. 221–6 (6 July 1789).   [95] Hill, *From Patriots to Unionists*, 145.

[96] Seamus Cummins, 'Extra-Parliamentary Agitation in Dublin in the 1760s', in R. V. Comerford, Mary Cullen, Jacqueline R. Hill, and Colm Lennon (eds.), *Religion, Conflict and Coexistence in Ireland: Essays Presented to Monsignor Patrick J. Corish* (Dublin, 1990), 120.

[97] James Kelly, 'Parliamentary Reform in Irish Politics: 1760–1790', in David Dickson, Daire Keogh, and Kevin Whelan (eds.), *The United Irishmen: Republicanism, Radicalism and Rebellion* (Dublin, 1993), 79.

These social and cultural dimensions bolstered volunteering's role as an instrument of popular politicization. Through participation in the volunteers 'thousands of Ulstermen acquired their first taste of active citizenship'.[98] Ordinary volunteers, predominantly men of the middling ranks of society, had grown accustomed to debating political issues, writing addresses, sitting on committees—and to having their ideas taken into account. Volunteering had given them a voice, a sense of their own importance, and now they wanted to ensure that they would be heard in the future. Parliamentary reform, if it could open up a largely closed system, promised to be the means of making the influence of the Irish 'middling sort' permanent rather than temporary.[99]

Accordingly, in June 1782 a volunteer convention at Dungannon, attended by delegates from more than three hundred corps, came out in favour of a more equal representation of the people in Parliament. At this stage, however, there was no agreement on what form any change should take. Volunteer reviews in 1782 and early 1783 enthusiastically endorsed the lead provided by the Dungannon convention, but there was still no move forward. Not until a meeting of volunteer delegates at Lisburn on 1 July 1783 did the campaign properly begin. The Lisburn meeting appointed a committee of correspondence to collect information on the best way to reform Parliament, and approached Britons as well as Irishmen known to be sympathetic.[100] It was agreed that the various plans would be considered at a general meeting of Ulster volunteer delegates at Dungannon in September.

Before the Dungannon meeting took place, there was a general election. The results were mixed and defy easy analysis. Some of the contests were influenced by the heated dispute that had erupted the year before about the formation of fencible regiments, the Irish administration's belated attempt to provide a military alternative to the volunteers. The volunteers were very hostile to the fencibles; in October 1782 the volunteers of Ennis, County Clare, for instance, refused to act with the fencibles in any military capacity; while the

---

[98] Ian McBride, *Scripture Politics: Ulster Presbyterians and Irish Radicalism in the Late Eighteenth Century* (Oxford, 1998), 10, 124–33.

[99] This, in essence, is the central theme of Maurice O'Connell, *Irish Politics and Social Conflict in the Age of the American Revolution* (Philadelphia, 1965).

[100] See e.g. York City Archives, Yorkshire Association MSS, M32/26, for Wyvill's correspondence with the Ulster reformers.

Doneraile, County Cork, volunteers threatened to suspend their assistance in raising men for the navy.[101] Volunteers who defected to the fencibles were regarded as traitorous 'mercenaries' who had deserted the cause of 'independency'.[102] This resentment seems to explain why Thomas Dawson, a former volunteer who had accepted a fencible command, was unseated in County Armagh in the 1783 election.[103] The defeat in County Down of Robert Stewart, a well-known volunteer colonel, seems to have been the consequence of a rather different dispute—a theological clash between the 'New Light' or liberal Presbyterians and the fundamentalist Seceders. Stewart was supported by many leading Ulster Presbyterians, but the local Seceders voted for a government candidate, Lord Kilwarlin, because they disliked Stewart's connection with a 'New Light' congregation and because Kilwarlin's father, the Earl of Hillsborough, had carefully cultivated links with the Seceders.[104] But in a few constituencies, at least, there were signs that there was public support for opening up the representative system. In Dundalk, a borough thought to be controlled by Lord Clanbrassill, opposition candidates appeared and Clanbrassill's nominees were successful only after a fierce contest. And in Lisburn two volunteer officers committed to reform defeated the candidates of the borough patron, the Earl of Hertford.

The general election results seem to have encouraged the Ulster volunteer delegates who met at Dungannon early in September. They proceeded to approve resolutions calling for annual parliaments, the secret ballot, abolition of rotten boroughs and redistribution of the seats to counties and populous towns, and the extension of the franchise.[105] There was some disagreement on whether to include Catholics on the same terms as Protestants, and the matter was therefore left for resolution by a Grand National Convention, which it was decided should meet in Dublin in November to draw up a comprehensive plan of reform for submission to Parliament. Thomas Conolly was dismayed by the radicalism of the Dungannon

[101] NLI, Minutes of the Ennis Volunteers, 13 Oct. 1782; Minutes of the Doneraile Rangers, 13 Oct. 1782.   [102] *General Evening Post*, 29 Aug. 1782.

[103] Smyth, 'Volunteers and Parliament', p. 129. For more on the dispute over the fencibles, see A. T. Q. Stewart, *A Deeper Silence: The Hidden Roots of the United Irish Movement* (London, 1993), 43, 62.

[104] Pieter Tesch, 'Presbyterian Radicalism', in Dickson, Keogh, and Whelan (eds.), *United Irishmen*, 44.

[105] This reflected the advice of the English reformers: O'Connell, *Irish Politics*, 380–4.

resolutions; the meeting, he wrote, 'seems determin'd to overturn all Government'.[106] But this radicalism was apparently to the taste of most volunteer delegates elsewhere, for the Dungannon resolutions were approved by volunteer meetings in Munster, Leinster, and Connacht.

The Grand National Convention proved much less radical. With more than fifty MPs and six peers among the delegates, this was perhaps only to be expected. Under the influence of moderates and conservatives, the Convention considerably diluted the Dungannon proposals. Annual parliaments and the secret ballot were dropped, and it was decided that rotten boroughs could best be dealt with by enlargement rather than abolition. A mischievous intervention by George Ogle, a determined anti-Catholic, who claimed to have evidence that Catholics did not want the vote, ensured that there was no serious discussion of the issue. The moderation of the Convention's plan of reform reflected the importance some delegates attached to tactical considerations as well as the caution of the more conservative spirits amongst them. Henry Flood, the patriot MP who brokered the agreement on the substance of the plan, was focused throughout on the need to come up with a set of proposals that had a realistic chance of approval in the Irish Parliament.

The moderation of the Convention's proposals was unable, however, to win over the Irish Parliament. The plan, when debated by the House of Commons on 29 November 1783, was decisively rejected by 158 to 49. Part of the problem was that Flood came straight from the Convention to Parliament and appeared, as did several other delegates, in volunteer uniform. This made it easy for opponents of reform, such as John Fitzgibbon, to argue that Flood's motion 'comes under the mandate of a military congress'. Yelvereton, now the attorney-general, declared that as the plan 'originates in an armed body, 'tis inconsistent with the freedom of debate for this House to receive it'.[107] Perhaps recognizing the tactical error of making their link with the volunteers too explicit, reformers turned in the next few months to more traditional avenues of protest. A petitioning campaign over the winter and spring, based on legally

---

[106] NLI, Heron Papers, MS 13049, Conolly to Buckinghamshire, 25 Sept. 1783.
[107] *The Parliamentary Register; or, History of the Proceedings and Debates of the House of Commons of Ireland* (17 vols., Dublin, 1781–97), ii. 226, 237.

constituted meetings in the counties and boroughs rather than volunteer gatherings, demonstrated continuing public interest. But this approach turned out to be scarcely more productive. Another reform bill presented to the Commons in March 1784 was defeated by almost as wide a margin. Flood defended his bill as an attempt 'to restore the constitution by moderate measures; not to introduce novelties, but to take them away'. But, despite the efforts to pursue conventional means of redress, the Dungannon volunteer resolutions were again brought up by opponents; John Monck Mason denounced the bill as 'the first of an alphabet of innovations, which the congress of Dungannon have voted . . . if you yield to them in this point', he told his fellow MPs, 'they will attack you upon some other, and so proceed from innovation to innovation, till they have subverted your constitution both in church and state; this is therefore the time to resist their encroachments'.[108]

Ulster's Presbyterians had provided the driving force for the campaign of 1783, but in 1784 Dublin's radicals led the way. In June Napper Tandy resurrected many of the elements of the Dungannon proposals, and a public meeting in the city even came out in favour of Catholic enfranchisement. The meeting also called on freeholders throughout Ireland to elect delegates to a National Reform Congress to be assembled in Dublin the following October. The Congress proved a great disappointment to its organizers. Less than half the expected delegates assembled. This was partly due to a concerted effort by the Irish administration and many leading aristocrats to prevent county sheriffs agreeing to the freeholder meetings that were required to elect the delegates. But perhaps as big a stumbling block was the issue of voting rights for Catholics. Although Catholic enfranchisement had been discussed before, it had always been possible to postpone a decision that was likely to divide reformers. The forthright commitment of Tandy and the Dublin radicals meant that it was bound to be debated thoroughly at the Congress. Once Catholic rights became a prominent issue, Ulster's enthusiasm for reform began to wane. Charlemont, who was a long-standing opponent of concessions to Catholics, used his enormous influence to encourage the Ulster volunteers to reject pro-Catholic resolutions at volunteer meetings in the province. The decision to drop Catholic enfranchisement enabled Ulster dele-

---

[108] Ibid., iii. 14, 48.

gates to participate more fully when the Congress reconvened in January, but by this stage all momentum had been lost. In the Irish Commons resistance was as strong as ever. Again, the allegedly unconstitutional pressure being exerted on Parliament was used as an argument against reform. John Toler, MP for Philipstown, was 'astonished at the patience of the House, to have remained so long unmoved when even some of its members have avowed their participating in the proceedings of a congress that presumed to usurp the authority of parliament, to call themselves the representatives of the people, and to question the right of your existence'. Denis Daly was 'convinced of a design . . . to plunge the nation into licentiousness, turbulence and anarchy'.[109]

Splits in the reforming camp were an obvious impediment to the realization of any reform initiative between 1783 and 1785. It was very difficult to meld moderates and radicals into a cohesive force. The issue of Catholic rights proved highly divisive. But concentration on the reformers distracts attention from the main obstacles. British governments had no interest in seeing an Irish Parliament that was more accountable to public opinion; in the patriotic mood of the early 1780s such a parliament might well have pressed for a further weakening of the Anglo-Irish connection. True, in 1784 Pitt, the new British prime minister, was prepared to consider a moderate reform of the Irish Parliament to complement the reform that he was advocating in Britain. But the Duke of Rutland, the new lord-lieutenant, warned him that nothing must be done that would 'materially interfere with the *system of Parliament* in this country, which, though it must be confessed it does not bear the smallest *resemblance to representation*, I do not see how quiet and good government could exist under any more popular mode'.[110] The Irish administration was naturally averse to any alteration in the constitution of a legislature that by careful use of patronage could usually be managed. What appeared to reformers as glaring defects were to the lord-lieutenant and his administration essential props. Of the 300 Irish MPs, 234 sat for boroughs, many of which were controlled by an individual borough owner. Reformers wanted to abolish 'pocket boroughs', but these seats were most useful to the

---

[109] Ibid. iv. 37–8.
[110] *Correspondence between the Right Honble. William Pitt and Charles Duke of Rutland Lord Lieutenant of Ireland 1781–1787* (Edinburgh, 1890), p. 17.

Castle, because they produced MPs who had little to fear from public opinion and were therefore more amenable to government blandishments. But the failure of the reformers was primarily caused by the determined opposition of the aristocratic elite that controlled many of the smaller boroughs. This was partly a natural consequence of their reluctance to yield up what they regarded as a species of property to be bought, sold, and inherited. It also reflected a more general concern that aristocratic authority everywhere was under threat. The great Ascendancy families had been uneasy about popular participation in politics from the time of the first stirrings of the volunteers over free trade. Many aristocrats and landed MPs had been volunteer officers, but a good number of them grew increasingly concerned at what they saw as illegitimate volunteer interference in political matters. So long as that interference was confined to mounting pressure for legislative independence, which was in the interests of the Ascendancy, it could be tolerated, even if with misgivings. But once interference extended to challenging the electoral influence of borough patrons and great landowners, resistance was bound to be open and determined. In the debate of 29 November 1783 Yelverton declared:[111]

I admire the volunteers, so long as they confine themselves to their first line of conduct; it was their glory to preserve the domestic peace of their country, and to render it formidable to foreign enemies—it was their glory to aid the civil magistrate, and to support their parliament; but when they turn aside from this honourable conduct, when they form themselves into a debating society, and with that rude instrument the bayonet, probe and explore a constitution which requires the nicest hand to touch, I own my respect and veneration for them is destroyed

Fifteen months later, on 18 February 1785, Luke Gardiner felt confident enough to go even further. 'I feel the highest gratitude to the volunteers for their exertions last war', he told the Irish Commons, 'but as occasion for their continuing in arms no longer exists, I would rather wish they should return to their former situation of citizens, and turn their attention to manufactures and industry'.[112] The aristocratic reaction identified by Eden in 1781 had reached its logical conclusion.

Reform, however, was only temporarily off the political agenda.

---

[111] *Parliamentary Register . . . Ireland*, ii. 226.   [112] Ibid. iv. 266.

The arguments heard in the agitation of the early 1780s were to be used again in the next decade. With the coming of the French Revolution, the Society of United Irishmen pursued reform with vigour—and to the point of open rebellion. In February 1797, when the United Irish agitation in Ulster was approaching its peak, an Anglican vicar told the Earl of Abercorn of his belief that the roots of the current troubles lay in the American war: 'talking with a Loyalist Farmer', the vicar wrote, 'on the novelty of some political Doctrines, he said they were not new, for they had been taught them all at Belfast at the great Volunteer Review in 1780'.[113] In England, the Society for Constitutional Information, after several years in the doldrums, revived its activities. It was reading some of the Society's literature that inspired Thomas Hardy, a shoemaker, to form the London Corresponding Society in 1792. This rapidly grew into a much larger body than the Society for Constitutional Information, and became an important vehicle for the transmission of the democratic programme first adopted by the Westminster Committee in 1780. There was also continuity in terms of personnel. A good number of those who played a prominent role in the events of the 1790s had cut their teeth in the earlier struggles. In England, this was most clearly the case with Major Cartwright, who continued to be in the forefront of reforming initiatives until the 1820s. In Ireland, continuity was personified by the likes of Napper Tandy and the Ulster Presbyterian radicals, William Drennan, William Steel Dickson, and Samuel Barber. They saw themselves as engaged in a continuing battle. In this respect, as in so many others, the American war gave a great boost to a process that was to reach its full flowering in the still more dramatic developments of the French Revolutionary Wars.

Economical Reform

We have seen how proposals for parliamentary reform in Britain developed out of the great campaign for economical reform of 1779–80. Let us now return to economical reform itself. It is no doubt tempting, given that parliamentary reform was to become one of the

---

[113] McBride, *Scripture Politics*, 113. See also Nancy J. Curtin, *The United Irishmen: Popular Politics in Ulster and Dublin 1791–1798* (Oxford, 1994), pp. 17–18, 204, 229, 249.

major issues of the nineteenth century, to assume that it was the more significant issue at the time of the American war; parliamentary reform, after all, seems to point the way forward, while economical reform might appear to be backward-looking. But the struggle for economical reform, though in many ways a reaffirmation of faith in traditional 'country' remedies for securing the independence of the legislature against executive encroachments, was to produce results that were scarcely less influential so far as nineteenth-century politics were concerned.

The campaign for economical reform, furthermore, was to be more immediately successful than the various efforts to change the representative system. No parliamentary reform was achieved in or just after the American war, but the war years saw the first steps towards the realization of a less corrupt and profligate means of political management. This is not to say that economical reform met with no resistance. Far from it. In Yorkshire, the epicentre of the campaign for retrenchment, critics of the county petition accused the organizers of using landlord pressure to secure signatures.[114] Defenders of the status quo argued that the time was not right for the kind of thoroughgoing overhaul of government and administration sought by the petitioners. In the words of the Revd John Butler, an outspoken supporter of Lord North: 'just as the Tide is turned in our favor we are to Stop the progress of the War, till the value of every man's place, the work he does for it, and the merits of every pension are ascertained'.[115] In parliament, Lord North's following remained fairly solid. True, the government experienced the humiliation of defeat in April 1780, when John Dunning, a Shelburnite, successfully carried a motion declaring that the 'influence of the crown has increased, is increasing, and ought to be diminished'.[116] But once the argument moved from theory to practice, North's troops rallied. By May 1780, John Pringle, a Scottish MP, was detecting a swing back to the government.[117] Burke's bill to abolish sinecures, introduced in February, was gradually emasculated as it passed through the Commons. Sir Philip Jennings Clerke's bill to prohibit contractors from sitting in the lower house passed the Commons without a division but was thrown out by the Lords.

---

[114] *Leeds Intelligencer*, 8 Feb. 1780.
[115] Surrey RO (Guildford Muniment Room), Onslow MSS, 173/2/1/184.
[116] *PH* xxi. 340–74.
[117] HMC, *Polwarth MSS* (5 vols., London, 1911–61), v. 371.

John Crewe's bill to prevent revenue officers voting in parliamentary elections was defeated without the government needing to rely on the safety net of the second chamber; it went down on second reading by 224 votes to 195.

All the same, the government faced a much more difficult task in holding back economical reform than in seeing off motions on parliamentary reform. To resist Burke's bills, for instance, the secretary at war was requested to ensure that every army officer who was an MP attended the Commons: 'we want every one I assure you, that it is possible to get', wrote John Robinson, North's secretary to the treasury. 'Not a man must be spared.'[118] The government's concern was partly caused by the undeniable strength of public feeling on retrenchment; thirty-seven petitions bearing about 60,000 signatures were weighty testimony, and might well sway wavering MPs who were conscious of the nearness of the next general election. But it was the cooperation of extra-parliamentary protesters and the parliamentary opposition that made this issue so tricky for North. Whereas the opposition—and particularly the Rockinghamites—were unable to work effectively with 'out of doors' reformers over changes to the representative system, economical reform seemed to bring together all opponents of the government, from the most extreme radicals to the ultra-cautious Burke. And the confidence of the parliamentary opposition was of course increased by the knowledge that behind them lay the associations in the counties and boroughs, representing an expectant public opinion. As Burke himself told the secretary of the Gloucestershire Committee on 28 February, in relation to his own endeavours in the Commons: 'The Watchful Attention, and temperate but unremitting Zeal of the people at large can alone carry this, or any other measure of Reform into Execution. To them and the intelligent Activity of their Committees I look for Support.'[119]

Burke was sure that it was to derail a potentially unstoppable attack on the existing order that North in March 1780 proposed a royal commission to examine the public accounts. The bill to establish the commission, Burke protested, would take away from parliament the right to scrutinize the accounts, and give it instead 'to some Tools of the Ministers nomination'. Consequently, he claimed, 'a

---

[118] BL, Liverpool Papers, Add. MS 38567, fo. 30.
[119] *Correspondence of Burke*, ed. Copeland et al., iv. 208.

Scheme [is] formed to frustrate all that enquiry into the publick expenditure, which the people have so strongly and so justly required of us in their petitions'.[120] Burke was no doubt right to suspect North's motives. But if North was trying to prevent meaningful progress in economical reform, he failed. The commission did not unduly delay the process of exposing the accounts; the Act appointing the commissioners received the royal assent on 5 July and by the end of November their first report, complete with numerous appendices of evidence, had been published.[121] Nor did the commissioners produce anodyne or obscure reports which let the government off the hook. The first report criticized the practice of receivers of the land tax and other revenue officers holding public money in their own hands rather than paying the collected revenue promptly into the exchequer. On 6 December, Robinson concluded with undisguised disappointment that the commissioners had provided the opposition with fresh opportunities to attack the government.[122] The detailed and very full reports that followed—fifteen of them had been published by the end of 1787—opened up to parliamentary and public view many of the unedifying aspects of the political system. The way was paved for an ongoing programme of administrative rationalization and financial retrenchment.[123]

More immediately, the opposition parties, on coming into office on North's fall, proceeded to implement the economical reform measures that they had put before parliament while in opposition. The new ministers were very conscious of public expectations. On being pressed to create a place for a friend of the Duke of Grafton, Rockingham protested that such a step would contradict 'the principles which . . . all of us have held in regard to necessary Oeconomy'.[124] Even in Ireland, where calls for retrenchment had regularly been heard in parliament over the years,[125] but there had

---

[120] Ibid. 222.   [121] *Journals of the House of Commons*, xxxviii. 74–85.

[122] BL, Liverpool Papers, Add. MS 38567, fo. 891.

[123] J. E. D. Binney, *British Public Finance and Administration 1774–1792* (Oxford, 1958), 282; Norman Baker, 'Changing Attitudes towards Government in Eighteenth-Century Britain', in Anne Whiteman, J. S. Bromley and P. G. M. Dickson (eds.), *Statesmen, Scholars and Merchants: Essays in Eighteenth-Century History presented to Dame Lucy Sutherland* (Oxford, 1973), 212–13; John Gascoigne, *Science in the Service of Empire: Joseph Banks, the British State and the Uses of Science in the Age of Revolution* (Cambridge, 1998), 1–4, 8–9, 11–12, 21–3, 34, 193, 198, 201.

[124] West Suffolk RO, Grafton Papers, Ac 423/479.

[125] e.g. *Cavendish Parliamentary Diary*, ed. Black, ii. 140.

been no serious external pressure for reform, the new lord-lieutenant and his chief secretary felt themselves committed to 'adhering to the economical system of England'.[126] So in Britain places were abolished—including the now redundant secretaryship of state for the American colonies—and money was saved. Burke's Civil List Act of 1782 axed some 134 offices, and Shelburne's ministry extinguished another 144. Pitt, who became prime minister after the brief interlude of the Fox–North coalition (April–December 1783), in effect carried forward the reforms of the Rockingham and Shelburne governments. There was a concerted attack on needless civil offices—in the revenue services alone some 440 places were abolished between 1784 and 1793. Pitt, it must be said, was almost certainly influenced above all by the enormous National Debt that he had inherited. In 1783 it stood at a towering, unprecedented, and, for many contemporaries, a frightening £232 million. Just to meet the interest charges required £9.5 million per year. Deep cuts in public expenditure were therefore inevitable, given the widespread wish to return as rapidly as possible to peace-time levels of taxation. In a sense, then, Pitt was doing no more than those of his predecessors who had been obliged to preside over the transition from war to peace. Similar cuts were instituted by Henry Pelham at the end of the War of Austrian Succession and by George Grenville after the Seven Years War. In real terms Pitt might in fact have achieved little more than either Pelham or Grenville. But he almost certainly wanted to do more. He sought a much bigger overhaul than he was eventually able to carry out—vested interests blocked some of his initiatives—and during his ministry there was, in John Brewer's rather measured language, an 'extension of a reformist sensibility'.[127]

Recent scholarship on this subject tends to downplay the importance of the American war, and focuses on the great stimulus to retrenchment given by the long and very expensive conflict with revolutionary and Napoleonic France.[128] Philip Harling, while conceding that the ingredients of the early nineteenth-century 'Old Corruption' critique of the British political system were already

---

[126] BL, Fitzpatrick Papers, Add. MS 47579, fo. 85.
[127] John Brewer, *The Sinews of Power: War, Money and the English State, 1688–1783* (London, 1989), 87.
[128] Philip Harling and Peter Mandler, 'From "Fiscal-Military" State to Laissez-Faire State', *Journal of British Studies*, 32 (1993), 44–70.

largely in place by 1780, argues that the movement for economical reform faded at the end of the American war, mainly due to the adoption of retrenchment by Rockingham and Pitt.[129] But if public clamour for economical reform slackened with the peace, or at least with the defeat of Fox's East India Bill, which temporarily revived fears of the expansion of government patronage and corruption,[130] one should not forget that the system continued to change, albeit quietly and incrementally, as a result of Pittite economies.

The process went dramatically into reverse, of course, with the coming of the next war in 1793. A protracted and very demanding struggle—a repetition of the American conflict but on a bigger scale—caused government patronage to expand exponentially as the army, navy, and revenue services again grew enormously. With the close of the Napoleonic wars in 1815, and especially with the repeal of the income tax the following year, pressure to reduce public expenditure was stronger than ever. Over the next few years the number of public offices was severely cut. By the 1820s governments could no longer rely on a large corps of placemen to form the solid basis of their support in parliament. Into the gap created by the contraction of patronage seeped party. By the 1830s—perhaps before—governments were based more on party loyalty than on patronage. The growth of party itself cannot be directly attributed to the American war; the process was a long and interrupted one. But the decline in patronage, which was certainly a spur to the development of party, can be traced back to the commissioners for examining the public accounts and the economical reforms of the Rockingham, Shelburne, and Pitt administrations.

[129] Philip Harling, *The Waning of 'Old Corruption': The Politics of Economical Reform in Britain, 1779–1846* (Oxford, 1996), 36.

[130] For details see below, Ch. 9.

7

Religious Reform
and Religious Reaction

IF THE AMERICAN war curbed the pretensions of the British
Parliament, increased the autonomy of the Irish Parliament, and
saw the emergence of campaigns to reform the constitution of
both legislatures, it also brought changes to the religious dispensation of the British Isles. Only in Scotland, where the established
church was Presbyterian, and anti-Catholic feeling amongst the
Protestant majority was particularly strong, did the religious framework remain the same as before the war. In England, Wales, and
Ireland, Catholics and Protestant Dissenters were beneficiaries of
legislation passed between 1778 and 1782. The changes were most
dramatic in Ireland, where the first steps towards the dismantling of
the penal laws directed against the Catholic majority led to a fall in
the number of Catholics converting to the established church,[1] and
Protestant Dissenters were even admitted to public office on the
same footing as Anglicans.

These reforms can be seen as carrying forward a process whereby
the British state gradually loosened its close ties to the Anglican
Church, a process culminating in the repeal of the Test and
Corporation Acts in 1828 and Catholic Emancipation in 1829.
From the close of the Seven Years War, when many new territories
were acquired with established non-Protestant and even non-
Christian populations, and as religious diversity was increasing
slowly at home and rapidly in the North American colonies (thanks
largely to a surge in non-English immigration after 1763), the
imposition of an Anglican model looked more and more problematic.
In 1760, when New France surrendered, the French Catholic
Canadiens were not subject to a policy of crude Anglicization, but

---

[1] Patrick Corish, *The Irish Catholic Experience: A Historical Survey* (Dublin, 1985),
128–9.

allowed to worship in their traditional ways.[2] Calls for an Anglican episcopal appointment in the old British colonies, voiced at various points in the 1760s by Anglicans on both sides of the Atlantic, caused much alarm in North America, but fell on deaf ministerial ears. 'Earnest and continued endeavors have been used with our successive ministries', the archbishop of Canterbury told Dr Samuel Johnson of New York in July 1766, 'but without obtaining more than promises to consider and confer about the matter; which promises have never been fulfilled.'[3] There are even signs that the relationship between church and state was becoming less intense under Lord North, who as chancellor of the university of Oxford, and the brother of a bishop, was widely seen as a friend to High Anglicanism. In 1772–3 relief bills for English and Welsh Protestant Dissenters, though defeated in the Lords, passed the Commons with comfortable majorities.[4] The Quebec Act of 1774, which formally acknowledged the special position of the Catholic Church in Canada, was evidence that North himself was essentially moderate and pragmatic on religious issues.[5] As he told the Commons during debate on the bill, 'it was a matter of indifference to him' if Catholicism were effectively established in Quebec, so long as 'it made the people happy'.[6]

The reforms of 1778–82 can equally well be seen, however, as war-induced concessions designed to build national unity and promote the recruiting of the armed forces. J. C. D. Clark sees the years preceding the American war as characterized by a good deal of hostility between Anglicans and Dissenters. He argues that the church's special relationship with the state was under attack from about 1760, when the final ending of the Jacobite threat freed the

---

[2] P. J. Marshall, 'A Nation Defined by Empire, 1755–1776', in Alexander Grant and Keith J. Stringer (eds.), *Uniting the Kingdom? The Making of British History* (London, 1995), 213.

[3] Herbert and Carol Schneider (eds.), *Samuel Johnson, President of King's College, His Career and Writings* (4 vols., New York, 1929), iii. 286.

[4] We should note, however, that John Seed, '"A Set of Men Powerful Enough in Many Things": Rational Dissent and Political Opposition in England, 1770–1790', in Knud Haakonssen (ed.), *Enlightenment and Religion: Rational Dissent in Eighteenth-Century Britain* (Cambridge, 1996), 144, following Horace Walpole, suggests that the 1772 bill passed the Commons because many MPs were fearful of the strength of the Dissenting vote at the next general election.

[5] See G. M. Ditchfield, 'Ecclesiastical Policy under Lord North', in John Walsh, Colin Haydon, and Stephen Taylor (eds.), *The Church of England, c.1689–c.1833: From Toleration to Tractarianism* (Cambridge, 1993), 228–46.   [6] *PH* xvii. 1395 (10 June 1774).

Nonconformists, and particularly heterodox 'Rational Dissenters', from a loyalty to the state based on fear of something worse—the restoration of Catholicism that it was imagined would accompany the return of the Stuarts to the throne. The new militancy of Dissent, Clark explains, provoked Anglican aggression, which in turn brought forth further attacks from the Nonconformists.[7] The outbreak of the fighting in North America in 1775 seems to have accentuated this religious struggle. In the early years of the American conflict, as we have seen, Dissenters tended to oppose the military coercion of the colonists, and Anglicans, especially High Churchmen, rallied to the support of government.[8] The wartime reforms, viewed in this light, appear not as continuations of an established pattern, but as measures of expediency dictated by an immediate crisis. With the broadening of the war from 1778, and the danger of invasion of the British Isles, the bitter sectarianism gave way to a more tolerant and inclusive attitude as senior churchmen accommodated themselves to the state's new priorities.[9] And the war, having called forth these concessions, can also be seen as shaping the reaction to them. Calls for national unity and arguments about the need to widen the scope of military mobilization were countered by assertions of the continuing unreliability and disloyalty of both Catholics and Protestant Dissenters.

Whichever perspective we adopt—whether we see the reforms as part of a long-drawn-out process of change or merely as expedient responses to a very pressing and peculiar situation—there can be no doubt that there was a strong Anglican reaction in the years following the war. This reaction continued into the next conflict against revolutionary and Napoleonic France, when further concessions were granted to Catholics but Protestant Dissenters were treated with particular suspicion.

---

[7] J. C. D. Clark, *English Society 1688–1832: Ideology, Social Structure and Political Practice during the Ancien Regime* (Cambridge, 1985) and *The Language of Liberty 1660–1832: Political Discourse and Social Dynamics in the Anglo-American World* (Cambridge, 1994).   [8] See above, Ch. 4.
[9] Paul Langford, 'The English Clergy and the American Revolution', in Eckhart Hellmuth (ed.), *The Transformation of Political Culture: England and Germany in the Late Eighteenth Century* (Oxford, 1990), 303.

The Religious Dispensation in 1775

We need first to be clear about the religious status quo on the eve of the American war and the various disabilities imposed on Catholics and Protestant Dissenters in the different countries of the British Isles. Scotland stood out, as we have seen, in the sense that its established church was Presbyterian in structure. Here the Protestant Nonconformists included the Episcopalians, who in England, Wales, and Ireland would have been members of the established church. The Act for the Toleration of Episcopacy, passed by the new British Parliament in 1712, secured the Scottish Episcopalians against prosecution or molestation; but in the aftermath of the Jacobite uprising of 1745–6 the Episcopalians, many of whom had sided with the Stuart Pretender, were subject to new restrictions. Episcopalian ministers were required to be ordained by English or Irish Anglican bishops; any who continued to act under authority conferred by a Scottish bishop would be liable to punishment, and members of their congregations could lose their right to hold public office.[10] Besides the Episcopalians there were also various Presbyterian Dissenting bodies that had broken away from the Church of Scotland, often over the contentious issue of lay patronage. The relationship between these Presbyterian Dissenters and the state church remained ambiguous, however. As Callum Brown has noted, those groups that left the Church of Scotland often called themselves 'Synods' or 'Presbyteries' rather than separate churches, implying 'historic unity with the one and universal kirk they hoped to reclaim'.[11] Nor were they subject to the kind of legal restrictions imposed on English, Welsh, and Irish Protestant Dissenters. Scottish Catholics, by marked contrast, were burdened with extensive disabilities; they were ineligible to hold public office, either at local or national levels; they were unable to vote in parliamentary elections; their right to own land was severely circumscribed. Even their right to worship peacefully was denied in law, though not usually in practice. The Church of Scotland was almost certainly the church of the majority of Scots, though Dissenting Presbyterian sects were growing in

---

[10] See F. C. Mather, 'Church, Parliament and Penal Laws: Some Anglo-Scottish Interactions in the Eighteenth Century', *English Historical Review*, 92 (1977), 540–72.

[11] Callum Brown, 'Religion and Social Change', in *People and Society in Scotland*, i. *1760–1830*, ed. T. M. Devine and Rosalind Mitchison (Edinburgh, 1988), 145.

strength, especially in the Lowlands, and Episcopalianism remained a force in the Highlands, where there was also a residual Catholic presence. Irish immigration into Glasgow and its satellite towns was in time to transform the religious map of Scotland. In 1778 there were said to be only twenty Catholics in Glasgow, and no more than about sixty in 1791; by 1820 there were 10,000 and ten years later some 27,000, or about 13% of the city's population.[12] But on the eve of the American war it seems that most of the Irish incomers were Protestants from Ulster who could trace their ancestors back to Scotland.[13]

In England and Wales the established church was even more obviously the national church, in that it commanded the loyalty, either nominally or, less usually, as regular communicants, of the vast majority of the population. According to recent estimates, only about 5% of the English and Welsh were members of the old Dissenting churches—the Presbyterians, Baptists, Congregationalists, and Quakers.[14] Methodism was beginning to make an impact, especially in Wales, but in 1775 it probably had no more than 30,000 adherents, or less than half a per cent of the population; its period of rapid growth was to come at the end of the century and the beginning of the next.[15] Catholics in England and Wales were likewise a small minority. There were about 80,000 of them in England, with around a third of this total concentrated in Lancashire, and scattered pockets in Wales. Catholic numbers were slowly increasing, largely, no doubt, due to the arrival of Irish economic migrants, though this movement across the Irish Sea was not to become marked until the next century.[16]

The dominance of the Anglican Church was at least partly a product of its established status and, by extension, of the disadvantaged position of its rivals. The close alliance of church and state, it must be said, provided critics of the establishment with useful ammunition; Anglican bishops sitting in the House of Lords

[12] Callum Brown, *Religion and Society in Scotland since 1707* (Edinburgh, 1997), 32.

[13] Such as William Miller, a Belfast weaver who enlisted in Glasgow in 1778 and deserted the following year (*Caledonian Mercury*, 7 Apr. 1779). See also Christopher A. Whatley, 'Labour in the Industrializing City, *c.*1660 to 1830', in T. M. Devine and Gordon Jackson (eds.), *Glasgow*, i. *Beginnings to 1830* (Manchester, 1995), 367.

[14] James E. Bradley, *Religion, Revolution and English Radicalism* (Cambridge, 1990), 93.

[15] David Hempton, *Methodism and Politics in British Society 1750–1850* (London, 1984), ch. 3.

[16] See John Bossy, *The English Catholic Community, 1570–1850* (London, 1975).

appeared to be reliable voting fodder for the government, and the presence of a significant number of Anglican clergymen amongst the more active magistrates in many counties was bound at times to make the church unpopular. But any difficulties associated with established status were, from the Anglican perspective, no doubt outweighed by the clear advantages. Full participation in public life was, in theory at least, confined to Anglicans. Catholics, as in Scotland, were completely excluded. They could neither vote nor hold office. Additionally, they were subject to economic penalties designed to remove any possibility of their exerting even the smallest influence; restrictions on Catholic landownership were predicated at least partly on the assumption that landownership brought some degree of political leverage. As in Scotland again, even Catholic worship was theoretically prohibited.

Protestant Dissenters were not subject to the same legal restrictions. The Toleration Act of 1689 allowed Trinitarian Protestant Dissenters freedom of worship, and though the Schism Act of 1714 had attempted to undermine this by proscribing the Dissenting academies, in the hope that this would eventually destroy Protestant Nonconformity, the concessions of the Toleration Act were effectively confirmed by the repeal of the Schism Act in 1719. Toleration, however, was by no means the same as equality. Dissenting ministers and schoolteachers still had to subscribe to nearly all of the Thirty-nine Articles of the Church of England. Dissenters, moreover, while free to vote in municipal and parliamentary elections so long as they met any property qualifications, were ineligible to hold public office. The Test and Corporation Acts of Charles II's reign operated to exclude Protestant Nonconformists as much as Catholics. There were ways round this restriction. Dissenters qualified for office by engaging in 'occasional conformity' to the established church. High Anglicans had succeeded in prohibiting this practice with the Occasional Conformity Act of 1711, but this was repealed, along with the Schism Act, in 1719. At the same time, the first of what were to become annual Indemnity Acts decreed that any Dissenter taking office who was not prosecuted within six months could hold his office thereafter without fear of legal action. Nonetheless, the Test and Corporation Acts remained a potent symbol of Anglican dominance and the second-class status accorded to Dissenters. As such they were regarded as a constant irritant by many Non-conformists, particularly by the heterodox Rational Dissenters, who strongly opposed all forms of subscription and state interference in religious matters.[17]

In Ireland the situation was superficially similar. The Anglican Church was the established church and enjoyed the same privileges and special status as its English and Welsh counterpart. Catholics were again subject to severe economic and political restrictions. Protestant Dissenters, very largely Presbyterians, were likewise in a position similar to their counterparts in England and Wales. The Irish Test Act of 1704 operated in the same way as the Test and Corporation Acts in England and Wales, at least theoretically debarring Protestant Nonconformists as well as Catholics from holding office at municipal and national levels.[18] But there was an important difference between Ireland and the rest of the British Isles. In England, Wales, and Scotland, the established churches could legitimately claim to be the national churches—the majority of people probably considered themselves to be adherents. But in Ireland the established Anglican Church undeniably served only a minority of the population. In 1786 Richard Woodward, bishop of Cloyne, in a vigorous defence of the establishment, claimed that about an eighth of the population were Anglicans.[19] It seems likely that even this was an overstatement, and that no more than 10% were members of the established church. Most of them were located in Ulster and Leinster, though everywhere they were in a decided minority. In Ulster, particularly in eastern Ulster, they were outnumbered by the Presbyterians of Scots descent, who were thickly clustered there but almost totally absent elsewhere. Somewhere in the region of 10% of the total Irish population was Presbyterian, putting Protestant Dissent on a par, numerically, with Anglicanism. The remaining 80% or so of the Irish were Catholics. Only in parts of Ulster were Catholics outnumbered by Protestants, and in the south and west of the country Catholic numerical superiority was overwhelming, there being about nineteen Catholics for every Protestant.[20] In Ireland, then, Dissenting and Catholic resentment was heightened by the perception that the established church was an alien institution,

---

[17] See Clark, *English Society*, 320, 341–2.

[18] For the operation of the 1704 Act see Toby C. Barnard, 'The Government and Irish Dissent, 1704–1780', in Kevin Herlihy (ed.), *The Politics of Irish Dissent, 1650–1800* (Dublin, 1997), 9–27.

[19] R. B. McDowell, *Ireland in the Age of Imperialism and Revolution, 1760–1800* (Oxford, 1979), 156 n.   [20] Ibid. 155–6.

foisted on Ireland by the English. For the Catholic majority this situation must have been particularly difficult to endure, though a sense of grievance amongst the Presbyterians was probably sharpened by the knowledge that in Scotland, the ancestral home with which many of them retained close connections, their coreligionists were not subject to any discrimination, because Presbyterianism was the established system of church government.[21]

Catholic Relief

The relief legislation passed by the British Parliament in April 1778 allowed English and Welsh Catholics to own and inherit land on the same basis as Protestants, and permitted Catholic priests to teach and officiate at religious services. The Act passed by the Irish Parliament in June was less generous, in that it was restricted to landownership issues and it fell short of enabling Catholics to acquire freeholds—they were permitted to take out 999-year leases on land, but not to purchase it outright. Both Relief Acts, however, removed the threat to Catholic ownership posed by the penal laws passed in William III's reign, which had decreed that on the death of a Catholic landowner his estate should be divided between his sons rather than inherited intact by the eldest, that children converting to the established church had a right to an immediate allowance from the family estate, and that a converting eldest son took immediate ownership of his father's land.

In the Irish context, the concessions of 1778 can be linked to the growth of the Catholic middle classes. Catholics, while debarred from most of the professions, could still exercise a trade, and Catholic merchants were the dominant element in Cork and Limerick, and formed about a third of the Dublin mercantile community by the time of the American war.[22] Middle- and upper-class Irish Catholics had been agitating, albeit with great politeness and

---

[21] On the close connections between the Ulster Presbyterians and the Church of Scotland see Ian McBride, *Scripture Politics: Ulster Presbyterians and Irish Radicalism in the Late Eighteenth Century* (Oxford, 1998), 26–34.

[22] Maureen Wall, 'The Rise of a Catholic Middle Class in Eighteenth-Century Ireland', *Irish Historical Studies*, 11 (1958), 91–115, is the seminal exposition; but see also David Dickson, 'Catholics and Trade in Eighteenth-Century Ireland: An Old Debate Revisited', in T. P. Power and Kevin Whelan (eds.), *Endurance and Emergence: Catholics in Ireland in the Eighteenth Century* (Dublin, 1990), 85–100.

moderation, for relaxation of disabilities since the establishment of the Catholic Committee in 1759. But the presence of a substantial and growing body of prosperous Catholics, and the arguments such 'respectable' Catholics advanced in favour of relief, were perhaps less important in changing Protestant attitudes than other influences. It used to be assumed that Catholic relief could be understood by reference to a gradual softening of Protestant hostility to Catholics, the growth of a more liberal approach associated with the Enlightenment, or what Lecky, the great nineteenth-century historian of Ireland, called 'a prevailing spirit of toleration'.[23] More recently, J. C. Beckett, in his introduction to the eighteenth-century volume of the *New History of Ireland*, argued that 'Tolerance . . . prepared protestant opinion for a gradual relaxation of the penal code'.[24] Perhaps more directly influential than the ideas of the Enlightenment was the effective ending of the Jacobite threat, for it was the fear of Jacobitism that had underpinned both the introduction and enforcement of many of the penal statutes in Britain and Ireland. The failure of the 'Forty-Five Rebellion was a significant landmark here, though a residual Jacobite challenge existed until 1759, when French invasion plans included provision for the restoration of the Stuarts. In 1766 even the pope ceased to be a Jacobite; on the death of James Edward Stuart, the Old Pretender, Rome refused to accept any further Stuart recommendations for Irish sees. There is, as well, an imperial dimension to consider. Once the French Canadian Catholics had been granted toleration, it became increasingly difficult to argue that the full range of penal laws must be retained in Ireland.[25]

But the impression of changing attitudes needs to be qualified by a recognition of continuing Protestant intransigence. Louis Cullen has argued that in Ireland Protestant opinion might even have hardened in the years preceding relief.[26] The early stages of the war certainly seem to have increased hostility. With the Catholic elite promoting enlistment in the army to prove their loyalty, Protestant

---

[23] W. E. H. Lecky, *A History of Ireland in the Eighteenth Century* (5 vols., London, 1913 edn.), ii. 208.

[24] *A New History of Ireland*, iv. *Eighteenth-Century Ireland 1691–1800*, ed. T. W. Moody and W. E. Vaughan (Oxford, 1986), liv.

[25] Jacqueline Hill, 'Religious Toleration and the Relaxation of the Penal Laws: An Imperial Perspective, 1763–1780', *Archivum Hibernicum*, 44 (1989), 98–109.

[26] See Louis Cullen, 'Catholics under the Penal Laws', *Eighteenth-Century Ireland*, 1 (1986), 23–36.

suspicions and fears were heightened. 'At present the Catholics are playing an artful game', an Ulster Protestant wrote in 1775. 'They are encouraging their people to enlist by public rewards and admonitions. I really believe in a short time our army will be mostly composed of this class'.[27] Two years later, Thomas Campbell, an advocate of Catholic relief, was clearly frustrated by the difficulty of persuading Protestants that the penal laws were the cause of Catholic disaffection, and not a protection against it. He, too, noted the alarm of Protestant gentlemen at Catholic recruitment.[28] And when the first instalment of relief came in 1778, it was not at all obvious that most Protestants welcomed it. In Scotland, as we shall see, there was determined resistance to any comparable concessions, and England, as we shall see also, experienced serious disturbances in 1780 inspired by the Scottish stand. In Ireland, David Dundas, the quartermaster-general, was convinced that the 1778 Act added to Protestant anxiety and was responsible for the take-off of the volunteer movement, which in many areas was essentially a response to the fear of a Catholic uprising.[29]

The demands of the war are now seen as central to an understanding of the Relief Acts of 1778.[30] The Act for England and Wales started life as a bill introduced by Sir George Savile, a prominent and well-respected opposition MP. Savile saw his initiative as designed to 'vindicate the honour, and to assert the principles of the Protestant religion, to which all persecution was, or ought to be, wholly adverse'.[31] It was government support, however, that ensured that the bill became law, and it passed through both houses and received the royal assent with remarkable speed. North's motives for backing the bill were no doubt mixed. He had already demonstrated, as we have noted, a willingness to look pragmatically at religious issues in the Quebec Act of 1774. He seems also to have

[27] W. H. Crawford (ed.), *Letters from an Ulster Land Agent 1774–1785* (Belfast, 1976), 5.
[28] Thomas Campbell, *A Philosophical Survey of the South of Ireland* (London, 1777), 254, 299, 301–2.
[29] NLI, MS 14306, 'Irish Military Associations', 2 Feb. 1780.
[30] R. Kent Donovan, 'The Military Origins of the Roman Catholic Relief Programme of 1778', *Historical Journal*, 28 (1985), 79–102; Thomas Bartlett, 'The Origins and Progress of the Catholic Question in Ireland, 1690–1800', in Power and Whelan (eds.), *Endurance and Emergance* 8–9; id., *The Fall and Rise of the Irish Nation: The Catholic Question 1690–1800* (Dublin, 1992), ch. 6; id., '"A Weapon of War Yet Untried": Irish Catholics and the Armed Forces of the Crown, 1760–1830', in T. G. Fraser and Keith Jeffery (eds.), *Men, Women and War* (Historical Studies, vol. xviii, Dublin, 1993), 70–1.
[31] *PH* xix. 1137.

acquired an appreciation of the essential conservatism of the Catholic Church; the Northite press started to carry pro-Catholic pieces in the early years of the war.[32] At a time when Protestant Dissent seemed to be supportive of the American rebels, Catholicism could be conceived as a possible prop for the constitutional order rather than, as in the past, a threat to it. A gesture to the Catholic elite—who would be the beneficiaries of the landownership provisions of the Relief Acts—might reinforce Catholic loyalty just when the war was about to broaden to include the traditional Catholic enemy, France. But, above all, ministers appear to have been influenced by the manpower needs of the British army. At the very beginning of the struggle, Germain wrote of the faith that the military authorities were placing in Catholic recruitment.[33] There was, as we have seen, a Catholic presence in Britain, and while the Scottish Highlands were yielding up significant quantities of men, the Catholics there were probably in the minds of ministers. But the Catholic population in Britain as a whole was tiny, and therefore of marginal military utility. The government's sights, we can be confident, were trained on the great mass of under-exploited Catholic manpower in Ireland. An Irish Act, based on the English and Welsh one, was accordingly necessary. It was duly introduced into the Irish Parliament by Luke Gardiner, and, after some initial hesitation, it was given backing by the Castle. But whereas the English and Welsh bill encountered virtually no resistance in its legislative passage, its Irish counterpart was brought to the statute book only after a fierce struggle, and in amended form. Prominent figures in the patriot opposition, such as Grattan and Charlemont, voted against the bill, as did Lords Shannon and Bellamont, who were regular government supporters.[34] Indeed, resentment at what was widely seen as the imposition by Britain of Catholic relief might well have furthered the growth of Protestant patriotism, and the agitation for free trade and then legislative independence, both within and beyond the Dublin Parliament.[35]

---

[32] James J. Sack, *From Jacobite to Conservative: Reaction and Orthodoxy in Britain, c.1760–1832* (Cambridge, 1993), 226.

[33] HMC, *Stopford Sackville MSS* (2 vols., London, 1904–10), i. 137.

[34] NLI, Heron Papers, MS 13060, list of MPs and Peers voting on Catholic relief, 1778.

[35] Robert E. Burns, 'The Catholic Relief Act in Ireland, 1778', *Church History*, 32 (1963), 204.

If many Protestants in Ireland disliked both the substance of the 1778 Act and the process that had led to its becoming law, the Catholics viewed it merely as a beginning. That May, Charles O'Conor, a leading Catholic gentleman, had predicted that the anticipated relief bill 'will be such a partial one as will defeat its own purposes'.[36] Once the bill passed, the Catholic Committee began to collect funds to lobby for further relief and took every opportunity to re-emphasize Catholic loyalty.[37] It was not until November 1781, however, that Gardiner announced his intention to introduce another relief measure in the Irish Parliament. The two bills that eventually became law in the 1782 session removed the remaining restrictions on Catholic landowners (except in parliamentary boroughs, where it was feared that landownership would lead to political influence) and allowed Catholic priests to teach and preach without fear of legal sanctions—in effect, the Catholics in Ireland were put on the same footing as those in England and Wales, where these reforms had been incorporated in the 1778 legislation.

Discussion of Gardiner's relief measures overlapped with the crucial phase of the battle for legislative independence. This has led some historians to imply that Gardiner's success owed something to the prevailing mood of national determination and inclusiveness. Richard Woodward, the bishop of Cloyne, spoke in favour of Gardiner's proposed land reforms, attacking the existing anti-Catholic laws as 'against nature' but, perhaps more significantly, as 'against national union, [and] against national unity'.[38] On the other hand, the timing might have encouraged the Irish administration to throw its weight behind the relief measures for precisely the opposite reason. Thomas Bartlett suggests that the Castle chose to support Gardiner in order to drive a wedge between the Protestant patriots and the Catholics, and to divide and distract the Protestants themselves. The aim, he argues, was to prevent the campaign for legislative independence receiving the tacit support of the Catholics by causing the predominantly Presbyterian Ulster Volunteers to give vent to their anti-Catholicism. The plan, Bartlett explains, failed. The willingness of the Ulster Volunteer delegates to adopt relaxation

---

[36] *The Letters of Charles O'Conor of Belanagare*, ed. Catherine Coogan Ward and Robert E. Ward (2 vols., Ann Arbor, 1980), ii. 121.

[37] R. Dudley Edwards (ed.), 'Minute Book of the Catholic Committee, 1773–1792', *Archivum Hibernicum*, 9 (1942), 37–9, 42, 47, 55, 60, 68, 75, 77.

[38] McDowell, *Ireland*, 191.

of the penal laws at their Dungannon meeting in February 1782 effectively scuppered the lord-lieutenant's attempt to play the Catholic card. But this does not undermine Bartlett's case that political calculation lay behind the Irish administration's original backing for Gardiner's initiatives.[39]

Bartlett's thesis is highly plausible. But perhaps other considerations also influenced British ministers and the Irish administration. If the need for Catholic manpower led to the introduction of the 1778 legislation, it was probably still relevant in 1781–2. Ireland's manpower potential continued to attract ministers long after 1778. In April 1779 Germain was telling the lord-lieutenant that he knew of 'no means of augmenting the army so Effectively as from Ireland'.[40] Shortly after the Dutch entry into the war at the end of 1780, the cabinet decided that 8,000 Irishmen should be recruited as speedily as possible.[41] But the immediate catalyst, from the point of view of British ministers, might have been the surrender of Cornwallis's army at Yorktown in October 1781. News of this catastrophe reached London on 25 November. It was to lead to a widespread conviction that the war in America had to be abandoned. By 13 December Lord Loughborough, the lord chief justice, was gloomily reporting to the Irish chief secretary that 'All the dissatisfied friends of govt. . . . blame the system of the war . . . & declare against its continuance'.[42] But ending the American aspect of the conflict did not reduce the need for more soldiers; almost everyone recognized that the struggle against the Bourbon powers and the Dutch would go on for some time. Accordingly, the first reaction of at least some of those in ministerial circles was to wonder how Cornwallis's troops could be replaced. On 30 November Loughborough himself wrote to Carlisle: 'A loss of seven thousand men can nowhere be supplied but from Ireland, and I am persuaded that if you had proper powers to animate and to direct the zeal of the Irish, a much greater army might soon be raised in a country that produces many stout men, to whom sixpence a day would be a fortune'. He continued: 'the pressure of the time may probably direct the view of Administration [i.e. Lord North's government]

---

[39] Bartlett, 'Origins and Progress of the Catholic Question', in Power and Whelan (eds.), *Endurance and Emergence*, 10–11; id., *The Fall and Rise of the Irish Nation*, 98–101.
[40] NLI, Heron Papers, MS 13052, Germain to Buckinghamshire, 17 Apr. 1779.
[41] Kent Archives Office, Amherst MSS, U1350 076/36.
[42] BL, Auckland Papers, Add. MS 34418, fo. 213.

towards Ireland; whether with sufficient liberality I doubt. But perhaps it may appear right to you to invite in some manner the attempt'.[43] In hinting at the need for concessions, Loughborough might, of course, have been thinking of the constitutional reforms demanded by the Protestant patriots—even perhaps of legislative independence. But, given that recruitment in Ireland had come to mean tapping the manpower potential of the Catholic majority, it seems distinctly possible that he was hoping for some concessions to the Catholic elite that would have the same stimulating effect as the 1778 Relief Act.

The Protestant Backlash

We have seen something of the Protestant reaction to the Catholic relief legislation in Ireland, but what of the rest of the British Isles? Scotland's anti-Catholic laws had been the work of the pre-union Edinburgh Parliament, which meant that Scottish Catholics could not share in the relief given to their English and Welsh co-religionists in 1778. Separate legislation was needed for Scotland, and during the progress of Savile's bill through the Commons, Henry Dundas, the Scottish lord advocate, announced that he would bring in a bill to repeal the Scottish legislation restricting Catholic landowning and subjecting Catholic priests and teachers to penalties.[44]

There can have been few greater misjudgments of the public mood. Protestants across Scotland reacted violently to the prospect of a Scottish relief bill. In Shetland, the Revd John Mill denounced concessions to Catholics as a threat to 'the nation's liberties and privileges sacred and civil'.[45] This view seems to have been widely shared. Catholics were attacked in Glasgow in October 1778. A body known as the Friends to the Protestant Interest was established in Edinburgh the following December. Very soon after, other Protestant associations were formed across Scotland, and burghs started to send in petitions to parliament. Serious rioting in Edinburgh led the city's lord provost to issue a proclamation claiming that all plans to introduce a Catholic relief bill for Scotland had been 'totally laid aside'.[46]

---

[43] HMC, 15th Report, app., pt vi, *Carlisle MSS* (London, 1897), 539.

[44] *PH* xix 1142.

[45] *The Diary of the Reverend John Mill*, ed. Gilbert Goudie (Scottish History Society, vol. v, Edinburgh, 1889), 56.   [46] SP 54/47, fo. 216.

Rioting took place in Glasgow a few days later. The commander-in-chief in Scotland, Sir James Adolphus Oughton, was convinced that if a Scottish relief bill passed into law 'a general insurrection would ensue'.[47] The government decided to back down. The lord justice clerk, Thomas Miller, let it be known that ministers had no intention of initiating or supporting any relief legislation.[48] But far from calming the situation, the retreat seems to have heightened the tension. Lord George Gordon, third son of the Duke of Gordon, and MP for an English pocket borough, had been prominent in the Scottish agitation, and in May 1779 he told the House of Commons that Scotland was on the verge of rebellion. In a debate on the king's speech the following November he went further, intervening to claim that he had 120,000 men ready to support him and that the king was regarded by the Scots as 'a papist'.[49]

By this stage, popular English anti-Catholicism was beginning to mobilize. The success of the Scottish Protestants in forcing the government to back down encouraged English opponents of Catholic relief to press for the repeal of Savile's Act. In February 1779 a Protestant Association was formed in London. In November Gordon became its president. Work began on drawing up a great petition. On 26 May 1780 Gordon announced that he would soon be presenting the petition to parliament. On 6 June some 60,000 people accompanied him to Westminster. That night serious rioting and looting occurred. The Protestant Association rapidly distanced itself from the rioters, but anti-Catholicism, allied it seems to other popular grievances and resentments,[50] led over the next few days to the destruction of property, attacks on public buildings and the homes of many prominent politicians, and extensive loss of life as the army and militia attempted to restore order. In the atmosphere of panic generated by the riots, rumours circulated that the troops were about to join the insurgents, and that 30,000 colliers were marching on London.[51] It was not until 8 June that the military was clearly in

---

[47] Ibid., fo. 228.
[48] Ibid., fo. 227 See Eugene Charlton Black, *The Association: British Extraparliamentary Political Organization 1769–1793* (Cambridge, Mass., 1963), 136–44. See also, for a more detailed account of the Scottish situation, Robert Kent Donovan, *No Popery and Radicalism: Opposition to Roman Catholic Relief in Scotland* (New York, 1987).
[49] *PH* xx. 622, 1108–9.   [50] See above, Ch. 3.
[51] *Memoirs of the Life of Sir Samuel Romilly* (3 vols., London, 1840), i. 125.

control of the situation and the riots subsided.[52] Even then, however, London continued for some time to look like an occupied city:
the West Yorkshire militia remained encamped in the grounds of the
British Museum at least until the end of July.[53] Nothing comparable
happened elsewhere in England, though there were disturbances on
a smaller scale in several towns.[54] In Birmingham, for instance, 'no
popery' was chalked on doors around the town, and about 1,500
people gathered menacingly to burn an effigy, but there was
apparently no descent into serious rioting and violence.[55]

Government ministers and their supporters claimed that the disturbances were part of a conspiracy. Lord Stormont told the king on
7 June that 'this is a deep laid Revlt. . . . the Ringleaders at least act
with Deliberate rage and Upon a predetermined plan',[56] while the
Revd John Butler hinted at an anti-ministerial design on the part of
those who had 'instructed' the mob.[57] Even Edmund Burke was later
to view the riots as a failed uprising, and Gordon as the demagogic
leader of a potential revolution. Burke's famous *Reflections on the
Revolution in France* of 1790, according to a recent account, was
heavily influenced by Gordon and the riots associated with his
name.[58] It seems unlikely, however, that ministerial accusations
and Burke's fears were well grounded. Radicals and reformers, as
Nicholas Rogers has shown, were greatly alarmed by the violent
activities of the rioters.[59] But there is no denying that in many cases

[52] The fullest account is still J. Paul de Castro, *The Gordon Riots* (Oxford, 1926). For
briefer coverage of the events see John Stevenson, *Popular Disturbances in England 1700–
1832* (2nd edn., London, 1992), 94–110; Colin Haydon, *Anti-Catholicism in Eighteenth-
Century England, c.1714–1780: A Political and Social Study* (Manchester, 1993), ch. 6; and
Nicholas Rogers, *Crowds, Culture, and Politics in Georgian Britain* (Oxford, 1998), ch. 5.

[53] *Daniel Solander: Collected Correspondence 1753–1782*, ed. and trans. Edward Duyker
and Per Tingbrand (Oslo, 1995), 389.

[54] Colin Haydon, 'The Gordon Riots in the English Provinces', *Historical Research*, 63
(1990), 354–9.

[55] HMC, *Dartmouth MSS* (3 vols., London, 1887–96), iii. 251. For the situation in
Bristol, where a new Catholic chapel and neighbouring houses were destroyed, see NLI,
Wicklow Papers, MS 3573, Diary, 9 June 1780.

[56] *The Correspondence of King George III*, ed. Sir John Fortescue (6 vols., London,
1927–8), v. 75.

[57] Surrey RO (Guildford Muniment Room), Onslow MSS, 173/2/1/193.

[58] Iain McCalman, 'Prophesying Revolution: "Mad Lord George", Edmund Burke
and Madame La Motte', in Malcolm Chase and Ian Dyck (eds.), *Living and Learning:
Essays in Honour of J. F. C. Harrison* (Aldershot, 1996), 53.

[59] Nicholas Rogers, 'Crowd and People in the Gordon Riots', in Eckhart Hellmuth
(ed.), *The Transformation of Political Culture: England and Germany in the Late Eighteenth
Century* (Oxford, 1990), 39–55.

those who were hostile to Catholic relief were hostile to North's ministry. A cartoon published on 10 June 1780 shows George III as a crypto-Catholic and North and Sandwich as fellow travellers.[60] In Yorkshire, in the aftermath of the Gordon Riots, a crowd assembled in the belief that North had fled London and was hiding with Lord Dartmouth in a nearby country house. A representative of the outraged locals called at the house to demand an audience with the prime minister. His intention, apparently, was to berate North for introducing a new malt tax and for encouraging 'popery'.[61] The composition of the Protestant Associations themselves adds credence to the idea of a close connection. The Newcastle Protestant Association included many well-known radicals and anti-ministerialists.[62] In London, the situation was much the same. Alderman Frederick Bull, MP for London, a Wilkite, and an outspoken opponent of the American war, was a conspicuous supporter of the Protestant Association. Gordon himself was a fierce critic of North and the struggle against the colonists; indeed, he resigned his naval commission in 1777, apparently to give himself greater freedom to condemn the war.[63]

Opposition to North and anti-Catholicism, in the minds of Bull, Gordon, and numerous others who thought like them, went hand in hand. North's ministry, its critics argued, was trying to establish an authoritarian system of government. Catholicism, as an authoritarian religious system, was seen as ideally suited to support such an attempt. Hence the deep hostility of much of the parliamentary opposition and many extra-parliamentary radicals to the passage of the Quebec Act in 1774, which gave a special status to the Catholic Church in Canada and continued the system of government without an elected assembly. One opposition MP pointed out that the Quebec Bill's being debated on 10 June, the birthday of the Stuart claimant to the throne, was wholly apposite; it reeked, in his view, of the authoritarian principles that underlay Jacobitism.[64] We should not be surprised, then, that when in December 1779 Archdeacon Francis Blackburne wrote to Wyvill to recommend a number of

---

[60] BM 5680, 'A Great Man at his Private Devotion'.
[61] HMC, *Dartmouth MSS*, iii. 252.
[62] Kathleen Wilson, *The Sense of the People: Politics, Culture and Imperialism in England, 1715–1785* (Cambridge, 1995), 266, 367.
[63] Sir Lewis Namier and John Brooke, *The History of Parliament: The House of Commons 1754–1790* (3 vols., London, 1964), ii. 513.   [64] *PH* xvii. 1393.

reforms necessary to check the power of the executive, he included repeal of the Quebec Act and amendment of the Catholic Relief Act of 1778.[65] Indeed, many anti-ministerialists seem to have regarded Catholicism and arbitrary, authoritarian government as so closely allied that the word 'popery' was often used not just in reference to Catholicism but also more broadly to signify authoritarianism in all its forms. It was on this basis that Lord North, a staunch defender of the Anglican Church, was accused of 'popery', as were government-supporting bishops of the established church—'the Popish episco-palians of the other House', as Gordon called them in one of his inflammatory speeches in the Commons.[66] Bull, for whom anti-Catholicism seems to have been the guiding principle of a long political career, put the case with characteristic clarity in the after-math of the Gordon Riots: 'The late toleration of Popery within the realm, I firmly believe, is a part of a deep-laid ministerial plan; a plan, which has for its objects the destruction of the liberties of the people, and the formation of an arbitrary, despotic government.'[67]

It would be a mistake, however, to assume that opposition to Catholic relief was merely an aspect of opposition to North and the American war. Savile, as we have seen, was against the conflict with the colonists and in favour of economical and parliamentary reform. The Rockinghamites, who supported his bill, might have been divided on the need for changes in the representative system, but they were united in their hostility to the American war and their commitment to financial retrenchment and securing the indepen-dence of the legislature from the executive. The Duke of Manchester's suggestion at the end of the Gordon Riots that the party try to accommodate itself to the prevailing anti-Catholic mood of the country seems to have had little or no impact on his colleagues: Richmond firmly declared that he was absolutely opposed to repeal of Savile's Act.[68] As a young lawyer wrote at the time of the riots, 'The opposition, in general, are entirely against the object of the [Protestant Association's] petition'.[69] On the other side, extra-parliamentary anti-Catholics were by no means always against North's ministry and the prosecution of the American war. John Wesley was a supporter of the Protestant Association, and a

[65] Christopher Wyvill, *Political Papers* (6 vols., York, 1794–1802), iii. 134–6.
[66] *PH* xxi. 386.   [67] Ibid. 707.
[68] *Memoirs of the Marquis of Rockingham*, ed. Earl of Albemarle (2 vols., London, 1852), ii. 417, 419.   [69] *Memoirs of Romilly*, i. 119.

pamphleteer on its behalf, but also a conservative defender of the established order and a critic of the rebel colonists and their friends and encouragers in Britain.[70] Nor was Wesley the exception that proves the rule. Newcastle's petition for reinstatement of the penal laws attracted 7,661 names. Kathleen Wilson, having sampled the signatories, concludes that 47% had voted for radical parliamentary candidates in the past, or would do so in the 1780 general election. But 19% were, or would shortly become, government supporters, and, perhaps more significantly, 33% had, or would, split their votes between ministerialists and anti-ministerialists. A majority of the petitioners in her sample, in other words, were by no means clearly committed to opposition to North's government.[71] In Scotland, likewise, anti-Catholicism was rife amongst supporters of North and the American war, as well as among opponents. Despite some reports that suggested Gordon's adherents were all pro-Americans,[72] Sir Lawrence Dundas, MP for Edinburgh, was told in January 1779 that the proposed Catholic relief bill for Scotland had 'given a very great Alarm, to the Best friends of Government in this Country'.[73] The strong opposition of Glasgow's leading lights to any extension of Catholic relief to Scotland likewise reveals the broad basis of anti-Catholicism; for Glasgow's burgh council, as we shall see, was fully committed to the war against the colonists.[74]

We should not be surprised that anti-Catholicism united otherwise antagonistic forces. Hostility to Catholicism was deep-rooted in Britain. The national calendar reflected the centrality of Protestantism, not least in the annual celebration of deliverance from Catholic conspiracy on Guy Fawkes's night.[75] William Dunne, a schoolmaster of Belbroughton, Worcestershire, whose political views are difficult to discern, regularly referred to 'Gunpowder Treason' or

[70] See David Butler, *Methodists and Papists: John Wesley and the Catholic Church in the Eighteenth Century* (London, 1995), ch. 5. For Wesley's support for government and condemnation of radicals and Americans, see Clark, *English Society*, 235–9. See also Eamon Duffy, 'Wesley and the Counter Reformation', in Jane Garnett and Colin Matthew (eds.), *Revival and Religion since 1700: Essays for John Walsh* (London, 1993), 1–19.

[71] Wilson, *Sense of the People*, 366–7.

[72] Hull University Library, Maxwell-Constable Papers, DDEV/60/20A, Alexander Strachan to William Haggerston Maxwell Constable, 17 Feb. 1781.

[73] North Yorkshire RO, Zetland (Dundas) MSS, ZNK X1/2/71.

[74] See below, Ch. 8.

[75] See David Cressy, *Bonfires and Bells: National Memory and the Protestant Calendar in Elizabethan and Stuart England* (London, 1989), ch. 9.

the 'Gunpowder Plott' in his diary entires for 5 November.[76] Nor
was it just a matter of public festivities, the original purpose of which
might have become obscure to those involved. Even humble readers
were likely to have been exposed to a good deal of directly or
indirectly anti-Catholic literature. John Bunyan's *The Pilgrim's
Progress*, first published in 1678–84, and John Foxe's *Book of
Martyrs*, a graphic portrayal of the execution of Protestants in the
reign of the Catholic Queen Mary, which originally appeared in
1563, were made available to a wide readership through repeated
reprints in cheap editions. The *Book of Martyrs*, for instance, came
out in a new edition of sixty instalments in 1776. In works such as
these, and in countless ballads and cheap chapbooks designed for the
popular market, the common people were led to believe that
Catholicism was by nature inimical to liberty. Continental European
Catholic states were despotic states, so it followed that British
liberties would be crushed if there was ever a re-establishment of
Catholicism as the state religion, or even if Catholics secured positions of power and influence. Catholicism was taken to be persecut-
ing and intolerant. Despite the toleration offered to Protestant
Dissenters by the Catholic James II in the 1680s, it was assumed
that Catholics could not rest until they had extirpated Protestantism.
Safeguards against Catholics acquiring any political leverage, and
against the growth of the Catholic community, were therefore seen
as imperative.[77]

Catholics were also assumed to be inherently disloyal because they
owed ultimate allegiance to the pope rather than to the British
crown. This made them, in the eyes of many Protestants, a kind
of religio-ideological 'fifth column'—the enemy within. Concern
about this aspect of Catholicism was bound to be amplified by
war, especially war against Catholic powers. A cartoon of February
1780 depicts the Catholic states of Europe leagued to propagate
Catholicism in the British Isles, with reminders of 'Popish Cruelty'
such as the burning of the Marian martyrs, the Gunpowder Plot,
and the massacre of Irish Protestants in 1641.[78] In 1778–80, then,
what gave particular piquancy to the appeal of militant anti-
Catholicism, and caused the Protestant Associations to attract such

---

[76] Bodleian Library, MS Don. C.76, fos. 126, 144, 177.

[77] See Linda Colley, *Britons: Forging the Nation, 1707–1837* (New Haven, 1992), ch. 1,
for the culturally ingrained anti-Catholicism that united Protestants in all the countries of
Britain. [78] BM 5643, 'The Times'.

substantial support, was surely the war situation. Shortly after Savile's bill became law, France entered the conflict. From June 1779 Britain was confronting the combined Bourbon powers. The threat of invasion in the summer of 1779, as we have seen, led to considerable alarm and seems to have contributed to a growing sense of Britishness.[79] It also revived deeply embedded memories of a beleaguered Protestant isle withstanding the attacks of advancing Catholicism.[80] As a half-pay officer explained to the commander-in-chief in July 1779, he was 'ready and Willing to Sacrifice his Life, for his King, Country, and Protestant Religion'.[81] The broadening of the war from 1778, in short, not only influenced the government to support Catholic relief, but also helped to condition the popular Protestant backlash against Savile's Act.

Concessions to Protestant Dissent

Sir Henry Hoghton, MP for Preston and himself a Dissenter, introduced a bill into the Commons in March 1779 to relieve English and Welsh Nonconformists. His bill was based on the ones he had brought before parliament in 1772 and 1773; it proposed simply that Dissenting ministers and schoolmasters should be freed from the requirement, imposed by the Toleration Act of 1689, that they subscribe to nearly all of the Thirty-nine Articles of the Church of England.

Whereas Catholic relief had met with no opposition within the Westminster Parliament in 1778, concessions to Protestant Non-conformists excited spirited resistance from some High Churchmen. Oxford University, that bastion of High Church Anglicanism, petitioned against any weakening of subscription, and Lord North, as the chancellor of the university, presented the petition to parliament.[82] Lewis Bagot, dean of Christ Church, condemned the bill even before it had been introduced on the grounds that the war situation made it dangerous. 'It cannot be prudent', he told his brother, 'to make essential alterations in your constitution at a

---

[79] See above, Ch. 5.   [80] Haydon, *Anti-Catholicism*, 203.
[81] WO 34/153, fo. 245.
[82] L. G. Mitchell, 'Politics and Revolution 1772–1800', in *The History of the University of Oxford*, v. *The Eighteenth Century*, ed. L. S. Sutherland and L. G. Mitchell (Oxford, 1986), 179.

time of public calamity.'[83] His brother, Sir William Bagot, MP for Staffordshire, used the same argument in the Commons, appealing for discussion of the issue to be 'postponed till quieter times'.[84] Sir Roger Newdigate, MP for Oxford University, and a recognized representative of its High Church traditions,[85] was also influenced by the war. He rejected Hoghton's description of the Dissenters as quiet and peaceful, and linked them with the American rebels, who had persecuted Anglican clergymen in the colonies. The conflict across the Atlantic, it seems, had sharpened Newdigate's hostility to Dissenters in general, though he reserved his bitterest comments for those heterodox anti-Trinitarians whom he feared would gain in influence if subscription were abandoned.[86] To meet this last point, North introduced an amendment requiring Dissenting ministers and schoolmasters to profess the Christian faith. This test clause was opposed by some supporters of the bill, on the grounds that any religious subscriptions were unacceptable, but it was successfully incorporated into the legislation, which then passed with remarkable ease.

Indeed, despite the protests of Bagot, Newdigate, and a handful of others in the Commons, when the bill went up to the Lords it was noticeable that none of the bishops offered any resistance.[87] This was in marked contrast to the situation in 1772–3, when episcopal opposition to Hoghton's bills was strong.[88] In 1779 a sense of Protestant solidarity had perhaps been fostered by Catholic relief. It certainly seems that many MPs accepted Hoghton's central argument that redress for Protestant Dissenters could not be denied once concessions had been given to the Catholics; after all, as Hoghton shrewdly stressed, the 'religious opinions' of the Dissenters 'came so much nearer the doctrines of the church of England' than did those of the Catholics.[89] North's government might well have felt that a gesture to the Nonconformists was necessary to mollify outraged

[83] Staffordshire RO, Bagot Papers, D 3259/13/18/1.
[84] *PH* xx. 240. See also ibid. 306–7.
[85] For his opposition to Hoghton's bills of 1772–3 see *The Correspondence of Sir Roger Newdigate*, ed. A. W. A. White (Dugdale Society Publications, vol. xxxvii, Hertford, 1995), 185, 192–5.   [86] Ibid. 246.
[87] Paul Langford, 'The English Clergy and the American Revolution', in Hellmuth (ed.), *Transformation of Political Culture*, 301–2.
[88] See *PH* xvii. 440, 790, and G. M. Ditchfield, 'The Subscription Issue in British Parliamentary Politics, 1772–1779', *Parliamentary History*, 7 (1988), 55–6.
[89] *PH* xx. 239.

Protestant sensibilities at a time when Savile's Act was causing such unrest. In proposing his amendment, North was probably also mindful of the advantages that could arise if doctrinally orthodox Dissenters could be separated from the anti-Trinitarian Rational Dissenters, who, though few in number, provided dynamic leadership for many radical and reforming causes, including opposition to the war against the Americans. Concessions to orthodox Dissenters, in other words, might have the effect of weakening heterodox Rational Dissent.[90] And, once again, the war almost certainly had a direct impact. With France now an open enemy, the need for national unity seemed more obvious than ever—especially when one recalls that Hoghton's bill was introduced just after the highly divisive Keppel affair had reached its dramatic climax.[91] Sir John Goodricke, a loyal Northite, put the matter very succinctly. Far from being, as Bagot argued, the wrong time to introduce such a bill, this was just the right time, because 'union was much wanted throughout the kingdom, and this would promote it'.[92]

Irish Protestant Dissenters saw their position improve rather more significantly during the war. In 1780 the Irish Test Act of 1704 was amended to allow Dissenters to hold public office. Recent scholarship suggests that this reform was essentially the result of the desire of the British government to reduce pressure for Irish legislative independence. James Kelly points out that an attempt was made in the Irish Parliament to tie repeal of the appropriate part of the Test Act to the 1778 Catholic relief bill, though it remains unclear whether the aim here was to advance the Dissenting cause or scupper concessions to Catholics. Either way, the British Privy Council struck out the tacked-on clauses relating to the Test Act, leaving the Act of 1778 dedicated to Catholic relief. But by the time that Sir Edward Newenham, a fervent Protestant, introduced the heads of a bill to relieve the Dissenters in the next parliamentary session, the political situation had changed. As the bill reached London, the volunteers, and especially those corps in Ulster that were mainly Presbyterian, were agitating for legislative independence for the Dublin Parliament. The British government decided to accept the bill, Kelly argues, in the belief that it would pacify the Dissenters and therefore help to preserve the existing constitutional

---

[90] Clark, *English Society*, 337–8, suggests that this might have been the intention.
[91] See above, Ch. 4.   [92] *PH* xx. 247.

framework for the Anglo-Irish relationship. The bill was returned to Dublin intact, and received the royal assent on 2 May 1780.[93]

This interpretation relegates the war to an indirect role, and so far as the politicking of 1780 is concerned, this may well be appropriate. But it was almost certainly the war that brought the issue on to the political agenda in the first place. Initially, it must be said, this outcome seemed unlikely, as the conflict clearly exacerbated the already strained relations between the Anglican established church and Protestant Dissenters. Lady Sarah Bunbury believed that the Bostonians, 'being chiefly Presbiterians, & from the north of Ireland', were inevitably 'quarrelsome, discontented, hipocritical, enthusiastical, lying people'.[94] She was wrong about the New Englanders, most of whom were Congregationalists rather than Presbyterians, who could trace their origins back to England not Ireland, but her comments on the Presbyterians of Ulster were revealing. And Lady Sarah, we should remind ourselves, was no government supporter; on the contrary, she opposed the war.[95] The Irish administration, as we have seen, took an even dimmer view of the Presbyterians, whose pro-American sympathies made them appear, from the government's perspective, as decidedly untrustworthy.[96]

But it was the very palpable disaffection of the Presbyterians at this time that caused repeal of the offending clauses of the Irish Test Act to become a political issue. The bishop of Derry, an advocate of all-round toleration, argued in 1778, with French invasion a real fear, that the Presbyterian was 'much more dangerous at this crisis than the Papist'. 'The Presbyterians', he continued, 'cannot believe that the K[ing] loves them'. Repeal of the Test Act, the bishop wrote, 'can disgust only a few ignorant High Churchmen among ourselves, and will reclame some thousands of ill dispos'd subjects among those sectaries'.[97] The bishop, to be sure, was a somewhat eccentric figure, and it is tempting to imagine that he had little or no influence in ministerial circles. But in the course of the next year, North appears to have come to accept that if the enemy landed in Ireland, they would immediately offer liberty of religion as well as free trade, which

---

[93] James Kelly, '1780 Revisited: The Politics of the Repeal of the Sacremental Test', in Herlihy (ed.), *Politics of Irish Dissent*, 74–92.

[94] *Life and Letters of Lady Sarah Lennox*, ed. Countess of Ilchester and Lord Stavordale (2 vols., London 1901), i. 246.   [95] See above, Ch. 3.

[96] See above, Ch. 4.   [97] HMC, *Stopford Sackville MSS*, i. 250.

could easily have the effect of attracting Protestant Dissenters.[98] Ireland, as North and his colleagues fully appreciated, would be lost if both Protestant Nonconformists and Catholics were won over by French promises. So, while buying off Dissenting pressure for legislative independence might have been uppermost in the minds of British politicians in 1780, their approach to concessions for Irish Dissenters had probably already been conditioned by defence and security considerations, which inevitably loomed large in ministerial thinking at a time when a Bourbon invasion seemed imminent.

The Anglican Reaction

Paul Langford has suggested that the more inclusive tone adopted by the British state and many leading Anglicans from 1778 was carried forward into the years following the war.[99] Eliga Gould has similarly argued that the American Revolution and its war stimulated amongst Britain's political and religious elite a new emphasis on moderate, civilized, multi-denominational tolerance as the hallmarks of British government, at home and in the empire.[100] But this move away from Anglican exclusivity, while undoubtedly discernible in certain spheres and in some individuals, needs to be set against evidence of a hardening of Anglican attitudes towards Dissent, and a reassertion of the special position of the church and its intimate relationship with the state.[101]

The departure of a large number of Dissenters from the empire with the independence of the United States can be said to have weakened Nonconformity in the British Isles, not least because Anglicanism emerged as unquestionably the dominant Protestant denomination in the remaining territories controlled by the British state. The kind of restraint and compromise that had seemed appropriate in the increasingly diverse Protestant world of the pre-war

---

[98] NLI, Heron Papers, MS 13038, North to Buckinghamshire, 19 July 1779.

[99] Langford, 'English Clergy', 303.

[100] Eliga H. Gould, 'American Independence and Britain's Counter-Revolution', *Past & Present*, 154 (1997), 107–41.

[101] See Clark, *English Society*, 247–76; Hugh Kearney, *The British Isles: A History of Four Nations* (Cambridge, 1989), 176–9; John Cannon, 'The Loss of America', in H. T. Dickinson (ed.), *Britain and the American Revolution* (London, 1998), 240–1.

empire now seemed rather less necessary. British ministers in the 1760s had resisted Anglican appeals for the creation of an American bishop on the grounds that it would be unduly provocative;[102] but in 1787 Pitt appointed a bishop to Nova Scotia, and in 1791 the Anglican Church was established in Upper Canada. The presence in Britain of exiled American Anglicans, small in number but vocal in their denunciations of the Dissenters across the Atlantic, no doubt increased the asperity. Colonial churchmen accustomed to the intensely competitive religious atmosphere of pre-war America, and who were used to identifying the American Revolution as the work of Presbyterianism, were not well suited to promoting toler-ance.[103] The Nonconformists in Britain made life more difficult for themselves by continuing to hold up America as an example to be followed, most famously when Richard Price published his *Observations on the Importance of the American Revolution* in 1784. Inspired by Virginia's adoption of religious freedom in 1786, the Dissenters began a campaign the following year for the repeal of the Test and Corporation Acts. In 1789 the repealers came within twenty votes of victory in the House of Commons, which would tend to support the line of Langford and Gould that the more inclusive approach of the later years of the American war continued after the peace. After all, the majority of those MPs voting for repeal in 1789 were themselves Anglicans.[104] Nor was the language of the opponents of repeal always harsh and unbending. Lord North was emollient. He cited the 'universal toleration' already established, and the 'free toleration' granted to the Dissenters, as proof of the essentially benign attitude of the church to Nonconformity.[105] But there were distinctly strident voices, which were perhaps more representative of the climate of the times. Pitt, who spoke powerfully against repeal, seems to have been influenced by the arguments of Bishop Sherlock's High Church tract, *A Vindication of the Test and Corporation Acts*, first published in 1718, but reprinted in 1787 and again in 1790. During the parliamentary debates in 1787, Sir William

---

[102] Schneider and Schneider (eds.), *Samuel Johnson*, iii. 259–60, 277–8.

[103] For examples of this logic, taken from wartime correspondence, see NLS, Fetter-cairn Papers, box 75, Dr Charles Inglis to Dr Myles Cooper, 24 July 1777, [Revd Peter Middleton] to Cooper, 7 Feb. 1778.

[104] See G. M. Ditchfield, 'The Parliamentary Struggle over the Repeal of the Test and Corporation Acts, 1787–1790', *English Historical Review*, 89 (1974), 551–77.

[105] For the 1787 debates, in which North made these statements, see *PH* xxvi. 780–832.

Dolben, a staunch High Churchman, vehemently denied the moderation of the Nonconformists, and to prove how dangerous they were he quoted an inflammatory passage from Joseph Priestly's recently published *Importance of Free Inquiry in Matters of Religion*. The same passage, in which Priestly referred to 'a train of gunpowder', laid carefully by the Dissenters, was quoted again triumphantly by Burke in 1790. This emphasis on Dissenting extremism was, to put it mildly, hardly the language of Anglican inclusiveness and a spirit of cross-denominational cooperation.[106]

Indeed, the closeness of the result in 1789 proved to be a false dawn for the Dissenters. In 1790, influenced in part, no doubt, by the contemporaneous convulsions in France, MPs decisively defeated a repeal motion by 294 to 105. The next year 'Church and King' mobs attacked Dissenters in Birmingham, and an attempt to exempt Scottish Presbyterians taking office in England and Wales from the provisions of the Test Act was heavily voted down.[107] In 1792 the penal laws directed against Scottish Episcopalians were repealed.[108] The Anglican reaction, it seems, was in full flood. There were, to be sure, concessions to Catholics during this period, notably a further Relief Act in 1791, the restoration of voting rights in Ireland in 1793, and the first state funding for the Catholic seminary at Maynooth in 1795. In this sense, the policy of greater inclusiveness identified by Langford and Gould did indeed live on after the crisis years of the American war. But Protestant Dissenters, it seems clear, were again regarded with deep suspicion. To many Anglicans, and particularly the High Churchmen amongst them, the Dissenters simply could not be trusted; they were tainted by association with French republicanism, just as they had been identified as friends and allies of the American rebels. In 1797 the Revd Jonathan Boucher, a refugee from Maryland, described the French Revolution as the 'giant offspring' of the American Revolution. The Dissenters, to churchmen like Boucher, were the leading figures in a long-running plot to destroy legally constituted and divinely ordained authority.[109] Not until 1813, when the threat of invasion had disappeared and

---

[106] Clark, *English Society*, 340–3.
[107] G. M. Ditchfield, 'The Scottish Campaign against the Test Act, 1790–1791', *Historical Journal*, 23 (1980), 37–61.
[108] See Mather, 'Church, Parliament and the Penal Laws'.
[109] Jonathan Boucher, *A View of the Causes and Consequences of the American Revolution; in Thirteen Discourses* (London, 1797), esp. p. vii.

success against Napoleon seemed likely, did Nonconformists receive their next instalment of state favour, in the form of the repeal of the clause directed against denials of the Trinity in the 1698 Blasphemy Act. Even this was less generous than it seemed; anti-Trinitarians continued to be subject to common law prosecutions for blasphemous libel for many years to come.[110] And it was not until 1828 that repeal of the Test and Corporation Acts was finally achieved.

[110] Clark, *Language of Liberty*, 179–80.

8

The Local Dimension

SEVERAL LOCAL STUDIES have been published that shed revealing light on the British side of the American war. London, Bristol, Manchester, Birmingham, Newcastle, and Norwich, in particular, have been the subjects of scholarly scrutiny.[1] It might therefore seem that little could be added by pursuing a similar approach with other localities. But there are at least two good reasons for focusing on the local dimension. First, the studies just mentioned are all concerned with large or medium-sized urban centres in England; they need to be supplemented by work on a wider range of communities, both in terms of type and geography. Second, many of the points made in preceding chapters can be brought out more sharply, and their relative significance both temporally and geographically can be better illustrated, by examining the impact of the war on various localities.

We will be looking at six very different places; one in Scotland, four in England and one in Ireland (see Map 8.1). We begin with Glasgow, a great commercial centre which had grown largely due to its transatlantic trade. Hull, an important English port with a north European orientation, is the subject of the second study. We then move to the English midlands to look at the cathedral city of Lichfield. In southern England we will concentrate on a small area in Essex profoundly affected by the war—Brentwood and its vicinity—and counterbalance this very localized study with an examination of the impact of the conflict on a whole county, Berkshire. The last community portrait is of Strabane in County Tyrone, a small market town notable for its linen trade.

---

[1] John A. Sainsbury, *Disaffected Patriots: London Supporters of Revolutionary America* (Kingston, 1987); Peter Marshall, *Bristol in the American War of Independence* (Bristol, 1977) and 'Manchester and the American Revolution', *Bulletin of the John Rylands University Library of Manchester*, 62 (1979), 168–86; John Money, *Experience and Identity: Birmingham and the West Midlands, 1760–1800* (Manchester, 1977); Kathleen Wilson, *The Sense of the People: Politics, Culture and Imperialism in England, 1715–1785* (Cambridge, 1995), 357–75, 417–33.

Map 8.1. Glasgow, Hull, Lichfield, Brentwood, Berkshire, and Strabane

Glasgow

Glasgow in 1775 had a population of about 40,000, making it one of the larger urban centres in Britain. The governing body was the city's council, selected annually by the magistrates, or baillies, from the burgesses in the Merchant House and the Trades House. Despite its size, Glasgow had only one MP—and this at a time when even the smallest English boroughs usually had two. In fact, Glasgow was even worse off than this comparison suggests, for the city's MP was meant to represent not just Glasgow but also the neighbouring burghs of Dumbarton, Renfrew, Rutherglen, and Lanark. The MP was selected by a very limited electorate under an indirect system: each burgh council chose a delegate; the delegates then met to choose the MP. At the start of the American war, the city's parliamentary representative was Lord Frederick Campbell, younger son of the Duke of Argyll. Campbell had held his seat, without a contest, since 1761, when he had succeeded his elder brother.[2]

The city had grown enormously since the Act of Union linking Scotland with England and Wales in 1707. The population was recorded as 12,766 in 1708 and had nearly doubled by 1755.[3] Thomas Pennant, the Welsh traveller, described Glasgow in 1769 as a major manufacturer of textiles that was beginning to rival Manchester.[4] But the city's expansion rested on the access Glasgow had gained to the English colonies across the Atlantic, and to the benefit it derived after the Union from the Navigation Acts, which stipulated that exports of the most lucrative colonial staples should come to the mother country before going on to any other market. Glasgow developed into a great entrepôt for colonial products. In particular, it became central to the tobacco trade of the Chesapeake. The city's merchant houses handled a large proportion of the tobacco exported from Virginia and Maryland, selling the bulk to continental European customers, especially the French and the Dutch.[5]

Small wonder, then, that the outbreak of war with the rebel colonies was greeted with trepidation in some quarters. In July 1775 the Virginia agent of a Glasgow tobacco house predicted that the conflict would have a 'direful effect' on business.[6] Glasgow's tobacco imports certainly declined precipitously, falling from forty-six million pounds weight in 1775 to only seven million in 1776. The next year they stood at a paltry 210,000 pounds.[7] Many companies lost stock and even land in America, and outstanding debts could not

[2] Sir Lewis Namier and John Brooke, *The History of Parliament: The House of Commons 1754–1790* (3 vols., London, 1964), i. 43–4, 505–6, ii. 182–3.

[3] *The New Statistical Account of Scotland* (15 vols., Edinburgh, 1845–58), vi. 129.

[4] Thomas Pennant, *A Tour in Scotland* (3rd edn., Warrington, 1774), 231–2.

[5] See T. M. Devine and Gordon Jackson (eds.), *Glasgow, Beginnings to 1830* (Manchester, 1995), ch. 4.

[6] T. M. Devine (ed.), *A Scottish Firm in Virginia: W. Cuninghame and Co.* (Scottish History Society, 4th ser. vol. xx, Edinburgh, 1984), 212.

[7] M. L. Robertson, 'Scottish Commerce and the American War of Independence', *Economic History Review*, 2nd ser., 9 (1956–7), 123.

of course be collected.[8] Not surprisingly, bankruptcies occurred among city merchants involved in the tobacco trade, the most notable casualties being in the Buchanan group of companies.[9]

The difficulties and anxieties generated by the conflict can be glimpsed through the letter-books of Alexander Houston and Company. Houstons was not primarily a tobacco house; it traded extensively with the West Indies, importing sugar, rum, cotton, and tobacco and sending back herrings and plantation stores. In the early years of the struggle, the company was concerned with the activities of American privateers and, more importantly, with the stagnation of sugar prices in Britain caused by the loss of the American market. Until General Howe was successful at New York, a correspondent at St Vincent was told in October 1776, 'Trade must be carried on with great risk and uncertainty'. The company's agent at Grenada was similarly informed: 'We look for great news from New York daily, which we hope will put an end to this disagreeable War quickly.' The prospect and then the reality of a French war caused considerable gloom ('the Consequences . . . may prove fatal to the Commerce of Britain') and offers from potential trading partners received polite refusals: no new business was the order of the day. The war in the Caribbean from 1778 was of course followed minutely; rumours and reports of troops movements and the loss of islands regularly appear in the company's letters. The capture by the French of St Vincent and Grenada was regarded as 'a severe blow to the West India trade of Britain, & to ourselves in particular'. With a weary fatalism, Houstons concluded 'we must submit to what has happened in hopes that 'ere long every thing will be as it was'.[10]

Not all of Glasgow's merchants were so downcast. The war brought opportunities as well as difficulties. 'Persons are come to Glasgow', a Scottish newspaper reported in January 1776, 'to contract for shipping, bedding &c. to carry over 3000 troops to America, who are to embark at Port Glasgow'.[11] Shipping contracts of this kind must have provided a most welcome compensation for the loss of the traditional tobacco trade. And we should note that for the

---

[8] See e.g. PRO, Audit Office Papers, Loyalist Claims Commission, AO 12/54, fos. 55–6; AO 12/55, fos. 23–30, 51–2; AO 12/56, fos. 143–57.

[9] T. M. Devine, 'Glasgow Merchants and the Collapse of the Tobacco Trade', *Scottish Historical Review*, 52 (1973), 65.

[10] NLS, Houston Papers, MS 8793, pp. 31, 36, 39, 73, 79, 83, 98, 315, 325; MS 8794, pp. 28, 321.   [11] *Caledonian Mercury*, 20 Jan. 1776.

bigger tobacco firms, which had stockpiled in anticipation of the crisis, the decline in imports was far from disastrous. Limited inflows of tobacco in 1776 and 1777 meant higher prices and increased profits for those with stocks to sell. As late as August 1777 Glasgow merchants were reported to have 'sold a great quantity of tobacco to the French at a very great price'.[12] Moreover, throughout the war some merchants were able to prosper by engaging in illicit trade with the rebel colonies through the neutral islands in the West Indies. The tobacco was purchased by agents in the Caribbean and then shipped in neutral vessels to ports such as Ostend, Amsterdam, and Hamburg.[13] Creative adaptation took others forms, too. Glasgow had at least 123 vessels commissioned as privateers between 1777 and 1783.[14] Glaswegians even invested in privateers operating from British bases across the Atlantic: Hector Macome and John Campbell were among the owners of a schooner which sailed against the rebels and the French from New York in February 1779.[15] And the British enclaves in North America provided opportunities of other kinds. As we have seen, the army, navy, and local population combined constituted a significant market. In 1779 Henry Ritchie asked a contact in a Scottish regiment to report back on prices, 'particularly provisions and liquors'. He added knowingly: 'provisions have sold of late very high at New York and a good deal of money has been made by them'.[16] Ritchie sent out an agent to purchase captured tobacco stocks and to handle the goods that he dispatched to the British bases. Other merchants, who were anxious to exploit these new opportunities effectively, took similar steps.[17] Robert Henderson sold fabrics, haberdashery, paper, footwear, shirts, and cutlery at New York for the Glasgow firm of Coventry and Henderson.[18] Nor was continued trade with America the only route to salvation for the Glasgow mercantile community. The Caribbean islands, largely cut off from their traditional source of food supplies in the mainland colonies, consumed more provisions sent out from Britain and Ireland, and Glasgow firms—Houstons

[12] Devine, 'Glasgow Merchants', 74.
[13] Id., *Exploring the Scottish Past* (East Linton, 1995), 101–2.
[14] J. Starkey, *British Privateering Enterprise in the Eighteenth Century* (Exeter, 1990), 200.
[15] PRO, High Court of Admiralty Papers, HCA 49/91, bundle iv, fo. 20.
[16] Library of Congress, Dunlop Family Papers, box 1, Ritchie to Lt. George Dunlop, 19 Feb. 1779.   [17] See SRO, Inglis Papers, GD 1/46/21/6.
[18] New York Public Library, Robert Henderson Papers, Day-book and Journal, 1779–1791.

among them—benefited from this development. And as continental European markets closed to British Caribbean products, increasing quantities were re-exported to Ireland. Scottish domestic exports also went across the Irish Sea in large volumes. A recent study concludes that Ireland's ability to absorb larger quantities of Scottish re-exports and Scottish domestic products did much to stabilize Scotland's economy and 'support the solvency' of many of the leading merchant houses.[19]

The success of Glasgow's merchants in finding new sources of profit might help to explain why so many of the city's leading lights displayed little sympathy for the Americans. This was somewhat surprising, given the support Glasgow's merchants had shown in earlier American crises, notably in 1765–6, when a petition was sent to the British Parliament suggesting the need for repeal of the Stamp Act,[20] and a Glasgow merchant, John Glassford, testified before the House of Commons that the Act was severely disrupting the city's commerce with the colonies.[21] Even at the beginning of 1775, just before the outbreak of fighting in America, many Glaswegian merchants seem to have been disposed to conciliation. A petition from merchants and traders, read to the House of Commons on 24 January 1775, asked the legislature 'to take into their Serious Consideration' the damage being done to trade with America by the colonial boycotts, which were themselves a result of the Coercive Acts passed by the British Parliament in 1774.[22] Glasgow, moreover, was a stronghold of the Popular party in the Church of Scotland, a party with an established record of sympathy for colonial grievances.[23] Yet the Trades House sent in a loyal address to the king in January 1776, expressing 'abhorrence and detestation at that unprovoked and unnatural rebellion now prevailing in some of your Majesty's colonys'.[24] The following November the burgh

---

[19] Robertson, 'Scottish Commerce', 127; L. E. Cochran, *Scottish Trade with Ireland in the Eighteenth Century* (Edinburgh, 1985), 7, 13, 15, 58, 77, 175.

[20] *Journals of the House of Commons*, xxx. 499.

[21] R. C. Simmons and P. D. G. Thomas (eds.), *Proceedings and Debates of the British Parliaments respecting North America, 1754–1783* (6 vols. to date, Millward, NY, 1982–), ii. 226–7. [22] *Journals of the House of Commons*, xxxv. 74–5.

[23] See Ned C. Landsman, 'Liberty, Piety and Patronage: The Social Context of Contested Clerical Calls in Eighteenth-Century Glasgow', in Andrew Hook and Richard B. Sher (eds.), *The Glasgow Enlightenment* (East Linton, 1995), 214–15.

[24] HO 55/11/60; Harry Lumsden (ed.), *The Records of the Trades House of Glasgow 1713–1777* (Glasgow, 1934), 572.

council offered bounties to local sailors joining the navy, and renewed the offer at regular intervals throughout the war.[25] The most conspicuous sign of the city's loyalty, however, was its response to the news of Burgoyne's capitulation at Saratoga. The council, meeting on 26 December 1777, unanimously resolved to 'give their aid and assistance to government at this critical time in order to enable them to quell the . . . rebellion'. Three days later, the council agreed to raise a battalion in the city 'by voluntary subscription'.[26] The council itself gave £1,000, and the Merchant and Trades Houses were encouraged to subscribe. We know that the Trades House provided £500, and recommended that each of its constituent trades make their own contribution also.[27] The bakers responded with £200, the weavers the same, and the barbers with £100.[28] To stimulate recruitment, the council offered to make enlistees burgesses of the city, a move endorsed by the Merchant House.[29] An address to the king from the council, shortly after the Spanish entered the war, reinforces the impression of loyalty;[30] while in 1782, when the new Rockingham administration consulted the counties and principal towns on a scheme for a reformed popular militia, Glasgow, along with many other towns that had supported the previous government, found fault with the proposals and declined to adopt them.[31]

But it would be a mistake to assume that Glasgow was solidly behind the North government. William Thom, minister at Govan, was a particularly outspoken critic of the American aspect of the war.[32] Nor was opposition confined to churchmen. Representations from the Merchant House scuppered a proposal that the council send in a loyal address in October 1775. According to newspaper

[25] Robert Renwick et al. (eds.), *Extracts from the Records of the Burgh of Glasgow* (11 vols., Glasgow, 1881–1916), vii. 486, 490, 505, 517, 521, viii. 6, 27, 57.
[26] Ibid. vii. 514.   [27] Lumsden (ed.), *Records of the Trades House*, 593–4.
[28] *The Incorporation of the Bakers of Glasgow* (Glasgow, 1937), 73; Robert D. McEwan (ed.), *Old Glasgow Weavers; Being the Records of the Incorporation of Weavers* (Glasgow, 1908), 129; James B. Tennent (ed.), *Records of the Incorporation of Barbers, Glasgow* (Glasgow, 1930), 188–9.
[29] Renwick et al. (eds.), *Records of Glasgow*, vii. 517, 526–7; *View of the Merchants House of Glasgow* (Glasgow, 1866), 200. Not many actually became burgesses: see James R. Anderson (ed.), *The Burgesses and Guild Brethren of Glasgow, 1751–1846* (Scottish Record Society, vol. lxvi, Edinburgh, 1935), 110.
[30] Renwick et al. (eds.), *Records of Glasgow*, vii. 557.   [31] Ibid. viii. 46, 48–50.
[32] Robert Kent Donovan, 'Evangelical Civic Humanism in Glasgow: The American War Sermons of William Thom', in Hook and Sher (eds.), *Glasgow Enlightenment*, 227–45.

reports, merchants threatened to send a counter-petition, opposing the war, if the address was forthcoming.[33] In January 1778, when money was flowing in to fund the raising of the Glasgow Regiment, the Merchant House was conspicuously not among the contributors, and a local newspaper reminded readers that many of the subscribers wished 'that the present dispute betwixt Britain and her Colonies may be amicably settled without further bloodshed'.[34] We might also note that the council and its supporters had mixed reasons for wanting to form the regiment. A sense of duty mingled with considerations of patronage and local politics. The council appointed a committee to make recommendations for junior officers in the corps;[35] and the bakers pressed the case for two candidates, both of whom were bakers themselves.[36] Similarly, when in 1778 Glasgow's council paid for the placing of cannon at Greenock to protect shipping in the Clyde estuary from enemy vessels,[37] its actions could be variously interpreted. Providing the battery at its own expense could be seen as another instance of the willingness of Glasgow's leading lights to support the war effort. But it can just as easily, and perhaps more accurately, be regarded as an implicit criticism of the government for itself failing to provide the necessary naval protection. Nor was the council prepared to support government if this entailed a sacrifice of what were perceived to be Glasgow's interests. The re-export trade to Ireland, important before the war and made still more so—as we have seen—by wartime developments, would clearly be jeopardized by any legislative concessions that allowed Ireland to trade directly with the colonies. Hence the council's opposition in 1778 to the measures designed to give freedom of trade to Ireland: Lord Frederick Campbell was requested to do all in his power to stop the relevant bills becoming law.[38] Another source of conflict with the North administration was the government's toleration policy, a policy intended, as we have seen, to promote recruitment into the armed forces. In January 1779 the council 'unanimously resolve[d] to take

[33] *York Courant*, 17 Oct. 1775.   [34] *Glasgow Mercury*, 15 Jan. 1778.

[35] Renwick et al. (eds.), *Records of Glasgow*, vii. 518–19.

[36] *Incorporation of Bakers*, 73. Neither of the nominees appears to have been given a commission. For their status see Anderson (ed.), *Burgesses and Guild Brethren*, 77.

[37] Renwick et al. (eds.), *Records of Glasgow*, vii. 514. See also Dr Williams's Library, Wodrow-Kenrick Correspondence, MS 24157 (65); *Glasgow Mercury*, 10 Sept. 1778.

[38] Renwick et al. (eds.), *Records of Glasgow*, vii. 527.

every legal and constitutional measure' to resist the extension of limited Catholic relief to Scotland. Campbell was again approached to use his influence against the proposals, and the assistance of Andrew Stewart, the MP for Lanarkshire, was also sought.[39] With tempers high, 'loyal' Glasgow was depicted by at least one government supporter as a hotbed of anarchy and disaffection.[40] Rioting in the city in February 1779, which led to claims for compensation for lost property, perhaps induced the council to adopt a more cautious line: in August 1780 the king was congratulated on his 'wisdom and prudence' in putting down the Gordon Riots.[41]

Even so, the city remained restless, not least because the presence of large numbers of soldiers caused great problems. Several Scottish regiments embarked for overseas service from Glasgow; the Western Fencible Regiment, commanded by Lord Frederick Campbell, was based in the city when it was first raised; and, as a populous urban centre that attracted men from a wide hinterland seeking work or other opportunities, Glasgow was an obvious place of resort for recruiting parties from many different regiments.[42] This considerable military activity no doubt brought some benefits to the city's shopkeepers and other traders; but, as elsewhere, army officers were often slow to settle their bills, leading to angry complaints and appeals for help from the War Office.[43] But the most obvious problem was the lack of accommodation to house the military visitors. As early as April 1776 the council paid the city's quartermaster £10 for his 'extraordinary trouble' in finding billets for recruiting parties and troops waiting for embarkation. Two years later he received £30 for further 'extraordinary trouble' in accommodating 'a great number of soldiers belonging to different corps that have been quartered in the city of Glasgow for a considerable time past'. By June 1780 the difficulties had become so acute that the council drew up regulations for quartering, which forbade the use of private homes without express permission from a magistrate, and limited all

---

[39] Ibid. 542.   [40] BL, Liverpool Papers, Add. MS 38212, fo. 271.
[41] Renwick et al. (eds.), *Records of Glasgow*, vii. 547, 549–51, 552–3, 607–8.
[42] Of the twenty-five men recruited in Glasgow by Lt. Allan Macdonald of the 76th Foot, only one came from Glasgow itself; the rest were from all over Scotland, or, in one case, from Ireland: Rammerscales House, Bell-Macdonald Papers, Letter-book, 1781–2. For the movement from the countryside to towns in this period see T. M. Devine, 'Urbanisation', in *People and Society in Scotland*, i. *1760–1830*, ed. id. and Rosalind Mitchison (Edinburgh, 1988), 27–52.   [43] e.g. WO 4/105, p. 56.

billeting to a maximum of six weeks.[44] In September 1782, however, the city's bakers still thought it necessary to consort with other trades to lobby for a more equitable distribution of quarters among the inhabitants.[45]

At a time when the war was posing multiple challenges, Glasgow's leading lights expected particularly attentive service from their MP.[46] Yet Campbell was tired of the burden and lost interest long before he decided not to stand again in 1780. His successor, John Crauford, was a government placeman well connected with the opposition, but he was no more inclined to exert himself on the city's behalf. No speech of Crauford's on a matter of concern to Glasgow is recorded. In these circumstances, dissatisfaction was perhaps bound to manifest itself. Perhaps an early symptom of this was the difficulty Crauford experienced in securing his seat; according to one report he beat off a challenge from William Fullarton only by spending large sums of money.[47] It was surely no coincidence that in the closing stages of a war that had high-lighted the need for a strong voice for the city, there was much discussion of reform of the burgh constitution and better represen-tation of Glasgow in Parliament. Even the council saw the need for change. In November 1782, Patrick Colquhoun, the lord provost, wrote to the Yorkshire Association supporting the principle of parliamentary reform. Colquhoun was careful to put the case for moderation, and to question whether 'the present moment is the best calculated for such objects of difficult discussion, in the midst of a formidable and complicated war'. Even so, he made it clear that the council was unhappy with a situation where 'the trading towns on the banks of the Clyde, forming a body of near 100,000 people, [are] represented only by one Member, and that Member elected by four Delegates, of which this City only sends one, who is chosen by the Corporation composed of no more than thirty individuals'.[48] Another symptom of the way in which the American war had

---

[44] Renwick et al. (eds.), *Records of Glasgow*, vii. 478, 529, 554, 589–90, 600–1.

[45] *Incorporation of Bakers*, 73.

[46] They did, to be sure, employ other avenues, such as the Convention of the Royal Burghs, a body which sought to lobby on behalf of the Scottish burghs. See Thomas Hunter (ed.), *Extracts from the Records of the Convention of the Royal Burghs of Scotland 1759–1779* (Edinburgh, 1918), 545–6.

[47] NLI, Fitzpatrick Papers, MS 8012, Lord Macartney to Lady Ossory, 13 Oct. 1780.

[48] Christopher Wyvill, *Political Papers* (6 vols., York, 1794–1802), ii. 84–5. See also *Incorporation of Bakers*, 73; Tennent (ed.), *Incorporation of Barbers*, 192–6.

increased dissatisfaction with the status quo was the formation in 1783 of the Glasgow Chamber of Commerce and Manufacturers. Colquhoun was again a leading light, and the chamber's brief was to oversee commercial matters pertaining to the Clyde valley, and 'to be the organ of all communications with His Majesty's government, or with the legislature, on subjects connected with the trade of the district'.[49]

Hull

'The Town & Port of Hull is so important an Object to All the trading & manufacturing Parts of Yorkshire, that I felt & shall always feel anxious to Assist & pay every Attention to its Welfare & security.' The Marquis of Rockingham, who wrote these words,[50] had good reason to be flattering—he was trying to increase his influence in the borough. But in fact he understated rather than exaggerated Hull's significance. Hull was not just vital to Yorkshire. The Trent, its tributaries, and an expanding canal network connected the port with the industrial areas of Lancashire, Derbyshire, Nottinghamshire, Leicestershire, and Staffordshire; Hull even handled goods produced in Birmingham.[51] The chief exports in 1768 were textiles, lead, tin plate, and earthenware, and the principal destinations of the outgoing vessels were the Low Countries, Germany, Scandinavia, and Russia. The return cargoes consisted mainly of timber and timber products, iron, hemp, flax, and raw Dutch linen yarn.[52] The port, moreover, was poised for expansion on the eve of the war. In 1774 an Act of Parliament incorporated the Hull Dock Company; construction started the following year. The dock, opened in 1778, was nearly ten acres in extent and capable of holding more than 100 sail.[53] In 1775 Hull had a population of about 13,500,

---

[49] Stana Nedadic, 'The Middle Ranks and Modernisation', in Devine and Jackson (ed.), *Glasgow*, i. 293.

[50] Hull RO, Borough Records, BRL 1386/11.

[51] VCH, *Yorkshire East Riding*, i. *The City of Kingston upon Hull*, ed. K. J. Allison (Oxford, 1969), 174–5.

[52] Gordon Jackson, *Hull in the Eighteenth Century: A Study in Economic and Social History* (Oxford, 1972), 333, 337, 339.

[53] Ibid. 245–7. The opening of the Grand Dock was, according to the *York Courant*, 29 Sept. 1778, 'such a Day of universal rejoicing as was never known in Hull before'.

making it a medium-sized town on a par with Chester, Nottingham, and Coventry.[54]

Politically, Hull was influenced by a number of different interests with patronage or favours to bestow. Trinity House, a guild established in the Middle Ages and dominated by the town's leading merchants and gentlemen, was of considerable importance. So was the corporation. Government also had some influence through the customs and excise and the garrison of the citadel. Local families such as the Wilberforces and the Etheringtons had some sway, and Sir George Savile and Rockingham, two great Yorkshire figures, carried weight in the town. The electorate, made up of the freemen, was probably about 1,400 strong,[55] but notoriously corrupt. Neither national nor local issues appear to have played a determining part in the political contests of the pre-war period. The ingredients that caused party turmoil elsewhere were largely absent; there was no established anti-corporation group, and Protestant Dissenters formed only a small portion of the general population and of the electorate. None of the five Dissenting ministers in the town—two Congregationalists, two Baptists, and a Presbyterian—played any discernible role in local politics. The 1774 general election saw the return of Lord Robert Manners, the lieutenant-governor of the citadel, MP since 1747, and an adherent of Lord North. But his colleague was David Hartley, a newcomer representing the Savile-Rockingham interest. Nearly half the electorate split their votes between the two successful candidates, apparently seeing nothing odd in voting for both a regular government supporter and an opposition nominee.[56]

The war seems to have brought party strife to Hull for the first time in more than twenty years. Hartley, whose political views were largely unknown in 1774, emerged as an outspoken critic of North's American policy. In March 1775 he introduced a motion in the Commons calling for conciliation of the colonies,[57] and over the next four years he put forward a further seven motions condemning

[54] Population figures for various towns are usefully tabulated in Geoffrey Holmes and Daniel Szechi, *The Age of Oligarchy: Pre-Industrial Britain 1722–1783* (London, 1993), 346–9.

[55] York City Archives, Yorkshire Association MSS, M83/4, Charles Pool to William Gray, 4 May 1782.

[56] Namier and Brooke, *History of Parliament*, i. 435; James E. Bradley, *Religion, Revolution and English Radicalism* (Cambridge, 1990), 289–98.

[57] *PH* xviii. 552–71, 574.

the conflict and seeking to promote a settlement.[58] In 1778 he published a pamphlet addressed to his Hull constituents, in which he sought to elaborate on his case against the war. Hartley's central theme was that the 'real purpose' of the war was 'to establish an influential dominion in the Crown, through the means of an independent American revenue, at the disposition of a royal sign manual, uncontrolled by Parliament'.[59] But these arguments seem not to have struck a chord in Hull. In October 1775 Manners, Hartley's fellow MP, presented to the king an address signed by 171 inhabitants supporting the coercion of the American rebels.[60] The corporation and Trinity House also sent in loyal addresses at this time,[61] and contributed to a subscription to provide material comforts for the British troops serving in America and their widows and orphans.[62] The corporation and Trinity House, furthermore, continued to demonstrate their loyalty and support for the war at almost every opportunity. In 1776 the corporation offered bounties to seamen joining the navy in the town, and renewed the offer at various points thereafter.[63] Trinity House offered its own bounties, and in 1777 made Captain James O'Hara, in charge of the naval impress service in the town, an honorary brother.[64] O'Hara was struck by the loyalty of both the corporation and Trinity House: in letters to the admiralty he described the mayor as having done 'every thing to further the service', adding that 'If in the Confusion of any night Work our [press] Gangs had any Accusation laid against them, we always found him our friend.'[65] In 1779 Trinity House again addressed the king expressing enthusiasm for the prosecution of the war,[66] and the following year Captain William Cumming, O'Hara's successor, again praised the brethren for their 'Zeal for the King's Service'.[67]

By this time, the conflict was clearly affecting Hull's economic

---

[58] Ibid. 1042–52, 1302–15; xix. 549–58, 1068–78, 1204–6, 1207–10; xx. 901–15.

[59] Hartley, *Letters on the American War* (London, 1778), 69, 70, 71, 73.

[60] HO 55/8/4.   [61] *London Gazette*, 10–14 Oct. 1775.

[62] Hull RO, WM/6, 'A Subscription', 3 Nov. 1775.

[63] *York Courant*, 26 Nov. 1776, 6 July 1779; ADM 1/2248, Capt. James O'Hara to Philip Stephens, 25 Nov. 1776; *Leeds Intelligencer*, 17 Mar. 1778; Hull RO, Borough Records, BRL 1386/149.

[64] *York Courant*, 19 Nov. 1776; Arthur Storey, *Trinity House of Kingston upon Hull* (Hull, 1967), 135.

[65] ADM 1/2248, O'Hara to Stephens, 17 May 1777; ADM 1/2249, O'Hara to Stephens, 6 Apr. 1778.   [66] SP 37/13, fo. 96.

[67] ADM 1/1613, Cumming to Stephens, 23 Dec. 1780.

life. For the first three years or so of the struggle, external trade carried on much as before. As an east coast town, Hull had less to lose from the interruption of Atlantic trade than had western ports such as Bristol, Liverpool, and Glasgow. Indeed, in 1772 only 7% of ships clearing Hull had been bound for America.[68] The entry of France into the war made Hull's North Sea trade more vulnerable to attack from enemy vessels—particularly privateers, whether French or American.[69] Requests for naval protection were accordingly dispatched to the admiralty,[70] and in 1780 a committee for convoys, established in the previous war, was revived to coordinate the sailing of merchant vessels and to establish an effective channel of communication with the local naval commanders and their superiors in London.[71] The town's MPs were also expected to lobby for trade protection, and by all accounts they devoted much energy to the task. In 1781, for instance, Manners and his new colleague William Wilberforce pressed for the Humber to be made the rendezvous for all naval vessels operating in the North Sea;[72] while in April 1782 Wilberforce spoke directly to admiralty officials about the need for ships to protect an important merchant convoy bound for the Baltic.[73]

The war, it must be said, offered opportunities for Hull, as for many other places. The garrison was much expanded from 1778. The two companies of invalids manning the citadel were reinforced by a militia regiment—first the Nottinghamshires, then the West Yorkshires, and later by the North Lincolns, and then the Northumberlands. While the pay of the militiamen was not sufficient to enable them to purchase much as individuals, the officers were often important consumers of local goods and services, either for themselves or for their units. The surviving accounts of Lieutenant-Colonel George Nevile of the Nottinghamshires provide a flavour of this kind of purchasing: stabling for horses, dinners at inns, miscellaneous items of clothing, wood for the use of his men.[74] The naval vessels protecting local shipping would presumably also

---

[68] Jackson, *Hull*, 339.   [69] See *York Courant*, 13 Oct. 1778.
[70] See Hull RO, Borough Records, BRL 1295.
[71] Hull RO, WM/3, Committee for Convoys Minute-book, 1757–82. For the protection of convoys see also ADM 1/2393, Capt. Stephen Rains to Stephens, 25 Apr., 30 June, 8 July, 22 Sept., 4 Nov. 1780, 23 Apr. 1781; ADM 1/1446, petition of Hull merchants to Capt. Alexander Agnew, Oct. 1780.   [72] Hull RO, Borough Records, BRL 1311.
[73] Ibid., BRL 1315.
[74] Nottinghamshire Archives, Nevile of Thomey MSS, DD N/215.

have added to the custom of the town's shopkeepers and tradesmen. Contracts to build ships for the navy must have given a welcome boost to the local economy, too.[75] Privateering may have provided another source of profit for some of the town's seafarers and merchants.[76] We should likewise note that coastal trade seems to have increased at this time, with more foodstuffs going to London and locally produced soap being shipped to other east coast ports such as Newcastle, Sunderland, and Boston.[77] And individual fortunes continued to be made from shipping goods across the North Sea: Francis Bine, a ship's master, was said to have amassed £20,000 during the American war from trade with Ostend, and to have used his profits to set himself up as a merchant and sugar-boiler.[78]

Against these positive features, however, we have to set the negative ones. Privateering may have benefited some townspeople, but the thirty privateers operating from Hull between 1777 and 1783 took only six prizes between them, which suggests that much of the investment in privateers yielded no return.[79] And, despite the profits made by Francis Bine, conventional overseas trade seems to have contracted. Increased risks and increased costs discouraged both producers and manufacturers from sending finished goods and raw materials across the North Sea. Burton upon Trent's beer sales to Scandinavia and Russia—which went through Hull—declined noticeably;[80] while John Wilson, a Leeds linen manufacturer, stopped buying foreign yarn in 1782 as a consequence of 'The additional Duties lately laid on all dry Goods imported together with the high Freights'.[81] The rise in seamen's wages would also

---

[75] See *Journals of the House of Commons*, xxxvii. 34; *The Private Papers of John, Earl of Sandwich*, ed. G. R. Barnes and J. H. Owen (4 vols., London, 1932–8), i. 423. On the other hand, there were probably fewer ships built at Hull than in previous and subsequent wars. See J. J. Sheahan, *History of the Town and Port of Kingston-upon-Hull* (2nd edn. Beverley, [1866]), 367–8, where vessels are listed for 1739–74 and 1803–15.

[76] The journal of Marmaduke Strother, a Hull clothier, refers to a privateer of twenty guns: BL, Egerton MS 2479, fo. 24.   [77] Jackson, *Hull*, 133.

[78] Strother's journal, BL, Egerton MS 2479, fo. 28. Bine seems to have been involved in shipping Dutch goods from Ostend for Boulton & Fothergills of Birmingham—even after the Dutch had become belligerents. See Birmingham City Archives, Matthew Boulton Papers, MBP 143, p. 547.

[79] David J. Starkey, *British Privateering Enterprise in the Eighteenth Century* (Exeter, 1900), 200, 221.

[80] C. C. Owen, *The Development of Industry in Burton upon Trent* (Chichester, 1978), app. 8, p. 203.

[81] Leeds Archives, John Wilson Papers, W/13/11, John Wilson & Sons to John and Daniel Lankenau, 17 Apr. 1782.

have put a dampener on trade: Hull mariners joined the navy, either as volunteers or through the efforts of the press-gangs, and this must have created a labour shortage.[82] The number of ships paying dock duties fell year by year from 1,012 in 1775 to 811 in 1779. Thereafter the recovery was only slight and faltering; not until 1786 was the 1775 level surpassed.[83] Hull's whaling fleet contracted even more dramatically: the twelve vessels based in the port in 1775 had shrunk to a mere three in 1781. Only with the coming of the peace was there any significant reversal of the downward trend.[84] Another indication of the difficulties experienced is the upward trajectory of the poor rates. After having remained steady since 1773, they rose in 1778, 1779, 1780, and 1781. By 1783 the assessment was 73% higher than ten years earlier.[85]

If the decline in trade and its consequences brought the war home to the people of Hull, the danger of an attack on the town itself made the conflict seem still more immediate. In November 1778 the inhabitants were thrown 'into a great Consternation' when an enemy privateer appeared in the mouth of the Humber. The mayor urgently requested further naval protection, and permission was given by the governor of the citadel to redeploy some of the cannon on the artillery ground.[86] The next year, the town was still more alarmed. That September John Paul Jones, with a small French and American force, was spotted off the Yorkshire coast. Jones had already established his reputation as a daring commander, willing to attack targets on land as well as at sea, and the deputy town clerk, Edward Codd, wrote immediately to Lord Weymouth requesting 'a Speedy Supply of Artillery and Small Arms' and asking permission for the mayor to appoint officers from amongst the townsmen willing to help defend the port and citadel.[87] The emergency passed when Jones and his squadron, having successfully engaged two Royal Navy vessels off Filey, sailed away with their prizes.

At this point, Rockingham intervened to further his influence in the town. Arriving in Hull when the alarm was at its height, he

---

[82] O'Hara sent regular reports to the admiralty of the number of men he had raised, but he searched far and wide, and even men impressed in Hull were not necessarily Hull mariners. See ADM 1/2248–9. We know from ships' musters, however, that Hull seamen joined the navy's vessels. There were at least four of them e.g. among the new entrants on the *Prince George* in Feb. and Mar. 1778: ADM 1/8205.   [83] Jackson, *Hull*, 344.

[84] Ibid. 417.   [85] Ibid. 428.

[86] Hull RO, Borough Records, BRL 1290, 1292–3. See also *York Courant*, 17 Nov. 1778.   [87] SP 41/33, fo. 111.

addressed a hastily convened public meeting. His 'chief object', he explained afterwards to his wife, 'was to persuade them—that *Govt* had *neglected them* & perhaps that they themselves had been too *flattering* & too *Courtly* in their late Addresses &c &c'.[88] To drive home his message, Rockingham offered to provide, at his own expense, cannon for the town's protection. He had already ordered six eighteen-pounders from Walker of Rotherham, he told the mayor on 7 October, and they could be delivered in less than three weeks.[89] Although Rockingham's offer was given official sanction by the government,[90] neither the corporation nor Trinity House was inclined to accept. Indeed, the mayor sought to turn their refusal to the town's advantage, by using it to encourage government to respond more positively to Hull's needs. The corporation had declined Rockingham's gift, the mayor informed Weymouth, 'as they have that Confidence in Government as to rest their Security and defence entirely on their attention'.[91] This confidence was not wholly justified by events—when the town called for improved defences after the Dutch joined the war, floating batteries were promptly promised, but several months later Wilberforce was still pressing for 'the immediate Execution of the Orders which have been given for putting the Town of Hull in a better State of Defence'.[92]

Even so, Rockingham's intervention had clearly failed to give him any political advantage. In the 1780 general election Hartley, who was associated with Rockingham's party, lost his seat. The result, admittedly, should not be interpreted simply as an affirmation of support for the government and the rejection of a pro-American. Manners was relatively secure as a long-serving member with strong local and ministerial backing; the real contest was between Hartley and Wilberforce, and Wilberforce entered the fray with considerable advantages, namely his local connections and a deep purse—he spent around £9,000 on his election.[93] But there was surely some truth to Hartley's claim that his opposition to the American war was an important factor—even before polling began he told the Duke of Portland of his fears 'that I have lost Hull in America, & by opposition

---

[88] Sheffield Archives, Rockingham MSS, R 1/1849.
[89] Hull RO, Borough Records, BRL 1386/11.
[90] Sheffield Archives, Rockingham MSS, R 1/1852a.   [91] SP 41/33, fo. 158A.
[92] Hull RO, Borough Records, BRL 1386/80, 87, 100. See also ADM 1/5118/21, fo. 564.
[93] Namier and Brooke, *History of Parliament*, iii. 636.

to the present system of Ministry'.[94] While a third of the loyal addressers of 1775 were still prepared to give one of their votes to Hartley, only one Anglican clergyman voted for him in 1780, compared with three out of five in 1774.[95] Not a single subscriber of 1775 favoured him—all but one of those who voted in 1780 opted for Manners and Wilberforce, and the exception, Henry Broadley, plumped for Wilberforce.[96] After the election, Rockingham wrote that he had 'no expectation that Mr. Hartley would succeed at Hull; some of our friends there had long said so'.[97] It would seem that it was not so much Wilberforce's superior spending power that cost Hartley his seat, as Hartley's own reputation as an outspoken— indeed, obsessive—opponent of the American war, which had turned Hull's voters against him long before the election was called.

The new MP, ironically, was soon to reveal his own hostility to the conflict across the Atlantic. After news of Yorktown reached Britain, Wilberforce became a regular supporter of the opposition. Still more ironically, Hartley was returned unopposed in the by-election of June 1782 that followed the death of Manners. But the corporation seems to have remained determinedly loyal to Lord North to the end, and ill-disposed to his successors. When Shelburne sent out his proposals for a reformed popular militia in May 1782, a meeting in Hull dismissed the scheme as 'impracticable';[98] yet only a few weeks later the corporation—as if to snub the new administration's initiative—launched a subscription to raise its own volunteer corps.[99]

In summary, then, the war, though it brought problems and detrimentally affected the commerce of the town, did not stimulate any significant opposition to North's government. The leading political forces—the corporation and Trinity House—remained steadfastly loyal. Indeed, Rockingham's attempt to exploit wartime discomfort seems to have backfired. Hartley's defeat owed much to local factors, but his well-known sympathy for the Americans almost certainly told against him, giving the 1780 poll a party flavour largely missing from contests in Hull since 1754.

[94] Nottingham University Library, Portland Papers, PWF 4875.
[95] Bradley, *Religion, Revolution and English Radicalism*, 295.
[96] Cf. Hull RO, WM/6, 'Subscription' and *A Copy of the Poll* (Hull, [1780]).
[97] HMC, 15th Report, app. pt. V, *Foljambe MSS* (London, 1897), 156.
[98] HO 42/205, fo. 171. See also Hull RO, WM/7/1.   [99] Hull RO, WM/7/6.

Lichfield

Thomas Pennant, the Welsh travel writer, passed through Lichfield towards the end of the American war. In a brief description in one of his publications he highlighted the city's 'considerable manufacture of sail-cloth, and small manufacture of saddle-cloths and tammies'.[100] A more recent and authoritative account adds coachmaking to the list of local trades.[101] But Lichfield could hardly be termed 'industrial', especially when compared with other Staffordshire towns such as Wolverhampton, Walsall, and Burton upon Trent. The cathedral dominated Lichfield's skyline, and gave a distinctive tone to life in the city. Dr Johnson, Lichfield's most famous son, may have found it dull after London ('this place grows more and more barren of entertainment', he complained during one of his visits),[102] but the city was widely regarded as a social centre. Indeed, Lichfield's multitude of retail outlets, and particularly the large number of bookshops, suggest that its primary function was to service the requirements of the leisured classes—an impression reinforced by the importance attached to the race meetings held at nearby Whittington Heath, which were accompanied with the usual round of dinners, concerts, and balls. Pennant's thumbnail sketch came nearer to capturing the flavour of Lichfield when he wrote of it as 'a place of great passage'.[103] To cater for the large number of travellers, the city had more than fifty inns, and this with a population in 1781 of less than 4,000.[104]

Lichfield was a parliamentary borough. The Anson and Gower families, local landowners of considerable standing, divided the representation between themselves from 1762. The hold of the two families might not have been quite as firm as it appeared from the outside. In 1775 Matthew Boulton lobbied Lord Gower for a government contract to be given to a nail-making firm owned by John Barker, a Lichfield banker, arguing that if the contract was secured Gower need never again fear any opposition in Lichfield elections, 'as Mr. Barkers consequence in those matters was more considerable than any other individual'.[105] But in fact no opposition

---

[100] *The Journey from Chester to London* (London, 1782), 114.

[101] VCH, *Staffordshire*, vol. xiv (Oxford, 1990), 21, 122–4.

[102] *The Letters of Samuel Johnson*, ed. Bruce Redford (5 vols., Oxford, 1992–4), iii. 49.

[103] Pennant, *Journey*, 114.   [104] VCH, *Staffordshire*, xiv. 125.

[105] William Salt Library, S.MS.478, Boulton to Barker, 20 Oct. 1775.

of any kind manifested itself either to Gower or to the Ansons in this period. George Anson and Thomas Gilbert, Lord Gower's land agent, were returned unopposed in 1774 and again in 1780. Gilbert generally supported Lord North, and was in favour of the war until February 1782, when he voted for Conway's motions to suspend operations in America. Anson, by contrast, was a Rockinghamite who had consistently opposed North's American policy. The city itself, however, had strong Tory traditions, and these seem to have found expression in the corporation's loyalty to government and preference in 1775 for a hard line against the colonists. That September, when the corporation was approached to join an association against North's administration, Charles Simpson, the town clerk, wrote to Lord Dartmouth, the city's recorder, expressing the corporation's disapproval of the proposed association and its willingness to contribute by all possible means to the suppression of the rebellion.[106] The next month the corporation formalized these sentiments by sending a loyal address to the crown.[107]

Thereafter, one could be forgiven for thinking that the war impinged remarkably little on genteel and somewhat somnolent Lichfield. The city had raised a volunteer company in 1745, at the time of the Jacobite uprising; in 1798, during the struggle against revolutionary France, a military association was formed, about 150 strong; and in 1803 a corps of 450 volunteers was established when invasion again threatened.[108] But in the American war Lichfield saw no need to form any volunteer unit, and in 1782 the city politely declined to cooperate with Shelburne's popular militia proposals.[109] It might seem appropriate that the commonplace book of Richard Greene, a local surgeon, which set out to record 'all the Mighty Events that have happened . . . in the City of Lichfield', has no entries for the American war period, save one for 6 August 1783, when 'The great window of the South Cross Aile of the Cathed [was] taken down in Order to be rebuilt'.[110]

Closer inspection reveals that the conflict intruded much more

---

[106] HMC, *Dartmouth MSS* (3 vols., London, 1887–96), ii. 376–7.
[107] HO 55/8/9. See also Lichfield RO, Corporation Records, D 77/5/2, Hall Book, vol. 2, fo. 182.
[108] VCH, *Staffordshire*, xiv. 24; *A Short Account of the Ancient and Modern State of the City and Close of Lichfield* (Lichfield, 1819), 77.   [109] HO 42/205, fos. 161–4.
[110] Lichfield RO, D 173, fos. 77–9.

than Green's highly selective account suggests.[111] Lichfield had very few conspicuous opponents of the war, perhaps because, as Jabez Maud Fisher wrote in 1776, the city was 'remarkable for having no Dissenters in the whole Place'.[112] At any rate, opponents of the conflict with the Americans lacked effective leadership. Lichfield's literati, while far from enthusiastic about coercion of the colonists, were unable, or unwilling, to raise the standard of opposition.[113] Erasmus Darwin, the physician, scientist, and writer, might have been pro-American, but he kept his views very much to himself.[114] He seems to have discussed the war only occasionally ('I never talk'd so much politics in my life before', he claimed at the end of his one recorded contemporary musing on the subject), and while clearly disliking violence on principle, he succeeded in arguing himself inside out on the merits of this particular conflict.[115] Anna Seward, the poet, looked back in 1801 on the American war as 'inscribed [with] injustice and tyranny'.[116] At the time itself, however, she was more ambivalent. Her early sympathy for the colonists was tempered by hostility towards the American alliance with the French ('our mutual Foe!') and above all by Washington's execution of her friend, the British officer and alleged spy John André.[117]

Supporters of the war, by contrast, were provided with clear and strong leadership, not just by the corporation, but more significantly by the city's clerical establishment. The loyal address from Staffordshire, which roundly condemned both 'an ungrateful and unnatural Rebellion in America' and those in the mother country who had 'encouraged and abetted it', was signed by two of the Lichfield

[111] Greene himself was surgeon to the Staffordshire militia, and by his brother's reckoning kept busy on militia business for much of the war. See *Correspondence of the Reverend Joseph Greene*, ed. Levi Fox (Dugdale Society Publications, vol. xxiii, London, 1965), 118, 130.

[112] *An American Quaker in the British Isles: The Travel Journals of Jabez Maud Fisher*, ed. Kenneth Morgan (Oxford, 1992), 251.

[113] For a recent account of Lichfield's cultural elite see John Brewer, *The Pleasures of the Imagination: English Culture in the Eighteenth Century* (London, 1997), ch. 15.

[114] Desmond King-Hele, *Doctor of Revolution: The Life and Genius of Erasmus Darwin* (London, 1977), 97, says that Darwin 'usually suppressed his own political opinions to avoid offending patients'. See also pp. 15, 150, 217, where Darwin's sympathy for the Americans is emphasized.

[115] *The Letters of Erasmus Darwin*, ed. Desmond King-Hele (Cambridge, 1981), 94–5. Darwin went on to contribute £20 to the Staffordshire subscription to strengthen the army in 1779: *Aris's Birmingham Gazette*, 27 Sept. 1779.

[116] Hesketh Pearson, *The Swan of Lichfield* (London, 1936), 236.

[117] *Monody on Major André* (Lichfield, 1781), 22–4.

Cathedral canons, James Falconer and Thomas Seward, Anna Seward's father.[118] The dean, Dr John Addingbrook, subscribed £10 to the fund to support the widows and orphans of British soldiers killed in America.[119] The churchwardens of St Mary's regularly paid for the church's bells to be rung to celebrate British victories—the capture of New York, the storming of Fort Washington, the repulsing of the French and Americans at Savannah, the seizure of Omoa from the Spanish, and Rodney's victory over the Spanish fleet.[120] The bishop of Lichfield and Coventry provided £1,000 for the Staffordshire subscription of 1779 to help recruit men for the army, and at least three other Lichfield clergymen also contributed—Addingbrook's successor as dean, the Revd Baptist Proby; Canon Seward; and John B. Pearson, the perpetual curate of St Michael's.[121]

The number of Lichfield men who joined the armed forces remains unknown, though we should note that recruiting parties were operating in the area and would almost certainly have tried to raise men in the city,[122] and that Lichfield was obliged to contribute its quota of men for the Staffordshire militia. For most townspeople, however, the war probably came home only when taxes rose and Lichfield became crowded with military visitors. On top of increases in national taxation, such as house duty, stamps, and excises, local demands also became greater. In St Michael's parish, the poor rate went up from an average of £132 per annum in 1774–7 to £157 in 1778–82, reaching a peak of £191. 19s. 11d. in 1782 itself.[123] The overseer's accounts for St Mary's parish suggest that a significant portion of such increases was attributable to the need from 1778 to support the families of embodied militiamen and to cover miscellaneous other militia expenses.[124]

From 1778, too, Lichfield became the temporary home to a multitude of military personnel. It might be supposed that the prospect of

[118] HO 55/21/40.   [119] Public Advertiser, 29 Nov. 1775.

[120] Lichfield RO, St Mary's Parish Records, D 20/4/3, Churchwarden's Accounts, 6 Nov. 1776, 2 Jan. 1777, 22 Dec. 1779, 14 Feb. 1780. According to Aris's Birmingham Gazette, 26 June 1780, news of the surrender of Charleston was greeted with 'incessant bell ringing, and the Evening with universal Illumination'.

[121] Aris's Birmingham Gazette, 27 Sept. 1779.

[122] See WO 4/96, p. 354; WO 1/1008, pp. 37–40.

[123] Stebbing Shaw, The History and Antiquities of Staffordshire (2 vols., London, 1798–1801), i, sub. 'Lichfield', 342.

[124] Lichfield RO, St Mary's Parish Records, D 173, fos. 77–9.

increased spending would have pleased those with goods to sell. Individual soldiers and militiamen might not have had much to spend, but their officers purchased both for themselves and for their units. Captain Richard Dyott's company of the Staffordshire militia, for instance, seems to have injected small but no doubt useful doses of cash into the local economy, boosting the beer sales of the city's publicans in particular.[125] But there are indications that at least some of the townspeople greeted the incomers with less than enthusiasm. In 1777 the corporation had been reluctant to allow the Staffordshire militia to come to Lichfield for its annual training, for fear that the burden of looking after any militiamen who were taken ill would fall on the city's ratepayers.[126] Similar concerns might have been influential when the military influx increased significantly in 1778. That French prisoners were amongst the arrivals probably added to local misgivings. True, this was not altogether a new experience—French prisoners had been accommodated in earlier wars—and there is some evidence of fraternization: Darwin employed one of the captive officers to teach French to his children.[127] But Darwin can hardly be said to have typified local attitudes. As we have seen, he took a decidedly detached and rather complicated view of the war, and was apparently unaffected by the prevalent xenophobia. For many townspeople the presence of the French was probably the cause of uneasiness, even anxiety. Symptomatic of this nervousness, surely, was the arrest in 1779 of a man thought to be employed by the French government to help rescue prisoners held in Lichfield and other neighbouring towns.[128]

The French were only part of the problem, though. Most of the military that came to Lichfield were wearing British redcoats rather than French white. The extent to which they intruded on local life can be glimpsed in the parish records. The register of births for St Mary's, for instance, includes entries for several children of militiamen and the son of an officer in the newly raised Ninety-sixth Foot;[129] whilst amongst those buried at St Michael's were 'John Hays a soldier belonging to the York. Volunteers', Jonathan

---

[125] Staffordshire RO, Dyott Papers, D 661/21/5, Dyott's accounts, e.g. 5 Nov. 1780.
[126] Lichfield RO, Corporation Records, D 77/5/2, Hall Book, vol. 2, fo. 100.
[127] *The Selected Letters of Josiah Wedgwood*, ed. Ann Finer and George Savage (London, 1965), 246–7.   [128] SP 37/13, Simpson to [Weymouth], 2 Dec. 1779.
[129] Lichfield RO, D 20/1/3, e.g., 24 May 1778; 4 Jan., 22 Aug., 10 Dec. 1779; 3 June 1780; 2, 6, 23 May 1782.

Houndsall, who was simply described as 'a soldier', and an unnamed 'Soldier in Captain North's Company'.[130] But the impact of the military becomes much more obvious when one reads the appeals to Dartmouth to use his influence with the secretary at war to relieve the overcrowding. In December 1779 William Inge, a local magistrate, wrote in support of the discontented city innkeepers; and the town clerk pointed out that even the smaller of Lichfield's taverns were obliged to accommodate at least ten military guests, and the larger, 'The George' and 'The Swan', had taken in seventy and sixty-five respectively.[131]

Brentwood and its Vicinity

Brentwood in Essex was little more than a village when the American war began. By 1784 it was still not sufficiently populous to merit an entry in *Bailey's British Directory*.[132] Yet from 1778 this small town had to come to terms with the sudden arrival on its doorstep, so to speak, of a military body comparable in size to the population of contemporary Hull or Coventry. Warley Common, parts of which were visible from Brentwood,[133] was used as a camp site in the summer and autumn months of 1778, 1779, and 1781. In its first year it was home to about 11,000 soldiers and militiamen, not to mention associated womenfolk and children, plus other camp followers.[134] The sheer scale of the camp—second only to Coxheath in Kent—meant that it was bound to exert a local influence that was both multifarious and profound.

For the gentry and nobility of the neighbourhood, the camp offered the chance to widen their social circle. Invitations to call, to take tea, or to dine, were dispatched to suitable officers in the militia or regulars. Several officers, for example, dined with Lord Petre, a Catholic peer keen to promote the interests of his coreligionists, whose estate was close to the camp.[135] And for local

---

[130] Lichfield RO, D 27/1/4.   [131] HMC, *Dartmouth MSS*, iii. 249.

[132] The nearest towns to be mentioned were Chelmsford and Romford.

[133] *The Correspondence of Jeremy Bentham*, ed. T. L. S. Sprigge et al. (10 vols. to date, London and Oxford, 1968–), ii. 153.

[134] John Houlding, *Fit for Service: The Training of the British Army, 1715–1795* (Oxford, 1981), 330.

[135] Essex RO, Petre Family Papers, D/DP F332/2, Petre's Diary, 4 Oct. 1778.

people of all ranks, the presence of significant bodies of troops, training and even conducting elaborate manoeuvres, made the camp an obvious source of fascination. Warley was drawing 'vast crowds' within a few weeks of its establishment—up to 20,000 on one Sunday in July 1778, according to the local press.[136] Many of these spectators, to be sure, came from London, which was close enough for a daytrip. But there were probably many people from the neighbourhood in the crowds, or at least from elsewhere in the county. An inspection by an eminent figure naturally added to local interest. In October 1778, when the king and queen went to Warley, John Crosier, a miller and farmer from Malden, travelled more than twenty miles to the camp to catch a glimpse of the royals and to witness 'a sham fight which was conducted in a very masterly manner and gave entertainment to one of the most innumerable multitudes I ever saw'.[137]

Some of the visitors were also attracted, no doubt, by less elevated residents of this tented town. Prostitutes plied their trade within the camp, catering for civilian sightseers as well as military personnel. Young Crosier, after another trip to Warley with two friends in September 1779, referred cryptically in his diary to 'adventures!'.[138] We can surmise, too, that other local people were less impressed, and saw such activities as confirmation of their worst fears about the moral dangers posed by the camp. Local complaints probably lay behind the attempt made by a parish constable to remove 'two Disorderly Women' from Warley—an attempt resisted by soldiers of the Monmouth militia, a unit that was upbraided by its commanding officer after several of the men caught 'the Foul Disease'.[139]

Venereal complaints were not the only public health problems associated with the camp. Although strenuous efforts were made by the military authorities to avoid insanitary conditions, significant numbers of the residents were likely to be laid low at any given time with bilious attacks. Warley and Coxheath were said to be 'very sickly' in November 1779, just before the camps broke up and the troops went into winter quarters.[140] It can hardly have been possible

---

[136] *Chelmsford Chronicle*, 17 July 1778.
[137] A. F. J. Brown (ed.), *Essex People 1780–1900 from their Diaries, Memoirs and Letters* (Chelmsford, 1972), 19.
[138] Essex RO, D/DQS 140, 'Memoirs relative to the life of John Crosier', 8.
[139] East Sussex RO, ABE/D 560/17, Monmouth Militia Order-book, 30 Apr. 1779.
[140] PRO, Chatham Papers, 30/8/25, fo. 206.

to confine such outbreaks to the camp itself; with so many visitors travelling to and fro, illness was bound to spread to neighbouring communities. This facet of the impact of the camp is, of course, difficult to measure. But it may be noteworthy that there was a marked increase in the number of burials recorded in the parish registers of the churches near Warley camp. This trend is discernible in the registers of St Peter, Little Warley, and St Thomas of Canterbury, Brentwood.[141] But it takes on striking proportions when we concentrate on St Mary the Virgin in Great Warley (see Fig. 8.1).[142] For the years 1775–7, before the camp was established, the average number of burials per annum was 14.7; in 1779 there were seventy-six. True, many of these were military personnel from the camp, or their dependants; but thirty-two were unconnected with the army or militia, and most members of this group appear to have been parishioners. In 1779, in other words, the death rate in Great Warley was more than double the yearly average for 1775–7. In 1780 the number of civilian deaths dropped back to around the 1775–7 average, and it was only slightly higher in 1782; but, as we have seen, in both these years the camp at Warley was not in use, and the only troops present would probably have been those confined to the hospitals established in various barns and outbuildings and those quartered in Brentwood itself. In 1781, when the camp was re-formed, there was another surge, though nowhere near as great as in 1779.

A comparison with the situation in other areas of England demonstrates that the pattern of mortality in Great Warley cannot be dismissed as part of a general trend. In Sutton-cum-Duckmanton in Derbyshire, an average of seven burials per year took place in 1775–7, ten in 1779, and thirteen in 1781.[143] In Wotton in Surrey, the average number of burials for 1775–7 was 8.3. There were eleven in 1779 and nine in 1781. The peak wartime year was 1780, with fifteen. In Abinger, also in Surrey, the average for 1775–7 was 10.6; there were fifteen burials in 1779 and 1781, and 1780 was again the peak wartime year with seventeen.[144] In short, in all these parishes 1779 and 1781 saw an increase over the average for 1775–7, but nothing like as steep a rise as in Great Warley.

---

[141] Essex RO, D/P 66/1/2 and D/P 362/1/2.   [142] Ibid., D/P 195/1/2.

[143] Pamela Kettle and Philip Riden (eds.), *Sutton-cum-Duckmanton Parish Register* (Derbyshire Record Society, vol. xviii, Chesterfield, 1992), 87–90.

[144] *The Parish Registers of Abinger, Wotton, and Oakwood Chapel* (Surrey Record Society, vol. ix, London, 1927), 123–6, 212–15.

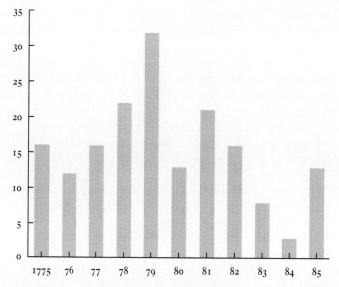

Fig. 8.1. Burials at St Mary the Virgin, Great Warley, 1775–1785. The totals exclude military personnel and their dependants

Source: Essex RO, D/P195/1/2

Another undesirable aspect of the presence of the camp was the damage to, and loss of, local property. At one end of the spectrum was the theft of fruit and vegetables, the unauthorized cutting-down of trees or pulling up of fences, and the shooting of rabbits on the Tower family estate at South Weald.[145] At the other was the killing of livestock and robbery on the highway.[146] But while such indiscipline led to a chorus of complaint from locals, the search for a solution to the problem seems to have benefited some of those who lived nearby. To keep their men in camp, commanding officers allowed the establishment of regular markets for the sale of fresh provisions to the troops. Local producers would presumably have required little encouragement; after all, Warley represented a considerable market, especially when its resident consumers were swelled by sightseers and other visitors. According to a local newspaper, beans, peas, cabbages, hot puddings and pies were all

---

[145] C. A. Markham, *The History of the Northamptonshire and Rutland Militia* (London, 1924), 19, 30, 31; East Sussex RO, ABE/D/560/17, Monmouth Militia Order-book, 5 May 1779.   [146] Markham, *History*, 21, 22–3.

sold at Warley by people who carried these items around with them, which suggests that such foodstuffs were freshly picked or prepared and brought straight to the camp.[147] We might also note that local brewers and distillers probably supplied a fair number of the drinking establishments that proliferated in and around the camp with the acquiescence, if not wholehearted approval, of the military authorities. At the reopening of Warley camp in the summer of 1779, it was calculated that there were 'one hundred and twenty eight houses (exclusive of the suttling houses within the lines) selling ale, beer and spiritous liquors without licence in the rear of the Camp'.[148]

Nor were the opportunities for local gain limited to the confines and immediate environs of the camp. The wives of soldiers and militiamen often supplemented the meagre pay of their husbands by taking in washing,[149] but there was still plenty of scope for local women to carry out the same service. 'The villagers wives round the country are employed in washing the officers linen', one report ran, 'and every garden looks like a bleaching ground'.[150] The officers also provided much business for local inns. The letters of Lord Althorp, a captain in the Northamptonshire militia, record numerous dinners in Brentwood;[151] while Lieutenant-Colonel Thomas Watson Ward of the Cambridgeshire regiment was one of a party of officers who attended a grand dinner at 'The Crown' in Brentwood when Lord Amherst came to Warley in October 1779.[152] Nor should we forget that visitors who came from many miles away often stayed overnight. Some, to be sure, were put up in the camp itself—Dr Johnson, calling to see his friend Bennet Langton, a captain in the North Lincolnshire militia, was accommodated in an officer's tent.[153] But it was probably more usual for visitors to sleep in Brentwood. When in September 1778 Althorp received a call from his kinsman Lord Charles Spencer, MP for Oxfordshire, and Frederick Montagu, another MP, his visitors stayed the night in one of the local inns, as had a party of Althorp's university friends who travelled from

---

[147] *Chelmsford Chronicle*, 7 Aug. 1778.   [148] WO 1/1009, p. 808.
[149] Northumberland RO, Ridley of Blagdon MSS, ZR1 30/4a, Accounts of Capt. John Ridley, provides an example from a regiment based in North America at this time.
[150] *Chelmsford Chronicle*, 7 Aug. 1778.
[151] BL, Althorp Papers, F 8, Althorp to his mother, 23–30 June 1778.
[152] BL, Hardwicke Papers, Add. MS 35660, fo. 229.
[153] *Boswell's Life of Johnson*, ed. George Birkbeck Hill and L. F. Powell (6 vols., Oxford, 1934–50), iii. 361.

Cambridge two months earlier.[154] Somewhat surprisingly, the number of licensed premises in Brentwood appears to have remained static while Warley Common was used as a camp site,[155] but the existing publicans must have had a profitable few years.[156] Other local people benefited, too. When the king and queen visited Warley in October 1778, they stayed not at Brentwood, but at Lord Petre's country house, Thorndon Place. Petre's expenditure on his guests, who were put up for two days, exceeded £1,000. Much of this, admittedly, was spent on goods purchased from London; but a significant proportion of the money found its way into the pockets of local women who were employed to help in the kitchens, local farmers who provided literally gallons of cream, and local shopkeepers like Thomas Davis, a grocer and tallow chandler of Brentwood.[157]

Berkshire

Eighteenth-century Berkshire was an overwhelmingly agricultural county. While textiles were produced in towns such as Newbury, Abingdon, Reading, and Wokingham, and breweries were to be found in most of the urban centres, the economy revolved around farming. Indeed, Reading, the chief town, was primarily notable for its corn market and Abingdon dispatched large quantities of

---

[154] BL, Althorp Papers, F 8, Althorp to his mother, 7–13 July, 27 Sept. 1778.

[155] Essex RO, Q/RL v. 32–6, Alehouse Recognizances, Chafford Hundred, 1775–82. It should be remembered, of course, that the number of unlicensed premises in or near the camp was considerable.

[156] The picture was not entirely rosy, however. When the camp broke up, and the troops were dispersed into winter quarters, publicans were obliged to accommodate soldiers at set rates. The innkeepers of Brentwood, for instance, had to cope with the 45th Foot in the months before the reopening of Warley camp in the summer of 1781 (BL, Liverpool Papers, Add. MSS 38438, fo. 10, 38439, fo. 9) and neighbouring towns, such as Romford, were similarly burdened at one time or another.

[157] Essex RO, Petre Family Papers, D/DP F332/2 and 5–37a. Petre himself, it should perhaps be added, had particular reason to be thankful for the presence of the military in his neighbourhood. Not only did it give him an opportunity to entertain the king and queen and therefore press the case of his co-religionists, it also enabled Thorndon Place to receive protection in June 1780, when it was feared that the Gordon Riots would inspire acts of violence against Catholics outside London. There were not many troops in the vicinity in the summer of 1780, because, as we have seen, Warley was not being used as a camp site. But a contingent of the Pembrokeshire militia, which was quartered at Brentwood, was posted at Petre's house 'to resist the Attempts of the Mobs'. NLW, Owen and Colby Papers, 436 and 438.

processed malt to London. The downlands were largely given over to sheep grazing, and the Vale of White Horse, Berkshire's fertile heartland, was famous for its cereal crops, beans, and the fattening of cattle. When the American conflict began, it seems that considerably less than half the land in the county was enclosed; forest—mainly to the east of the River Loddon—common fields and downs accounted for the rest.[158]

Berkshire's farmers and landowners seem not to have suffered acutely during the war. In 1779 Edward Loveden Loveden, apparently undeterred by the credit crisis and high rates of interest prevalent at the time, began the construction of the great mansion at Buscot Park near the Thames.[159] The more humble Badcock family, farmers of Radley, were able to gain a good income from their sale of crops, particularly in 1777–8 and 1782–3, when prices were high due to generally poor harvests but Berkshire fared better than other areas.[160] James Roberts of Steventon Farm was similarly able to send large quantities of wheat and barley to nearby Abingdon, and his accounts convey no impression of crisis; nor, indeed, of any great change in routine.[161] Sources such as these suggest that wartime developments impinged remarkably little on life in rural Berkshire.

Yet, if we look elsewhere, there are signs that the conflict had a disruptive effect on economic life. The number of bankruptcies in the county rose noticeably in the years 1777–81.[162] Enclosure activity seems to have halted abruptly in 1781 and not resumed until after the war. Given that this halt to enclosure activity coincided with rising wheat prices in 1781–3,[163] it can hardly be explained by price movements—a fall in prices might be expected to reduce the rate of land enclosure, while a rise in cereal prices might, by the same reasoning, act as the trigger to enclosure initiatives.[164] If crop price considerations were not the primary factor, it seems likely that government borrowing was deflecting investment from the

---

[158] VCH, *Berkshire*, ed. P. H. Ditchfield and William Page (4 vols., London, 1906–24), i. 394–6, 407–8; ii. 219, 221.

[159] Berkshire RO, Loveden Papers, D/ELV E1, building accounts, Buscot Park.

[160] Reading University Library, BER 13/3/1, Farm Account-book.

[161] Ibid., BER 16/1/1.

[162] See the lists of bankrupts regularly produced in the contemporary periodical press: for instance, *Gentleman's Magazine*, 45–53 (1775–83).

[163] See ibid. for monthly listings of cereal prices in Berkshire and other counties.

[164] See above, Ch. 2.

land.[165] Even Berkshire farmers like the semi-literate Thomas Johnson of Hampstead Norreys were encouraged by high interest rates and attractive discounts to tie up resources in government stock: Johnson purchased £350-worth of the new four per cents in 1780 (paying only £255. 18s. 9d. for them) and made further investments during the remainder of the war and thereafter.[166] And in some areas of the county poor rates rose significantly, in part due to the expenses associated with the embodying of the militia and support for militiamen's families. In Tilehurst, near Reading, for instance, the overseer's accounts include frequent references to militia expenditure,[167] while in St Nicholas, Abingdon, payments to militiamen's families, both in the parish and elsewhere, seem to have made a notable contribution to the poor rate.[168] In Peasemore parish on the Berkshire downs £208 was expended in 1778, compared with only £81 in 1774.[169] Newbury's poor relief disbursements similarly rose from £1,833 in 1773–4 to £2,432 in 1782–3.[170]

The manpower demands of the armed forces also brought the war home to Berkshire. Boatmen on the Thames and others employed in riverine activities were liable for naval impressment and ships' musters make occasional reference to sailors from Berkshire, such as the Reading man on the *Cumberland* in June 1778.[171] But as an inland county Berkshire contributed few men compared with the coastal districts. The marines, however, were another matter, and we know that they sent recruiting parties to Reading.[172] Captain Bolton Power of the Twentieth Foot was also there in 1779, and enlisted some pardoned convicts in the gaol;[173] in 1782 Captain John Moore of the newly raised One-hundred and fourth Foot was advertising for men in one of the local newspapers.[174] In Abingdon, a recruiting party of the Forty-eighth Foot clashed violently with townspeople, leading the secretary at war to recommend to the commanding officer the

---

[165] See the chronological list of inclosure awards and agreements in Berkshire RO's guide to collections.
[166] Berkshire RO, D/EX 62/2, Account-book of Thomas Johnson, 11 May, 8 and 28 Nov. 1780; 13 Feb. 1781; 20 Nov. 1782; 18 Nov. 1783; 15 Jan. and 30 June 1784; etc.
[167] Ibid., Tilehurst Parish Records, D/P 132/12/7.
[168] Ibid., Abingdon St Nicholas Parish Records, D/P 2/17/1.
[169] Ibid., Peasemore Parish Records, D/P 92/9/1.
[170] Ibid., Newbury Corporation Records, N/AP 3/1, 2, Overseers' Accounts.
[171] ADM 36/9026.   [172] WO 1/1004, p. 103.
[173] Ibid., pp. 415, 485; WO 4/106, p. 196; WO 4/107, p. 339.
[174] See above, Ch. 1.

withdrawal of the detachment, on the grounds that 'after what has passed', it was unlikely that 'you can expect any further success from Recruiting in Abingdon'.[175]

Military activity was evident in other senses, too. In August 1779, when invasion threatened, Lord Barrington, the former secretary at war, whose estate was in Berkshire, used his position as foreman of the grand jury of the Abingdon Assizes to launch a subscription for the defence of the county. Around 1,000 persons contributed and Barrington himself embodied about 240 volunteers in Shrivenham Hundred, in which his country house was located. The volunteers, whom Barrington described as 'Gentlemen, Clergymen and Day Labourers', wore a cockade in their hats, provided their own weapons, and assembled for target practice on Sundays.[176] These volunteers were far removed from an armed manifestation of the movement for reform that some radicals sought to promote. On the contrary, Barrington's association was a conservative response to the fear of disorder, and as such serves as a reminder of the diverse nature of volunteering in the American war. As he explained to his friend the Duke of Buckinghamshire, the lord-lieutenant of Ireland, a dread of the mob lay behind the association; with the outbreak of the war against Spain, Barrington believed that there would not be enough troops available in the county to preserve the public peace and so it was incumbent on property-owners to take the necessary steps themselves.[177]

Barrington's concern perhaps stemmed in part from the movement out of the county of the Berkshire militia. The regiment was embodied in May 1778, and after assembling at Reading set off for Coxheath. It returned home for the winter, but in early June 1779 marched out of the county again, this time for Warley camp.[178] Yet there was a good deal of compensatory movement into the county. Many of the towns were host to regulars or militia. The Oxfordshire militia was quartered in Reading in October and November 1778, then in Newbury until the end of May 1779.[179] The newly raised Eighty-ninth Foot was based in Newbury during the following

---

[175] WO 4/106, pp. 453–6.   [176] HO 42/205, fos. 136–7.
[177] NLI, Heron Papers, MS 13038, Barrington to Buckinghamshire, 29 Aug. 1779. See also Tony Hayter, *The Army and the Crowd in Mid-Georgian England* (London, 1978), 73.
[178] Berkshire RO, Neville and Aldworth Papers, D/EN F55/1, Diary of Richard Neville.
[179] *Jackson's Oxford Journal*, 3 Oct., 7 Nov. 1778; 17 April, 8 and 29 May 1779.

autumn,[180] and in 1782 the Dorsetshire militia was in Reading, the West Kents at Newbury, and the Cheshires in Abingdon and Wallingford. The presence of soldiers or militiamen offered opportunities for spectacular public celebrations at various points in the war. In January 1779, when the Berkshire militia was back home, the queen's birthday was marked by a parade in Reading and 'It having been reported in the neighbourhood that the cannon were to be fired . . . the number of people that were present is almost incredible'.[181] Rodney's victory at the Saints was greeted with still more excitement. The normal forms of celebration were pursued—in Reading 'the bells of the different churches were set a ringing';[182] at Abingdon there were 'Great Eluminations'[183]—but again the availability of the militia added a further dimension. At Newbury the West Kents fired a *feu de joie* in the market place and then the officers were entertained to dinner by the mayor and corporation.[184] A military presence could also be good for business: George Miller, a musical instrument maker of Windsor, sold his wares to Lord Fauconberg's Yorkshire fencible regiment while it was based in the county in October 1781.[185]

Even so, the military was not always welcome. Soldiers might add lustre to public festivities and stimulate local trade, but they could also cause public health problems. We have seen already that the presence of large numbers of the military and their dependants could have consequences for death rates in the vicinity of camps. But attempts to reduce the spread of disease could also create difficulties. In November 1778 Newbury's corporation protested at the inoculation of the Oxfordshire militia based in the town, arguing that the smallpox would spread to the residents and dampen local trade. The same issue was vexing the corporation in January 1780, when the Somerset militia was quartered in Newbury and Speenhamland, and again in March 1782 when the West Kents were being inoculated. In May 1783 the corporation was pressing for the permanent removal of the Seventh Dragoons, and

---

[180] Ibid., 23 Oct. 1779. The regiment went to the West Indies thereafter (BL, Liverpool Papers, Add. MS 38434, fo. 23).
[181] *Reading Mercury and Oxford Gazette*, 25 Jan. 1779.   [182] Ibid., 20 May 1782.
[183] Horsham Museum, Medwin Papers, MS 543/26.
[184] *Reading Mercury and Oxford Gazette*, 27 May 1782.
[185] North Yorkshire RO, Zetland (Dundas) MSS, ZNK X2/2/19.

alluded to 'the many grievances sustained by this Borough during the War'.[186]

But the American conflict's most obvious impact was on the county's politics. Berkshire returned nine MPs; two for the county, one for Abingdon, and two each for New Windsor, Reading, and Wallingford. On the eve of the war, the parliamentary representation was divided almost evenly between government and opposition supporters. The main electoral influence in the county was the joint interest of Baron Craven and the Earl of Abingdon, both of whom were prominent and enthusiastic oppositionists. Craven and Abingdon effectively nominated the MPs for the shire, but elsewhere they were less dominant. In Abingdon borough, the Earl was high steward, yet despite his efforts, and those of the town's Dissenters, John Mayor had won the seat in the 1774 general election with support of government and the corporation. Wallingford also failed to succumb to the Earl's influence, even though here, too, he was high steward. A venal borough with an electorate of about 200, Wallingford had as its representatives John Cator, a Southwalk timber merchant, and Sir Robert Barker, a recently returned nabob. Both were government supporters. New Windsor's MPs were Admiral Keppel, a well-known oppositionist, and John Hussey Montagu, who, though returned with government backing in a by-election in 1772, by 1774 seems to have been in the opposition camp. Reading's representation was split. John Dodd, who had held one of the seats since 1755, received government money to help him secure re-election in 1774, while Francis Annesley, who topped the poll in that election, was a consistent critic of North's administration.[187]

In a sense, then, it would be wrong to suggest that the American war was the cause of party conflict in Berkshire. Such conflict already existed. In Abingdon, particularly, the contest was heated, not least because there was a significant body of Dissenters in the town.[188] A broadsheet published after the 1774 general election strongly attacked 'Jo Baptist and Jack Presbyter', and exulted that 'the *Elect* were not *elected*'; another depicted the rival candidates as

---

[186] Berkshire RO, Newbury Corporation Records, N/AC1/1/2, Minute-book, 565, 588, 617, 629.

[187] Namier and Brooke, *History of Parliament*, i. 208–13.

[188] James E. Bradley, 'Nonconformity and the Electorate in Eighteenth-Century England', *Parliamentary History*, 6 (1987), 239–41.

representatives of the 'Patriot' and 'Court' parties.[189] A poll book for the local elections of that year demonstrates a remarkable degree of disciplined party voting and a great consistency in political behaviour; many of those who declared themselves to be supporters of the war in 1775 are identifiable as adherents of the 'Court' party in 1774.[190] Elsewhere it seems very likely that the partisanship of Lords Craven and Abingdon, who occupied the extreme wing of their party, contributed to the contentious nature of Berkshire politics on the eve of the war. But we can say that the conflict across the Atlantic deepened the divisions and introduced a new level of acrimony. Terms of abuse such as the 'Jacobites' and the 'Americans' came into common use, and the editor of *Jackson's Oxford Journal* decided not to publish letters from the two sides because they were so 'replete with personal Invective'.[191]

In the autumn of 1775 government supporters started to send in loyal addresses, condemning the Americans and the opposition alike. An address was drawn up by the corporation of Maidenhead,[192] and another, praying that the almighty would 'disappoint the secret designs' of the king's enemies 'both at Home and Abroad', by the corporation of New Windsor.[193] The first of these was unsigned and the second bore the names only of the mayor, aldermen, bailiffs, and other members of the council. But Abingdon's address was signed by 115 persons.[194] Amongst them were the mayor and the borough MP, together with the rector of St Nicholas, the lecturer of St Helen's, the master of the grammar school, and various other members of the town's clerical establishment. Most of those who appended their names, however, appear to have been local tradesmen and manufacturers.[195] The county address attracted over 300 signatures.[196] Again, prominent churchmen were well represented —

---

[189] Berkshire RO, Preston MSS, D/EP 7/150, 'How are the Mighty Fallen!' and 02/4/1, 'Much a do about Nothing'.

[190] Ibid., Abingdon Borough Records, A/Eb 1. Cf. Abingdon's address and petition, discussed below. See also Bodleian Library, MS Top. Berks. d. 18, fo. 11, where John Payne, William Bowles, and James Rose are mentioned as supporters of Mayor at the time of his adoption as a candidate in Oct. 1773; all three went on to sign the town's loyal address in 1775.

[191] *Public Advertiser*, 29 Nov. 1775; *Jackson's Oxford Gazette*, 18 Nov. 1775.

[192] HO 55/10/4.   [193] HO 55/11/67; *London Gazette*, 2–5 Dec. 1775.

[194] HO 55/11/23; *London Gazette*, 28–31 Oct. 1775.

[195] Occupations are taken from *Bailey's British Directory . . . for the Year 1784* (4 vols., London, 1784), ii. 341–2, which is probably a reasonably accurate guide.

[196] HO 55/12/8; *London Gazette*, 18–21 Nov. 1775.

the archdeacon of Berkshire; three canons of Windsor; the rectors of Childrey, East Hendred, and East Lockinge; and the vicars of Sutton Courtney and St Giles, Reading. Leading political figures were there also, such as Lord Barrington; the MPs John Dodd and John Mayor; Arthur Vansittart, a former MP for the county; Richard Aldworth Neville of Stanlake and Billingbear, MP for Grampound in Cornwall; together with many well-known Berkshire names: James Stonehouse of Radley; Peniston Powney of Maidenhead; Clement Saxton of Abingdon; Edward Loveden Loveden of Buscot; Bartholomew Price, the county sheriff; and various members of the Pye family of Great Farringdon.

Opponents of the war were slower off the mark, but by the end of 1775 they were able to demonstrate a greater level of public support for their position. There were some disappointments—Newbury's corporation refused to accede to Lord Craven's request that the town submit an anti-war petition.[197] On the whole, however, the efforts of the opposition were fruitful. Wallingford produced a petition, signed by the mayor, aldermen burgesses, and principal inhabitants, which was critical of the addressers, referred to 'our Brethren in America', and called for the redress of colonial grievances. A petition from Abingdon was signed by 117 'of *the most respectable Inhabitants*'; 'many more would have signed', it was claimed, 'had they not before inadvertently signed the Corporation Address, deceived by the Misrepresentations of those who applied to them'. All the same, the Abingdon petition bore two more names than the town's address.[198] The county petition was still more of a triumph. With nearly 1,000 signatures it easily outshone the Berkshire address.[199] Opponents of the war, furthermore, argued again that weight of property as well as numbers was on their side. Whereas the addressers had relied on the signatures of the Abingdon tradesmen to inflate their numbers ('poor Fellows, Journeymen and 'Prentice Boys' according to one report)[200] it was claimed that none of the petitioners was 'below the dignity of a freeholder, and many of them persons of high distinction and great opulence'.[201] Considered

[197] Berkshire RO, Newbury Corporation Records, N/AC1/1/1, Minute-book, 511.

[198] *Jackson's Oxford Journal*, 25 Nov. 1775. For the role of the opposition nationally in helping with the Abingdon petition, see *The Correspondence of Edmund Burke*, ed. Thomas W. Copeland et al. (10 vols., Cambridge, 1958–78), iii. 234–5.

[199] HO 55/12/9.   [200] *Public Advertiser*, 29 Nov. 1775.

[201] *Jackson's Oxford Journal*, 25 Nov. 1775.

in these terms, it was indeed an impressive display. The Earl of Abingdon and Lord Craven naturally headed the long list, followed by such notables as Nathaniel Bayley, MP for Abingdon, 1770–4; Avery Tyrrell of Stanford in the Vale; Winchcombe Henry Hartley of Bucklebury; and Benjamin Tomkins, a wealthy Abingdon Dissenter.

The next trial of strength between the two parties was the by-election of February 1776, caused by the death of Christopher Griffith, one of the county MPs. Two candidates emerged: Winchcombe Henry Hartley and Richard Aldworth Neville. Neville's draft election address made no political points, and did not identify him with government,[202] while Hartley's campaign slogans ('Hartley & Independence—no placemen—Berks ever will be free') made no direct reference to the war. But America was the central issue. In a letter canvassing support for Hartley, Neville was attacked on the basis that 'His Vote is always given for carrying on a ruinous War against his fellow subjects in America'. Hartley, on the other hand, was described as 'an Enemy to these Measures'.[203] A meeting at Abingdon on 14 February of 'the Gentlemen of the Vale' resolved to support Neville.[204] Three days later, however, a meeting in Reading backed Hartley, as did another meeting at Abingdon on 21 February, where he was nominated by the Earl's brother, Captain the Hon. Peregrine Bertie, MP for Oxford and himself a noted opponent of the war.[205] Neville could see that he had little chance of success, and with Lord North opposed to his giving up his seat at Grampound, he decided not to pursue his candidacy. At this late stage, Henry James Pye was approached to stand for government, but, fearful of the likely outcome, he declined. Hartley was therefore returned without a formal contest.

After this major defeat, the friends of the administration seem to have lapsed into sullen silence for a time. But they had not given up. The next major clash came with the Yorkshire Association's attempt to coordinate a petitioning campaign in favour of economical reform. The divisions within Berkshire were again laid bare. Wallingford,

---

[202] Berkshire RO, Neville and Aldworth Papers, D/EN 020/1.
[203] Ibid., Hartley Russell Papers, D/EHy 044.
[204] *Jackson's Oxford Gazette*, 17 Feb. 1776.
[205] Ibid., 24 Feb. 1776. Bertie had refused to serve against the Americans, and resigned his command of the *Shannon* in 1776.

which had petitioned against the war in 1775, submitted a petition in favour of the reform of public expenditure and a reduction in the influence of the crown.[206] In Reading the mayor and corporation refused to call a meeting of the town to decide whether to support the Yorkshire Association;[207] a meeting nevertheless took place, as did one in Abingdon, at which the county freeholders supported the Yorkshire Association's proposals and registered their own hostility to the war.[208] Berkshire's loyalists were unwilling to accept this, and submitted their own 'Dissent' to parts of the county petition. The signatories to the 'Dissent' included many of those who had been loyal addressers in 1775—Barrington, R. A. Neville, Dodd, Mayor, Vansittart, Powney, Loveden, H. J. Pye.[209] And as if to emphasize its continued commitment to the war, the staunchly loyal corporation of Abingdon paid the bellringers of St John's Church for their services 'on the taking of Charlestown by the British Forces'. To celebrate victory over the French or Spaniards was politically uncontentious; but to ring church bells in praise of a triumph over the Americans was to make a clear political statement.[210]

The tensions generated by the war made their mark on the 1780 general election, although with mixed results.[211] In the county election there was again some effort to mount a challenge to the Craven-Abingdon interest, but this failed to make any headway and the sitting members were returned unopposed. 'We are quite peaceable in this County', Craven wrote contentedly to the Duke of Portland.[212] In Reading there was a contest, but no change in the split representation. Temple Luttrell, standing for the opposition, was an outsider and he failed to displace Dodd. Annesley, as in 1774,

---

[206] *Journals of the House of Commons*, xxxvii. 783. Wallingford continued to be supportive: see Wyvill, *Political Papers*, ii. 120.

[207] Berkshire RO, Reading Corporation Records, R/ACI/1/23, Diary, 28 Jan. 1780.

[208] *Jackson's Oxford Journal*, 5 Feb. 1780; *Journals of the House of Commons*, xxxvii. 606.

[209] *Jackson's Oxford Journal*, 22 Apr. 1780. The continuing political division was also reflected in the voting in the House of Commons on Dunning's motion. Those Berkshire MPs who were opposed to the war against the Americans—John Elwes, Hartley, Annesley, Keppel, and Montagu—all voted for the motion; while those who supported North's government and the prosecution of the American war—Dodd, Mayor, Barker, and Cator—all voted against. See *PH* xxi. 367, 371.

[210] Berkshire RO, Abingdon Corporation Records, A/ACa1, Minute-book, 19 Jan. 1781.

[211] The following account is heavily indebted to Namier and Brooke, *History of Parliament*, i. 208-13.

[212] Nottingham University Library, Portland Papers, PWF 3167.

topped the poll. Abingdon was the scene of another heated contest, but Mayor, supported by the corporation, easily beat off the threat posed by Thomas Wooldridge, a London alderman representing the opposition.[213] In Wallingford and New Windsor, however, the election brought change. Wallingford's corporation had made its views on the war and economical reform perfectly clear in 1775 and 1780, and these views were at odds with those of Cator and Barker, the sitting members. Barker decided not to stand in 1780, but Cator was keen to keep both seats for government and asked the ministry to provide him with a suitable running-mate. Another nabob, Richard Barwell, was accordingly put forward as a man with the requisite money to spend on winning over the borough's electorate. But the war had increased the political temperature in Wallingford, and two opposition candidates came forward—John Aubrey, who had been one of the town's MPs in the 1768–74 Parliament, and Chaloner Arcedeckne, a Suffolk gentleman with no obvious connection with the borough. Both men were backed by the Earl of Abingdon and no doubt by the corporation. Cator, who might have saved himself had he compromised with the Earl about the second seat, recognized the hopelessness of his situation and he and Barwell declined the poll.

If the opposition triumphed in Wallingford, administration was successful in New Windsor, where the bitterest and most controversial of polls took place. Montagu and Keppel, as two opposition members sitting for a constituency on the king's very doorstep, were perhaps bound to be put under pressure. The king was particularly averse to Keppel, who had become a hero of the opposition both in Parliament and beyond, but in the run-up to the election government had hopes of taking both seats. In the end, however, it was decided that Montagu was secure and administration's efforts were concentrated on toppling the admiral. Initially, the king saw Major-General William Phillips, imprisoned in America as part of Burgoyne's defeated army, as 'the properest and most acceptable candidate';[214] but Peniston Portlock Powney, one of the loyal addressers of 1775, who was a substantial property-owner in the Maidenhead area, came forward as the government's candidate. He was paid

---

[213] In Apr. 1780, Captain Bertie, adopting a racing metaphor, told a potential candidate for Abingdon that 'there is only one Villainous *Mare* to Start against you, if the course is good, you will certainly win, but if Dirty, the *Mare* (who is famous for going through thick & thin & Dirty Courses) will certainly overreach you' (Bodleian Library, MS Top. Berks. d. 18, fo. 28).   [214] BL, Abergavenny MS 252.

£2,600 from the king's own private account to help him with his election expenses, and George personally canvassed tradesmen in the town who were dependent on the castle. Keppel 'complained of undue Influence made Use of against him' in a speech before the poll began, adding that 'it was novel in its Kind, and could it be proved . . . struck at the very Root of the Constitution'.[215] Despite his national reputation, Keppel could not withstand the combined weight of the corporation and a particularly determined monarch; all the same, Powney beat him only by 174 votes to 158. Among those who voted against Keppel were those Windsor voters who had signed the loyal address five years earlier, including Richard Jephson, the Revd Edward Tew, and William Tyrrell.[216]

The war intruded again when John Dodd's death brought a by-election in Reading in February 1782. A fierce battle was anticipated. With North's government under much pressure, local opposition supporters were said to be determined to block a ministerial candidate. In the event there were two contestants: John Simeon, the recorder of Reading, and the seemingly ubiquitous R. A. Neville. Neville won comfortably, by 267 votes to 179. Given his role as candidate in the county by-election of February 1776, and the strong support he had expressed for the war in Parliament, Neville's success might be taken as an indication of the relative weakness of the opposition. But this would surely be a mistake. Lavish spending undoubtedly contributed to his victory, but Neville was shrewd enough to know that a deep purse was not sufficient to guarantee that he would win. A gesture to the opposition was necessary, and Neville made it in fulsome terms when he pledged henceforth to vote against the continuation of the American war.

Strabane

Located twelve miles south-south-east of Londonderry, on the east bank of the River Mourne, Strabane was essentially a product of the Protestant plantation of Ulster in the early seventeenth century. The

---

[215] *Jackson's Oxford Journal*, 16 Sept. 1780. After the election, the opposition hoped that the doubtful tactics of the king could help them: 'Kepple has good Grounds to petition', Lord Edward Bentinck wrote on 11 Sept., '& it is thought Powney will be thrown out if he does' (Nottingham University Library, Portland Papers, PWF 652).

[216] Compare the Berkshire address and the New Windsor printed *Poll*.

original settlement was transformed by the influx of English and Scottish colonists, and by 1622 there were more than 200 British adult males in the town.[217] The population by around 1780 has been estimated at about 5,000 persons,[218] many of whom—though precisely how many is unknown—must have been Protestants. There had been an episcopal church in the town since 1618, and the leading townspeople, we can be fairly confident, were Anglicans. There was a Presbyterian congregation, too, and its minster at the time of the American war, William Crawford, was later to run an academy in Strabane for the training of Presbyterian ministers.[219] By the mid-eighteenth century the town had become notable as 'the principal Mart in the North West for the Linen Manufacture',[220] and trade in linens and local agricultural produce gave Strabane an air of modest prosperity.[221] The town's links with the American colonies were strong. The linen industry benefited from flaxseed imports from North America, which had been developed by Samuel Carson, a native of Strabane who became a leading merchant in Philadelphia.[222] Carson was just one of many local migrants to the colonies; indeed, Strabane was in an area that has been described as 'the emigration hinterland' of Londonderry.[223] John Dunlap, publisher of the *Pennsylvania Packet* and first printer of the Declaration of Independence, was born in Strabane, and in 1780 his father, a saddler, was still resident in the town.[224]

The first Earl of Abercorn had been granted the land in and around Strabane by James I, and his lineal descendant, the eighth Earl, remained the leading landowner in the area at the time of the American war. The Abercorns had promoted the development of the

---

[217] Philip S. Robinson, *The Plantation of Ulster: British Settlement in an Irish Landscape, 1600–1670* (Dublin, 1984), 156.
[218] J. H. Andrew, 'Land and People, c. 1780', in *A New History of Ireland*, iv. *Eighteenth-Century Ireland 1691–1800* (Oxford, 1986), 256.
[219] *A History of the Congregations of the Presbyterian Church in Ireland 1610–1982* (Belfast, 1982), 761.
[220] Dean William Henry, cited in G. Kirkham, 'Economic Diversification in a Marginal Economy: A Case Study', in Peter Roebuck (ed.), *Plantation to Partition: Essays in Ulster History in Honour of J. L. McCracken* (Belfast, 1981), 65.
[221] W. H. Crawford, 'The Evolution of Ulster Towns, 1750–1850', in Roebuck (ed.), *Plantation to Partition*, 140–1; *Richard Pococke's Irish Tours*, ed. John McVeigh (Dublin, 1995), 55.
[222] Thomas M. Truxes, *Irish-American Trade, 1660–1783* (Cambridge, 1988), 172.
[223] R. J. Dickson, *Ulster Emigration to Colonial America 1718–1775* (London, 1966), 139 n. 1. [224] PRONI, T 1336/1/17, Will of John Dunlap, Snr.

town, playing a leading role in establishing the linen industry.[225] The family, however, had not always enjoyed unchallenged sway. The second Earl was a Catholic, and the fourth Earl, also a Catholic, died in the service of James II. This was hardly likely to have endeared the family to Strabane's Protestants. But the fifth Earl and his successors were Protestants themselves, and they were able to exercise considerable influence over the election of the borough's two MPs. After a period when the Abercorn interest felt obliged to concede one seat to local merchants, the eighth Earl regained full control of Strabane's parliamentary representation in 1764.[226] The franchise was confined to the thirteen-strong corporation, and Abercorn was able to ensure that his nominees were returned unopposed. In 1775 the two MPs were John Hamilton of Dunnamanagh and Claudius Hamilton of Beltrim. A contemporary survey of the Irish Parliament identifies them as consistent opponents of the lord-lieutenant's administration.[227] John Hamilton was returned again at the 1776 Irish general election, but Abercorn replaced Claudius Hamilton with Henry Pomeroy of Newbery, County Kildare, a distant relative of the Earl's family. Pomeroy duly pledged himself to act in accordance with his patron's wishes.[228]

The war's impact on Strabane was multifarious. The linen trade was immediately affected. Events in America pushed linen prices down, as the colonies had been a major market before the outbreak of hostilities and British linen merchants and manufacturers were reluctant to purchase more cloth than they could sell. In February 1776 James Hamilton, Abercorn's agent in Strabane, reported that 'the linen drapers from these parts . . . told me that they were considerable losers . . . they attribute the fall of Cloth to the troubles in America'.[229] Similarly, after Cornwallis's surrender at Yorktown

---

[225] G. E. Kirkham, '"To Pay the Rent and Lay up Riches": Economic Opportunities in Eighteenth-Century North West Ulster', in Rosalind Mitchison and Peter Roebuck (eds.), *Economy and Society in Scotland and Ireland 1500–1939* (Edinburgh, 1988), 96–7.

[226] See A. P. W. Malcomson, 'The Politics of "Natural Right": The Abercorn Family and Strabane Borough, 1692–1800', *Historical Studies*, 10 (1976), 43–90.

[227] William Hunt (ed.), *The Irish Parliament 1775* (London, 1907), 24–5.

[228] Malcomson, 'Politics of "Natural Right"', 88.

[229] PRONI, Abercorn Papers, D/623/A/43/5. The letters from Hamilton to Abercorn form the basis of what follows. Arguably, they tell us more about Hamilton than about Strabane. A source of this nature is bound to be partial; his preoccupations and predilections must necessarily distort the picture. But the letters remain the best documentary evidence available. Strabane Corporation Minutes, though they survive in a continuous run from 1755 (PRONI, Mic 159/1) are rather unilluminating.

finally put paid to any lingering hopes of reclaiming the rebel colonies, Hamilton informed the absentee Earl that 'Our linnen market was dulled by the late unfavourable accounts from America'.[230] But there were compensations. During the first year of the war it seems that 'a great quantity' of local linen was sold for 'Soldiers Shirts'.[231]

Uncertain times for the linen trade, combined with the effective suspension of large-scale emigration to America, meant that Strabane was identified by the army as an area of military potential. A party from the Third Foot was based in the town from early 1776; but by January 1778 it was said to have had 'very bad success'.[232] Over the next two years, however, the situation seems to have changed dramatically. Another recruiting party, seeking to raise men after the French entered the conflict, was reported to have been 'very successfull'. Indeed, in March 1780 Hamilton claimed that 'this Town and neighbourhood, have afforded more soldiers I believe than any other part of the Kingdom'. While he argued that 'this country is vastly drained', Hamilton was happy to give every assistance to James Gage, who arrived at this time to enlist men into the One-hundredth Foot.[233] Gage's regiment was on the British establishment, and so he had no official beating orders to recruit in Ireland; but, as was often the case, officers trying to raise men for rank in a new regiment saw Ireland as a rich resource to be tapped, especially if the would-be officers had Irish connections themselves.[234] Gage remains a shadowy figure. He might, however, have been related to the Gages of Bellarena, County Londonderry; he certainly had an uncle who was a doctor at Ennishown, County Donegal.[235] Gage made the city of Derry his headquarters, but he left a sergeant to raise as many men as he could at Strabane. The sergeant seems to have been ably assisted by Hamilton and other local worthies. The men recruited in the area were shipped over

---

[230] PRONI, Abercorn Papers, D/623/A/44/153.   [231] Ibid., D/623/A/42/103.
[232] Ibid., D/623/A/43/88.
[233] Ibid., D/623/A/44/15. Compare the situation with that in 1759, during the Seven Years War, when the local linen industry could not spare men for the army. See Kirkham, '"To Pay the Rent . . . "', 102.
[234] Moses Kinkead recruited the men he needed for a commission in the Eighty-fifth Foot, another corp on the British establishment, remarkably quickly in Ulster in 1779: see BL, Liverpool Papers, Add. MS 38344, fo. 3.
[235] PRONI, Abercorn Papers, D/623/A/44/15.

to England and in August 1780 Gage obtained his captain's commission.[236]

The sources available provide some possible explanations for the greater ease with which men were recruited from the spring of 1778. In 1775–6 a good harvest and low provision prices may have made enlistment an unattractive option; whereas from late 1777 the linen trade throughout Ireland went into a deep depression.[237] But if the economic background is relevant, so are the political and religious dimensions. Ulster Presbyterians were said to be reluctant to fight their co-religionists in America,[238] and in a town like Strabane, with its close ties with the colonies, this might have been an especially important consideration. Once the character of the war changed in 1778, the fierce Protestantism of the Presbyterians probably pushed them in a different direction. The principal enemy was now the Catholic French, supported from 1779 by the equally Catholic Spanish, and an invasion was widely feared.[239] The enlistees themselves may or may not have been moved in this way—some of them were probably Catholics themselves—but there are some indications that the influential community figures whose support was vital to successful recruiting responded positively to the coming of the Bourbon war. It was surely notable that the Protestants of the middling sort who formed volunteer companies for local defence in and around Strabane enthusiastically celebrated Rodney's victorious engagement in January 1780 with the Spanish fleet.[240]

The volunteers loom large in Hamilton's correspondence with Abercorn, and his letters form an eloquent testimony to their ambiguous nature. Strabane, along with many other communities in Ulster, formed a volunteer company in July 1778. Hamilton explained that 'the most respectable people' of the town had approached him

And sayed they wished to be imbodied, that others had begun and thought it was very proper for our internall safety, and to prevent any risings or disorder among us, they at the same time offered me the command, and have pressed me to write to our representatives [i.e., the borough's MPs] to endeavour to procure for us from Government, a hundred stand of Arms Colours Drums &c, they have fixed on their uniforms.

---

[236] PRONI, Abercorn Papers, D/623/A/44/29.   [237] See above, Ch. 2.
[238] See above, Ch. 6.   [239] PRONI, Abercorn Papers, D/623/A/43/236.
[240] Ibid., Stewart of Killymoon Papers, D/3167/2/26.

Hamilton was uneasy, even at this early stage, fearing that volunteering might promote 'idleness'. More significantly, he confessed that he did not wish to see 'a Country in arms'. It was too late, however, 'to diswade them from it', and so he was obliged to go along with the scheme.[241]

A year later, Hamilton was still more nervous. He told Abercorn that he had accepted command of Strabane's company because 'I found they were determined to have one, and that I was sure they never wd. have got one more inclined to preserve peace and order'. But even the assurances of the dean of Derry, who approved of the volunteers, failed to convince Hamilton, who did nothing to encourage the growth of Strabane's company. 'I must own that I did not wish to see the Country all learning the use of arms, nor did I immagine it was thoroughly agreeable to your Lordship', he reported to Abercorn, 'else my company would not have been the smallest' in the area.[242] We can surmise that Hamilton's lukewarm attitude contributed to the emergence of a second volunteer company in Strabane in the summer of 1779. This development would no doubt have added to his alarm, partly because the uniform of the new company, according to a newspaper report, was 'wisely calculated for young men of lesser circumstances',[243] but also because the chaplain was none other than William Crawford, Strabane's Presbyterian minister.

By December 1779 Hamilton was reporting that 'the volunteers are certainly driving at something more than defending us from invaders'. His efforts to prevent the Strabane volunteers joining with others in the barony to form a battalion were in vain.[244] Worse still, the battalion, once established, proceeded to choose as its colonel not Abercorn's nephew and heir, but James Stewart of Killymoon, one of the MPs for County Tyrone. Hamilton was convinced that Stewart was exploiting the situation for his own political purposes—having donated 100 guineas, and promising to provide colours and even two field pieces, he had every reason to expect support from the volunteers in the next election.[245] But if Stewart recognized the value of cultivating the volunteers, the volunteers clearly saw him as a more appropriate patron than

---

[241] Ibid., Abercorn Papers, D/623/A/43/146. [242] Ibid., D/623/A/43/236.
[243] *Belfast News-letter*, 3–7 Sept. 1779.
[244] PRONI, Abercorn Papers, D/623/A/43/260. [245] Ibid., D/623/A/44/22.

Abercorn. The Earl was much slower than Stewart in making a donation, and Strabane's two MPs had by early 1780 moved into the government camp, especially on constitutional issues.[246] Their new political stance presumably reflected Abercorn's own views, but it was starkly at variance with those of the volunteers.

The language adopted by the Strabane barony volunteers makes it obvious that they saw themselves as a political as much as a military organization. A meeting of the battalion in March 1780 thanked Stewart profusely, and observed:[247]

Long have the Inhabitants of this Island complained of political restrictions inconsistent with their natural rights and highly prejudicial to their happiness—But, in the vicissitudes of human affairs, a favourable period has arrived, when they have it in their power, in some measure to obtain deliverance from these Injuries.

Or, as Hamilton told Abercorn the following May: 'every thing seems to go on, in a settled determined way, the first cause given for their associating (to oppose invaders) not even spoken of now, but openly declared to have, the Laws reformed, to what they think their right'.[248]

The local volunteers continued to watch closely events in Dublin and London, and to seek to influence developments. In December 1781 Crawford, by now chaplain to the First Tyrone Regiment of Volunteers, was expressing his 'grief and disappointment' at the failure of the Irish Parliament to approve the required changes, and looking forward to a fresh administration at Dublin Castle.[249] The next summer there was a review of the volunteers near Strabane, at which the participants celebrated Ireland's new status as an independent kingdom, congratulated Lord Charlemont for his part in this achievement, and expressed their loyalty to the crown and the lord-lieutenant, the Duke of Portland.[250] But if the focus was mainly national, there were local repercussions. The volunteers had already, in effect, declared their independence of Abercorn by choosing Stewart as colonel of the barony's battalion. Now the Earl's stranglehold on the politics of the borough became a cause of complaint. Distress caused by poor harvests and high provision

[246] Malcomson, 'Politics of "Natural Right"', 64.
[247] PRONI, Stewart of Killymoon Papers, D/3167/2/25.
[248] Ibid., Abercorn Papers, D/623/A/44/34.
[249] HMC, *Charlemont MSS*, i. 390.   [250] *Belfast News-letter*, 30 July–2 Aug. 1782.

prices no doubt added to the disquiet: by the summer of 1783 Hamilton was writing of the numbers of beggars in the streets and pointing out that 156 of the town's households were in receipt of from one to three shillings' relief per week.[251] That December some of the townspeople petitioned Abercorn to protest at their exclusion from decisions on local taxation and regulation; and in March 1784 Richard Charleton, lieutenant-colonel of the barony battalion, convened a meeting in the town to consider an address to the Irish Parliament 'to open the corporation'.[252] This may have owed something to family resentment. Charleton was related to William Maxwell, a Strabane merchant who had wanted to become one of the borough's MPs in 1768, but had failed to persuade the Earl to support him. But perhaps it would be more appropriate to see Charleton, like Maxwell before him, as representing the concerns of the merchant community—when Maxwell attempted to stand in 1768 he had the backing of about ninety of the town's principal businessmen.[253] Either way, nothing seems to have come of either of these expressions of discontent, and the Abercorn family remained in control, perhaps, as Anthony Malcomson suggests, because in the final analysis the residents recognized that only the Abercorns possessed the necessary capital and influence to promote the interests of the town.[254] But the successful outcome, from the Abercorns' point of view, should not obscure the rumblings of discontent brought on by the American war.

These local studies, viewed collectively, confirm many of the points made in earlier chapters. They highlight the importance of recruitment for the armed forces; the seemingly ubiquitous presence of the military, and the problems and opportunities that they created; the varied nature and meaning of the volunteers; the economic dislocations and adaptations; the embittering effect of the war on political divisions, reflected in petitions, addresses, subscriptions, and public celebrations; and the challenge posed to the existing political and even social status quo. They demonstrate, too, that the war impinged upon very different communities, the length and breadth of the

---

[251] James Kelly, 'Scarcity and Poor Relief in Eighteenth-Century Ireland: The Subsistence Crisis of 1782–1784', *Irish Historical Studies*, 28 (1992–3), 51.
[252] Malcomson, 'Politics of "Natural Right"', 62.
[253] John H. Gebbie (ed.), *An Introduction to the Abercorn Letters* (Omagh, 1972), 85, 113.   [254] Malcomson, 'Politics of "natural right"', 76–8.

British Isles. It pressed, of course, more heavily on some than on others. In Hull, for instance, there was a genuine fear of an enemy attack; the war threatened to come home quite literally. But even in sleepy and genteel Lichfield, deep in the heart of the English midlands, far from vulnerable coastlines, the war intruded, bringing forth expressions of loyalty to the government, bell-ringing to celebrate British victories, and complaints about military overcrowding. Indeed, whether we are looking at Glasgow, Hull, Lichfield, Brentwood, Berkshire, or Strabane, the American war emerges as intrusive and disruptive.

9

War, Peace, and Empire

THE AMERICAN WAR was for the British a long, arduous, and ultimately unsuccessful struggle. The stout defence of Gibraltar and Rodney's victory at the Saints helped to restore national pride, but the outcome of the conflict was unquestionably bruising. Vast sums had been spent, and many lives lost, to little or no good purpose. The war was intended to preserve the sovereign rights of the British Parliament over the rebellious colonies, yet in the end the complete independence of those same colonies had to be acknowledged, and territorial concessions were made to France and Spain, the vanquished powers in the previous war. To many contemporaries the hubris of 1763 had been followed by the nemesis of 1783.[1] It seems reasonable to ask, therefore, whether the experience of the American conflict altered British attitudes to war and to empire?

In many senses the answer must be no. Continuity is often the dominant impression. But in certain respects attitudes did change. The American war saw the first sustained and large-scale public criticism of the use of military force as an instrument of policy. While the criticism was directed, for the most part, at the justice and wisdom of fighting fellow subjects, rather than a genuine expression of hostility to war as such, it prepared the ground for the more clearly anti-war campaigns in the struggle against revolutionary and Napoleonic France. Attitudes to empire also underwent change. Opposition to the possession of overseas territories, while gaining converts in intellectual circles, remained very much a minority view, but the loss of America accentuated a process of change in the nature of the empire, and with this change came an important shift in public perceptions. After 1783 there were fewer colonies of British settlement and more areas where non-Britons were subject to imperial rule, particularly in India. As India became more significant, the old idea of the British empire as an empire of liberty was increasingly

---

[1] See e.g. NLS, Stuart Stevenson Papers, MS 8327, fo. 93.

supplanted by a new and more authoritarian version of empire—
humane and in many senses enlightened, no doubt, but authoritarian
nevertheless.[2] And the British public, after having for many years
worried about the domestic implications of expansion of empire in
the east, seems to have accepted the change with remarkable ease.

War and Peace

Many obstacles existed to the emergence of widespread opposition
to war on principle. There was, to be sure, no shortage of regret
about the destruction, expense, and suffering caused by the
American conflict. Looking back in 1783, the Revd John Mill, a
Church of Scotland minister, lamented the squandering of 'an
hundred millions Ster. with the loss supposed of an 100,000 lives'.[3]
Hannah More, the author, actuated by the same concerns, wrote in
1776 of her wish for an 'accommodation with America . . . before
more human blood is spilt'.[4] Even those far from the brutal reality of
the theatres of operations were exposed to graphic descriptions of
the struggle. John Lloyd of South Carolina related to his English
correspondents 'all the horrid effects concomitant to intestine wars'.
'Blood and Slaughter—Desolation and Ravage make rapid progress', he wrote in January 1781.[5] At the end of the conflict, John
Lucas of Maryland similarly detailed for his brother-in-law in
Cambridgeshire the ordeal of his 'near neighbours', whose homes,
possessions, and crops had been 'burnt and wantonly destroyed'. 'I
cou'd never have believed', Lucas concluded, 'that Old England

---

[2] See esp. P. J. Marshall, 'Empire and Authority in the Later Eighteenth Century',
Journal of Imperial and Commonwealth History, 15 (1987), 105–22. Eliga H. Gould,
'American Independence and Britain's Counter-Revolution', *Past & Present*, 154 (1997),
107–41, also has interesting things to say on this subject.

The move to a more authoritarian empire, it should be noted, is not simply the
perception of modern historians. The British empire in India was perceived to be despotic
by contemporaries, and an empire centred increasingly on India was seen to be very
different from an empire centred on the North American colonies. In 1772 Harry Verelst
described British rule in Bengal as a despotism, albeit a civilized as opposed to an
'oriental' despotism, a despotism similar to that 'assumed by the prince in the absolute
monarchies of Europe'. See *A View of the Rise, Progress and Present State of the English
Government in Bengal* (London, 1772), 146.

[3] *The Diary of the Reverend John Mill*, ed. Gilbert Goudie (Scottish History Society,
vol v, Edinburgh, 1889), 69.

[4] *The Letters of Hannah More*, ed. R. Brinsley Johnson (London, 1925), 44.

[5] Gloucestershire RO, John Lloyd Letters, D 1628, bundle 2.

wou'd have descended to such a mean, barbarous way of carrying on a war.[6] Military men engaged in fighting the Americans were probably less likely than their compatriots at home to shed tears for the suffering brought on by the war—indeed, some of them pressed for a more vigorous approach that would bring the full horror of armed conflict home to more of the colonists in order to persuade them to submit. Brigadier Charles O'Hara of the Guards, to give just one example, called repeatedly for 'a war of desolation . . . where the object is only to Ruin & devastate'.[7] 'Fire & Sword', he wrote, should be employed against the most disaffected of the colonies '& every Man Experience in himself, & dearest connections, the Rude & mercyless hand of war'.[8] But even soldiers could be moved by the distress of civilians. Captain John Peebles of the Royal Highland Regiment noted in his journal while he was based at Rhode Island that 'many of the Inhabitants of this Country are to be pitied'. At Dorchester, near Charleston, he spared time to reflect on the way in which the war had 'reduced many wealthy people to shifting circumstances, & the poor negroes to a starving condition in many places hereabout'.[9] Captain William Congreve of the Royal Artillery was similarly affected by the suffering of the inhabitants of Long Island, New York: 'Never was War so dreadful as this', he wrote to a relative back in England.[10] To Lord Dunglass, a subaltern in the Guards, the impact of the war on the area around Philadelphia was truly shocking: 'this once happy Country exhibits a scene of desolation to[o] horrible for language to express'.[11]

In an age when the cultivation of sensibility was very much in vogue,[12] such expressions of pity, horror, and dismay were perhaps only to be expected, especially given that the war could be seen as a

---

[6] Cambridgeshire RO, Huddleston of Sawston Papers, 483/C2/L2, Lucas to Ferdinand Huddleston, 7 Nov. 1783.

[7] West Suffolk RO, Grafton Papers, Ac 423/190.

[8] Hull University Library, Hotham Papers, HO 4/19, O'Hara to Sir Charles Thompson, 20 Sept. 1778. For the strength of the 'fire and sword' lobby, see Stephen Conway, 'To Subdue America: British Army Officers and the Conduct of the Revolutionary War', *William & Mary Quarterly*, 3rd ser. 48 (1986), 381–407.

[9] *John Peebles' American War; The Diary of a Scottish Grenadier, 1776–1782*, ed. Ira D. Gruber (Mechanicsburg, Penn., 1998), 71, 377.

[10] Staffordshire RO, Congreve Papers, D 1057/M/F/1–2.

[11] The Hirsel, Douglas-Home Muniments, box 187, bundle 5, Dunglass to the Earl of Home, 29 Jan [1778].

[12] See G. J. Barker-Benfield, *The Culture of Sensibility: Sex and Society in Eighteenth-Century Britain* (Chicago, 1992) for a consideration of the various ramifications.

conflict between fellow subjects, or even fellow Britons.[13] But fashionable sympathy has to be set against the powerful pull of traditional views of war. It was still regarded by many as a divine visitation, much like plague and pestilence, or famine. We have seen that sermons preached during the conflict, by both opponents and supporters of the North government's American policies, generally laid stress on war as a sign of the Almighty's disapproval.[14] Our vices and transgressions, the dean of Canterbury informed his listeners on 4 February 1780, had brought 'the divine displeasure upon us'.[15] The next year, Walter Kerrich, canon of Salisbury, reminded his congregation that 'the judgments of the Lord are upon this land, that the inhabitants thereof may learn righteousness'.[16] Seen as punishment for sin, war appeared not so much as an evil but as a necessary corrective. As Bishop Porteus told the House of Lords in 1779, the successes of the Seven Years War had proved 'too great for our feeble virtue to bear'. The wealth created by victory had 'produced a scene of wanton extravagance and wild excess, which called loudly for some signal check; and that check it has now received'.[17] Nor was this just the message of clerics in their pulpits. Letters from across the Atlantic, describing the sufferings of the war zones, frequently expressed the same view. Thomas Lightfoot of Pennsylvania, writing to a fellow Quaker in Britain, reported in October 1777 the 'great desolation in this land' and the terrible plight of their co-religionists, yet concluded that all of this 'loudly proclaims the necessity of learning Righteousness'.[18] And in the British Isles themselves, much the same view seems to have been widely diffused. An Irish Quaker, bracing himself for war against France and the danger of invasion, recorded in his diary the same biblical justification (Isaiah 26: 9) with which Walter Kerrich sought to explain the perils and turmoil confronting Britain.[19]

There were, of course, other ways of thinking about war. Quakers

---

[13] See above, Ch. 3, for the literary response to the war.

[14] See above, Ch. 3.

[15] James Cornwallis, *A Sermon Preached at the Cathedral and Metropolitan Church of Christ, Canterbury, on Friday, February 4, 1780* (Canterbury, n.d.), 16.

[16] Walter Kerrich, *A Sermon Preached at the Cathedral Church of Sarum, on Wednesday, February 21, 1781* (Salisbury, 1781), 4.

[17] Beilby Porteus, *A Sermon Preached before the Lords Spiritual and Temporal, . . . February 10, 1779* (London, 1779), 12.

[18] Friends House Library, Misc MSS, Port.34.180.

[19] NLI, MS 4242, Diary of a Cork Quaker, 7 June 1778.

might accept war as a judgement, but for more than a century they had consistently stressed the scriptural arguments for non-violence and non-resistance. Their influence in this regard, however, was limited. Absolute pacifism was most definitely a minority taste. On a more secular level, the years prior to the American conflict saw political economists attempting to establish that war was profoundly damaging. Sir James Steuart, for instance, wrote in 1767 of war as 'inconsistent with the prosperity of a modern state', and regretted the cultural influences that led generation after generation to regard armed struggle as normal and natural.[20] There is some evidence that such ideas were making headway: Sir Charles Whitworth, an MP loyal to Lord North, was to include similar sentiments in a book that appeared at the beginning of the American war.[21] But it would be a mistake to assume that Steuart represented a general Enlightenment hostility to war. Enlightenment thinkers did not necessarily come to irenical conclusions. Adam Ferguson, in a work published in the same year as Steuart's, maintained that violence was inherent in man and that mankind was addicted to war.[22] Lord Kames went further, arguing that it was wrong to regard war as always a misfortune. War was necessary, he claimed, as 'a school for improving every manly virtue'. While perpetual war was clearly undesirable given the suffering and loss that all conflicts caused, 'perpetual peace', he wrote, would be worse because it would promote selfishness and turn men 'into beasts of burden'. Alternating war and peace, in Kames's view, was the ideal.[23] Indeed, it was far from uncommon for peace and commerce to be seen as threats to liberty, and war as its preservative. The wealth, or 'luxury', created by commerce was held by some to have made the nation soft and effeminate and concerned only with self-gratification, making many of the people unable and unwilling to exert themselves to defend their liberties against foreign and domestic oppressors. During the War of Austrian Succession James Burgh, in *Britain's Remembrancer, or the Danger Not Over* (1746), had identified a slide into 'effeminacy', which he linked to

[20] Sir James Steuart, *An Inquiry into the Principles of Political Oeconomy* (2 vols., London, 1767), i. 448.

[21] Sir Charles Whitworth, *State of the Trade of Great Britain in its Imports and Exports, Progressively from the Year 1697* (London, 1776), pref.

[22] Adam Ferguson, *An Essay on the History of Civil Society*, ed. Duncan Forbes (Edinburgh, 1966), 20–5, 98.

[23] Henry Homes, Lord Kames, *Sketches of the History of Man* (2 vols., Edinburgh, 1774), i. 426–38.

the influence of trade, and in the Seven Years War the Revd John Brown of Newcastle had forcefully repeated the charge in his *Estimate of the Manners and Principles of the Times* (1757), though he attributed the problem to the aristocracy ('the Higher Ranks') and their following the cultural lead of their French counterparts.[24] Military service, on the other hand, was widely portrayed as a means by which liberty may be protected—especially military service in the militia, and still more so in the volunteers. During the American war, the Irish volunteers, in particular, made much of their role as 'citizen soldiers', willing to sacrifice personal comfort and risk danger for the sake of their communities. They were depicted, indeed, as the very embodiment of 'republican virtue'.[25] As if all of this were not sufficient to make war seem a positive rather than a negative experience, some contemporary writers chose to stress the changing character of conflict, and to advance this as a reason for regarding war as more acceptable than in earlier ages. William Robertson, the great Scottish historian, expressed the view that there was an enormous difference between the wars of 'barbarians' and the wars of modern 'Civilized nations', which 'carry on their hostilities with so little rancour, or animosity, that war amongst them is disarmed of half its terrors'.[26] This might have failed to accord with the grim actuality of warfare in the eighteenth century, but for those distant from the battlefields it no doubt chimed pleasingly with the idea of progress and improvement.

Against this background, with providential religion and many of the fruits of social-scientific, philosophical, and historical enquiry pointing broadly to the same conclusion, it was clearly going to be no easy matter to change minds in a more peace-loving direction. Is it possible, however, that this process was furthered by the arguments deployed by British and Irish opponents of the military coercion of the Americans? Martin Ceadel, the foremost historian of British pacifism, sees the anti-war petitions of the early years of the conflict as embodying an 'embryonic *pacificism*', by which he means that some of the petitions contained arguments against war in

---

[24] Kathleen Wilson, *The Sense of the People: Politics, Culture and Imperialism in England, 1715–1785* (Cambridge, 1995), 187.

[25] Ian McBride, *Scripture Politics: Ulster Presbyterians and Irish Radicalism in the Late Eighteenth Century* (Oxford, 1998), 123–33.

[26] William Robertson, *The History of the Reign of the Emperor Charles V* (3 vols., London, 1769), i. 9.

general, though not condemnation of all wars.[27] Ceadel is measured in his claims, and he endorses Paul Langford's view that it was not until the 1790s and the great struggle against revolutionary France that a sustained and genuine anti-war movement emerged.[28] This is surely correct. The anti-war petitions, and the anti-war sentiments of those who sympathized with the colonists, need to be placed in the context of the American war. The aim of those who opposed the war against the Americans was to stop what they saw as a civil war within the British empire, not to protest at the use of military force per se. When Charles James Fox condemned as 'cruel and intolerable' the 'sacrifice of thousands of lives', he added tellingly 'almost without prospect of advantage'.[29] This was falling a long way short of opposing war as an instrument of policy. His language suggests that in different circumstances he would have raised no objection to the use of force. Indeed, once in power as a minister in the Rockingham administration of 1782, Fox had no qualms about using British military and naval resources against the Bourbons. That May he was reporting to the king on preparations for the 'ensuing Campain [sic] in the West Indies'.[30] Joshua Toulmin, attacking the American war in a fast-day sermon, noted that the conflict was 'pregnant with peculiar evils'. The outcome, whoever triumphed, would be disastrous. The only winners, he predicted, would be the French, whom he went on to identify as 'our natural enemies'.[31] In condemning the American war, then, Toulmin was not condemning war in general, but rather comparing it unfavourably with conflict against Britain's true foe. Likewise, the independent congregation at Isleham, Cambridgeshire, asked the Lord to 'put an end to this bloody and unnatural war' against the Americans, but once the struggle broadened in 1778 they prayed that the Almighty would

[27] Martin Ceadel, *The Origins of War Prevention: The British Peace Movement and International Relations, 1730–1854* (Oxford, 1996), 164–5.
[28] Paul Langford, *A Polite and Commercial People: England 1727–1783* (Oxford, 1989), 626–7. For the peace campaigns of the French wars of 1793–1815 see J. E. Cookson, *The Friends of Peace* (Cambridge, 1982).
[29] *Memorials and Correspondence of Charles James Fox*, ed. Lord John Russell (4 vols., London, 1853–7), i. 140.
[30] *The Correspondence of King George III*, ed. Sir John Fortescue (6 vols., London, 1927–8), vi. 41.
[31] Joshua Toulmin, *The American War Lamented* (London, 1776), 3, 8–11.

appear 'for us against the French'.[32] Such examples could be multi-plied. The sentiments of many of those who opposed the coercion of the colonists were probably most pithily summed up in a toast of the Newtonards Volunteers at a dinner in July 1778: 'Reunion to the British empire, and disgrace to them who oppose it. Speedy peace with America, and war with France.'[33]

Yet there was, as Ceadel suggests, the germ of a more generally applicable critique to be found in some of the arguments deployed against the American aspect of the war. Out of the case against the American war, in other words, emerged a case against war in general—even if opponents of the struggle against the Americans often seem to have failed to recognize the wider implications of what they were writing and saying. This is not to claim that the arguments employed during the American war were novel in themselves; as we have seen, political economists had already been trying to persuade their readers of the practical merits of peace. But during the American war a concerted attempt was made to construct a convin-cing case against the coercion of the colonists, and the impact of this effort was likely to have been much greater than that of the writings of the pre-war political economists. Anti-war arguments were now receiving much wider exposure in pamphlets, newspapers, and periodicals. But the war not only increased the diffusion of such arguments, it gave many of them more immediacy. Theoretical speculations in the pages of the political economists came alive, and seemed all the more relevant, because in many respects they were beginning to reflect current experience.

So, when Joshua Toulmin sought to convince his congregation of the evils of the American war by mentioning the 'calamities common to the devastating sword', he was, perhaps unwittingly, doing some-thing more than criticize this particular conflict.[34] When the Presbyterian Synod of Ulster addressed the king in June 1782 to rejoice that 'Brother will no more rise up against Brother', the delegates no doubt had in mind the ending of hostilities with the Americans, amongst whom were many Presbyterians of Scotch-Irish origin. But the Synod's address, by referring to 'the pleasing prospect now opened of having the sword sheathed', contained

---

[32] Kenneth A. C. Parsons (ed.), *The Church Book of the Independent Church . . . Isleham 1693–1805* (Cambridge Antiquarian Records Society, vol. vi, Cambridge, 1984), 97–8, 102, 111; see also 120.   [33] *Belfast News-letter*, 3–7 July 1778.
[34] Toulmin, *American War Lamented*, 3, 8.

sentiments that could easily be applied to the wider war against Britain's other enemies, and indeed to all wars.[35] Equally, when Matthew Robinson Morris told his readers that 'Commerce is the offspring of peace and war is her irreconcilable enemy', he was presenting an argument against war in general and not just the American war.[36] The same point can be made about some of the criticisms voiced in the oppositionist pamphlet *The Letters of Valens*. To state that 'The influence of the Crown, considerable in peace, in war is boundless' is to advance a proposition against war in principle on constitutional grounds, even though it was clearly intended merely as an argument against the conflict with the Americans.[37] And when David Hartley, that most zealous of pro-Americans, wrote to the Yorkshire Association that high and general taxation were the inevitable consequences of the contest with the colonists, he was likewise laying stress on a point that could be made about almost every large-scale war.[38] All of these arguments, we should note— that war brought great and intolerable suffering, damaged commerce, expanded the patronage available to the government, and increased taxation—became the stock-in-trade of pacifically inclined writers of the following generations.[39]

The American war seems also more directly to have influenced a number of writers, who were themselves to be influential. We can perhaps mention in this context the claim of James Silk Buckingham, a nineteenth-century anti-war campaigner, that he had been converted to the cause of peace by reading Benjamin Franklin's account of the horrors of a naval battle between the British and the French in the American war.[40] But more immediately important is the impact of the conflict on Richard Price. We have seen that Price was a vocal opponent of the war against the colonists. In 1784 he published a tract that was designed to show that the American Revolution could act as an example to the world. One of his points was that an arbitral body, like the American Congress, could settle disputes between 'any

---

[35] Synod of Ulster, *Records of the Synod of Ulster* (3 vols., Belfast, 1890–8), iii. 46.

[36] Matthew Robinson Morris, *Peace the Best Policy* (2nd edn., London, 1777), 9.

[37] [William Burke], *The Letters of Valens* (London, 1777), p. iii. The letters had first been published in the *London Evening Post*.

[38] Christopher Wyvill, *Political Papers* (6 vols., York, 1794–1802), iii. 184.

[39] See e.g. James Mill, *Commerce Defended* (London, 1808), 97–100, 119; Jonathan Dymond, *An Enquiry into the Accordancy of War with the Principles of Christianity* (London, 1823), 15.

[40] *Autobiography of James Silk Buckingham* (2 vols., London, 1855), ii. 359–61.

number of confederated states', and that it was 'not impossible' that 'by such means universal peace may be produced and all war excluded from the world'.[41] This idea was not, to be sure, particularly new: the Abbé Saint-Pierre had called for a European confederation at the end of the War of Spanish Succession, and William Penn, the duc de Sully, and Emeric Crucé had done the same at various points in the seventeenth century.[42] But the example of America, where a confederation had just been established, was recent enough to give the idea freshness, and seems to have influenced not just Price but other pacifically inclined observers. Similar sentiments were to be expressed a few years later by Thomas Paine, the famous supporter of the American and French Revolutions. In the first part of his *Rights of Man*, Paine looked forward to a 'European Congress' settling quarrels between nations. He also, we might add, repeated the arguments about the link between patronage, corruption, and war that had gained currency during the American conflict.[43]

The key figure here, however, was Josiah Tucker, the dean of Gloucester. Jeremy Bentham, who wrote on peace, war, and international relations in the mid-1780s, cited Tucker approvingly as one of his intellectual inspirations,[44] and the dean's ideas seem to have been widely read and provoked much controversy. Tucker had already been predisposed to view war unfavourably as a result of his experiences as a clergymen in Bristol during the Seven Years War. He had been appalled by the moral degeneration that he associated with privateering and service in the armed forces, which he had witnessed at first hand in the great western seaport.[45] It was during the American conflict, however, that he emerged as a notable figure in the public arena. Tucker adopted a distinctly unusual position. He was a supporter of government, a vehement anti-Lockian,

---

[41] Richard Price, *Observations on the Importance of the American Revolution* (London, 1784), 14–15.

[42] See F. H. Hinsley, *Power and the Pursuit of Peace* (Cambridge, 1963), chs. 1 and 2.

[43] Thomas Paine, *Rights of Man*, pt. I (London, 1791: Harmondsworth, 1984 edn.), 145–7.

[44] University College London, Bentham MSS, UC xxv. 121. See also *The Works of Jeremy Bentham*, ed. John Bowring (11 vols., Edinburgh, 1838–43), ii. 546 n. For Bentham's influence, see Stephen Conway, 'Bentham, the Benthamites, and the Nineteenth-Century British Peace Movement', *Utilitas*, 2 (1990), 221–43.

[45] J. G. A. Pocock, *Virtue, Commerce, and History: Essays on Political Thought and History, Chiefly in the Eighteenth Century* (Cambridge, 1985), 159.

and an opponent of parliamentary reform along the lines urged by the Association movement—the only change to the representative system that he was willing to contemplate was a tightening-up of the franchise qualifications to *reduce* the number of electors and thereby diminish popular influence.[46] But this conservative, or even reactionary, side to his character was blended with a curious radicalism. Tucker was a trenchant opponent of the American war, who argued that the independence of the rebellious colonies should be welcomed, not resisted. In part, it must be said, this radical prescription was a logical (if rather eccentric) outgrowth of his conservatism. He wanted to immunize Britain from the revolutionary contagion emanating from the rebellious colonies: if the connection continued, he wrote in 1775, 'the sound Parts of our Constitution will be in great Danger of being tainted by the Gangerene of *American* Republicanism'.[47] But not long afterwards he accepted Dunning's motion that the influence of the crown was expanding and needed to be diminished. 'The Causes of this encreasing Influence', Tucker wrote in 1781, 'are the vast Territories abroad, and those ruinous Wars, and immense Expence which they occasion whilst we are connected with them'.[48]

Empire

Tucker's opposition to war was clearly linked to his opposition to overseas possessions. Colonies caused jealousy between nations and so led to armed conflict. Yet fighting to keep colonies was a waste of resources, because colonies themselves were an encumbrance rather than an asset. Possession of colonies was not vital to secure trade, Tucker argued, as 'The Trade of *Great-Britain* with the Colonies rests on a much firmer Foundation, than that of a *nominal* Subjection by Means of *Paper* Laws and *imaginary* Restrictions'.[49] The true foundation, he explained, was the superiority of British

---

[46] His political views found their fullest expression in his *Treatise Concerning Civil Government* (London, 1781).

[47] Tucker, *An Humble Address and Earnest Appeal to those Respectable Personages in Great Britain and Ireland, who . . . are the Ablest to Judge, and the Fittest to Decide, Whether a Connection with, or a Separation from the Continental Colonies of America, be most for the National Advantage, and the Lasting Benefit of these Kingdoms* (2nd edn., Gloucester, 1775), 75.   [48] Id., *Treatise Concerning Civil Government*, 248.

[49] Id., *A Series of Answers to Certain Objections, Against Separating from the Rebellious Colonies* (Gloucester, 1776), 30.

manufactures over those of any rivals. The colonies, as independent states, would continue to trade with Britain because it was in their interest to do so. While dominion over America appeared to be Tucker's main objection, it should be stressed that he broadened his attack to include overseas dependencies in general. '*Gibraltar* and *Portmahon* [Minorca] are very expensive, and very useless Things', Tucker wrote, and 'Colonies of every Sort or Kind are, and ever were, a *Drain* to, and an *Incumbrance* on the *Mother-Country*'.[50] In a pamphlet published in 1782 he maintained that the best plan for Britain would be to give up all imperial possessions (though not, it seems, Ireland, which he saw in a very different light) and trust to the 'Goodness and Cheapness' of British manufactures.[51] Adam Smith, whose famous *Wealth of Nations* appeared in March 1776, just as the American war was beginning, made much the same points. Britain, he maintained, 'derives nothing but loss from the dominion which she assumes over her colonies'.[52] In a paper written in February 1778 he suggested the possibility of a federal union with the rebel colonies as a useful way forward: by this means, Smith wrote, 'we should certainly incur much less expense, and might, at the same time, gain as real advantages, as any we have hitherto derived from all the nominal dominion we have ever exercised over them'.[53]

Smith, like Tucker, was to influence Bentham, and the views that they and their followers advanced in various publications were gradually to gain ground. The Navigation Acts were not repealed until 1849, but Shelburne and Pitt were well disposed to the ideas of the political economists, and the Jay Treaty of 1794 effectively gave the independent Americans the same commercial rights as British subjects and represented a major breach in the Navigation system. The 1794 treaty, however, probably owed much to a generational

---

[50] Id., *Treatise Concerning Civil Government*, 252.

[51] Id., *Cui Bono? Or, an Inquiry, what Benefits can Arise Either to the English or the Americans, the French, Spaniards, or Dutch, from the Greatest Victories, or Successes, in the Present War* (3rd edn., London, 1782), 129. In his *Treatise Concerning Civil Government*, 252, Tucker had looked forward to 'renouncing all foreign Possessions, and cultivating the Arts of peace in the two fruitful Islands of *Great-Britain* and *Ireland*'.

[52] Smith, *An Inquiry into the Nature and Causes of the Wealth of Nations*, ed. R. H. Campbell, A. S. Skinner and W. B. Todd (2 vols., Oxford, 1976), ii. 616.

[53] *The Correspondence of Adam Smith*, ed. Ernest Campbell Mossner and Ian Simpson Ross (Oxford, 1987), 383.

change in Pitt's ministry.[54] During and immediately after the American war the situation appears to have been very different. The purveyors of the new political economy were acutely aware that they faced an uphill struggle. When Tucker argued that 'the Glory of Conquest,—and the Jealousy of Trade' were amongst the most serious errors that had 'perverted the Judgement of a great part of Mankind', he was accepting that it was going to be no easy matter to change minds.[55] Smith's work might have been praised by fellow intellectuals as likely to 'Enlarge and rectify' generally held ideas, but as Smith himself pointed out, 'The real futility of all distant dominions, . . . is, I think, the subject upon which the public prejudices of Europe require most to be set right'.[56] It would take time, he tacitly acknowledged, for the verities of political economy to be widely diffused.

Meanwhile, traditional ideas continued to hold sway. Shelburne had hoped to build on his generosity to the United States in the peace negotiations by agreeing to reciprocal trading arrangements. But a bill to allow the Americans to be regarded as British subjects for the purposes of the Navigation Acts ran aground in a hostile House of Commons in March 1783. Allowing the Americans to carry goods to and from the British islands in the Caribbean, it was widely feared, would undermine the British mercantile marine and therefore lead, in the words of William Eden, to 'the absolute destruction of our navy'.[57] Lord Sheffield's *Observations on the Commerce of the American States*, which put the case for excluding the former colonists from the benefits of the navigation system, had provided Eden with the arguments he deployed against Shelburne's American Intercourse Bill. And the views of Sheffield and those who thought like him continued to be immensely influential over the next few years. During the short lifetime of the Fox–North coalition (April–December 1783), a series of orders in council allowed the Americans to trade with the British West Indies only in British ships. One of the authors of the original order, William Knox,

---

[54] D. L. Mackay, 'Direction and Purpose in British Imperial Policy, 1783–1801', *Historical Journal*, 17 (1974), 499. John E. Crowley argues along rather different lines, suggesting that the framers of post-war policy were 'neomercantalists', who fused the old economic nationalism with the new political economy (*The Privileges of Independence: Neomercantilism and the American Revolution* (Baltimore, 1993), esp. 75–87).

[55] Tucker, *Cui Bono?*, 33–4.

[56] *Correspondence of Adam Smith*, ed. Mossner and Simpson, 186, 262.

[57] *PH* xxiii. 604.

who had been under-secretary for the colonies in North's government, was so convinced of its importance that he wished to have a copy 'engraved on my tombstone, as having saved the navigation of England'.[58] Pitt, as is well known, was receptive to the idea of freer trade, but even his administration chose to subordinate new economic doctrines to traditional maritime and strategic considerations. In 1786 Pitt's president of the Board of Trade, Lord Hawkesbury, who as Charles Jenkinson had been in the governments of George Grenville and Lord North, carried through the British Parliament a new Navigation Act that specifically denied the ships of the United States access to trade with Britain's overseas territories.

Public opinion, so far as it can be assessed, seems to have been in favour of the maintenance of the protectionism that was central to the Navigation Acts. Many British merchants and manufacturers were interested in colonial North America before the war.[59] A good number of these merchants and manufacturers expressed opposition to the disturbance of trade brought on by the Stamp Act crisis, and their objections seem to have played a big part in persuading the British Parliament to accept the necessity for repeal. Some of the same merchants and manufacturers continued to press for a conciliatory line towards the Americans in 1775. But very few of them, we can be fairly confident, looked forward to the dismantling of the regulatory system that had brought them healthy profits; indeed, keeping the colonies *within* that regulatory system was the very objective of many of those who urged conciliation.[60] The hostility of merchants and manufacturers to a new and more competitive commercial environment was revealed by their reaction to the proposed concessions to the Irish in 1778. The protests of trading and manufacturing towns, it will be recalled, were so strong that North felt obliged to retreat, and he only returned to the British Parliament with measures to conciliate the Irish once the bayonets of

---

[58] William Knox, *Extra-Official State Papers* (2 vols., London, 1789), ii. 53.

[59] Jacob Price, 'Who Cared about the Colonies?', in Bernard Bailyn and Philip D. Morgan (eds.), *Strangers in the Realm: Cultural Margins of the First British Empire* (Chapel Hill, NC, 1991), 405–11. See also David Hancock, *Citizens of the World: London Merchants and the Integration of the British Atlantic Community* (Cambridge, 1995).

[60] For division within the merchant community over coercion, see James E. Bradley, *Religion, Revolution, and English Radicalism* (Cambridge, 1990), 376–7. For the petition of London merchants fearful of the effects of the war on trade, see *Journals of the House of Commons*, xxxv. 405 (27 Oct. 1775).

the volunteers compelled him to respond positively to Irish griev-ances.[61] In 1785, when Pitt was trying to negotiate new commercial arrangements 'to put Ireland still more completely on an equal footing with this country in point of trade',[62] British mercantile and manufacturing interests reacted in much the same way. Historians of the episode emphasize that the merchants and man-ufacturers misunderstood Pitt's intentions—a misunderstanding encouraged by the parliamentary opposition, and particularly by Sheffield and Eden, the prime movers in the defeat of Shelburne's American commercial proposals.[63] But, even though the govern-ment's Irish proposals were nowhere near as radical as they were portrayed, many of the responses to the scheme indicate a strong commitment to protectionism and the maintenance of the special position of British subjects in trade with the empire. Cartoons conveyed images of shuttered shops, with 'Removed to Dublin' on the doors,[64] and Liverpool's petition asked that 'the privilege of supplying her own Markets with the produce of her Colonies may be preserved inviolate to this Kingdom'.[65] A year earlier, Richard Price had written dispiritedly of 'the prejudices in this Country against a relaxation of the Navigation Act' as the impediment to 'any settlement between us and America with respect to com-merce'.[66] As if to justify Price's remarks, the Liverpool Chamber of Commerce was at that very time busily opposing the 'destructive and ruinous' proposal of the West Indian planters and merchants that American ships be allowed to carry goods to and from the British Caribbean islands.[67]

Continuity can be discerned in other areas. Imperial policy gen-erally, it could be argued, was little affected by the loss of America. Perhaps, in the long term, the departure of the rebel colonies had the psychological effect of encouraging British politicians to be more cautious about pressing constitutional disputes to breaking point,

---

[61] See above, Chs. 6 and 8.

[62] PRO, Granville Papers, 30/29/3, Pitt to Lord Gower, 2 Jan. 1785.

[63] See e.g. John Ehrman, *The Younger Pitt: The Years of Acclaim* (London, 1969), 209 and n.

[64] BM 6794, 'The Maid Servants Address to Master Billy Pitt', 22 May 1785. See also BM 6787, 'The Hibernian Attempt', 1 Apr. 1785, and BM 6799, 'Paddy O'Pitts Triumphal Exit!!', 20 June 1785.   [65] *Journals of the House of Commons*, xl. 576.

[66] *The Correspondence of Richard Price*, ed. W. Bernard Peach and D. O. Thomas (3 vols., Durham, NC, 1983–94), ii. 221.

[67] PRO, Chatham Papers, 30/8/182, John Tarleton to George Rose, 23 June 1784.

and more aware of the transience of empire.[68] But in many respects the constitutional settlement of Canada enacted by the British Parliament in 1791 demonstrated the consistency of British official thinking. Just as in the 1760s and 1770s, when the old British North American colonies were the primary focus of concern, the objectives were to strengthen executive authority, curb the pretensions of local legislatures, and transfer at least some of the costs of empire on to colonial peoples.[69] On a grander scale, it has been suggested that the decision to fight for America—first against the French in the Seven Years War and then against the American colonists themselves in the War of Independence—and the commitment to maintain and expand influence in India were part of the same process.[70] As the British economy and public finances seemed to become more and more reliant on imperial trade, successive governments from the middle of the eighteenth century recognized the necessity of protecting Britain's imperial possessions as markets for British products and as sources of raw materials and valuable re-exports. The Seven Years War, the American war, and wars in India from the 1760s to the 1790s can all be seen as linked by a common concern to defend British interests in an increasingly competitive world. France, Britain's great commercial and imperial rival, was regarded as the principal threat, even after the defeat of the Bourbon powers in the Seven Years War. Fear of France could, of course, lead to the conclusion that a harmonious relationship with America must be restored to deny the French an opportunity; in February 1766 General Henry Seymour Conway argued that 'a civil war in America' would inevitably be followed by a war with the Bourbon powers, 'and this connected with an American war would be absolute ruin to this country'.[71] But fear of France could just as easily lead to the opposite conclusion—that America must be compelled, by force if necessary, to remain within the commercial and

---

[68] See Eliga H. Gould, 'A Virtual Nation: Greater Britain and the Imperial Legacy of the American Revolution', *American Historical Review*, 104 (1999), 476–89.

[69] See Stephen Conway, 'Britain and the Revolutionary Crisis, 1763–1791', in *The Oxford History of the British Empire*, ii: *The Eighteenth Century*, ed. P. J. Marshall (Oxford, 1998), 345–6.

[70] See P. J. Marshall, 'Britain and the World in the Eighteenth Century: I, Reshaping the Empire', *Transactions of the Royal Historical Society*, 6th ser. 8 (1998), 1–18.

[71] R. C. Simmons and P. D. G. Thomas (eds.), *Proceedings and Debates of the British Parliaments respecting North America, 1754–1783* (6 vols. to date, Millward, NY, 1982–), ii. 281.

maritime system created by the Navigation Acts. In this sense, the looming presence of France influenced the decision of Lord North's government to fight for America in 1775; Britain without America, it was widely assumed, would be no match for its powerful continental neighbour. Fear of French influence likewise encouraged a forward policy in India. In October 1772 the cabinet discussed 'the schemes we have reason to suspect the French are meditating' in the East Indies.[72] In January 1778, before Britain and France had become formal enemies in the American war, the Bombay presidency of the East India Company was justifying intervention in the politics of a neighbouring state on the grounds that 'nothing but a change in the present Administration at Poonah can secure the Company from the Dangerous & serious Consequences which must ensue from an alliance between the French and the Marathas and that there is no other Method to avert them but by the Company immediately taking a decisive Part'.[73] Twenty years later, similar concerns were expressed about French intrigue in India, and were used to justify further British involvement.[74]

If we look at the level of public perceptions, certain continuities are also evident. The empire and imperial structures were of interest to many people who were not responsible for the formulation of imperial policy, or engaged in colonial commerce or manufacturing for imperial markets. In many ways the empire had become part of the daily experience of countless inhabitants of the British Isles. Kathleen Wilson has shown how prominently imperial themes featured in the press, theatre, and the arts in the years before the American conflict.[75] There seems to have been little diminution in public interest after the loss of the American colonies. This is not to say that America itself remained a preoccupation. Far from it; the number of books and pamphlets on the new republic was very limited compared with the number of publications that had appeared before the war on the North American colonies.[76] But other areas of

---

[72] PRO, Granville Papers, 30/29/1, minutes of the cabinet meeting of 7 Oct. 1772.

[73] India Office Library and Records, Bombay Letters Received, E/4/467, 384.

[74] Michael Duffy, 'World-Wide War and British Expansion 1793–1815', in *Oxford History of the British Empire*, ii. *The Eighteenth Century*, ed. Marshall, 197.

[75] Kathleen Wilson, 'Empire of Virtue: The Imperial Project and Hanoverian Culture c.1720–1785', in Lawrence Stone (ed.), *An Imperial State at War: Britain from 1689 to 1815* (London, 1994), 128–64.

[76] John Cannon, 'The Loss of America', in H. T. Dickinson (ed.), *Britain and the American Revolution* (London, 1998), 240.

the empire came to the forefront in place of America. The *Gentleman's Magazine*, a barometer of middling and upper-class tastes and interests, continued to carry plenty of items connected with empire. In 1785, for instance, a year in which there were no major imperial issues to stimulate heightened awareness, the *Gentleman's Magazine* included a sketch of the life of Captain Cook, reviews of works on the slave trade, the treatment of British troops captured at Bednur by Tipu Sultan, the caves at Elephant Island, near Bombay, and Charles Wilkins's translation of the *Bhagvat Geeta*, together with regular pieces of 'Intelligence' or 'Advice' from the East and West Indies, and notices on plays such as *The West Indian*, which was performed at Drury Lane in April and Covent Garden in September.[77]

There were changes in attitude, however. Anti-imperialism might not have been a significant force for many years to come, but there were alterations in the way in which empire was viewed. It was a commonplace observation before the American Revolution that the British empire, based primarily on the colonies in North America, was an empire of liberty, while the other European powers had established empires of authority and despotism. British self-congratulation in this regard might seem grotesquely inappropriate when one pauses to consider that the British empire, like the other European empires, relied to a significant extent on slave labour. But the British claim to distinctiveness was based on the role played by elected assemblies at home and in all the areas of British settlement. The liberty contemporary Britons had in mind was the liberty that consisted in freedom from arbitrary rule, a freedom secured, it was believed, by the presence of independent local legislatures. Each of the old British colonies had their own representative institutions and their peoples—or at least their peoples of British origin—regarded themselves as entitled to all the liberties of Englishmen. Even British politicians who were keen to assert the authority of the Westminster Parliament in America were careful to respect this cherished legacy. George Grenville, whose ministry brought in the American Stamp Act, referred approvingly in 1764 to the spirit of liberty in America,

---

[77] *Gentleman's Magazine*, 55 (1785), 18–20, 33–6, 67, 114–16, 148, 229, 311–13, 377, 382, 395–6, 414–16, 478–9, 553, 655–6, 740, 825, 901–3, 912, 976–7, 999.

and the need to consult the colonists on details of his proposed tax.[78] And we should note that the argument that the colonists, though not actually represented in the British Parliament, were 'virtually' represented by MPs who could speak on their behalf—an argument propagated with much industry by ministerial writers at the time of the Stamp Act—was itself an acknowledgement of the strength of the American case that taxation and representation were inextricably linked. Taxation of British subjects in America was best justified, it seemed to British ministers and their apologists, by trying to show the colonists that they were represented in the legislature that was levying the tax.[79] In 1766, when repeal of the Stamp Tax was being debated, Burke pronounced that without liberty the empire 'would not be the British Empire'.[80]

In the aftermath of the American war it was more difficult to sustain this claim. After all, more than two million free whites had left the empire with the creation of the United States. Even though 60,000 or more American loyalists had decamped to Canada, the loss of the thirteen colonies tipped the balance within the empire away from colonies of British settlement. As British-controlled territories expanded in Asia, and particularly in India, it became more an empire of conquest and annexation, involving rule over an increasing number of non-British peoples. Before 1776 a significant portion of the inhabitants of the empire were protected by their own local legislatures; after 1783, even taking account of developments in Canada—where representative institutions were established in New Brunswick in 1784 and Upper and Lower Canada in 1791— the proportion was much smaller. The association of liberty and

---

[78] Simmons and Thomas (eds.), *Proceedings and Debates of the British Parliaments respecting North America*, i. 489. There has been considerable scholarly controversy over Grenville's sincerity on this point; but whether or not he intended to give the Americans any real say is perhaps less important than his evident wish to be seen to be respecting their right to be consulted.

[79] The most well-known exposition of the theory of 'virtual representation' came in *The Regulations Lately Made Concerning the Colonies and the Taxes Imposed on them Considered* (London, 1765), a pamphlet by Grenville's secretary to the treasury, Thomas Whately. See esp. pp. 108–9. For a recent assessment of Whately's work, which places this argument in a broader context, see Ian R. Christie, 'A Vision of Empire: Thomas Whately and *The Regulations Lately Made Concerning the Colonies*', *English Historical Review*, 112 (1998), 300–20.

[80] Jack P. Greene, 'Empire and Identity from the Glorious Revolution to the American Revolution', in *Oxford History of the British Empire*, ii. *The Eighteenth Century*, ed. Marshall, 223.

empire did not wither completely; indeed, it was given a new lease of life in a rather different form, for as the British public warmed to the evils of slavery and the slave trade it became possible to compare favourably the British commitment to freedom for slaves with the continuing existence of slavery in the United States.[81] But at least some of the enthusiasm for slave emancipation can be viewed also as part of a new paternalism, a paternalism that was based on concern and care for subject peoples and that was itself an aspect of an empire based more on authority than on liberty.

The roots of a more authoritarian empire can perhaps be traced back to the Seven Years War.[82] In North America, the acquisition of Quebec in 1760 brought some 70,000 French Canadian Catholics under British jurisdiction. While the new British rulers prided themselves on their tolerance of French ways, and avoided any policy of crude 'Anglicization', Quebec was judged to be unready for a representative assembly on the model established in the old British colonies. An assembly was promised in the royal proclamation of 7 October 1763, though it seems that there was no intention to honour this promise until such time as a significant British (or British American) Protestant population had been established. Attempts to promote anglophone settlement, however, bore little fruit. In recognition of this failure, the 1774 Quebec Act, as we have seen, perpetuated government without an assembly. And it was assumed that Quebec's white population, so long as it remained overwhelmingly French Canadian, had to be held in check by a military presence; a large portion of the British army in North America after the Seven Years War was stationed in the St Lawrence Valley.[83] Significant numbers of Native Americans—perhaps about 100,000—were also present in territories acquired as a result of victory in the Seven Years War, and no one contemplated even the remotest prospect of their being given representative assemblies. The Indians, though left largely to their own devices, were to come under the paternal authority of the British crown. The proclamation of 7 October 1763 referred to 'the several nations or tribes

---

[81]   Linda Colley, *Britons: Forging the Nation 1707–1837* (New Haven, 1992), 354.

[82]   See Marshall, 'Empire and Authority in the Later Eighteenth Century'.

[83]   John Shy, *Toward Lexington: The Role of the British Army in the Coming of the Revolution* (Princeton, 1965), 55, 116, 238, 328. See also F. Ouellet, 'The British Army of Occupation in the St Lawrence Valley, 1760–1774', in A. H. Ion and R. A. Prete (eds.), *Armies of Occupation* (Waterloo, Ont., 1984), 17–54.

of Indians . . . who live under our protection', and insisted on the prevention of the expansion of white settlement into lands reserved for the Native Americans.[84] At the same time, there were British churchmen who saw it as their duty to convert the people that God had delivered into their hands. The archbishop of Canterbury and the Society for the Propagation of the Gospel were reported to be keen 'that some attention should be paid to the Indians'.[85]

In the east, meanwhile, conquest and annexation were bringing much greater numbers of non-Britons into the empire. Robert Clive's victory at Plassey in 1757 opened the door to a dramatic expansion of the territories of the East India Company. In 1765 the Mughal emperor granted the Company the *diwani*, or right to collect revenues, of Bengal, which contemporaries estimated to have a population of between ten and twenty million.[86] The Company effectively became a territorial power, with authority over a vast number of Indians, who, like the French Canadians and Native Americans, were to be ruled without recourse to representative institutions. In the case of India, however, there was a further dimension to the general theme of change from an empire of liberty to an empire of authority. The accretion of riches promised with the grant of the *diwani* greatly exacerbated concerns in Britain that the luxury, corruption, and authoritarian habits of India were infecting Company servants. The immediate cause of anxiety was the way in which returning 'nabobs', as they were called, used their ill-gotten gains to advance themselves socially and politically. Samuel Foote's well-known play *The Nabob* (1768) gave voice to this unease. But there was also a gnawing fear that 'Asiatic principles of government', imported by the nabobs, would undermine the constitution, destroying British liberty.[87]

It was not just rule over an increasing number of non-Britons that gave the empire a more authoritarian flavour. In the aftermath of the Seven Years War, pride at the growth of British territorial dominion

---

[84] *English Historical Documents*, ix. *American Colonial Documents to 1776*, ed. Merrill Jensen (London, 1969), 642–3.

[85] See e.g. *The Papers of Sir William Johnson*, ed. James Sullivan, Alexander C. Flick, et al. (14 vols., Albany, NY, 1921–65), v. 221, 383.

[86] P. J. Marshall, 'Empire and Opportunity in Britain, 1763–1775', *Transactions of the Royal Historical Society*, 6th ser. 5 (1995), 112.

[87] Id., *'A Free though Conquering People': Britain and Asia in the Eighteenth Century* (London, 1981), 7; Philip Lawson and Jim Phillips, '"Our Execrable Banditti": Perceptions of the Nabobs in Mid-Eighteenth Century Britain', *Albion*, 16 (1984), 225–41.

was tempered by anxiety about the vulnerability of Britain's overseas possessions. It was assumed that an expanded British empire needed to be guarded jealously against any inclination on the part of France and Spain to recover lost territories and lost influence. France, in particular, as we have seen, continued to be regarded with much suspicion. The security of the empire could only be ensured, it was imagined, if the metropolitan core took a more active role. Hence the new emphasis on the British Parliament's supervision and control; an imperial legislature, able to bind the empire more closely together, seemed more necessary than ever before. The result was a conviction amongst most British politicians that the superintending power of the British Parliament had to be asserted at the expense of the independence of the local legislatures of the empire. In this way, the British Parliament, though itself a representative institution, added to the authoritarian drift.[88]

Yet if the Seven Years War can be seen as starting the move towards a more authoritarian empire, the American war made a significant contribution to its development. At first this was perhaps not at all obvious, since among the outcomes of the conflict was a marked intensification of concern about the arbitrary and despotic behaviour of the East India Company's servants and a heightened alarm about the ways in which the wealth of the east could be used to corrupt British politics. But this increased public concern and alarm, paradoxically, seems merely to have been the necessary precondition of the final acceptance, among both politicians and public, of a more authoritarian version of empire. A growth in interest in the Indian part of the empire was central to this whole process. India had since the 1760s been an issue in British politics, and in 1773 it was even being claimed that the loss of India would be catastrophic for Britain's national finances.[89] But it was in and immediately after the American war that India assumed a high profile.

This was partly, and most obviously, a consequence of the loss of the American colonies. Even before the war was over, the expectation that the rebel colonies would never be brought back into the empire was encouraging some British politicians to take India more seriously. As Burke wrote to Philip Francis in December 1778, 'I

---

[88] P. J. Marshall, 'Britain and the World in the Eighteenth Century: II, Britons and Americans', *Transactions of the Royal Historical Society*, 6th ser. 9 (1999), 1–16.

[89] H. V. Bowen, *Revenue and Reform: The Indian Problem in British Politics, 1757–1773* (Cambridge, 1991), 22–3.

assure you that all your Wisdom, diligence and fortitude will be wanting to compensate to us in the East, what we have lost irrecoverably in the West'.[90] Once the independence of the United States had formally been conceded, this line of thinking became more compelling. In a speech to the House of Commons in February 1786 Burke hyperbolically described India as 'that remaining and last part of our foreign possessions'.[91] Nor was this just the perspective of a politician who was obsessed with India. Shelburne, who was loathed by Burke, expressed very similar sentiments during the peace negotiations of 1782: 'it was not to be expected', he told a French emissary pressing for concessions in India, 'that the King could cede two continents'.[92] And in 1784 Pitt the Younger told the House of Commons how the loss of America had highlighted the importance of India.[93]

Parts of the public, as well as politicians, increasingly turned their attention to India after the loss of the North American colonies. Prior to the American war, the colonies across the Atlantic had provided an outlet not just for British and Irish families looking for a new life, but also for individuals whose relatives remained in the British Isles. Younger sons of gentry and middling families, in particular, saw America as the place to make a fortune, often in trade, or in the law or medicine, or in an official capacity, or just by acquiring land and drawing an income from it. Henry Rugeley, for instance, was the son of a linen draper from St Ives, Huntingdonshire. He went to South Carolina in 1769, and within a short time established himself as a merchant at Charleston. He was reported to have been able in 1775 to pay all his debts and be left with 'an Overplus of Twenty thousand Sterling'.[94] America, of course, continued to attract migrants from the British Isles after 1783, and continued to be viewed by at least some British and Irish families as the place to send younger sons to secure their fortunes.[95] But the

---

[90] *The Correspondence of Edmund Burke*, ed. Thomas W. Copeland *et al.* (10 vols., Cambridge, 1958–78), iv. 33.

[91] *The Writings and Speeches of Edmund Burke*, vi. *India: The Launching of the Hastings Impeachment 1786–1788*, ed. P. J. Marshall and W. B. Todd (Oxford, 1991), 46.

[92] Bedfordshire RO, Grantham Papers, L 30/14/307, Shelburne to Lord Grantham, [14 Sept. 1782].

[93] H. V. Bowen, 'British India, 1765–1813: The Metropolitan Context', in Marshall (ed.), *Oxford History of the British Empire*, ii: *The Eighteenth Century*, 542.

[94] Bedfordshire RO, Rugeley Family Papers, MS X311/112.

[95] See Rosane Rocher and Michael F. Scorgie, 'A Family Empire: The Alexander Hamilton Cousins, 1750–1830', *Journal of Imperial and Commonwealth History*, 23 (1995), 189–210.

experience of losses in the war—Rugeley in 1782 was said to have been 'reduced to Beggary'[96]—and the fact that the colonies had become independent states, the governments of which might look less than favourably on property held by British subjects, almost certainly persuaded some families to consider other destinations for their junior members. India was an obvious alternative.[97] As the territories under British control increased, so did opportunities in the East India Company's service. The Company's armies expanded and so needed more officers, its ships needed more mariners as trade increased, doctors were required in significant numbers, and there were more posts for administrators. The Scots, who had taken up many of the opportunities both in colonial North America and in pre-war India, were particularly notable in India after the American conflict.[98] By the beginning of the nineteenth century, most of the Company's doctors and botanists were graduates of the University of Aberdeen, Scots were the most active figures in the Indian press, and Church of Scotland missionaries had established schools and colleges on the subcontinent.[99] In short, a great many British families, sensing that opportunities had diminished in North America, had good reason to look benignly, even enthusiastically, on the expansion of empire in India.

The American war also heightened awareness of India in a very direct way. Nothing is more likely to make possessions seem important than the prospect of their being taken away, and during the American conflict Britain's very presence in India seemed under threat. Simultaneous struggles against the Maratha confederacy and Haidar Ali of Mysore, revolts in the East India Company's northern territories, and then the intervention of the French, appeared to endanger both trade and dominion. The Company's armies suffered a number of humiliating defeats. In January 1779 the Marathas

[96] Bedfordshire RO, Rugeley Family Papers, MS X311/112. For Rugeley's losses see PRO, Audit Office Papers, Loyalist Claims Commission, AO 12/52, fos. 130–2, 155. He remained in America after the war, becoming a citizen of the United States.

[97] For an example of a family shifting its focus as a result of the American Revolution, see Jacob M. Price, 'One Family's Empire: The Russell-Lee-Clerk Connection in Maryland, Britain and India, 1707–1857', *Maryland Historical Magazine*, 72 (1977), 165–225.

[98] We should note, however, that G. J. Bryant concludes that although the absolute number of Scots going to India increased dramatically in the 1780s, there was no increase in the proportion of Scots employed. 'Scots in India in the Eighteenth Century', *Scottish Historical Review*, 64 (1985), 23, 40.

[99] John M. MacKenzie, 'Empire and National Identities: The Case of Scotland', *Transactions of the Royal Historical Society*, 6th ser. 8 (1998), 221–2.

compelled the forces of the Bombay presidency to conclude the unfavourable convention of Wadgaon. Reinforcements from Bengal restored British fortunes, but in March 1781 a contingent of the Company's troops was severely mauled as it withdrew to Panwell. In what seems like an Indian version of the retreat from Lexington and Concord, the Company's soldiers, according to Captain Richard Gomond, were pursued 'close from Bush, to Bush, with a very brisk Fire'.[100] Some 400 of the Company's troops were killed or wounded. Meanwhile, on the other side of India, in September 1780 Haidar's forces inflicted a crushing defeat on Lieutenant-Colonel Baillie's detachment at Polilur, and Madras itself looked likely to fall. At Calcutta, a British medical officer, writing on the situation in southern India, commented that 'There appears to be nothing wanting but an European enemy to act in concert with the country powers, to hurl destruction among the company's possessions in that part of the world.'[101] From the British perspective it was fortunate indeed that effective French intervention was delayed, and Eyre Coote, a Seven Years War veteran, was able to inflict a series of defeats on Haidar in 1781. But in February 1782 Tipu Sultan, Haidar's son, embarrassed the British again, wearing down and then compelling the surrender of Colonel Braithwaite's forces in Tanjore. The war against the French ended with the British in distinctly nervous mood. The Company's decision to suspend operations in June 1783, before news of the signing of the peace preliminaries in Europe had been confirmed, while having the appearance of 'an indecent haste', was viewed by one of its officers as 'most judicious and wise', given the precariousness of the position of the British forces near Cuddalore.[102] The previous month Tipu had captured General Matthew's army at Bednur, and he was confident enough to continue the struggle without the French. Tipu finally came to terms in March 1784, but not before he had delivered another blow to British pride by breaching the defences of Mangalore in January. These military failures, which contrasted so unfavourably with the victories of the Seven Years War, almost certainly encouraged British politicians and the wider public to recognize afresh the value of India and the need to secure it.

---

[100] Centre of South Asian Studies, Cromartie Papers, Gomond to Major William Sydenham, 24 Apr. 1781.
[101] BL, Benenden Letters, Add. MS 41665, fos. 14–15. See also India Office Library and Records, Munro Collection, MSS Eur. F. 151/140, Thomas Munro to Alexander Munro, 11 Oct. 1780.   [102] Devon RO, Kennaway Papers, 961 M/F1, 59–60.

Intensified interest in India manifested itself in 1781 when the British Parliament began a series of investigations into the East India Company's administration. A select committee was appointed to consider the situation in Bengal, and over the next few years it produced nine substantial reports. A secret committee probed into British involvement in various parts of India.[103] Between them, these committees uncovered maladministration and corruption on a considerable scale. Their damning indictments of the conduct of the Company's servants in India paved the way for resolutions in 1782 calling for the recall of Warren Hastings, the governor-general of Bengal; the prosecution of Sir Thomas Rumbold, former governor of Madras ('The Nabob Rumbled' was the fitting title of a Gillray cartoon);[104] Fox's India Bill of 1783, which attempted to take supervision of Indian government away from the Company's directors in London; Pitt's India Act of 1784, which established a board of control to oversee the Company's activities in India; and finally the impeachment of Hastings.

The American war and its outcome, then, increased anxieties about the governance of British India, and the ill-effects that the Indian empire was having on Britain's own government. Indeed, Fox's bill, while intended to remedy the problems, added considerably to the alarm. Fox proposed to place control over Indian affairs in the hands of a body of commissioners appointed by the government, and he wanted to give the commissioners all the patronage powers of the Company for five years. This new regime was justified by its advocates on the grounds that the Company, by its own mismanagement, had almost brought ruin on itself and the territories in its charge, and that drastic action was therefore necessary to address the situation.[105] The Company, unsurprisingly, protested at this level of interference, and its supporters spoke darkly of a violation of charter rights. But the public generally seem to have been alarmed. Rather than curing the disease, Fox's bill appeared to many contemporaries as a means of ensuring that it took a firm grip in Britain itself. A cartoon appeared on 5 December 1783 entitled 'Carlo Khan's Triumphal Entry into Leadenhall Street'. It depicted Fox ('Carlo Khan') as an oriental prince riding an elephant into the

---

[103] Jim Phillips, 'Parliament and Southern India, 1781–1783: The Secret Committee of Inquiry and the Prosecution of Sir Thomas Rumbold', *Parliamentary History*, 7 (1988), 81–97.   [104] BM 6169, 21 Jan. 1783.
[105] See e.g. the speech of John Nicholls, 8 Dec. 1783, *PH* xxiv. 14.

East India Company's headquarters.[106] The image, which was widely copied and disseminated, seems to have both influenced and reflected the public mood. It was feared that a ministry in possession of the patronage of India would soon be able to buy the support of the House of Commons and turn the legislature into a rubber stamp for the decisions of government. The bill, in the words of one of its opponents, had filled 'the nation with apprehensions of the consequences of the enormous patronage vested in the ministers'.[107] It was, in the view of Pitt, then in opposition, 'the boldest and most unconstitutional measure ever attempted, transferring at one stroke . . . the immense patronage and influence of the East to Charles Fox'.[108] All the fears about the growth of executive power that had led to the great wartime campaign for 'economical reform' were revived.[109]

But once the Company's activities were brought under closer state supervision, in Pitt's more acceptable India Act of 1784, and once the misconduct of senior Company officials in India had been brought into the limelight and duly censured, it was as if the public conscience were salved. The turning point probably came during the lengthy and ultimately unsuccessful impeachment of Hastings, which formally began in February 1788, after two years of preliminaries. At first there was considerable public interest. Cartoonists warmed to their task, one of them inevitably describing the affair as 'The Battle of Hastings'.[110] Newspapers carried full reports of the proceedings, and the public galleries were packed. James Oakes, a Suffolk businessman, was one of those who came to see the trial; his diary entry for 20 May 1788 suggests that it was still the fashionable thing to do.[111] But as the proceedings became bogged down in technicalities, and the issues became more and more complex, the public seems to have wearied of Burke's obsessive attacks and increasingly sympathized with Hastings. From the very beginning, of course, Hastings had his supporters; a cartoon first published in 1786 described the former governor-general as 'the Saviour of India' and his opponents as 'Political Banditti'.[112] But it seems that pro-Hastings sentiment, encouraged by his agents and friends, grew

---

[106] BM 6276.   [107] BL, Hardwicke Papers, Add. MS 35381, fo. 174.
[108] Earl Stanhope, *Life of the Rt. Hon. William Pitt* (4 vols., London, 1861–2), i. 140–1.
[109] See above, Ch. 6.   [110] BM 7139, 9 Feb. 1787.
[111] *The Oakes Diaries*, ed. Jane Fisk, vol. i (Suffolk Record Society, vol. xxxii, Woodbridge, 1990), 252.   [112] BM 6955.

as the trial proceeded.[113] In another cartoon of February 1790 Burke was criticized for his '*Persecution of Mr. H*'.[114] Burke, in short, by going too far appears inadvertently to have created a more forgiving attitude towards the Company's wayward servants.

The new public mood was also influenced, no doubt, by the outbreak of further war in India in 1789. This fresh conflict, another round in the long-drawn-out struggle against the rulers of Mysore, was not initially greeted with much enthusiasm. There still seems to have been much fear in Britain about the consequences of expansionism in India. In December 1791 a London debating society decided 'almost unanimously' that the war was 'unjust, disgraceful and ruinous'.[115] But newspapers carried extensive reports on the campaigns and when news arrived that in February 1792 Tipu had been defeated, and that he had been obliged to sue for peace and accept the loss of some of his territory, there were widespread celebrations in Britain. Books appeared to capitalize on public interest, broadsheets were published containing songs and poems, and all manner of artefacts were produced to cater for public enthusiasm—even tin trays were decorated with pictures of Tipu's surrender. The public euphoria, as Peter Marshall has pointed out, can be variously explained. It owed something, in all probability, to anxieties about the French Revolution and the threat it posed to Britain: 'large sections of the British public by celebrating the downfall of Tipu were bidding defiance to their enemies both within and without'.[116] But it was also, as Marshall stresses, a product of a new attitude towards the empire in India.

Tipu's reputation was important here. He was widely seen as an ambitious rival to the British. Mysore itself was an expansionist state, and Tipu was regarded as a fanatical anti-Christian, determined to spread his influence across India. 'He was resolved', a British officer wrote at the end of the American war, 'to establish his empire over all Hindostan by the united terrors of the Koran and

---

[113] See the assessment in the introd. to *Writings and Speeches of Burke*, ed. Marshall and Todd, vi. 13.   [114] BM 7627, 'Peachum and Lockit'.

[115] Donna T. Andrew (ed.), *London Debating Societies, 1776–1799* (London Record Society, vol. xxx, London, 1994), 19.

[116] P. J. Marshall, '"Cornwallis Triumphant": War in India and the British Public in the Late Eighteenth Century', in Lawrence Freedman, Paul Hayes, and Robert O'Neill (eds.), *War, Strategy, and International Politics: Essays in Honour of Sir Michael Howard* (Oxford, 1992), 69.

the sword.'[117] Tipu was also viewed as a powerful and skilful military practitioner. His successes in the American war years earned him much admiration. He was, according to a British periodical, 'ardent, eager, enterprising'.[118] Even one of the officers captured by Tipu's father at Polilur wrote of him as 'an expert soldier'.[119] At the same time, however, respect was tempered by the perception that Tipu was cruel and despotic. His handling of his own people was criticized; in 1786 a British account compared him unfavourably with his father, arguing that Tipu, 'from his tyrannical disposition don't stand so well in the affections of his subjects as old Hyder did'.[120] But it was his maltreatment of British prisoners that above all marked him out, in British eyes, as a stereotypical oriental despot. In 1785, as we have seen, the *Gentleman's Magazine* had reviewed Captain Henry Oakes's *Authentic Narrative of the Treatment of the English who were Taken Prisoners on the Reduction of Bednore*. The review, while placing some of the blame on the British forces themselves for their ill-conduct prior to the fall of Bednur, roundly condemned the 'hardships and cruelties' Tipu had inflicted on his defenceless prisoners.[121] Another periodical, equally prepared to view the episode in a balanced manner, was no less critical of the fate of General Matthews and his fellow officers, murdered by poisoning, or, according to some accounts, by having melted lead poured down their throats.[122]

With the coming of another war against Mysore, Tipu naturally acquired still more notoriety. In June 1792, before news reached Britain of Cornwallis's triumph, General Richard Smith, himself a nabob, told the House of Commons that Tipu, having murdered 'our gallant countrymen' in the previous war, was 'so faithless a tyrant' that he could never be trusted.[123] Tipu became, and was to remain for long after his death in 1799, in the next Mysore war, a 'bogeyman' for the British public, comparable, in the view of a leading historian of India, to such twentieth-century hate-figures as Colonels Nassar of Egypt and Gaddhafi of Libya,[124] and, we might

---

[117] Earl of Crawford (ed.), *Lives of the Lindsays* (2nd edn., 3 vols., London, 1858), iii. 319.
[118] *New Annual Register . . . for the Year 1784* (London, 1785), 98.
[119] Earl of Crawford (ed.), *Lives of the Lindsays*, iii. 319.
[120] HMC, *Palk MSS* (London, 1922), 393.
[121] *Gentleman's Magazine*, 55 (1785), 553. See also ibid., 54 (1784), 949–50.
[122] *New Annual Register . . . for 1784*, 99–100.   [123] *PH* xxix. 1553.
[124] C. A. Bayly, *Imperial Meridian: The British Empire and the World 1780–1830* (London, 1989), 114.

add, to carry forward the analogy, Saddam Hussein of Iraq. And as Tipu's character and alleged crimes preoccupied the public in Britain, they started, unsurprisingly, to look more favourably on those East India Company officials who had been trying to provide government in India. The offences of Hastings and his colleagues seemed to pale into insignificance beside the outrages committed by Tipu.

Tipu's inhumane despotism, moreover, could now be contrasted with the more restrained and civilized paternalism of Company rule, epitomized by the new governor-general of Bengal, Earl (later Marquis) Cornwallis. Cornwallis, who led the forces that defeated Tipu in 1792, was a highly plausible representative of a new style of British authority in India. As a patrician aristocrat he seemed both to embody paternalism and to elevate the reputation of British rule, distancing it appreciably from the shabby and squalid money-grabbing of the past. While Hastings liked to stress his noble lineage, Cornwallis exuded aristocratic ease. His kindly treatment of Tipu's sons, who were taken into his care as a pledge for the fulfilment of the terms of the peace, was widely interpreted as a sign of the essentially moderate and benevolent nature of British power. Robert Home's painting of this event, completed in 1794, pleasingly captured its symbolism. At the centre of the canvas is an avuncular-looking Cornwallis, smiling gently as he takes the hand of one of Tipu's sons, while Tipu himself, or more probably Tipu's representative, his face in shadow, ushers the boy forward. Enormous elephants, meant no doubt to represent India, provide a suitable backdrop, and fluttering triumphantly above the scene is the inevitable Union Flag.[125]

The American war, then, saw the first sustained criticism of war as an instrument of policy, and prepared the ground for the more thoroughly irenical movements that flourished during and after the long conflict with revolutionary and Napoleonic France. It no doubt also created some converts to the view that fighting to maintain overseas dominion was a waste of resources, not least because the value of territorial empire was itself questionable. Of more immediate importance was the way in which the American war

---

[125] For more on the iconography of British India at this time see Mildred Archer, *India and British Portraiture 1770–1825* (London, 1979).

furthered the process whereby the British empire became increasingly associated with authoritarian rule over subject peoples and less with largely self-governing British settlements abroad. It contributed to a change in attitudes, at both official and public levels, about the nature of the empire and the desirability of dominion in the east. With America gone, the focus naturally turned to India. And once India was at the forefront of political concern, the language of an empire of liberty seemed peculiarly inappropriate. Once the British state was able to exert a degree of control over the East India Company, and bring its wayward servants to book, it was possible for the British public to look more favourably on British rule on the subcontinent. Despotic it might be, but it was a humane, civilized, and regulated despotism—a despotism that seemed to an increasing number of contemporaries in the British Isles to be an acceptable means of governing India, not least because it could be portrayed as an altogether gentler and superior form of despotism to the oriental variety practised by Indian rulers like Tipu Sultan.

Conclusions

THE AMERICAN WAR was an important event not just in the history of North America but also in the history of the British Isles. Different chapters in this book have examined its imprint, both ephemeral and longer-lasting, on the economy, society, culture, politics, religion, the constitution, and attitudes to war and the empire. A series of local studies has underlined the varied manner in which the war impinged upon very different communities the length and breadth of the British Isles. In many respects, of course, the conflict merely intensified or carried forward developments associated with earlier armed struggles—especially with the Seven Years War—or accelerated existing trends. At the same time, however, the American war was responsible for much that was new and distinctive in eighteenth-century terms—a prolonged recession in overseas trade; legislative independence for Ireland; the creation of a broadly based movement for political reform; the start of a process of administrative change that helped to alter the nature of the political system—and it influenced thinking on issues as diverse as the role of women, penal policy, and provision for the poor. Here was an armed conflict that touched the lives, in one way or another, of almost all of George III's British and Irish subjects.

The scale and many dimensions of the impact of the war have not been fully appreciated by historians. The conflict used to be dismissed as very different from the long struggle against revolutionary and Napoleonic France that followed it. Piers Mackesy, in a memorable phrase, described it as 'the last great war of the *ancien régime*'. He implied that it was a limited conflict that could not be put in the same class as the French Revolutionary and Napoleonic Wars, which should be seen as anticipations of the 'total' wars of the twentieth century. Mackesy acknowledged elements of novelty in the American war's American aspect, but he argued that for Britain it was remarkable more for its lack of intrusion than for its transforming effects.[1] More recently some attention has been given to the way in which developments earlier in the eighteenth century prefigured the impact of the wars of 1793–1815. J. E. Cookson's thought-provoking work on British and Irish mobilization in the French Revolutionary and Napoleonic Wars includes some helpful pointers to anticipations of his 'British armed nation', and he gives the experience of the war of 1775–83 honourable if brief mention.[2] But even Cookson underplays the significance of the American conflict. The wars of 1793–1815 were undeniably longer and more demanding than the American war, bringing forth a greater mobilization of manpower and resources. But rather than viewing this as proof of the distinctiveness of the wars against the French Revolution and Napoleon—as an indication of a qualitative change in the nature and impact of warfare—we should perhaps see the struggle of 1793–1815 as the culmination of a process of greater mobilization and more intrusiveness that had been fitfully lurching forward as the eighteenth century progressed, and was given a considerable boost by the American war.

War and the State

What does this book tell us about the nature and power of the late eighteenth-century British state? John Brewer's thesis that a strong 'fiscal-military state' underpinned Britain's emergence during the eighteenth century as an undisputed Great Power has been criticized, as we have seen, by Cookson, who in his study of mobilization during the wars of 1793–1815 presents a picture of a weak British state, dependent upon a great number and variety of interests beyond its control, even for the organization of national defence.

The preceding pages provide some evidence to suggest that much the same could be said of the British state in the American war. Mobilization was a complex and contested process. The number of men in uniform was a consequence not just of the will of government, but of the extent of grass-roots resistance and, perhaps more

[1] Piers Mackesy, *The War for America 1775–1783* (London, 1964), 4. Mackesy, to be fair, made this statement in his introductory, scene-setting remarks. His book concentrates on British strategy, and does not attempt to explore the impact of the war on British society.
[2] J. E. Cookson, *The British Armed Nation 1793–1815* (Oxford, 1997), ch. 1.

importantly, of the independent efforts of a whole host of local interests, many of which were deeply antagonistic to ministerial management. In Ireland, where the militia could not be revived for lack of public money, the volunteers emerged as an armed force beyond the control of either the Dublin or London governments. And if the very existence of the Irish volunteers was a sign of the weakness of central authority, we might also note that by 1783 the volunteers, by playing a crucial role in securing greater autonomy for the Irish Parliament, had been instrumental in *reducing* the power of the British state. In Britain, too, volunteer units, largely composed of the 'middling sort', emerged in ways that were usually unamenable to central direction and control, and were sometimes expressly hostile to the government. At the very least, volunteer bodies represented vigorous localism rather than loyalty to central institutions, and in that sense demonstrated the limited power of the state.

Even the vast expansion of the regular armed forces was not in itself a sign of the power of the state. In fact the initiative for forming most of the new corps came from beyond government. Highland chiefs, English and Irish peers, Welsh gentlemen, town corporations, and West Indian merchants and planters all offered to provide regiments at little or no cost to the state. In making such offers, these bodies and individuals looked, unsurprisingly, to their own interests. As the lord-lieutenant wrote from Dublin in 1779, 'Proposals for raising corps crowd in upon me from every side, which very, very few instances excepted, are dictated by idea's of military rank, county influence, or emolument.'[3] When the state was unwilling to accommodate local interests, the offers tended to be withdrawn. That the king and his ministers were often obliged reluctantly to accept such offers, is surely a reflection of the weakness of the state's position. The king's preferred policy of augmenting existing regiments rather than raising new ones, more or less maintained while the war was simply an Anglo-American struggle, had to be abandoned once the war became a worldwide conflict and the British Isles were themselves threatened with invasion.

Similar points could be made about the mobilization of resources. The securing of food and other supplies for the armed forces was not simply a matter of ministerial diktat, but involved often lengthy discussions with contractors, many of whom were able to secure

---

[3] HMC, *Lothian MSS* (London, 1905), 352.

distinctly favourable terms. The raising of money to fund the war effort was likewise the subject of hard bargaining. Lord North, as we have seen, secured ever larger loans to finance the war, but he did so only by offering all manner of inducements to investors and by engaging in negotiations with the 'monied men'. The outcome, so far as North was concerned, was not always satisfactory. More importantly perhaps, increases in taxation, which Brewer and others have seen as a vital element of the 'fiscal-military state', became a major political issue in the American war. The existence of the House of Commons as a representative institution had, according to Brewer, reconciled Britons to relatively high levels of taxation in previous wars.[4] In the American war, however, as the tax burden increased, and defeats and setbacks brought discontent and uncertainty, parliament came to be seen by a significant section of the political nation as corrupted and unrepresentative. And we should remember, of course, that the Association movement, while failing to secure even a modest change in the representative system, did succeed in pushing North's government into beginning a process of administrative overhaul and financial retrenchment that was to have far-reaching effects on the nature of the British state.

On the other hand, the state's role and effectiveness should not be minimized. Some apparent signs of weakness can, on further reflection, appear as evidence of growing strength. The East India Company provided the bulk of Britain's military presence in India, directly through its own large armies and indirectly by paying for the British and Hanoverian regular regiments employed on the subcontinent. That a private company was responsible for providing most of the men and nearly all of the money for the war in India would seem to confirm the limited power of the British state. Yet, looked at in a different way, the opposite can be said to be the truth. The Company paid for British regular regiments because the British state insisted that it did so, a statute of 1781 formalizing the arrangement.[5] British ministers, moreover, oversaw the activities of the Company's servants in India, who were required, under the terms of the Regulating Act of 1773, to submit reports to a secretary of state. Eyre Coote, a British regular army commander, took charge of

---

[4] See Brewer, *Sinews of Power*, esp. 132.

[5] See P. J. Marshall, 'Britain and the World in the Eighteenth Century: I, Reshaping the Empire', *Transactions of the Royal Historical Society*, 6th ser. 8 (1998), 15.

Company troops in southern India and successfully exerted his authority, despite the attempts of the Madras council to interfere in his operations.[6] The Company, in other words, was increasingly becoming an arm of the state rather than an autonomous body, and shortly after the war, as we have seen, state control was increased by Pitt's India Act of 1784. Even the process of 'economical reform' within Britain, which on the face of it involved cutting back the power of government, can be interpreted as strengthening rather than weakening the state in the medium to long term. A leaner and cheaper state was in many ways a more efficient state, and therefore to many Britons a more acceptable state. As it gradually shed the taint of corruption, and acquired a reputation for probity and economy, the stage was set for an expansion of its activities into new areas of regulation and intervention in the course of the nineteenth century.

More immediately, we can see that military and naval mobilization during the war, at least so far as the regular armed forces are concerned, owed much to state direction and control. The total numbers employed and paid were determined by the estimates submitted annually to the British and Irish Parliaments. And recruitment itself, while leaning heavily on voluntary endeavour at the local level, was significantly influenced by the activities of the state. The navy's expansion owed much to the willingness of many landmen and mariners to volunteer, but the number of men serving could never have reached the heights that it did without the activities of the press-gangs. Here we see in very stark terms the importance of compulsion by the state. Resistance, both from the intended targets and from local magistrates, might have diminished the quantity of men forced to join the navy, but pressing proved overall to be a successful means of raising trained mariners. An indication of this, surely, is the way in which the new ministers in 1782, having criticized pressing while in opposition, had no hesitation in continuing the practice once in power. The expansion of the army, we should not forget, also owed something to compulsion, with the Recruiting Acts of 1778 and 1779 allowing the forcible enlistment of the able-bodied unemployed, and convicted criminals and even accused men were encouraged, through conditional pardons or judicial discretion, to become soldiers. The numbers in these

---

[6] For Coote's complaints see BL, Liverpool Papers, Add. MS 38405, fo. 124.

categories may not have been large in the context of the expansion of the army, but in the case of the Recruiting Acts the stimulation provided to voluntary recruitment by the threat of compulsion is perhaps a more appropriate way of assessing their impact. Indeed, the state's role as a provider of inducements was probably much more important than its role as a coercive force. The Recruiting Act of 1779, by offering entrants into the army the chance to exercise their trade in any town in the kingdom once they had been discharged, probably helped to stimulate enlistment amongst artisans and small traders. And it did so, we should note, at the expense of entrenched local interests. Corporate bodies wishing to restrict trading activity to their own members were naturally aggrieved, but their likely resistance was ignored when the legislation was framed, and seems to have been overcome when ex-servicemen sought to exercise the rights given them by the legislature. The state, furthermore, offered inducements to Catholic elites in Ireland to promote recruitment; the Catholic Relief Acts of 1778 are now widely recognized as an attempt to tap the manpower potential of Irish Catholicism, and the further measures of 1782 can be seen in a similar light.

We might also reflect that sustaining most of the greatly enlarged military and naval forces was the responsibility of the state, and a responsibility that it discharged remarkably successfully. The army in America—the biggest that any British government had ever sent abroad—had to be supplied for the most part from the British Isles. Assembling the provisions and the ships to carry food, fuel, equipment, money, and men across 3,000 miles of ocean was an immense logistical exercise, involving the government not just in negotiations with contractors but also in attempting to safeguard stocks and control prices, as in 1776 when an embargo was placed on the export of Irish provisions. Given the scale of the task, we should not be surprised at occasional crises. The army in besieged Boston was forced on to reduced rations in the winter of 1775–6; General Clinton complained in November 1778 that since he had been in command his army had four times been 'within 3 weeks of Starving';[7] and in 1782 a lack of shipping delayed the movement of troops from New York to the Caribbean. Yet the achievement, considered overall, was striking. In 1776, when the British army in America was substantial, Howe was delighted with his logistical

[7] Nottingham University Library, Newcastle of Clumber MSS, NeC 2646.

support. 'The Supplies of Provisions from Europe have been so wisely planned and so well executed', he wrote, that his forces could 'be under no Apprehension of Want'.[8]

The large-scale mobilization of manpower and the provision of appropriate logistical back-up cost a great deal of money. Even though public subscriptions and private initiatives reduced the potential charge on the state, and the East India Company paid for the troops employed in India, the British government had to take responsibility for the bulk of the necessary expenditure. Again, it should be said that this responsibility was discharged remarkably successfully. It might have been increasingly difficult to raise loans, and opposition to mounting taxation was encountered, but successive governments secured vast sums of money—more than had ever been raised before in Britain and Ireland. They did so, moreover, in a safer manner and on better terms than the governments of their enemies. The printing of paper money by the American Congress and by the various independent American states led to hyperinflation, destroyed public confidence, and very nearly brought the war effort of the rebel colonies to a standstill. Lord North might have had to offer free stock and other inducements to attract investment in the national debt, but he was able to negotiate loans at lower rates of interest than were the Spanish and French governments. The French debt in 1783 was only 62% of the British, yet French interest payments were 75% of the British. Indeed, it would seem that Britain's financial capacity to pursue the war was much greater than that of the Americans, the French, the Spanish, and even the Dutch.[9]

The power of the state was evident in other senses. As government expenditure rose significantly, the state found itself, at least temporarily, playing a bigger part in the economic life of the British Isles. The large-scale buying of foodstuffs, military equipment, uniforms, and so on had an impact on prices and production. When an Irish merchant wrote in January 1781 that the Dutch war would have the effect of 'keep[ing] up provisions', he was reflecting on the enormous purchasing power of government.[10] Indeed, as we have seen, the stimulus to home production provided by war-related

[8] T 64/108, fo. 73.

[9] Stephen Conway, *The War of American Independence 1775–1783* (London, 1995), chs. 3 and 10.

[10] NLI, Blake Papers, MS 10816, John Blake to Isidore Blake, 2 Jan. 1781.

government spending seems to have been sufficient almost to offset the depressive effects of the slump in overseas trade. At the end of the war, when the government had surplus food stocks on its hands, it was able to relieve extreme hardship in the Scottish Highlands. Provisions originally purchased for the army were distributed to help counter a subsistence crisis caused by the poor harvests of 1782 and 1783.[11]

Where, then, do we strike the balance? The Cookson perspective, by emphasizing the limitations on the state, provides a useful corrective to some of the more extravagant ideas that can flow from the Brewer thesis, and presents us with a more subtle and variegated picture of the distribution of power in the eighteenth-century British Isles. But, as Cookson himself recognizes, too much concentration on the localities can lead one to overlook the controlling influence of central authority. In truth, even in our own times, when no one would deny that the state plays a big role in shaping our lives, society functions only through the efforts and energies of a vast array of voluntary bodies and organizations independent of the state. In the late eighteenth century the scales were obviously tipped much more in favour of local elites and initiatives, but the state still showed itself to have formidable war-making capacity—a capacity that defeat in the American war should not be allowed to obscure.

Division and Unity

Linda Colley's picture of the widespread adoption of a British national identity, as we have seen, stresses the important role played by war, and particularly war against France, in forging a common sense of Britishness. We have seen, too, that Colley has been criticized for presenting too one-dimensional and unsophisticated a vision of British patriotism, which Cookson contends was multifaceted and often based more on self-interest than a commitment to the nation.[12] Colley has also been attacked by several

---

[11] T. C. Smout, 'Famine and Famine Relief in Scotland', in L. M. Cullen and T. C. Smout (eds.), *Comparative Aspects of Scottish and Irish Economic and Social History 1600– 1900* (Edinburgh, n.d.), 27.

[12] He treads cautiously, however, acknowledging that in a section of *Britons* Colley 'says sensible things about the different motivations that operated' when it came to volunteering in the wars of 1793–1815. See Cookson, *British Armed Nation*, 9 and n.

historians for what they see as her presentation of Britishness as a unifying force that smothered divisions within contemporary society. Her critics maintain that war not only failed to paper over the cracks, but actually deepened them. The experience of war itself, they suggest, caused division.

Was this the case in the American conflict? The war was clearly divisive. Most familiarly, it divided along political lines, with opponents and supporters of the coercion of the colonists often adopting extreme positions and even engaging in acts of violence towards each other. In 1780 William Cowper was fearful that his country was on the brink of an internecine conflict; the political tensions, he suggested, appeared alarmingly like those in the period of Charles I's reign immediately prior to the last civil war.[13] Other divisions were opened up as well: between Protestants and Catholics; between the sexes, in the sense that traditional gender roles, while challenged in some respects, were ultimately reinforced; and between different social groups, particularly between landed elites and the middling ranks, but also between parts of the manufacturing middling sort and their plebeian workforces. The war even divided along lines of economic interest. The wartime fall in wool prices, good news for the hard-pressed textile industries, was decidedly unwelcome for wool producers. The result was a vigorous campaign to allow, if only temporarily, the export of raw wool, which was successfully countered by a still more vigorous defence of the prohibitory legislation by the manufacturers.

But if division is evident enough, what of unity? Unity is certainly far more elusive. Yet it is part of the story. War against the Americans polarized opinion in Britain and Ireland; but then war against the Bourbon powers provided an opportunity for the creation of a new unity. This unity, it should be said, was based on a conception of Britishness that was in an important sense very different from what had gone before. The American colonists, prior to declaring their independence, had regarded themselves—and been regarded by many of the British and Irish—as part of the extended British nation. Once the Americans departed from the empire, national identity had to be reconfigured. But if Britishness

---

[13] *The Letters and Prose Writings of William Cowper*, ed. James King and Charles Ryskamp (5 vols., Oxford, 1979–86), i. 314–15, 337. But see also i. 340, where he changes his mind.

could no longer incorporate the Americans, and was therefore more geographically confined, it could be argued that the experience of the war made it enter deeper into the consciousness of the peoples of the British Isles. To say this is not to deny or even to minimize the ways in which the conflict opened up and at times magnified divisions between the component countries. Due consideration has been given to these tensions, I trust, in the course of this book. But the war also had the effect, it seems, of bringing the English, Welsh, Scots, and Irish together in a great British struggle against their European enemies. Important in this respect were the demands of the war from 1778. The armed services were themselves melting pots and, perhaps more tellingly, they presented to the wider public an image of Britishness at work. The threat of invasion was a significant influence, too, intensifying, as it did, hostility to outsiders. But a peculiar feature of the American conflict should be highlighted. Britain had fought several wars against France earlier in the eighteenth century, which had brought forth a considerable, if lesser, mobilization of manpower and had threatened the home territory with invasion. But never before had Britain been faced with such a combination of enemies. The previous pattern, indeed, was for Britain to be part of a coalition of states formed to check French power. Now the tables had been turned. In the American war it was the British who found themselves confronted by a multiplicity of foes as first the French, then the Spanish, and finally the Dutch joined the conflict. The sense of a beleaguered nation seems to have captured the public imagination. Hence the euphoria when news arrived of Rodney's victory at the Saints. It was not just that Jamaica had been saved, important as that undoubtedly was believed to be. More significantly, Britain now appeared to be reviving, even against formidable odds. This perception, as we have seen, was a great source of comfort and national pride, which seems to have affected people across the British Isles.

Bibliography

UNPUBLISHED PRIMARY SOURCES

Aberdeen University Library
Duff of Braco Muniments

Alnwick Castle, Northumberland
Percy Papers (now on deposit in the Northumberland Record Office)

American Philosophical Society, Philadelphia
Thomas Sullivan Journal

Ardchattan Priory, Connell, Argyll
Campbell Preston of Ardchattan Papers

Ballindalloch Castle, Banffshire
Macpherson Grant of Ballindalloch Papers

Beaulieu, Hampshire
Montagu Estate Papers

Bedfordshire Record Office, Bedford
Grantham Papers
Polwarth Papers
Robinson Papers
Rugeley Papers

Berkshire Record Office, Reading
Abingdon Corporation Records
Abingdon St Nicholas Parish Records
Barrett and Belson Family Papers
Butler Papers
Downshire Papers
Hartley Russell Papers
Thomas Johnson Account-book
Loveden Papers
Maidenhead Borough Records

Neville and Aldworth Papers
Newbury Corporation Records
New Windsor Borough Records
Peasemore Parish Records
Preston MSS
Quarter Sessions Records
Reading Corporation Records
Shrivenham Parish Records
Stevens of Bradfield Papers
Sutton Courtney Parish Records
Thatcham Parish Records
Tilehurst Parish Records
Wallingford Borough Records
Wokingham Corporation Records

Birmingham City Archives

Matthew Boulton Papers
Galton Papers
James Watt Papers

Bodleian Library, Oxford

Abingdon Election Papers
Bertie Papers
Diary of William Dunne
North Papers

Boston Public Library, Boston, Massachusetts

Miscellaneous Papers
Percy Letters
Thomas Stanley Letters

The British Library, London

Abergavenny MSS
Althorp Papers
American Papers (Egerton MSS)
Auckland Papers
Benenden Letters
Blenheim Papers
Buckingham Papers
Diary of William Digby
Fitzpatrick Papers
Fox Papers
Journal of Midshipman James Francis Grant

Haldimand Papers
Hamilton and Greville Papers
Hardwicke Papers
Hastings Papers
Hutchinson and Oliver Papers (Egerton MSS)
Leeds Papers
Liverpool Papers
Loudoun Papers
Macartney Papers
Mackenzie Papers
Martin Papers
Miscellaneous Papers (microfilm)
Napier Papers
Nelson Papers
Newcastle Papers
Pelham Papers
Rainsford Papers
William Vassell Letter-books (microfilm)
Westminster Committee Papers

The Brotherton Library, University of Leeds

Jonathan Akroyd Account-books
John Jowitt Jnr. Debtor and Creditor Ledger
James Lister Day-book

Buckinghamshire Record Office, Aylesbury

Howard-Vyse Deposit

Calderdale Archives, Halifax

Lister of Shibden Hall MSS
Ovenden Parish Records

Cambridgeshire Record Office, Cambridge

Huddleston of Sawston Papers
Quarter Sessions Records

Canna House, Isle of Canna, Scotland

Campbell of Inverneill Papers

Centre of South Asian Studies, Cambridge

Cromartie Papers (photocopies)

Cornwall Record Office, Truro

Journal of Thomas Hawkins

Ilogan Parish Records
Militia Papers
Ordnance Office Letter-book
Rogers of Penrose Papers
St Erme Parish Records
Tremayne of Heligan Papers
Wynell-Mayow Papers

Corporation of London Record Office

Sir John Langham's Charity Papers
Press Act Papers
Quarter Sessions Records

Cumbria Record Office, Kendal

Robert Rauthmell Letters

Devon Record Office, Exeter

Drake of Buckland Abbey Papers
Kennaway Papers
Quicke Papers
Miscellaneous Shipping Papers

Dr Williams's Library, London

Wodrow-Kenrick Correspondence

East Suffolk Record Office, Ipswich

Barrington Papers
Saumarez Papers

East Sussex Record Office, Lewes

Lieutenancy Papers
Miscellaneous Additional MSS
Monmouthshire Militia Order-book
Newick Parish Records
Diaries of William Poole
Sheffield Papers

Essex Record Office, Chelmsford

John Crosier's Memoirs
Ilford Militia Records
Petre Family Papers
Quarter Sessions Records
Round MSS

St Mary the Virgin, Great Warley, Parish Records
St Peter, Little Warley, Parish Records
St Thomas of Canterbury, Brentwood, Parish Records
Smyth Family Papers

Friends House Library, London

Miscellaneous MSS

Glasgow University Library

Bannerman MSS

Gloucestershire Record Office, Gloucester

Blathwayt Papers
Ducie and Morton Muniments
Hale Papers
John Lloyd Letters
Rooke Papers

Hampshire Record Office, Winchester

Banbury Papers
Diary of Revd Richard Ford
Jervoise Collection
Quarter Sessions Records
Diaries of John Thorp of Preston Candover

Hertfordshire Record Office, Hertford

Ashbridge II MSS
Baker MSS
Ratcliffe MSS
Verulam MSS

The Hirsel, Berwickshire

Douglas-Home Muniments

Historical Society of Pennsylvania, Philadelphia

Clifford Papers
Tench Coxe Papers
Dreer Collection: Daniel Weir Letter-book
Pemberton Papers
Sir John Wrottesley Notebook

Horsham Museum

Medwin Papers

Hull Record Office

Borough Records
Minute-book of Committee for Convoys
Miscellaneous MSS

Hull University Library

Hotham Papers
Maxwell-Constable Papers
Sykes Papers

India Office Library and Records, London

Bombay Letters Received
Diary of an Unidentified Officer
Home Miscellaneous Papers
Hughes MSS
Madras Letters Received
Munro Collection

Kent Archives Office, Maidstone

Amherst MSS
Pratt MSS
Twisden Family Papers

Lancashire Record Office, Preston

Grundy Papers
Hoghton Papers

Leeds Archives

Ramsden Papers (Rockingham Letters)
John Wilson Papers

Leicestershire Record Office, Leicester

Lieutenancy Papers
Turville Constable Maxwell MSS

Library of Congress, Washington, DC

Colebrooke, Nesbitt, Colebrooke and Franks Papers
Stephen Collins & Son Collection
Dunlop Family Papers
Peter Force MSS
Christopher French Journals
Miscellaneous MSS Collection

Lichfield Record Office

Corporation Records
Commonplace-book of Richard Greene
St Mary's Parish Records

Lincolnshire Archives Office, Lincoln

Diary and Account-book of Matthew Flinders the Elder
Journal or Day-book of John Mells
Stubton Papers

Liverpool Record Office

Parker Papers
Tarleton Papers

Massachusetts Historical Society, Boston

Coffin Family Papers
Gardiner, Whipple and Allen Papers
Miscellaneous MSS

National Army Museum, London

Services of James Green
Laye Papers
Maitland Papers

National Library of Ireland, Dublin

Blake Papers
Dobbs Papers
D'Olier Papers
Minutes of the Doneraile Volunteers
Minutes of the Ennis Volunteers
Fitzpatrick Papers
Heron Papers
Vere Hunt Papers (microfilm)
Papers relative to the defence of Ireland
Diary of a Cork Quaker
Kilmainham Papers
O'Hara Papers
Order-book, 32nd Foot
Diaries of Mary Shackleton
Shannon Papers
Wicklow Papers

National Library of Scotland, Edinburgh

Fettercairn Papers
Halkett Papers
Houston Papers
John Macleod Letters
Robertson-MacDonald Papers
Steuart Papers
Stuart Stevenson Papers
William Wilson Papers

National Library of Wales, Aberystwyth

Bodrhyddan Papers
Bute MSS
Glynllifon Papers
D. T. M. Jones Collection
Nassau Senior Papers
Noyadd Trefawr Papers
Owen and Colby Papers
Peniarth MSS
Powis Castle Papers
Spence Colby Papers
Tredegar MSS
Wigfair Papers

New-York Historical Society

Bancker Papers
Beekman Papers
Byvant-Bleeker Papers
Andrew Elliot Letters
Miscellaneous MSS
Frederick and Philip Rhinelander Papers

New York Public Library

Bayard-Campbell-Pearsall Papers
Robert Henderson Day-book

Norfolk Record Office, Norwich

Great Yarmouth Corporation Records

Northumberland Record Office, Newcastle

Ridley of Blagdon MSS

North Yorkshire Record Office, Northallerton

Chaytor Papers
Scarborough Corporation Records
Wyvill MSS
Zetland (Dundas) MSS

Nottingham University Library

Mellish of Hodsock MSS
Newcastle of Clumber MSS
Portland Papers

Nottinghamshire Archives

Nevile of Thorney MSS

Pembrokeshire Record Office (Dyfed Archives), Haverfordwest

Daniel Gwynne Letters

The Public Record Office, London

Admiralty Papers
Audit Office Papers
Carleton Papers
Chatham Papers
Clerk of Assize Papers
Colonial Office Papers
Cornwallis Papers
Documents of Unknown Ownership
Foreign Office Papers
Granville Papers
High Court of Admiralty Papers
Hoare (Pitt) Papers
Home Office Papers
Rodney Papers
State Papers
Treasury Papers
War Office Papers

The Public Record Office of Northern Ireland, Belfast

Abercorn Papers
Notebook of a Coleraine merchant
Downshire Papers
Drennan Letters
Account-book of James Ferguson
Greer Papers

Hart Papers
Diary of an Irish linen merchant
Miscellaneous MSS
Minute-book of the First Newry Volunteers
O'Hara Papers
Shannon Papers
Stewart of Killymoon Papers
Stabane Corporation Records (microfilm)

Queen's Lancashire Regiment Museum, Warrington

Plymouth Citadel Orderly-book

Rammerscales House, Dumfries

Bell-Macdonald Papers

Reading University Library

Elliot Family Papers
Farm Records
Diary of Richard Hayes

Royal Fusiliers Museum, The Tower of London

Recruiting Instructions
Regimental Records

The Royal Society, London

Blagden Papers

The Scottish Record Office, Edinburgh

Broughton and Cally Muniments
Campbell of Barcaldine Muniments
Cuninghame of Thorntoun Muniments
Dalguise Muniments
Henderson of Fordell Muniments
Inglis Papers
Lindsay of Dowhill Muniments
Logan Home of Edrom Muniments
Miscellaneous Gifts and Deposits

Sheffield Archives

Rockingham MSS
Spencer Stanhope of Cannon Hall Muniments

Somerset Record Office, Taunton

Caleb Dickinson's Journal
Strachey MSS

Staffordshire Record Office, Stafford

Bagot Papers
Congreve Papers
Dartmouth MSS
Diary of Samuel Pipe Wolferstan
Dyott Papers
Gower Papers
Hanbury Parish Records
Littleton Papers
Paget Papers
Sneyd Papers

Surrey Record Office (Guildford Muniment Room)

Borough Records
Onslow MSS

Trinity College Library, Dublin

Conolly MSS

University College London Library

Bentham MSS

Warwickshire Record Office, Warwick

Quarter Sessions Records
Ward-Boughton-Leigh of Brownsover Collection

West Suffolk Record Office, Bury St Edmunds

Grafton Papers

West Sussex Record Office, Chichester

Goodwood MSS
Kirdford Parish Records
Lytton MSS
Diaries of John Marsh (microfilm)
Northchapel Parish Records
Minute-book of Petworth Turnpike Trustees
Diary of John Tompkins

West Yorkshire Archives Service, Bradford
Spencer Stanhope Collection

Whitehaven Library, Cumbria
John Bragg Collection

William L. Clements Library, Ann Arbor, Michigan
Clinton Papers
Gage Papers
Germain Papers
Mackenzie Papers
Miscellaneous MSS
Simcoe Papers
Wray Papers

William Salt Library, Stafford
Congreve Papers
Miscellaneous MSS

Wiltshire Record Office, Trowbridge
Diary of Jonathan Adams
Savernake MSS
Wansey Papers

Worcestershire Record Office, Worcester
Quarter Sessions Records

York City Archives
Dr William White's Diary
York Assembly Rooms Papers
Yorkshire Association MSS

PUBLISHED PRIMARY SOURCES

1. Newspapers and Periodicals
Adams's Weekly Courant (Chester)
Annual Register
Aris's Birmingham Gazette
Bath Chronicle
Belfast News-letter

Berrow's Worcester Journal
British Chronicle, Or, Pugh's Hereford Journal
Caledonian Mercury
Chelmsford Chronicle
Chester Chronicle
Cumberland Pacquet, and Ware's Whitehaven Advertiser
General Advertiser (Liverpool)
General Evening Post (Dublin)
Gentleman's Magazine
Glasgow Mercury
Gloucester Journal
Ipswich Journal
Jackson's Oxford Journal
Leeds Intelligencer
Leeds Mercury
Limerick Chronicle
London Chronicle
London Gazette
Morning Chronicle, and London Advertiser
Morning Post, and Daily Advertiser
New Annual Register
Public Advertiser
Reading Mercury and Oxford Gazette
York Courant

2. *Selected Diaries, Journals, Memoirs, Correspondence, and Contemporary Publications*

Anderson, James R. (ed.), *The Burgesses and Guild Brethren of Glasgow, 1751–1846* (Scottish Record Society, vol. lxvi, Edinburgh, 1935).

Andrew, Donna T. (ed.), *London Debating Societies, 1776–1799* (London Record Society, vol. xxx, London, 1994).

Ayde, Stephen Payne, *Treatise on Courts Martial* (London, 1778).

Bailey's British Directory . . . for the Year 1784 (4 vols., London, 1784).

Balderston, Marion, and Syrett, David (eds.), *The Lost War: Letters from British Officers during the American Revolution* (New York, 1975).

Banks, Sir Joseph, *The Sheep and Wool Correspondence of Sir Joseph Banks*, ed. Harold B. Carter (Norwich, 1979).

Barrington, Shute, *The Political Life of William Wildman, Viscount Barrington* (London, 1814).

Bateson, Mary, Stocks, Helen, and Chinnery, G. A. (eds.), *Records of the Borough of Leicester* (7 vols., London, Cambridge, and Leicester, 1899–1974).

Bedfordshire Country Records, *Notes and Extracts from the . . . Quarter Sessions Rolls* (Bedford, n.d.).

Bentham, Jeremy, *The Correspondence of Jeremy Bentham*, ed. T. L. S. Sprigge et al. (10 vols. to date, London and Oxford, 1968–).

Beresford, John, *The Correspondence of the Right Hon. John Beresford* ed. William Beresford (2 vols., London, 1854).

Beresford, John (ed.), *The Diary of a Country Parson* (5 vols., Oxford, 1924–31).

Boswell, James, and Temple, William Johnson, *The Correspondence of James Boswell and William Johnson Temple*, i, ed. Thomas Crawford (Edinburgh, 1997).

Boucher, Jonathan, *A View of the Causes and Consequences of the American Revolution; in Thirteen Discourses* (London, 1797).

Brown, A. F. J. (ed.), *Essex People 1750–1900 from their Diaries, Memoirs and Letters* (Chelmsford, 1972).

Brown, John, *An Estimate of the Manners and Principles of the Times* (2 vols., London, 1757).

Brown, Nicholas, 'The Diary of Nicholas Brown', *Surtees Society Publications*, 118 (1910), 230–323.

Burke, Edmund, *The Correspondence of Edmund Burke*, ed. Thomas W. Copeland et al. (10 vols., Cambridge, 1958–78).

[Burke, William], *The Letters of Valens* (London, 1777).

Burney, Fanny, *The Early Journals and Letters of Fanny Burney*, ed. Lars E. Troide and Stewart J. Cooke (3 vols. to date, Kingston, 1988–).

Butcher, E. E. (ed.), *Bristol Corporation of the Poor: Selected Records 1696–1834* (Bristol Record Society, vol. iii, Bristol, 1932).

Campbell, Thomas, *A Philosophical Survey of the South of Ireland* (London, 1777).

Cartwright, John, *Take Your Choice!* (London, 1776).

Caulfield, Richard, (ed.), *The Council Book of the Corporation of the City of Cork* (Guildford, 1876).

—— (ed.), *The Council Book of the Corporation of Youghal* (Guildford, 1878).

Cavendish, Sir Henry, *An Edition of the Cavendish Irish Parliamentary Diary 1776–1778*, ed. Anthony R. Black (3 vols., Delavan, Wis., 1984).

Cobbett, William, and Wright, J. (eds.), *The Parliamentary History of England* (36 vols., London, 1806–20).

Cornwallis, James, *A Sermon Preached at the Cathedral and Metropolitan Church of Christ, Canterbury, on Friday, February 4, 1780* (Canterbury, n.d.).

Cowper, William, *The Poems of William Cowper*, ed. John D. Baird and Charles Ryskamp (3 vols., Oxford, 1980–95).

Crabbe, George, *Poems of George Crabbe*, ed. William Adolphus Ward (3 vols., Cambridge, 1905–7).

Crawford, W. H. (ed.), *Letters from an Ulster Land Agent 1774–1785* (Belfast, 1976).

Crawford, Earl of (ed.), *Lives of the Lindsays* (2nd edn., 3 vols., London, 1858).

Darwin, Erasmus, *The Letters of Erasmus Darwin*, ed. Desmond King-Hele (Cambridge, 1981).

Davies, J. Barry (ed.), *The Freemen and Ancient Borough of Llantrisant* (Gloucester, 1989).

Davies, K. G. (ed.), *Documents of the American Revolution* (21 vols., Shannon, 1972–81).

Day, Thomas, *The Desolation of America: A Poem* (London, 1777).

Debates Relative to the Affairs of Ireland; in the Years 1763 and 1764 (2 vols., Dublin, 1766).

Devine, T. M. (ed.), *A Scottish Firm in Virginia: W. Cuninghame and Co.* (Scottish History Society, 4th series, vol. xx, Edinburgh, 1984).

Dobbs, Francis, *A Letter to the Right Honourable Lord North* (Dublin, 1780).

Drinkwater, John, *A History of the Late Siege of Gibraltar* (London, 1785).

Dudley Edwards, R., (ed.), 'Minute Book of the Catholic Committee, 1773–1792', *Archivium Hibernicum*, 9 (1942), 3–172.

Durie, Alastair J. (ed.), *The British Linen Company 1745–1775* (Scottish History Society, 5th series, vol. ix, Edinburgh, 1996).

Durrant, Peter (ed.), *Berkshire Overseers' Papers 1654–1834* (Berkshire Record Society, vol. iii, Reading, 1997).

Elwin, Malcolm (ed.), *The Noels and the Milbankes* (London, 1967).

Ferguson, Adam, *The Correspondence of Adam Ferguson*, ed. Vincenzo Merolle (2 vols., London, 1995).

Fisher, Jabez Maud, *An American Quaker in the British Isles: The Travel Journals of Jabez Maud Fisher*, ed. Kenneth Morgan (Oxford, 1992).

Fletcher, Isaac, *The Diary of Isaac Fletcher*, ed. Angus J. L. Winchester (Cumberland and Westmorland Antiquarian and Archaeological Society, extra ser., vol. xxvii, Kendal, 1994).

Fox, Charles James, *Memorials and Correspondence of Charles James Fox*, ed. Lord John Russell (4 vols., London, 1853–7).

Gawthern, Abigail, *The Diary of Abigail Gawthern*, ed. Adrian Henstock (Thoroton Society Record Series, vol. xxxiii, Nottingham, 1980).

Gebbie, John H. (ed.), *An Introduction to the Abercorn Letters* (Omagh, 1972).

George III, *The Correspondence of King George III*, ed. Sir John Fortescue (6 vols., London, 1927–8).

Gibbon, Edward, *The Correspondence of Edward Gibbon*, ed. J. E. Norton (3 vols., London, 1956).

Gilbert, J. H., and Gilbert, R. M. (eds.), *Calendar of Ancient Records of Dublin* (19 vols., Dublin, 1889–1944).

Gilbert, Thomas, *Plan for the Better Relief and Employment of the Poor* (London, 1781).

Godshall, William Man, *A General Plan of Parochial and Provincial Police* (London, 1787).

Grafton, Duke of, *Autobiography and Political Correspondence of Augustus Henry Third Duke of Grafton*, ed. Sir William R. Anson (London, 1898).

Grant, Francis J. (ed.), *The Commissariot of Edinburgh: Consistorial Processes and Decrees, 1658–1800* (Scottish Record Society, vol. xxxiv, Edinburgh, 1909).

Greene, Revd. Joseph, *Correspondence of the Reverend Jospeh Greene*, ed. Levi Fox (Dugdale Society Publications, vol. xxiii, London, 1965).

Guttridge, G. H. (ed.), *The American Correspondence of a Bristol Merchant* (Berkeley and Los Angeles, 1934).

Hamwood Papers, ed. Eva Mary Bell (London, 1930).

The Harcourt Papers, ed. E. W. Harcourt (14 vols., Oxford, 1880–1905).

Hardy, Mary, *Mary Hardy's Diary*, ed. Basil Cozens-Hardy (Norfolk Record Society, vol. xxxvii, Norwich, 1968).

Hartley, David, *Letters on the American War* (London, 1778).

Hembry, Phyllis (ed.), *Calendar of the Bradford-on-Avon Settlement Examinations and Removal Orders 1725–98* (Wiltshire Record Society, vol. xlvi, Trowbridge, 1990).

Herbert, Dorothea, *Retrospections of Dorothea Herbert* (2 vols., London, 1929–30).

Historical Manuscripts Commission, *Bath MSS.* (4 vols., London, 1904–68).

—— *Carlisle MSS* (London, 1897).

—— *Charlemont MSS*, i (London, 1891).

—— *Dartmouth MSS* (3 vols., London, 1887–96).

—— *Denbigh MSS* (London, 1911).

—— *Donoughmore MSS* (London, 1891).

—— *Du Cane MSS* (London, 1905).

—— *Emly MSS* (London, 1895).

—— *Foljambe MSS* (London, 1897).

—— *Hastings MSS* (4 vols., London, 1928–47).

—— *Laing MSS* (2 vols., London, 1914–25).

—— *Lothian MSS* (London, 1905).

—— *Palk MSS* (London, 1922).

—— *Pembroke MSS* (London, 1884).

—— *Polwarth MSS* (5 vols., London, 1911–61).

—— *Rutland MSS* (4 vols., London, 1888–1905).

—— *Stopford Sackville MSS* (2 vols., London, 1904–10).

—— *Verulam MSS* (London, 1906).

Hobson, M. G., (ed.), *Oxford Council Acts 1752–1801* (Oxford Historical Society, NS, vol. xv, Oxford, 1962).

Horne, George, *A Sermon Preached before the Honourable House of Commons, at the Church of St. Margaret's, Westminister, on Friday, Feb. 4, 1780* (Oxford, 1780).

—— *A Sermon Preached before the University of Oxford, at St. Mary's, on Wednesday, Feb. 21, 1781* (Oxford, 1781).

Hunt, William, (ed.), *The Irish Parliament 1775* (London, 1907).

Hunter, Martin, *The Journal of Gen. Martin Hunter*, ed. Ann Hunter and Elizabeth Bell (Edinburgh, 1894).

Hunter, Thomas (ed.), *Extracts from the Records of the Convention of the Royal Burghs of Scotland 1759–79* (Edinburgh, 1918).

The Inchiquin Manuscripts, ed. John Ainsworth (Dublin, 1961).

The Incorporation of the Bakers of Glasgow (Glasgow, 1937).

John, A. H. (ed.), *The Walker Family: Ironfounders and Lead Manufacturers, 1741–1893* (London, 1951).

Johnson, Samuel, *The Letters of Samuel Johnson*, ed. Bruce Redford (5 vols., Oxford, 1992–4).

—— *The Temple of Fashion: A Poem in Five Parts* (Shrewsbury, 1781).

Jones, Sir William, *The Letters of Sir William Jones*, ed. Garland Cannon (2 vols., Oxford, 1970).

Jones, Revd. William, *The Diary of the Revd. William Jones*, ed. O. F. Christie (London, 1929).

Journals of the House of Commons.

Journals of the House of Commons . . . of Ireland.

'Kentishman, A', *Thoughts on the Present State of the Poor* (London, 1776).

Kenyon, R. L., and Wakeman, O. (eds.), *Abstracts of the Orders of the Shropshire Quarter Sessions* (Salop County Records, vols. xiv–xvii, Shrewsbury, n.d.).

Kerrich, Walter, *A Sermon Preached at the Cathedral Church of Sarum, on Wednesday, February 21, 1781* (Salisbury, 1781).

Knight, R. J. B. (ed.), *Portsmouth Dockyard Papers 1774–1783* (Portsmouth Record Series, Portsmouth, 1987).

Knox, William, *Extra-Official State Papers* (2 vols., London, 1789).

Lamb, Roger, *An Original and Authentic Journal* (Dublin, 1809).

—— *Memoir* (Dublin, 1811).

Lambert, Sheila (ed.), *House of Commons Sessional Papers of the Eighteenth Century* (145 vols., Wilmington, Del., 1975).

Langton, Thomas, *The Letters of Thomas Langton*, ed. Joan Wilkinson (Chetham Society, Manchester, 1994).

Le Hardy, William (ed.), *Notes and Extracts from the Sessions Records of the Liberty of St. Alban Division 1770 to 1840* (Hertfordshire County Records, vol. iv, Hertford, 1923).

—— *Calendar to the Sessions Books, Sessions Minute Books and other Sessions Records . . . 1752 to 1799* (Hertfordshire County Records, vol. viii, Hertford, 1935).

Leinster, Duchess of, *Correspondence of Emily, Duchess of Leinster*, ed. Brian Fitzgerald (3 vols., Dublin, 1949–57).

Lennox, Lady Sarah, *Life and Letters of Lady Sarah Lennox*, ed. Countess of Ilchester and Lord Starvordale (2 vols., London, 1901).

Lowe, J. A. (ed.), *Records of the Portsmouth Division of Marines, 1764–1800* (Portsmouth Record Series, Portsmouth, 1990).

Lumsden, Harry (ed.), *The Records of the Trades House of Glasgow 1713–1777* (Glasgow, 1934).

McEwan, Robert D. (ed.), *Old Glasgow Weavers; Being the Records of the Incorporation of Weavers* (Glasgow, 1908).

Macmahon, K. A. (ed.), *Beverley Corporation Minute Books* (Yorkshire Archaeological Society, record ser., vol. cxxii, Wakefield, 1958).

[Macpherson, James], *A Short History of the Opposition during the Last Session of Parliament* (London, 1779).

Mann, Julia DeL. (ed.), *Documents Illustrating the Wiltshire Textile Trades in the Eighteenth Century* (Wiltshire Archaeological and Natural History Society, Records Branch, vol. xix, Devizes, 1964).

Mill, Revd. John, *The Diary of the Reverend John Mill*, ed. Gilbert Goudie (Scottish History Society, vol. v, Edinburgh, 1889).

Moore, John, *A Sermon Preached before the Lords Spiritual and Temporal, in the Abbey-Church, Westminster; on Wednesday, February 21, 1781* (London, 1781).

Morgan, Kenneth (ed.), *Calendar of Correspondence from William Miles . . . to John Tharp* (Bristol Record Society Publications, vol. xxxvii, Bristol, 1985).

Morris, Matthew Robinson, *Peace the Best Policy* (2nd edn., London, 1777).

Murray Keith, Sir Robert, *Memoirs and Correspondence of Sir Robert Murray Keith*, ed. Mrs Gillespie Smyth (2 vols., London, 1849).

Neville, Sylas, *The Diary of Sylas Neville, 1767–1788*, ed. Basil Cozens-Hardy (Oxford, 1950).

Newdigate, Sir Roger, *The Correspondence of Sir Roger Newdigate*, ed. A. W. A. White (Dugdale Society Publications, vol. xxxvii, Hertford, 1995).

Nottingham, Borough of, *Records of the Borough of Nottingham* (9 vols., Nottingham, 1882–1956).

Oakes, James, *The Oakes Diaries*, ed. Jane Fisk (Suffolk Record Society, vol. xxxii, Woodbridge, 1990).

O'Conor, Charles, *The Letters of Charles O'Conor of Belanagare*, ed. Catherine Coogan Ward and Robert E. Ward (2 vols., Ann Arbor, 1980).

Ode on the Taking of Minorca (London, 1782).

'Officer, An', *A New System . . . for the Army* (London, 1775).

Orton, Job, *Letters from the Rev. Job Orton* (2 vols., Shrewsbury, 1800).

Parliamentary Register (66 vols., London, 1775–1804).

Parliamentary Register; or, History of the Proceedings and Debates of the House of Commons of Ireland (17 vols., Dublin, 1781–97).

Parsons, Kenneth A. C. (ed.), *The Church Book of the Independent Church . . . Isleham 1693–1805* (Cambridgeshire Antiquarian Records Society, vol. vi, Cambridge, 1984).

Peebles, John, *John Peebles' American War: The Diary of a Scottish Grenadier, 1776–1782*, ed. Ira D. Gruber (Mechanicsburg, Penn., 1998).

The Pembroke Papers, ed. Lord Herbert (2 vols., London, 1939–50).

Picton, Sir James A. (ed.), *City of Liverpool: Municipal Archives and Records* (Liverpool, 1897).

Pitt, William, *Correspondence between the Right Honble. William Pitt and Charles Duke of Rutland, Lord Lieutenant of Ireland 1781–1787* (Edinburgh and London, 1890).

Porteus, Beilby, *A Sermon Preached before the Lords Spiritual and Temporal, . . . February 10, 1779* (London, 1779).

—— *A Charge Delivered to the Clergy of the Diocese of Chester* (Chester, 1779).

Price, Richard, *The Correspondence of Richard Price*, ed. W. Bernard Peach and D. O. Thomas (3 vols., Durham, NC, 1983–94).

—— *Observations on the Importance of the American Revolution* (London, 1784).

Renwick, Robert, et al. (eds.), *Extracts from the Records of the Burgh of Glasgow* (11 vols., Glasgow, 1882–1916).

Robertson, E. Arnot (ed.), *The Spanish Town Papers* (London, 1959).

Rockingham, Marquis of, *Memoirs of the Marquis of Rockingham*, ed. Earl of Albemarle (2 vols., London, 1852).

Sandwich, Earl of, *The Private Papers of John, Earl of Sandwich*, ed. G. R. Barnes and J. H. Owen (4 vols., London, 1932–8).

Schneider, Herbert, and Schneider, Carol, (eds.), *Samuel Johnson, President of King's College, His Career and Writings* (4 vols., New York, 1929).

Scotland, Church of, *Acts of the General Assembly of the Church of Scotland* (Edinburgh, 1843).

Scott, James, *A Sermon Preached at York on 21st of February, 1781* (York, [1781]).

Seward, Anna, *Monody on Major André* (Lichfield, 1781).

Sheridan, Richard Brinsley, *The Dramatic Works of Richard Brinsley Sheridan*, ed. Cecil Price (2 vols., Oxford, 1973).

Simmons, R. C., and Thomas, P. D. G. (eds.), *Proceedings and Debates of the British Parliaments respecting North America, 1754–1783* (6 vols. to date, Millward, NY, 1982–).

Sinclair, Sir John, *Considerations on Militias and Standing Armies* (London, 1782).

Smith, Adam, *An Inquiry into the Nature and Causes of the Wealth of Nations*, ed. R. H. Campbell, A. S. Skinner, and W. B. Todd (2 vols., Oxford, 1976).

—— *The Correspondence of Adam Smith*, ed. Ernest Campbell Mossner and Ian Simpson Ross (Oxford, 1987).

Smith, V. (ed.), *The Town Book of Lewes, 1702–1837* (Sussex Record Society, vol. lxix, Lewes, 1973).

Solander, Daniel, *Daniel Solander: Collected Correspondence 1753–1782*, ed. and trans. Edward Duyker and Per Tingbrand (Oslo, 1995).

Stinton, George, *A Sermon Preached before the Honourable House of Commons, at St. Margaret's, Westminster, on Wednesday, February 10, 1779* (London, 1779).

[Tasker, William], *Ode to the Warlike Genius of Great Britain* (London, 1778).

Tayler, Alistair, and Tayler, Henrietta (eds.), *Lord Fife and his Factor* (London, 1925).

Tennent, James B. (ed.), *Records of the Incorporation of Barbers, Glasgow* (Glasgow, 1930).

Thomas, William, *The Diary of William Thomas of Michaelston-super-Ely, near St Fagans Glamorgan 1762–1795*, ed. R. T. W. Denning (Cardiff, 1995).

Tracts, Concerning the Ancient and Only True Legal Means of National Defence, by a Free Militia (London, 1781).

Torrington, Viscount, *The Torrington Diaries*, ed. C. Bruyn Andrews (4 vols., London, 1934–8).

Toulmin, Joshua, *The American War Lamented* (London, 1776).

Tucker, Josiah, *An Humble Address and Earnest Appeal* (2nd edn., Gloucester, 1775).

—— *A Series of Answers to Certain Objections Against Separating from the Rebellious Colonies* (Gloucester, 1776).

—— *Treatise Concerning Civil Government* (London, 1781).

—— *Cui Bono? Or, an Inquiry, What Benefits can Arise . . . from the Greatest Victories, or Successes, in the Present War* (3rd edn., London, 1782).

Twining, Thomas, *A Selection of Thomas Twining's Letters 1734–1804*, ed. Ralph S. Walker (2 vols., Lampeter, 1991).

Ulster, Synod of, *Records of the Synod of Ulster* (3 vols., Belfast, 1890–8).

Victoria County History, *Berkshire*, vols. i and ii, ed. P. H. Ditchfield and William Page (London, 1906–7).

—— *Staffordshire*, vol. xiv (Oxford, 1990).

—— *Yorkshire East Riding*, i. *The City of Kingston upon Hull*, ed. K. J. Allison (Oxford, 1969).

Warren, John, *A Sermon Preached before the Lords Spiritual and Temporal . . . on Friday, February 4, 1780* (London, 1780).

Watson, Richard, *A Sermon Preached before the University of Cambridge, on Friday, February 4th, 1780* (2nd edn., Cambridge, 1780).

Wedgwood, Josiah, *The Selected Letters of Josiah Wedgwood*, ed. Ann Finer and George Savage (London, 1965).

White, Gilbert, *Journals of Gilbert White*, ed. Walter Johnson (London, 1982 edn.).

Williams, A. H. (ed.), *John Wesley in Wales 1739–1790* (Cardiff, 1971).

Windham, William, *Windham Papers* (2 vols., London, 1913).

Wood, Beavis, *Georgian Tiverton: The Political Memoranda of Beavis Wood*, ed. John Bourne (Devon & Cornwall Record Society, NS, vol. xxix, Torquay, 1986).

Woodward, Richard, *An Address to the Public on the Expediency of a Regular Plan for the Maintenance and Government of the Poor* (Dublin, 1775).

Wyvill, Christopher, *Political Papers* (6 vols., York, 1794–1802).

Young, Arthur, *A Tour in Ireland* (London, 1780).

Zouch, Henry, *Remarks upon the Late Resolutions of the House of Commons, respecting the Proposed Changes of the Poor Laws* (Leeds, [1776]).

SELECTED SECONDARY SOURCES

Albert, William, *The Turnpike Road System in England 1663–1840* (Cambridge, 1972).

Andrew, Donna T., 'Popular Culture and Public Debate: London 1780', *Historical Journal*, 39 (1996), 405–23.

Andrew, J. H., 'Land and People, c.1780', in *A New History of Ireland*, iv. *Eighteenth-Century Ireland 1691–1800* (Oxford, 1986), 236–64.

Archer, Mildred, *India and British Portraiture 1770–1825* (London, 1979).

Ashton, T. S., *An Economic History of England: The Eighteenth Century* (London, 1955).

—— *Economic Fluctuations in England, 1700–1800* (London, 1959).

Baker, Norman, *Government and Contractors* (London, 1971).

—— 'Changing Attitudes towards Government in Eighteenth-Century Britain', in Anne Whiteman, J. S. Bromley, and P. G. M. Dickson (eds.), *Statesmen, Scholars and Merchants: Essays in Eighteenth-Century History presented to Dame Lucy Sutherland* (Oxford, 1973), 202–19.

Barnard, Toby C., 'The Government and Irish Dissent, 1704–1780', in

Kevin Herlihy (ed.), *The Politics of Irish Dissent, 1650–1800* (Dublin, 1997), 9–27.

Bartlett, Thomas, 'The Augmentation of the Army in Ireland, 1767–1769', *English Historical Review*, 96 (1981), 540–59.

—— 'Army and Society in Eighteenth-Century Ireland', in W. A. Maguire (ed.), *Kings in Conflict: The Revolutionary War in Ireland and its Aftermath, 1689–1750* (Belfast, 1990), 173–82.

—— *The Fall and Rise of the Irish Nation: The Catholic Question 1690–1800* (Dublin, 1992).

—— '"A Weapon of War Yet Untried": Irish Catholics and the Armed Forces of the Crown, 1760–1830', in T. G. Fraser and Keith Jeffery (eds.), *Men, Women and War* (Historical Studies, vol. xviii, Dublin, 1993), 66–85.

Baugh, Daniel A., 'The Politics of British Naval Failure, 1775–1777', *American Neptune*, 52 (1992), 221–46.

Bayly, C. A., *Imperial Meridian: The British Empire and the World 1780–1830* (London, 1989).

Beattie, John, *Crime and the Courts in England 1660–1800* (Princeton, 1986).

Beckett, Ian J. F., *The Amateur Military Tradition 1558–1945* (Manchester, 1991).

Berg, Maxine, *The Age of Manufactures* (London, 1985).

Binney, J. E. D., *British Public Finance and Administration 1774–1792* (Oxford, 1958).

Black, Eileen, 'Volunteer Portraits in the Ulster Museum, Belfast', *Irish Sword*, 13 (1977–9), 181–4.

Black, Eugene Charlton, *The Association: British Extraparliamentary Political Organization 1769–1793* (Cambridge, Mass., 1963).

Black, Jeremy, *War for America* (Stroud, 1991).

—— *Britain as a Military Power, 1688–1815* (London, 1999).

Boime, Albert, *Art in an Age of Revolution 1750–1800* (Chicago, 1987).

Bonwick, Colin, *English Radicals and the American Revolution* (Chapel Hill, NC, 1977).

Botham, F. W., and Hunt, E. H., 'Wages in Britain during the Industrial Revolution', *Economic History Review*, 2nd ser., 40 (1987), 380–99.

Bowen, H. V., *War and British Society, 1688–1815* (Cambridge, 1998).

—— 'British India, 1765–1813: The Metropolitan Context', in *The Oxford History of the British Empire*, ii. *The Eighteenth Century*, ed. P. J. Marshall (Oxford, 1998), 530–51.

Bowler, R. A., *Logistics and the Failure of the British Army in North America* (Princeton, 1975).

Boyer, George R., *An Economic History of the English Poor Law 1750–1850* (Cambridge, 1990).

Bradley, James E., *Popular Politics and the American Revolution in England* (Macon, Ga., 1986).

—— *Religion, Revolution and English Radicalism* (Cambridge, 1990).

—— 'The British Public and the American Revolution: Ideology, Interest and Opinion', in H. T. Dickinson (ed.), *Britain and the American Revolution* (London, 1998), 124–54.

Brewer, John, *The Sinews of Power: War, Money and the English State 1688–1783* (London, 1989).

—— *The Pleasures of the Imagination: English Culture in the Eighteenth Century* (London, 1997).

Brown, Callum, 'Religion and Social Change', in *People and Society in Scotland*, i. *1760–1830*, ed. T. M. Devine and Rosalind Mitchison (Edinburgh, 1988), 143–62.

—— *Religion and Society in Scotland since 1707* (Edinburgh, 1997).

Bruce, Anthony, *The Purchase System in the British Army, 1660–1871* (London, 1980).

Bryant, G. J., 'Scots in India in the Eighteenth Century', *Scottish Historical Review*, 64 (1985), 22–41.

Buel, Richard, Jnr., 'Time: Friend or Foe of the Revolution?', in Don Higginbotham (ed.), *Reconsiderations on the Revolutionary War: Selected Essays* (Westport, Conn., 1978), 124–43.

Bulloch, John Malcolm, *Territorial Soldiering in the North-East of Scotland during 1759–1814* (Aberdeen, 1914).

Burns, Robert E., 'The Catholic Relief Act in Ireland, 1778', *Church History*, 32 (1963), 181–206.

Butterfield, Herbert, *George III, Lord North and the People* (London, 1949).

Bythell, Duncan, 'Women in the Workforce', in Patrick O'Brien and Ronald Quinault (eds.), *The Industrial Revolution and British Society* (Cambridge, 1993), 31–53.

Cannon, John, *Parliamentary Reform, 1640–1832* (Cambridge, 1972).

—— *Aristocratic Century* (Cambridge, 1984).

—— 'The British Nobility, 1660–1800', in *The European Nobilities in the Seventeenth and Eighteenth Centuries*, i. *Western Europe*, ed. H. M. Scott (London, 1995), 53–81.

—— 'The Loss of America', in H. T. Dickinson (ed.), *Britain and the American Revolution* (London, 1998), 233–57.

Ceadel, Martin, *The Origins of War Prevention: The British Peace Movement and International Relations, 1730–1854* (Oxford, 1996).

Chartres, John, 'English Landed Society and the Servants Tax of 1777', in Negley Harte and Roland Quinault (eds.), *Land and Society in Britain, 1700–1914: Essays in Honour of F. M. L. Thompson* (Manchester, 1996), 34–56.

Christie, Ian, *The End of North's Ministry* (London, 1958).

—— *Wilkes, Wyvill and Reform* (London, 1962).

Clark, Dora Mae, *British Opinion and the American Revolution* (New Haven, 1930).

Clark, J. C. D., *English Society, 1688–1832: Ideology, Social Structure and Political Practice during the Ancien Regime* (Cambridge, 1985).

—— *The Language of Liberty 1660–1832: Political Discourse and Social Dynamics in the Anglo-American World* (Cambridge, 1994).

Clay, Christopher, 'The Price of Freehold Land in the Seventeenth and Eighteenth Centuries', *Economic History Review*, 2nd ser. 27 (1974), 173–89.

Clayton, Timothy, *The English Print 1688–1802* (New Haven, 1997).

Cochran, L. E., *Scottish Trade with Ireland in the Eighteenth Century* (Edinburgh, 1985).

Cole, W. A., 'Factors in Demand', in Roderick Floud and Donald McCloskey (eds.), *The Economic History of Britain since 1700* (2 vols., Cambridge, 1981), i. 36–65.

Colley, Linda, 'Whose Nation? Class and National Consciousness in Britain 1750–1830', *Past & Present*, 113 (1986), 97–117.

—— *Britons: Forging the Nation 1707–1837* (New Haven, 1992).

—— 'The Reach of the State, the Appeal of the Nation', in Lawrence Stone (ed.), *An Imperial State at War: Britain from 1689 to 1815* (London, 1994), 165–84.

Connolly, S. J., 'Varieties of Britishness: Ireland, Scotland and Wales in the Hanoverian State', in Alexander Grant and Keith J. Stringer (eds.), *Uniting the Kingdom? The Making of British History* (London, 1995), 193–207.

Conway, Stephen, 'The Recruitment of Criminals into the British Army, 1775–1781', *Bulletin of the Institute of Historical Research*, 58 (1985), 46–58.

—— *The War of American Independence* (London, 1995).

Cookson, J. E., *The British Armed Nation 1793–1815* (Oxford, 1997).

Corish, Patrick, *The Irish Catholic Experience: A Historical Survey* (Dublin, 1985).

Corvisier, André, *Armies and Societies in Europe 1494–1789* (Bloomington, Ind., 1979).

Crafts, N. F. R., *British Economic Growth during the Industrial Revolution* (Oxford, 1985).

Crowley, John E., *The Privileges of Independence: Neomercantilism and the American Revolution* (Baltimore, 1993).

Cullen, L. M., *An Economic History of Ireland since 1660* (London, 1972).

—— 'Catholics under the Penal Laws', *Eighteenth-Century Ireland*, 1 (1986), 23–36.

Curtin, Nancy J., *The United Irishmen: Popular Politics in Ulster and Dublin 1791–1798* (Oxford, 1994).

Davis, Ralph, *The Rise of the English Shipping Industry in the Seventeenth and Eighteenth Centuries* (Newton Abbot, 1972).

Devine, T. M., 'Glasgow Merchants and the Collapse of the Tobacco Trade', *Scottish Historical Review*, 52 (1973), 50–74.

—— 'Urbanisation', in *People and Society in Scotland*, i. *1760–1830*, ed. id. and Rosalind Mitchison (Edinburgh, 1988), 27–52.

—— *Exploring the Scottish Past* (East Linton, 1995).

—— and Jackson, Gordon (eds.), *Glasgow*, i. *Beginnings to 1830* (Manchester, 1995).

de Vries, Jan, 'Between Purchasing Power and the World of Goods: Understanding Household Economy in Early Modern Europe', in John Brewer and Roy Porter (eds.), *Consumption and the World of Goods* (London, 1993), 85–132.

Dickinson, H. T., 'Radicals and Reformers in the Age of Wilkes and Wyvill', in Jeremy Black (ed.), *British Politics and Society from Walpole to Pitt 1742–1789* (London, 1990), 123–46.

Ditchfield, G. M., 'The Parliamentary Struggle over the Repeal of the Test and Corporation Acts, 1787–1790', *English Historical Review*, 89 (1974), 551–77.

—— 'The Scottish Campaign against the Test Act, 1790–1791', *Historical Journal*, 23 (1980), 37–61.

—— 'The Subscription Issue in British Parliamentary Politics, 1772–1779', *Parliamentary History*, 7 (1988), 45–80.

—— 'Ecclesiastical Policy under Lord North', in John Walsh, Colin Haydon and Stephen Taylor (eds.), *The Church of England, c.1689–c.1833: From Toleration to Tractarianism* (Cambridge, 1993), 228–46.

Donovan, Robert Kent, 'The Military Origins of the Roman Catholic Relief Programme of 1778', *Historical Journal*, 28 (1985), 79–102.

—— *No Popery and Radicalism: Opposition to Roman Catholic Relief in Scotland* (New York, 1987).

—— 'The Popular Party of the Church of Scotland and the American Revolution', in B. Sher and J. R. Smitten (eds.), *Scotland and America in the Age of the Enlightenment* (Edinburgh, 1990), 81–99.

—— 'Evangelical Civic Humanism in Glasgow: The American War Sermons of William Thom', in Andrew Hook and Richard B. Sher (eds.), *The Glasgow Enlightenment* (East Linton, 1995), 227–45.

Doyle, David Noel, *Ireland, Irishmen and Revolutionary America, 1760–1820* (Dublin, 1981).

Duffy, Michael, 'The Foundations of British Naval Power', in id. (ed.), *The Military Revolution and the State* (Exeter, 1980), 49–85.

Floud, Roderick, Wachter, Kenneth, and Gregory, Annabel, *Height, Health and History: Nutritional Status in the United Kingdom, 1750–1980* (Cambridge, 1990).

Foreman, Amanda, 'A Politician's Politician: Georgiana, Duchess of Devonshire and the Whig Party', in Hannah Parker and Elaine Chalus (eds.), *Gender in Eighteenth-Century England* (London, 1997), 179–204.

French, David, *The British Way in Warfare* (London, 1990).

Frey, Sylvia, *The British Soldier in America: A Social History of Military Life in the Revolutionary Period* (Austin, Tex., 1981).

Gascoigne, John, *Science in the Service of Empire: Joseph Banks, the British State and the Uses of Science in the Age of Revolution* (Cambridge, 1998).

Gilboy, E. W., *Wages in Eighteenth-Century England* (Cambridge, Mass., 1934).

Gill, Conrad, *The Rise of the Irish Linen Industry* (Oxford, 1924).

Gould, Eliga H., 'American Independence and Britain's Counter-Revolution', *Past & Present*, 154 (1997), 107–41.

—— 'A Virtual Nation: Greater Britain and the Imperial Legacy of the American Revolution', *American Historical Review*, 104 (1999), 476–89.

Greene, Jack P., 'Empire and Identity from the Glorious Revolution to the American Revolution', in *The Oxford History of the British Empire*, ii. *The Eighteenth Century*, ed. P. J. Marshall (Oxford, 1998), 208–30.

Guy, Alan J., 'The Irish Military Establishment, 1660–1776', in Thomas Bartlett and Keith Jeffrey (eds.), *A Military History of Ireland* (Cambridge, 1996), 211–30.

Gwyn, Julian, 'The Impact of British Military Spending on the Colonial American Money Markets, 1760–1783', Canadian Historical Association, *Historic Papers / Communications historiques* (1980), 77–99.

Hancock, David, *Citizens of the World: London Merchants and the Integration of the British Atlantic Community* (Cambridge, 1995).

Harling, Philip, *The Waning of 'Old Corruption': The Politics of Economical Reform in Britain, 1779–1846* (Oxford, 1996).

—— and Mandler, Peter, 'From "Fiscal-Military" State to Laissez-Faire State', *Journal of British Studies*, 32 (1993), 44–70.

Hastings, Adrian, *The Construction of Nationhood: Ethnicity, Religion and Nationalism* (Cambridge, 1997).

Hay, Douglas, 'War, Dearth and Theft in the Eighteenth Century: The Record of the English Courts', *Past & Present*, 95 (1982), 117–60.

—— and Rogers, Nicholas, *Eighteenth-Century English Society* (Oxford, 1997).

Haydon, Colin, 'The Gordon Riots in the English Provinces', *Historical Research*, 63 (1990), 354–9.

—— *Anti-Catholicism in Eighteenth-Century England, c.1714–1780: A Political and Social Study* (Manchester, 1993).

Hayter, Tony, *The Army and the Crowd in Mid-Georgian England* (London, 1978).

Heaton, H., *Yorkshire Woollen and Worsted Industries from the Earliest Times up to the Industrial Revolution* (2nd edn., Oxford, 1965).

Heim, C. E., and Mirowski, P., 'Interest Rates and Crowding Out during Britain's Industrial Revolution', *Journal of Economic History*, 47 (1987), 117–39.

Hill, Bridget, *Women, Work and Sexual Politics in Eighteenth-Century England* (Oxford, 1989).

Hill, Jacqueline, 'Religious Toleration and the Relaxation of the Penal Laws: An Imperial Perspective, 1763–1780', *Archivum Hibernicum*, 44 (1989), 98–109.

—— *From Patriots to Unionists: Dublin Civic Politics and Irish Protestant Patriotism, 1660–1840* (Oxford, 1997).

Hoppit, Julian, *Risk and Failure in English Business* (Cambridge, 1987).

—— 'Patterns of Parliamentary Legislation, 1660–1800', *Historical Journal*, 39 (1996), 109–31.

Hoskins, W. G., *Industry, Trade and People in Exeter* (Manchester, 1935).

Houlding, John, *Fit for Service: The Training of the British Army, 1715–1795* (Oxford, 1981).

Humphreys, Melvin, *The Crisis of Community: Montgomeryshire, 1680–1815* (Cardiff, 1996).

Innes, Joanna, 'Politics and Morals: The Reformation of Manners Movement in Later Eighteenth-Century England', in Eckhart Hellmuth (ed.), *The Transformation of Political Culture: England and Germany in the Late Eighteenth Century* (Oxford, 1990), 57–118.

—— 'Parliament and the Shaping of Eighteenth-Century Social Policy', *Transactions of the Royal Historical Society*, 5th ser. 40 (1990), 63–92.

—— 'The Domestic Face of the Military-Fiscal State: Government and Society in Eighteenth-Century Britain', in Lawrence Stone (ed.), *An Imperial State at War: Britain from 1689 to 1815* (London, 1994), 96–127.

—— 'The Local Acts of a National Parliament: Parliament's Role in Sanctioning Local Acts in Eighteenth-Century Britain', *Parliamentary History*, 17 (1998), 23–47.

Jackson, Gordon, *Hull in the Eighteenth Century: A Study in Economic and Social History* (Oxford, 1972).

James, F. G., *Ireland in the Empire 1688–1770* (Cambridge, Mass., 1973).

Jameson, Alan G., 'American Privateers in the Leeward Islands, 1776–1778', *American Neptune*, 43 (1983), 20–30.

—— 'The Return to Privateering: Channel Island Privateers, 1739–1783', in id. (ed.), *A People of the Sea: The Maritime History of the Channel Islands* (London, 1986), 148–72.

Jenkins, Geraint H., *The Foundations of Modern Wales 1642–1780* (Oxford, 1987).

Joslin, D. M., 'London Bankers in Wartime, 1739–1784', in L. S. Presnell (ed.), *Studies in the Industrial Revolution presented to T. S. Ashton* (London, 1960), 156–77.

Kearney, Hugh, *The British Isles: A History of Four Nations* (Cambridge, 1989).

Kelly, James, *Prelude to Union: Anglo-Irish Politics in the 1780s* (Cork, 1992).

—— 'Scarcity and Poor Relief in Eighteenth-Century Ireland: The Subsistence Crisis of 1782–1784', *Irish Historical Studies*, 28 (1992–3), 38–62.

—— 'Parliamentary Reform in Irish Politics: 1760–90', in David Dickson, Daire Keogh, and Kevin Whelan (eds.), *The United Irishmen: Republicanism, Radicalism and Rebellion* (Dublin, 1993), 74–87.

—— '1780 Revisited: The Politics of the Repeal of the Sacramental Test', in Kevin Herlihy (ed.), *The Politics of Irish Dissent, 1650–1800* (Dublin, 1997), 74–90.

Kennedy, Liam, and Dowling, Martin W., 'Prices and Wages in Ireland, 1700–1850', *Irish Economic and Social History*, 24 (1997), 62–104.

Kent, D. A., '"Gone for a Soldier": Family Breakdown and the Demography of Desertion in a London Parish, 1750–1791', *Local Population Studies*, 45 (1990), 27–42.

Kidd, Colin, 'North Britishness and the Nature of Eighteenth-Century British Patriotisms', *Historical Journal*, 39 (1996), 361–82.

King-Hele, Desmond, *Doctor of Revolution: The Life and Genius of Erasmus Darwin* (London, 1977).

Lammey, David, 'The Growth of the "Patriot Opposition" in Ireland during the 1770s', *Parliamentary History*, 7 (1988), 257–81.

Langford, Paul, *A Polite and Commercial People: A History of England 1727–1783* (Oxford, 1989).

—— 'The English Clergy and the American Revolution', in Eckhart Hellmuth (ed.), *The Transformation of Political Culture: England and Germany in the Late Eighteenth Century* (Oxford, 1990), 275–307.

—— *Public Life and the Propertied Englishman 1689–1798* (Oxford, 1991).

Lawson, Philip, and Phillips, Jim, '"Our Execrable Banditti": Perceptions of the Nabobs in Mid-Eighteenth Century Britain', *Albion*, 16 (1984), 225–41.

Lemire, Beverly, *Dress, Culture and Commerce: The English Clothing Trade before the Factory, 1660–1800* (London, 1997).

McBride, Ian, 'William Drennan and the Dissenting Tradition', in David Dickson, Daire Keogh, and Kevin Whelan (eds.), *The United Irishmen: Republicanism, Radicalism and Rebellion* (Dublin, 1993), 48–61.

—— *Scripture Politics: Ulster Presbyterians and Irish Radicalism in the Late Eighteenth Century* (Oxford, 1998).

McCalman, Iain, 'Prophesying Revolution: "Mad Lord George", Edmund Burke and Madame La Motte', in Malcolm Chase and Ian Dyck (eds.), *Living and Learning: Essays in Honour of J. F. C. Harrison* (Aldershot, 1996), 52–65.

McCusker, John J., and Menard, Russell R., *The Economy of British America, 1607–1789* (Chapel Hill, NC, 1991 edn.).

McDowell, R. B., *Ireland in the Age of Imperialism and Revolution 1760–1800* (Oxford, 1979).

McFarland, E. W., *Ireland and Scotland in the Age of Revolution* (Edinburgh, 1994).

Mackay, D. L., 'Direction and Purpose in British Imperial Policy, 1783–1801', *Historical Journal*, 17 (1974), 487–501.

McKendrick, Neil, 'Josiah Wedgwood and the Commercialization of the Potteries', in id., John Brewer, and J. H. Plumb, *The Birth of a Consumer Society* (London, 1982), 100–45.

MacKenzie, John M., 'Empire and National Identities: The Case of Scotland', *Transactions of the Royal Historical Society*, 6th ser. 8 (1998), 215–31.

Mackesy, Piers, *The War for America 1775–1783* (London, 1964).

Mackillop, Andrew, *'More Fruitful than the Soil': Army, Empire and the Scottish Highlands 1715–1815* (East Linton, 1999).

Macpherson, David, *Annals of Commerce* (4 vols., London, 1805).

Malcolmson, R. W., *Life and Labour in England 1700–1780* (London, 1981).

Malcomson, A. P. W., 'The Politics of "natural right": the Abercorn Family and Strabane Borough, 1692–1800', *Historical Studies*, 10 (1976), 43–90.

—— *John Foster: The Politics of the Anglo-Irish Ascendancy* (Oxford, 1978).

Markham, C. A., *The History of the Northamptonshire and Rutland Militia* (London, 1924).

Marshall, Peter, *Bristol in the American War of Independence* (Bristol, 1977).

—— 'Manchester and the American Revolution', *Bulletin of the John Rylands University Library of Manchester*, 62 (1979), 168–86.

Marshall, P. J., *'A Free though Conquering People': Britain and Asia in the Eighteenth Century* (London, 1981).

—— 'Empire and Authority in the Later Eighteenth Century', *Journal of Imperial and Commonwealth History*, 15 (1987), 105–22.

—— '"Cornwallis Triumphant": War in India and the British Public in the Late Eighteenth Century', in Lawrence Freedman, Paul Hayes, and Robert O'Neill (eds.), *War, Strategy, and International Politics: Essays in Honour of Sir Michael Howard* (Oxford, 1992), 57–74.

—— 'A Nation Defined by Empire, 1755–1776', in Alexander Grant and

Keith J. Stringer (eds.), *Uniting the Kingdom? The Making of British History* (London, 1995), 208–22.

—— 'Empire and Opportunity in Britain, 1763–1775', *Transactions of the Royal Historical Society*, 6th ser. 5 (1995), 111–28.

—— 'Britain without America—A Second Empire?', in *The Oxford History of the British Empire*, ii. *The Eighteenth Century*, ed. P. J. Marshall (Oxford, 1998), 576–95.

—— 'Britain and the World in the Eighteenth Century: I, Reshaping the Empire', *Transactions of the Royal Historical Society*, 6th ser. 8 (1998), 1–18.

—— 'Britain and the World in the Eighteenth Century: II, Britons and Americans', *Transactions of the Royal Historical Society*, 6th ser. 9 (1999), 1–16.

Mather, F. C., 'Church, Parliament and Penal Laws: Some Anglo-Scottish Interactions in the Eighteenth Century', *English Historical Review*, 92 (1977), 540–72.

Mathias, Peter, *The Brewing Industry in England 1700–1830* (Cambridge, 1959).

—— *The Transformation of England* (London, 1979).

—— and O'Brien, Patrick, 'Taxation in Britain and France, 1715–1810', *Journal of European Economic History*, 5 (1976), 601–50.

Mitchell, B. R., *British Historical Statistics* (Cambridge, 1988).

Mitchell, L. G., 'Politics and Revolution 1772–1800', in *The History of the University of Oxford*, v. *The Eighteenth Century*, ed. L. S. Sutherland and L. G. Mitchell (Oxford, 1986), 163–90.

—— *Charles James Fox* (Oxford, 1992).

Money, John, *Experience and Identity: Birmingham and the West Midlands, 1760–1800* (Manchester, 1977).

Namier, Sir Lewis, 'Anthony Bacon MP, an Eighteenth-Century Merchant', in W. E. Minchinton (ed.), *Industrial South Wales 1750–1914* (London, 1969), 59–106.

—— and Brooke, John, *The History of Parliament: The House of Commons 1754–1790* (3 vols., London, 1964).

Newman, Gerald, *The Rise of English Nationalism: A Cultural History 1740–1830* (London, 1997 edn.).

Norris, John, *Shelburne and Reform* (London, 1963).

O'Brien, Patrick, 'The Political Economy of British Taxation, 1660–1815', *Economic History Review*, 2nd ser. 41 (1988), 1–32.

—— and Hunt, P. A., 'The Rise of a Fiscal State in England, 1485–1815', *Historical Research*, 66 (1993), 129–76.

O'Connell, Maurice, *Irish Politics and Social Conflict in the Age of the American Revolution* (Philadelphia, 1965).

O'Flaherty, Eamon, 'Ecclesiastical Politics and the Dismantling of the Penal Laws in Ireland, 1774–1782', *Irish Historical Studies*, 26 (1988–9), 33–50.

O'Gorman, Frank, *The Rise of Party in England: The Rockingham Whigs 1760–1782* (London, 1975).

—— 'The Parliamentary Opposition to the Government's American Policy 1760–1782', in H. T. Dickinson (ed.), *Britain and the American Revolution* (London, 1998), 97–123.

O'Shaughnessy, Andrew J., 'The Formation of a Commercial Lobby: The West Indian Interest, British Colonial Policy and the American Revolution', *Historical Journal*, 40 (1997), 71–95.

Owen, C. C., *The Development of Industry in Burton upon Trent* (Chichester, 1978).

Philips, David, 'Good Men to Associate and Bad Men to Conspire: Associations for the Prosecution of Felons in England 1760–1860', in Douglas Hay and Francis Snyder (eds.), *Policing and Prosecution in Britain 1750–1850* (Oxford, 1989), 113–70.

Phillips, Jim, 'Parliament and Southern India, 1781–1783: The Secret Committee of Inquiry and the Prosecution of Sir Thomas Rumbold', *Parliamentary History*, 7 (1988), 81–97.

Pittock, Murray G. H., *Inventing and Resisting Britain: Cultural Identities in Britain and Ireland, 1685–1789* (London, 1997).

Pocock, J. G. A., *Virtue, Commerce, and History: Essays on Political Thought and History, Chiefly in the Eighteenth Century* (Cambridge, 1985).

Price, Jacob, 'One Family's Empire: The Russell-Lee-Clerk Connection in Maryland, Britain and India, 1707–1857', *Maryland Historical Magazine*, 72 (1977), 165–225.

—— 'Who Cared about the Colonies?', in Bernard Bailyn and Philip D. Morgan (eds.), *Strangers in the Realm: Cultural Margins of the First British Empire* (Chapel Hill, NC, 1991), 395–436.

Ritcheson, Charles R., *British Politics and the American Revolution* (Norman, Okla., 1954).

Robertson, John, *The Scottish Enlightenment and the Militia Issue* (Edinburgh, 1985).

Robertson, M. L., 'Scottish Commerce and the American War of Independence', *Economic History Review*, 2nd ser. 9 (1956–7), 123–31.

Robins, Keith, *Great Britain: Identities, Institutions and the Idea of Britishness* (London, 1998).

Rocher, Rosane, and Scorgie, Michael F., 'A Family Empire: The Alexander Hamilton Cousins, 1750–1830', *Journal of Imperial and Commonwealth History*, 23 (1995), 189–210.

Rodger, N. A. M., *The Wooden World: An Anatomy of the Georgian Navy* (London, 1986).

—— *The Insatiable Earl: A Life of John Montagu, 4ᵗʰ Earl of Sandwich* (London, 1993).

Rogers, Nicholas, 'Crowd and People in the Gordon Riots', in Eckhart Hellmuth (ed.), *The Transformation of Political Culture: England and Germany in the Late Eighteenth Century* (Oxford, 1990), pp. 39–55.

—— *Crowds, Culture and Politics in Georgian Britain* (Oxford, 1998).

Rule, John, *The Experience of Labour in Eighteenth-Century Industry* (London, 1981).

Russell, Gillian, *The Theatre of War: Performance, Politics and Society, 1793–1815* (Oxford, 1995).

Sack, James J., *From Jacobite to Conservative: Reaction and Orthodoxy in Britain, c.1760–1832* (Cambridge, 1993).

Sainsbury, John A., *Disaffected Patriots: London Supporters of Revolutionary America* (Kingston, 1987).

Scott, H. M., *British Foreign Policy in the Age of the American Revolution* (Oxford, 1990).

Seed, John, '"A Set of Men Powerful Enough in Many Things": Rational Dissent and Political Opposition in England, 1770–1790', in Knud Haakonssen (ed.), *Enlightenment and Religion: Rational Dissent in Eighteenth-Century Britain* (Cambridge, 1996), 140–68.

Slack, Paul, *The English Poor Law 1531–1782* (Basingstoke, 1990).

Smith, Annette M., 'The Administration of the Forfeited Annexed Estates, 1752–1784', in G. W. S. Barrow (ed.), *The Scottish Tradition: Essays in Honour of Ronald Gordon Cant* (Edinburgh, 1974), 198–210.

Smith, D. J., 'Army Clothing Contractors and the Textile Industries in the 18ᵗʰ Century', *Textile History*, 14 (1983), 153–64.

Smout, T. C., 'Famine and Famine Relief in Scotland', in L. M. Cullen and T. C. Smout (eds.), *Comparative Aspects of Scottish and Irish Economic and Social History 1600–1900* (Edinburgh, n.d.), 21–31.

Smyth, Peter, '"Our Cloud-Cap't Grenadiers": The Volunteers as a Military Force', *Irish Sword*, 13 (1977–9), 185–207.

—— 'The Volunteers and Parliament, 1779–1784', in Thomas Bartlett and D. W. Hayton (eds.), *Penal Era and Golden Age: Essays in Irish History, 1690–1800* (Belfast, 1979), 113–36.

Snell, K. D. M., *Annals of the Labouring Poor: Social Change and Agrarian England 1660–1900* (Cambridge, 1985).

Solkin, David H., *Painting for Money: The Visual Arts and the Public Sphere in Eighteenth-Century England* (New Haven, 1993).

Starkey, David J., *British Privateering Enterprise in the Eighteenth Century* (Exeter, 1990).

Stewart, A. T. Q., *A Deeper Silence: The Hidden Roots of the United Irish Movement* (London, 1993).

Syrett, David, *Shipping and the American War* (London, 1970).

—— 'The Navy Board and Merchant Shipowners during the American War', *American Neptune*, 47 (1987), 5–13.

—— 'The Victualling Board Charters Shipping, 1775–1782', *Historical Research*, 68 (1995), 212–24.

—— 'Procurement of Shipping by the Board of Ordnance during the American War, 1775–1782', *Mariner's Mirror*, 81 (1995), 409–16.

Tesch, Pieter, 'Presbyterian Radicalism', in David Dickson, Daire Keogh, and Kevin Whelan (eds.), *The United Irishmen: Republicanism, Radicalism and Rebellion* (Dublin, 1993), 33–48.

Thomas, P. D. G., 'Society, Government and Politics', in Donald Moore (ed.), *Wales in the Eighteenth Century* (Swansea, 1976), 9–26.

—— 'A Welsh Political Storm: The Treasury Warrant of 1778 concerning Crown Lands in Wales', *Welsh History Review*, 18 (1997), 430–49.

Thorold, James E., *A History of Agriculture and Prices in England* (7 vols., London, 1866–1902).

Tilly, Charles, *Popular Contention in Great Britain 1758–1834* (Cambridge, Mass., 1995).

Tracy, Nicholas, *Navies, Deterrence and American Independence* (Vancouver, 1988).

Truxes, Thomas M., *Irish-American Trade, 1660–1783* (Cambridge, 1988).

Turner, Michael, *Enclosures in Britain 1750–1830* (London, 1984).

Wahrman, Dror, '*Percy*'s Prologue: From Gender Play to Gender Panic in Eighteenth-Century England', *Past & Present*, 159 (1998), 113–60.

Walker, Graham, *Intimate Strangers: Political and Cultural Interaction between Scotland and Ulster in Modern Times* (Edinburgh, 1995).

Ward, J. R., *The Finance of Canal Building in Eighteenth-Century England* (Oxford, 1974).

Western, J. R., *The English Militia in the Eighteenth Century* (London, 1965).

Whetstone, Ann E., *Scottish County Government in the Eighteenth and Nineteenth Centuries* (Edinburgh, 1981).

Wickens, Peter L., 'The Economics of Privateering: Capital Dispersal in the American War of Independence', *Journal of European Economic History*, 13 (1984), 375–95.

Williamson, Jeffrey G., 'Why was British Growth So Slow during the Industrial Revolution?', *Journal of Economic History*, 44 (1984), 687–712.

Wilson, Kathleen, 'Empire of Virtue: The Imperial Project and Hanoverian Culture c.1720–1785', in Lawrence Stone (ed.), *An Imperial State at War: Britain from 1689 to 1815* (London, 1994), 128–64.

—— *The Sense of the People: Politics, Culture and Imperialism in England, 1715–1785* (Cambridge, 1995).

Wilson, Richard, 'Newspapers and Industry: The Export of Wool Controversy in the 1780s', in Michael Harris and Alan Lee (eds.), *The Press in*

English Society from the Seventeenth to the Nineteenth Centuries (London, 1986), 80–104.

York, Neil Longley, 'The Impact of the American Revolution on Ireland', in H. T. Dickinson (ed.), *Britain and the American Revolution* (London, 1998), 205–32.

Index